PMP® Exam Prep

PMP® Exam Prep

Feb 14-20 → round 1
Feb 20-28 → register &
        fill in data
Feb 28 → exam 1
March 1-15 → round 2
March 15 → exam 2
March 16-20 → round 3
March 20 → exam 3
March 20-30 → round 4
March 30 → exam 4

April 15 → exam

Accelerated Learning
to Pass PMI's PMP Exam —
On Your FIRST Try!

Rita Mulcahy, PMP

RMC
Publications, Inc.

Thank you to new readers of this book who put up with my humor and laughter as I show you the tricks for learning, rather than memorizing, to pass the PMP exam.

Thank you to the thousands of people who used earlier editions to make this the best selling and most effective way to get ready to pass the PMP exam! Your support and encouragement since this book was first published in 1998, creating the PMP exam prep industry, has been overwhelming. After five editions, you have helped to make this a truly unique and effective product.

To Tim, who always encourages me to make a great thing better. To Jeff and Mary, who help make that a reality! To Kerry and Connor, whose little smiles make me realize why I work this hard.

To the rest of the spectacular team at RMC Project Management and RMC Publications. When I am running around like a tornado, it is great to have such a strong anchor!

Printed in the United States of America.

Third Printing

ISBN   1-932735-00-3

Library of Congress Control Number: 2005900659

RMC Publications, Inc.

Phone: 952.846.4484
Fax: 952.846.4844
E-mail: info@rmcproject.com
Web: www.rmcproject.com

Table of Contents

Introduction to the Fifth Edition of PMP Exam Prep

by Rita Mulcahy, PMP

Thank you for purchasing the latest edition of the original PMP Exam prep book, which paved the way for accelerated learning in the industry. Our materials have been used in more than 40 countries as the primary tool for passing the exam since we created the PMP exam prep book market in 1998.

I am glad that you chose to let us help you get ready for the exam faster, and without focusing on memorization. I have enjoyed coming up with devilish ways for you to get ready for the exam faster and easier. I hope you enjoy this edition!

I have a particular aversion to using memorization to pass an exam, don't you? That is why this book is full of learning, not memorization. The funny thing is that while others force you to memorize, you can actually spend the same amount of time learning instead and pass the exam.

After working with thousands of people, I have perfected what my students say is the most efficient and shortest process for studying for the exam! You should not need to study more than 120 hours using our products if you have had project management training.

Although you will certainly learn a lot about project management, this book is <u>not</u> designed to teach you all you need to know about how to manage a project, or the art and science of project management. You must have project management training before you take the exam.

In order to get the most out of your efforts and save time studying, this book has been specifically designed to accomplish the following:
- Help you learn, not just memorize
- Focus you on the areas where others commonly score the worst
- Help you determine your knowledge gaps
- Provide insider tips about the exam that are not readily available elsewhere
- Review topics not in the PMBOK® Guide
- Identify and define PMI-isms
- Help you to gain familiarity with the types of exam questions
- Provide page references to PMBOK® Guide content
- Increase your probability of passing the exam on your first try

If you have had training in project management, you should not need any materials other than this book, RMC's *PM FASTrack*® exam simulation software, our *Hot Topics* flashcards (audio or hard copy format) and PMI's *A Guide to the Project Management Body of Knowledge, Third Edition* (called the *PMBOK® Guide* in this book) to pass the PMP Exam. If you do not have all of these materials, I invite you to visit RMC's online store at www.rmcproject.com to purchase them before beginning your study.

Free Updates Purchase of this book includes access to updates regarding the PMP exam, as well as additional tricks, tips and information to help you prepare for the exam. Access this information at www.rmcproject.com/extras. Have this book with you when you go to the Web site.

We Need You to Help Us Stop Copyright Infringement As the author of the best-selling PMP exam prep book on the market, RMC is also, unfortunately, the most illegally copied. It is true that many people use our materials legally and with our permission to teach PMP exam preparation. However, from time to time, we are made aware of others who copy our exam questions, Tricks of the Trade® and other content illegally and use them for their own financial gain.

If you recognize any of RMC's proprietary content being used in other PMP exam prep materials or courses, please notify us at copyright@rmcproject.com immediately. We will do the investigation. Please also contact us at the address above for clarification on how to use our materials in your class or study group without violating any laws.

Contact Us We love to hear your feedback. Is there anything in this book that you wish was expanded, that is too much, anything not covered that you think should be here? We would love to hear from you. Send us an e-mail at pmp@rmcproject.com.

About the Author

Rita Mulcahy, PMP, is an internationally recognized expert in project management and a sought-after project management speaker, trainer and author. She has six project management books and products to her credit, and was a Contributor and Reviewer to the *PMBOK® Guide, Third Edition*. Rita has taught thousands of project managers from around the world and helped about 80,000 people prepare for the PMP exam. She is the winner of the 2004 Professional Development Product of the Year award from the Project Management Institute for her book, *Risk Management Tricks of the Trade® for Project Managers* and its companion, *SIRK-Kit® Risk Analysis Kit*.

Rita's speaking engagements draw record crowds. People have stated: "Rita makes you think! The most informative presentation I have ever seen." In fact, Rita has spoken at PMI's annual project management symposium to standing room only crowds and has been asked to present encore presentations at the symposium for an unheard of four years!

She has over 15 years and U.S. $2.5 billion of hands-on project experience on hundreds of IS, IT, new product, high-tech, service, engineering, construction and manufacturing projects. She has served as an acting PMI Chapter President and Vice President for more than seven years and has taught project management courses for four major universities.

Rita is the founder of RMC Project Management, an international project management speaking, training and consulting firm, and a Global Registered Education Provider with PMI. RMC specializes in real-world project management training; in interpreting the *PMBOK® Guide* for real-world use and helping companies use the latest project management tools and techniques to complete projects faster, with less expense, better results and fewer resources. RMC provides training in basic and advanced project management for team members, project managers, project management offices and senior management. Since its founding in 1991, RMC has provided many quality courses and products to prepare you for the exam. Courses offered include:

- PMP Certification Training
- Project Management Tricks of the Trade®
- Tricks of the Trade® for Risk Management
- Tricks of the Trade® for Determining and Managing Project Requirements
- What Makes a Project Manager Successful?
- Why Projects Fail and How to Prevent Failure
- Tricks for Avoiding Common Project Problems
- Avoiding Common Stumbling Blocks in Risk Management
- Project Management for Teams, Senior Management, Sales and Functional Managers
- Executive Briefing on Project Management
- Setting Up and Managing the Project Office
- All PMI *PMBOK® Guide* Subjects

The PMP Exam

Why Take the PMP Exam?

Let me quote one of my students. "The exam has changed my life. (Could I be more dramatic?) The process of studying for the exam, taking your class and passing the exam has changed how others look at my abilities."

By passing the exam, you can say that you have passed an international exam designed to prove your knowledge of project management. That is impressive. Since the exam focuses on situations you might see in the real world, passing also indicates that you are experienced. The PMP certification is a way to set yourself apart. There are other benefits.

PMI's salary survey has found that PMPs are paid at least 10 percent more than non-PMPs in the United States (and even more in some other countries). I have had many students who have received a U.S. $15,000 bonus AND a 15 percent raise when they passed the exam. Others have said they got a job over 200 others because they were a PMP. These are good reasons to finally get around to taking the exam.

Are You Ready for the PMP Exam?

From my experience, 50 percent of those who fail the exam do so because they have not had project management training that uses PMI terminology. Take this seriously! Real-life experience or just reading the *PMBOK® Guide* is not enough to pass this exam! Books cannot help you answer questions like, "You are in the middle of creating a work breakdown structure for the project. Which of the following problems is most likely to occur?" To pass this exam, you need training as well as experience using what you learn in that training. Since 2002, project management training has been required by PMI before one can take the PMP exam.

Do you know enough about project management to take this exam? You do not know enough if you experience two or more of the following problems on projects:
- Large cost or schedule overruns
- Unrealistic schedules
- Excessive changes to the scope or schedule
- Poor communications and increased conflict
- Running out of time near the end of the project
- Unsatisfactory quality
- Low morale
- People on the team are unsure of what needs to be done

- Excessive rework and overtime
- Too many project meetings

You do not know enough about project management to take this exam if you do not understand or do not use five or more of the following:
- A step-by-step process for managing projects and why each step is necessary
- Project manager, sponsor and team roles
- Historical information from previous projects
- Lessons learned from previous projects
- Creation of lessons learned on your projects
- Project charter
- What is a work breakdown structure, how to create it, and that it is not a list in a bar chart
- How to manually create a network diagram
- Critical path—how to find it and what benefits it provides the project manager
- Three-point estimating
- Monte Carlo analysis
- Earned value
- Schedule compression, crashing and fast tracking
- An unrealistic schedule is the project manager's fault
- Creating a realistic and approved project management plan that you would be willing to be held accountable to achieving
- Measuring and implementing corrective action
- Risk management process and that risk management is not just using a checklist
- Expected monetary value
- Calculating budget reserves and their relationship to risk management
- Controlling the project to the project management plan

If you don't know or do many of the items listed above, I encourage you to consider taking RMC Project Management's three day Tricks of the Trade® for Project Management course, in addition to our two day PMP Exam Prep course. Combining these courses into a one week experience will give you the 35 contact hours that PMI requires to take the exam. You may also wish to consider enrolling in RMC's e-Learning based PMP Exam Prep course, which also meets PMI's 35 contact hour requirement.

How to Use This Book

Be Sure You Have Current Materials for the Exam

RMC products are frequently updated to give you the latest information available. This book takes into account the latest changes to the exam. Previous editions of this book are now out of date and should not be used to try to pass the exam.

How This Book Is Organized
Each chapter is organized the same: an introductory paragraph, a list of Quicktest topics (listed in order of importance), Rita's Process Chart, review materials and a practice exam. All page references in this document refer to the *PMBOK® Guide, Third Edition* unless otherwise stated! This book works with the other components of RMC's *PMP Exam Prep System*.

Introduction to Each Chapter
The introductory paragraph provides an overview of the chapter.

Quicktest The list at the beginning of each chapter gives you an understanding of what topics are most important and my impression as to their order of importance. Refer to this list when you are finished with each chapter to test your knowledge of the chapter contents and to review what is most important.

Rita's Process Chart Created in 1998 for the first edition of this book, this chart has been greatly expanded to help you integrate knowledge areas and process groups in a unique and easy-to-understand way. Study this chart in the Project Management Processes chapter. Use the repeated chart at the beginning of each chapter to know where you are in the project management process as you work though each knowledge area.

Review Materials and Exercises The review materials contain the latest updates on the PMP exam. (See our *CAPM Exam Prep Kit* if you have less experience and are interested in taking that exam.) Feedback from students indicates that the review material covers all the major items on the exam.

The review materials are more than just words. Throughout this book you will see many exercises. These have been developed based on accelerated learning theory and an understanding of difficult topics on the exam. They will be more helpful to you than you might think. It is important to make sure you do these exercises, rather than jumping right to the answers. Do not skip them, even if their value does not seem evident to you. The exercises and activities are a key benefit of this book. You will see the results when you pass the exam. The answers are listed right after the exercises. Although you may wish the answers were shown later in the book, analysis shows that it is better for you to have them where they are. Here is a trick: Keep a blank paper handy to cover the answers until you have completed each exercise and are ready to review.

Also included in the review material are tricks to passing the exam. They are designated by this image. Tricks of the Trade® are so important to RMC that it is actually our registered trademark. You will find these tricks helpful to focus your study on what you need to know for the exam.

Occasionally throughout the book, you will see a "memory finger." This indicates information you must memorize for the exam. As we have said, most of the exam does not depend on memorization. However, there are certain things that you will need to memorize in order to pass the exam.

Practice Exam The practice exam at the end of each chapter allows you to review the material and test your understanding. On page 5, you will find a score sheet to use as you take the practice exams. Make a copy of it for each set of sample questions in the book.

NOTE: The questions in this book are tests on the chapter content. They do not simulate the complete range and depth of the PMP Exam questions. You can find such a simulation in the *PM FASTrack*®, PMP exam simulation software.

Other Materials to Use to Study for the PMP Exam

Throughout this book, we will from time to time refer to other PMP exam preparation resources offered by RMC. To increase your chances of passing the exam and decrease your overall study time, we recommend that you seriously consider acquiring one or more of the valuable tools listed here. Note that all of these resources are available for purchase online at www.rmcproject.com.

PMBOK® Guide—Third Edition

PM FASTrack® Exam Simulation Software,
by Rita Mulcahy

RMC's best-selling PMP exam simulation software, offering over 1,300 questions—including tricky situational questions with more than one right answer. Sample exams can be sorted by Knowledge Area, Process Group, Keyword, PMP Simulation and even Super PMP Simulation. All questions are cross-referenced with this book or the *PMBOK® Guide*, making it easy to go back and study your weak areas. Students say these questions are harder than the ones on the actual exam! Upgrades from previous versions include new questions and scenarios, more "wordy" questions to match the actual exam, automatic question updates, and comprehensive grading and reporting capability.

Hot Topics Flashcards (hard copy or audio CD),
by Rita Mulcahy

Are you looking for a way to prepare for the PMP exam that fits into your busy schedule? Now you can study at the office, on a plane or even in your car with RMC's portable and extremely valuable *Hot Topics* flashcards— in hard copy or audio CD format! Over 600 pages of the most important and difficult to recall PMP exam-related terms and definitions are now available for study as you drive, fly or take your lunch break. Our *Hot Topics* flashcards will enhance your ability to recall and understand PMP exam-related terms, as well as improve your recall of the information you will need to answer those dreaded situational questions. Add instant mobility to your study routine.

Test Tactics Session #1: Approaching and Answering Difficult Questions, by Rita Mulcahy
In this unique e-Learning based online strategy session, Rita Mulcahy breaks down in detail extremely difficult PMP exam sample questions. In interactive fashion, Rita reviews never before published techniques for interpreting questions, eliminating choices, spotting traps, handling questions with multiple correct answers and choosing the "best" answer when it is not immediately evident. Upon completion of this session, you will be able to read and interpret difficult questions, analyze the answer choices and determine the most correct answers. No more boring online training experiences!

Only products purchased directly from RMC are supported by RMC.

© 2005 Rita Mulcahy, PMP • Phone: (952) 846-4484 • E-mail: info@rmcproject.com • Web: www.rmcproject.com

Question Number	Third Time	Second Time	First Time
1.			
2.			
3.			
4.			
5.			
6.			
7.			
8.			
9.			
10.			
11.			
12.			
13.			
14.			
15.			
16.			
17.			
18.			
19.			
20.			
21.			
22.			
23.			
24.			
25.			
26.			
27.			
28.			
29.			

Question Number	Third Time	Second Time	First Time
30.			
31.			
32.			
33.			
34.			
35.			
36.			
37.			
38.			
39.			
40.			
41.			
42.			
43.			
44.			
45.			
46.			
47.			
48.			
49.			
50.			
Total Score	**Third Time**	**Second Time**	**First Time**

What will you do different next time?

© 2005 Rita Mulcahy, PMP • Phone: (952) 846-4484 • E-mail: info@rmcproject.com • Web: www.rmcproject.com

How to Study for the PMP Exam

There are two serious mistakes you can make in preparing for this exam. The first is reading every book you can find. The second is studying too long. This book is part of the fast way to pass the exam. It is designed to save you time and increase your understanding. If you feel the need to read more books to make sure you pass the exam, simply take a PMP simulation exam using *PM FASTrack®* and see how you score. (See "Using This Book With the PMP Exam Prep System," on the next page.)

If you purchased this book directly from RMC, you received extra study materials free. You should read this book first before using those materials.

The Magic Three

Studies have shown that if you visit a topic three times, you will remember it. Therefore, you should read this book and use our products three times before you take the exam.

Be in Test-Taking Mode

Get used to jumping from one topic to another and practice taking an exam for four hours. Do not underestimate the physical aspects of taking an exam lasting that long.

Your Step-by-Step Study Plan

We recommend that you use one of the following study plans. Follow Plan A if you do not own RMC's complete PMP Exam Prep System. Follow Plan B if you own the entire system.

Plan A: Using This Book As a Stand-alone

1. Before you review the book, take the practice exams in one sitting—as you would during the actual exam. This will give you a baseline to tell you how much you have learned after using the book. It will also help you determine how much study time you need and what chapters to read more carefully. Do not analyze your right and wrong answers at this point; just note the chapters where you have the most and least difficulty. If you are too excited to get started, skip this step and go to Step 2.
2. Read the material in this book for the first time, (focusing on the chapters where you had the most errors in Step 1). Refer to Rita's Process Chart for each chapter, and at the same time, skim through the corresponding chapter in the *PMBOK® Guide* to get an understanding of the flow of the processes.
3. As you finish each chapter, review the Quicktest terms listed on the first page of the chapter.
4. If it is at all possible, form a study group any time after you have read the book for the first time on your own. This will actually make your study time shorter and more effective! You will be able to ask someone questions and the studying (and celebrating afterward) will be more fun. A study group should consist of only three or four people. (See "How to Use This Book in a Study Group" on the next page.)
5. Spend more time reviewing any topics you score poorly on before moving to Step 6.
6. PASS THE EXAM!

Plan B: Using This Book With the PMP Exam Prep System

1. Before you review the materials, take 20 questions in each process group and knowledge area using *PM FASTrack®*. This will give you a baseline to tell you how much you have learned after using the materials. It will also help you determine how much study time you need and what chapters to read more carefully. Do not analyze your right and wrong answers at this point; just note the chapters where you have the most and least difficulty. If you are too excited to get started, skip this step and go to Step 2.

2. Read the material in this book for the first time, focusing on the chapters where you had the most errors in Step 1. Refer to Rita's Process Chart for each chapter, and at the same time, skim through the corresponding chapter in the *PMBOK® Guide* to get an understanding of the flow of the processes.

3. As you finish each chapter, review the Quicktest terms listed on the first page of the chapter, use the *Hot Topics* flashcards to improve recall and test your understanding of that chapter. Then take an exam on the chapter in *PM FASTrack®*. You are doing well if you score over 70 percent.

4. If it is at all possible, form a study group any time after you have read the book for the first time on your own. This will actually make your study time shorter and more effective! You will be able to ask someone questions and the studying (and celebrating afterward) will be more fun. A study group should consist of only three or four people. (See "How to Use This Book in a Study Group" topic below.)

5. Spend more time reviewing any topics you score poorly on before moving to Step 6.

6. Retake the practice tests until you score over 85 percent on a PMP simulation exam. You should be careful not to become too familiar with the questions. *PM FASTrack®* and its over 1,300 questions will help make sure you do not see the same question too often, giving you the most representative evaluation of your knowledge. YOU ARE OVERSTUDYING if you see too many of the questions repeated in *PM FASTrack®*!

7. Use the *Hot Topics* flashcards, if you have them, to retain the information you have learned until you take the exam.

8. PASS THE EXAM!

How to Use This Book in a Study Group

I am honored that you have chosen my book for your group. Pick someone to lead the discussion of each chapter (preferably someone who is *not* comfortable with the chapter). Each time you meet, go over questions about topics you do not understand and review the hot topics on the exam using the *Hot Topics* flashcards, if you have them. Most groups meet for one hour per chapter. Either independently or with your study group, do further research on questions you do not understand or answered incorrectly.

Each member of the study group will need his or her own copy of the book. Notice that you do not have to create exercises, homework or even class activities; they are already provided for you. Make sure you are not violating international copyright laws by creating any derivative works from this copyrighted book. The best thing is to follow the book content. If you are leading or teaching a structured PMP exam preparation course using RMC products, I encourage you to contact RMC for information on our Corporate Partnership program, which may give you the right to create overheads or other materials using content from this book.

I also encourage you to contact RMC about other tools we offer to study groups and independent instructors, or to receive quantity discounts on this book, *PM FASTrack®* exam simulation software or *Hot Topics* flashcards.

Qualifying to Take the Exam

To take this exam you must meet requirements as outlined by the Project Management Institute. The current requirements are described below.

Category	General Education	PM Education	PM Experience	Experience	Number of Questions
One	Bachelors degree	35 contact hours	4,500 hours	Three years within last six years	*200
Two	High School graduate	35 contact hours	7,500 hours	Five years within last eight years	

Consider taking PMI's CAPM® Exam if you do not meet the above requirements. The requirements can be found at www.pmi.org. Currently, test takers must document 1,500 hours of experience or 23 hours of project management education to qualify for this exam. See our *CAPM Exam Prep Kit* to help you prepare.

Applying to Take the Exam

You must submit an application to PMI. Applications may be submitted by mail or electronically. Submit online if at all possible, since PMI's response time is faster for electronic submissions. When your application is accepted, you will receive a letter authorizing you to make an appointment to take the exam. PMI is quickly moving to offer computerized testing around the world in many languages.

Watch out! ONCE YOU RECEIVE YOUR AUTHORIZATION LETTER, YOU MUST PASS THE EXAM WITHIN ONE YEAR! In some instances, testing centers may not have openings for several weeks.

* See the next page for details about the breakdown of questions on the PMP exam.

What Is the PMP Exam Like?

Keep in mind three very important things about this exam. First, THE PMP EXAM IS NOT A TEST OF THE INFORMATION IN THE *PMBOK® Guide*! Second, you cannot rely only on real-world experience. Third, training in professional project management based on the *PMBOK® Guide* is critical! However, do not let any organization fool you into thinking you need weeks of training or a master's certificate in project management to take the exam.

The PMP exam includes 200 multiple-choice questions with four answers per question. The exam must be completed in four hours. (NOTE: If your study material has five choices per question, do not use it! It is either related to an old exam and therefore out of date, or it has not been created using the same modern test creation standards as the exam.)

Twenty-five of the 200 exam questions are "pre-release questions," meaning they are not included in your score for the exam. These questions will be randomly placed throughout the exam. You will not know which ones are which. They will be used by PMI to validate the questions for future inclusion in the master database. **Your score will be calculated based on your response to the remaining 175 questions. Passing score on the exam is now 106 out of 175, approximately 61 percent.**

The questions are randomly generated from a database containing hundreds of questions. The questions may jump from topic to topic and cover multiple topics in a single question. You get one point for each correct answer. There is no penalty for wrong answers.

The following table breaks out the percent of scored questions currently on the exam in each process group:

PM Process	Percent of Questions
Project Initiating	11
Project Planning	23
Project Executing	27
Project Monitoring and Controlling	21
Project Closing	9
Professional and Social Responsibility	9

For many people the toughest knowledge areas on the exam are Framework, Integration, Procurement, Risk, and Time. The toughest process groups are Executing, Monitoring and Controlling, and Professional and Social Responsibility. Make sure you study these carefully.

PMI occasionally makes changes to many aspects of the exam, including qualification requirements, the application process, passing score, and breakdown of questions in each process group. For the latest information, please visit www.pmi.org and read your authorization letter carefully. Any differences between what is listed here and what is communicated by PMI should be resolved in favor of PMI's information.

WARNING: THE PMP EXAM IS NOT LIKE ANY MULTIPLE QUESTION EXAM YOU HAVE TAKEN BEFORE. The exam is designed to weed out those who should not be PMPs and passing it is a major achievement. The questions can be tricky and wordy. If you know what you are doing as a project manager, you pass the exam. If you do not know what you are doing, you do not pass.

Be aware of the following for the exam:
- The PMP exam tests knowledge, application and analysis. This makes the PMP exam more than a test of memory. You must know how to apply the information in this book and be able to analyze situations involving this information. Do not expect the exam to have all straightforward, definition-type questions.
- It is important to realize that the PMP exam deals with real-world use of project management. It contains about 150 "What would you do in this situation?" questions (situational questions). These questions are extremely difficult if you have not used project management tools in the real world or if your project management efforts include common errors. You have to have been there to pass the exam.
- There may be instances where the same data is used for multiple questions. This is particularly true of network diagram questions.
- It always feels like more for the test taker, but only a few questions require you to MEMORIZE the step-by-step *PMBOK® Guide* processes. Only 10 to 12 questions require you to MEMORIZE the inputs or outputs from the *PMBOK® Guide*. These are discussed in later chapters.
- Expect only eight to 10 formula-related calculations on the exam.
- Expect only 10 to 12 earned-value questions on the exam. Not all of these require calculations using the formulas.
- Most acronyms (e.g., WBS for work breakdown structure) will be spelled out.
- The correct answers should not include direct quotations from the *PMBOK® Guide*.
- Most students feel uncertain of only 40 or fewer questions of the 200 questions on the PMP exam.
- Many students have needed only 2½ hours to finish the PMP exam and then taken the rest of the time to review their answers.

Watch whose advice you take. I am often surprised about what people say about the exam, versus what the exam is really like. When you also consider the fact that the exam has changed over the years, it is best to be wary of advice that does not come from a recognized authority.

The questions are mostly situational, many are ambiguous and very wordy and some even seem like they have two right answers. Be prepared for the following types of questions so you will not waste time or be caught off guard when you are taking the exam.

1. **Situational questions** These questions require you to have "been there."

     You receive notification that a major item you are purchasing for a project will be delayed. What is the BEST thing to do?
     A. *Ignore it, it will go away.*
     B. *Notify your boss.*
     C. *Let the customer know about it and talk over options.*
     D. *Meet with the team and identify alternatives.*
        Answer *D*

2. **Questions with two or more right answers** Questions that appear to have two, three or even four right answers are a major complaint from many test takers. Most of the questions will list choices that all could reasonably be done, or that less experienced or less qualified project managers might choose. To those people, it looks like there is more

than one right answer. To more experienced project managers, the same questions may appear to have one or maybe two right answers. Honestly, the more of a problem you have with this, the less you really know about project management.

As you go through questions and review the answers in this book or in our other products, look for instances where you think there is more than one right answer and try to figure out why you think so. I have intentionally put questions like these into my products for PMP exam preparation. The explanations will be key to understanding why your right answer is not the right answer.

Let's look again at question number one. Couldn't we really do all of the choices? The right answer is certainly D, but isn't it also correct to tell the customer? Yes, but that is not the first thing. Essentially this question is really saying, "What is the BEST thing to do *next?*"

3. **Questions with extraneous information** It is very important to realize that not all information included in a question will be used to answer the question. Can you imagine multiple paragraphs of information for each question on the exam? Most of the data provided will NOT be needed to answer the question. In the following question, the numbers are extraneous.

> *Experience shows that each time you double the production of doors, unit costs decrease by 10 percent. Based on this, the company determines that production of 3,000 doors should cost $21,000. This case illustrates:*
> A. *learning cycle.*
> B. *law of diminishing returns.*
> C. *80/20 rule.*
> D. *parametric cost estimating.*
> **Answer** *D*

4. **Out of the blue questions,** or words that you have never seen before. Many people taking the exam expect that all the terms used as choices should mean something. They do not! There are often made-up terms used on the exam. Perhaps the question writer needed another choice, perhaps they are intentionally added to trick those who do not know the answer. If you consider yourself well trained and see a term you do not know on the exam, chances are it is not the right answer.

No matter how well you study, there will ALWAYS be questions where you have no idea what the question is asking. Here is an example that will seem out of the blue until you finish reading this book.

> *The concept of "optimal quality level is reached at the point where the incremental revenue from product improvement equals the incremental cost to secure it" comes from:*
> A. *quality control analysis.*
> B. *marginal analysis.*
> C. *standard quality analysis.*
> D. *conformance analysis.*
> **Answer** *B*

5. **Questions where understanding is important** In order to answer many of the questions on the exam, you must understand all the topics. Memorization is not enough!

   The process of decomposing deliverables into smaller, more manageable components is complete when:
   A. project justification has been established.
   B. change requests have occurred.
   C. cost and duration estimates can be developed for each work element at this detail.
   D. each work element is found in the WBS dictionary.
      Answer C.

6. **Questions with new a approach to known topic** There will be many instances where you understand the topic, but have never thought about it in the way the question describes.

   In a matrix organization, information dissemination is MOST likely to be effective when:
   A. information flows both horizontally and vertically.
   B. the communications flows are kept simple.
   C. there is an inherent logic in the type of matrix chosen.
   D. project managers and functional managers socialize.
      Answer A.

On Exam Day

You must bring your authorization letter from PMI to the test site, as well as two forms of ID with exactly the same name you entered on the exam application.

You will be given scratch paper, pencils (and possibly even earplugs or headphones) and have the chance to do a 15 minute computer tutorial, if your exam is given on computer, to become familiar with the computer and its commands. NOTE: The testing center will require you to exchange your used scratch paper if you need more during the exam.

When you take the exam, you will see one question on the screen at a time. You can answer a question and/or mark it to return to it later. You will be able to move back and forth throughout the exam.

You will have multiple chances to indicate that you have completed the exam. The exam will not be scored until you indicate that you are ready, or your time is up. You will receive a printed summary of your test results. If you pass, the computer will print out a certificate, and you will officially be certified. If you do not pass, PMI will send you information on retaking the exam. You will have to pay an additional fee to retake the exam.

 ## Tricks for Taking the PMP Exam

1. Keys to answering PMI's questions:
   - Understand the material cold. Do not assume this exam tests memorization; it tests knowledge, application and analysis! You must understand the items in this book, how they are used in the real world and how they work in combination with each other.
   - Have real-world experience using all the major project management techniques.

- Read the *PMBOK® Guide*.
- Understand the areas PMI emphasizes (PMI-isms, explained later in this book).
- Be familiar with the types of questions.
- Practice interpreting ambiguous and wordy questions.
- Practice being able to pick an answer from what appears to be two or three right answers.
- Get used to the idea that there will be questions you cannot answer.

2. Control the exam, do not let it control you. How would you feel if you read the first question and had no idea of the answer? The second question? And the third question? For many reasons, this is likely to occur! Here is what to do. If you do not immediately know the answer to the question, use the Mark for Review function and come back to it later. This will mean that your first pass through the exam will be generally quick. More prepared now? Imagine how good you will feel when all you have to do is go through a few questions that were confusing to you. Remember this. It could be a big stress reliever for you on the exam.

3. Control your frustration. You might very well dislike or disagree with some of the questions on this exam. You might also be surprised at how many questions you mark for review. If you are still thinking about question 20 when you reach question 120, there will have been 100 questions that you will not have looked at closely enough. Take care to control your frustration.

4. Answer the question from PMI's perspective, not the perspective you have acquired from your life experience. If this approach does not give you an answer, rely on your training and, lastly, your life experience.

5. First identify the actual question in the words provided (it is often the last sentence), then read the rest of the question. Note the topics discussed in the question and the descriptors (e.g., "except," "includes," "not an example of"). This should help you understand what the question is asking and reduce the need to reread questions. Determine what your answer should be, and then look at the answers shown.

6. One of the main reasons people answer incorrectly is because they do not read all four choices. Do not make the same mistake! Practice reading the questions and all four choices when you take the practice exams. It is best to practice reading the choices backwards (choice D first, then C, etc.). Practice in this area will help you select the BEST answer.

7. Practice quickly eliminating answers that are highly implausible. Many questions have only two plausible options and two obviously incorrect options.

8. There may be more than one "correct" answer to each question, but only one "BEST" answer. Practice looking for the BEST answer.

9. Be alert to the fact that information in one question is sometimes given away in another question. Write down things that you do not understand as you take the exam. Use any extra time at the end of the exam to go back to these questions.

10. Attempts have been made to keep all choices the same length. Therefore, do not follow the old rule that the longest answer is the right one.

11. A concerted effort has been made to use "distracters"—choices that distract you from the correct answer. These are plausible choices that less knowledgeable people will pick. Distracters make it appear as though some questions have two or more right answers. To many people, it seems as though there are only shades of differences between the choices. Look for this type of question as you take practice exams.

12. Look for words like "first," "last," "next," "best," "never," "always," "except," "not," "most likely," "less likely," "primary," "initial," "most," etc. Make certain you clearly read the question, and take note of these words, or you will answer the question incorrectly! There are many questions that require you to really understand the process of project management and its real-world application.

13. Watch out for choices that are true statements but not the answer to the question.

14. Watch out for choices that contain common project management errors. They are intentionally there to determine if you really know project management. Therefore, you may not know that you answered a question incorrectly! Look for errors in your knowledge and practice as you go through this book. (See "Common Project Management Errors and Pitfalls" list at the end of this chapter.)

15. Options that represent broad, sweeping generalizations tend to be incorrect, so be alert for "always," "never," "must," "completely" and so forth. Alternatively, choices that represent carefully qualified statements tend to be correct, so be alert for words such as "often," "sometimes," "perhaps," "may," and "generally."

16. When a question asks you to fill in a blank space, the correct answer may not be grammatically correct when inserted in the sentence.

17. As soon as you are given scratch paper when you arrive at the exam, write down anything you were having trouble remembering. This will free up your mind to handle questions once the information you are concerned about is written down.

18. Visit the exam site before your exam date to determine how long it will take to get there and to see what the testing room looks like. This is particularly helpful if you are a nervous test taker.

19. Just because you are taking an exam, do not expect the exam site to be quiet. A student from one of my PMP Exam Prep courses had a band playing outside the testing center for three hours. Others have had someone taking an exam that required intensive typing, and thus more noise, right next to them. Many testing sites will have earplugs or headphones available.

20. Look for the "rah, rah" answer (e.g., "The project manager is so important," "The WBS is so useful").

21. Take the night off before the exam to do something relaxing and get a little extra sleep. DO NOT STUDY! You will need time to process all you have learned so you can remember it when you take the exam.

22. Make sure you are comfortable during the exam. Wear layered clothing and bring a sweater to sit on in case the chairs are uncomfortable.

23. Bring snacks! Bring lunch! You will not be able to bring snacks into the exam room, but having them stored close by may stop hunger pains.

24. Use deep breathing techniques to help relax. This is particularly helpful if you are very nervous before or during the exam and when you notice yourself reading the same question two or three times.

25. Use all the exam time. Do not leave early unless you have reviewed each question twice.

26. Remember that it is okay to change your answers as long as you have a good reason.

27. Create a test-taking plan and stick to it. This may mean, "I will take a ten minute break after every 50 questions because I get tired quickly," or "I will answer all the questions as quickly as possible and then take a break and review my answers."

Recurring Themes—PMI-isms to Know for the PMP Exam

"PMI-ism" is a term I coined to refer to the items PMI stresses on the exam that most project managers do not know. PMI-isms are not stressed and sometimes not even mentioned in the *PMBOK® Guide*! Those who write questions on the exam know what most project managers do wrong. This knowledge helps them to write questions that weed out those who should not be PMPs.

Understanding PMI-isms will help you pick the best answer from what seems like more than one correct answer. Some of the topics are listed only here and others are summarized here and described more fully later in the book. Review this list again just before you take the exam and make sure you understand all these PMI-isms.

1. There is a basic assumption that you have records (historical information) for all previous projects that include what the work packages were, how much each work package cost, and what risks were uncovered. These are now referred to in the *PMBOK® Guide* as part of organizational process assets. You are probably laughing because you do not have such information. You may even be saying, "That is a good idea!" For the exam, assume that you have them for all projects and that you create them for existing projects. Organizational process assets are an input to almost every project management process.

   Why would PMI stress historical records? They are exceedingly valuable (like gold) to the project manager, the team, the performing organization and even the customer.

2. Project cost and schedule cannot be finalized without completing risk management.

3. PMI stresses the fact that a project manager must work within the existing systems and culture of a company. They call these enterprise environmental factors and they are inputs to many processes.

4. The word "task" is not used in the *PMBOK® Guide*. There are work packages, activities and/or schedule activities.

5. The term Gantt chart is not used, only bar chart.

6. You must understand the process of project management; e.g., what to do first, second, etc., and why! See Rita's Process Chart and Rita's Process Game in the Project Management Processes chapter.

7. A project manager's job is to focus on preventing problems, not to deal with them. ✳ What do you spend time doing every day? If you spend all your time dealing with problems, you are not a great project manager. You should have planned the project to address the problems or to prevent the problems you knew would be coming.

8. ✳ Percent complete is an almost meaningless number. Project managers should not spend time collecting useless information. It is better to control the project and know the status through other actions.

9. A great project manager does not hold meetings where you go around the room asking all attendees to report. Such meetings are generally, but not always, a waste of time, as such information can be collected through other means. There are more important topics for team meetings.

10. A project manager has authority and power. She can say "No" and work to control the project to the benefit of the customer.

11. The project must be completed on time and on budget and meet any other project objectives; otherwise it is the project manager's fault. ✳

12. Delays must be made up by adjusting future work.

13. Know the following about the project management plan:
    - The project management plan is approved by all parties, is realistic and everyone believes it can be achieved.
    - The project is managed to the project management plan.
    - A project management plan is not a bar chart, nor is a WBS created in a bar chart or a list in a bar chart.
    - Make sure you know what actions it takes to create a real project management plan.
    - Most project managers have never developed a project management plan that contains all the items in the *PMBOK® Guide*'s definition of a project management plan. Make sure you are familiar with what goes into a project management plan and what each component includes.

14. If at all possible, all the work and all the stakeholders are identified before the project begins.

15. Stakeholders are involved in the project and may help identify and manage risks. They are involved in team building and their needs are taken into account while planning the project and in the communications management plan.

16. Many people fail the exam because their vision of what a project manager is and what he should do is different from that outlined in the *PMBOK® Guide*. They often do not exercise the power and perform the activities described in the *PMBOK® Guide*. Others fail the exam because they think the project manager is supposed to plan the project on his own and TELL everyone what to do.

17. All roles and responsibilities must be CLEARLY assigned to specific individuals on the project. Such responsibilities may include things like attending meetings, as well as project work. In my studies, lack of clear assignment is the number one complaint of team members. This is therefore worth thinking about a little more.

18. The work breakdown structure (WBS) is the foundation of all project planning and should be used on every project.

19. You cannot get something for nothing. A change in scope MUST be evaluated for impact to time, cost, quality, risk and customer satisfaction. Project managers must have enough data about their projects to do this analysis. Do you?

20. Project managers can save the universe, are "wonderful," "great," and must be very skilled (a "rah! rah! for project management" topic).

21. PMI does not approve of gold plating (adding extra functionality).

22. The definition of "kickoff meeting" used on the exam may be different from a "kickoff meeting" you might hold.

23. The project manager must be proactive. Correct answers indicate that the project manager must find problems early, look for changes, prevent problems, etc.

24. Planning is very important and all projects must be planned.

25. Project managers should always plan before they do. Therefore, there should be management plans for every knowledge area except Integration and Framework. Use of management plans is discussed throughout the *PMBOK® Guide* and yet most people have never been taught them, nor do they create them. Look for management plans in each chapter and make sure you have an understanding of each.

26. One should always follow the plan-do-check-act cycle stressed in quality management.

27. All changes must flow through the change request process and integrated change control.

28. The constraints the project manager must manage (often called the "triple constraint") include more than three items. They include scope, time, cost, quality, risk, and customer satisfaction. Any change to one must be investigated for impacts to all as part of integrated change control.

29. The *PMBOK® Guide* talks about what is needed for a larger project. Therefore, many of the items described in the *PMBOK® Guide* are inappropriate for some projects, maybe yours. Make sure you understand why the processes and work described in the *PMBOK® Guide* would be necessary on larger projects in order to pass the exam. The *PMBOK® Guide* is real-world; you just might work on small projects.

30. If you do not manage cost on your projects, you should be more careful studying cost.

31. Most companies have a project management office and that office has important authority over the project.

32. The project manager should decide which processes in the *PMBOK® Guide* should be used on each project.

33. The project manager is assigned during project initiating.

34. Notice how many times corrective action and preventive action are mentioned in the *PMBOK® Guide.* They are there because most project managers spend all their time dealing with problems rather than preventing them. Make sure you understand these two concepts exceedingly well.

35. Many project managers do not properly plan their projects. Therefore, the work they do while the project work is ongoing is vastly different from what should be done,

and different from what is outlined in the *PMBOK® Guide*. Make sure you check your knowledge of what activities are included in the project executing and project monitoring and controlling process groups. The exam will give you the most trouble in these areas.

36. There is a basic assumption on the exam that you have company project management policies (don't laugh, we will get there) and that you will adapt them for use on your projects. These may include project management methodologies, risk procedures, and quality procedures. So, assume you have them when you take the exam.

37. The project manager has some human resource responsibilities of which you might not be aware.

38. The project manager should recommend improvements to the performing organizations's standards, policies and processes. Such recommendations are expected and welcomed by management.

39. Quality should be considered whenever there is a change to any component of the "triple constraint."

40. Quality should be checked before an activity or work package is completed.

41. The project manager must spend time trying to improve quality.

42. The project manager must determine metrics to be used to measure quality before the project work begins.

43. The project manager must put in place a plan for continually improving processes.

44. The project manager must make sure the authorized approaches and processes are followed.

45. Some of the quality activities could be done by a quality assurance or quality control department.

46. You are required to understand that people must be compensated for their work. (I am serious, this question has appeared on the exam.)

47. A project manager creates a reward system during the planning process group.

48. You should spend time documenting who should do what.

49. Since most projects are managed in a matrix environment, such seemingly easy topics as motivational theories and powers of the project manager become quite serious on the exam.

50. All roles and responsibilities on the project must be clearly assigned and closely linked to the project scope statement.

51. Lessons learned (as part of historical records) is a PMI-ism.

Common Project Management Errors and Pitfalls

If you were reading this chapter carefully, you noted that common errors in project management are often listed as choices on the exam. Here is a summary of some of the major errors even experienced project managers make, so that you can be sure you will not make the same mistakes.

Errors include:

- Focusing on asking for percent complete
- Holding "go around the room" type status meetings
- Spending most of your time babysitting team members by constantly checking on them
- Asking to cut 10 percent off the estimate
- Thinking a bar (Gantt) chart is a project management plan
- Not attempting to obtain finalized requirements
- Not getting real resource commitments
- Not having a reward system
- Not focusing on quality
- Not having a control system
- Not having management plans
- Not measuring against the project management plan, or even creating metrics
- Not spending time finding and eliminating root causes of problems or deviations
- Not implementing corrective action to keep the project in line with the project management plan
- Not reevaluating the effectiveness of the project management plan
- Not reevaluating the accuracy or completeness of schedule, cost, scope
- Ignoring resource managers' need to have their people do their own departments' work
- Not realizing the project can affect the reputation of team members
- Not realizing the project manager has some human resource responsibilities to the project team, such as project job descriptions and adding letters of recommendation to team members' human resource files
- Blaming unrealistic schedules on management instead of realizing they are the project manager's responsibility

Project Management Framework

The trick to reading this chapter is to make sure you keep an open mind and specifically look for things you do not know. You will find lots of small things. These can add up on the exam. Just knowing the true definition of a project can get you up to four questions right on the exam. Most importantly, read this chapter (and the rest of this book) with an open mind to finding out what you do not know. You will LEARN, rather than just MEMORIZE to pass the exam. You will be a better project manager when you are finished. My purpose is to help you to learn!

Definition of a Project (page 5; all page number references are to the *PMBOK® Guide—Third Edition*):
You must understand the definition of a project.
- Temporary endeavor with a beginning and an end
- Creates a unique product, service or result
- Is progressively elaborated—distinguishing characteristics of each unique project will be progressively detailed as the project is better understood

Think this is on the exam? No it is not, at least not on the exam the way you might think. Let me explain.

What is a project? If your boss walked in to your office today and said, "The system is broken. Can you figure out what is wrong with it and fix it?" would this be a project?

Are you reading on before you have thought through the question I asked? Please read it again and think of your answer. Make the wrong decision and your career may be over.

I have taught thousands of students and almost no one has been taught the concept that you must take what you are given and organize the work into appropriate projects. If you know the definition of a project, then you know that the planning process will produce schedules and budgets. Can you schedule "fix it" if you do not know what is wrong? Of course you cannot, so there are at least two projects in the previous story.

Remember that a project manager must come up with a project management plan that can be agreed to, that people believe is realistic, and most importantly, that they can stake their reputations on. It is time someone said this out loud: Excluding approved changes for additional work, if the project manager does not get the project completed for the time and cost they agreed to (in addition to meeting other objectives) he should be relieved of his position! Why so dramatic? Studies conducted by the Standish Group in 2004 show that only 34 percent of projects are successful. This means we are doing a bad job of project management and things need to change.

The exam will give you situations which you will need to analyze. It may describe issues where more than one project is being managed as a single project, or there is not a real, authorized project at all. This should be easy to see, now that I have warned you.

There is another major issue that may be a problem for you on the exam. Do you know what a project is? Are you really working on projects? If your "projects" are less than three months long and have less than 20 people on the team, you might not be working on projects. For example, let's say you work on a help desk. Someone contacts you about a problem they are having and your job is to fix it. Certainly such things as a WBS will be of great help, but do you need a network diagram? How about management plans for scope, time and cost? Probably not. What about hardware installation projects? Are they all the same? Maybe they are not really projects at all.

TRICKS OF THE TRADE In order to pass this exam, you will need to get your mind around things that are definitely projects. I suggest that you think of much larger projects than your own. When you do that, more of what is described here will make sense and you will better understand what is intended.

Operational Work (page 6) Operational work is different than project work. You must be able to tell the difference for the exam. You may see instances where the real problem in the question is that someone is attempting to manage ongoing work, like manufacturing, rather than a project.

What Is Project Management (page 8) Many people think project management is just managing, or even worse, that one can buy some software and be a project manager. Project management is a profession which is growing extremely fast. It is both a science and an art, and follows a systematic process. The Project Management Institute breaks project management into Professional and Social Responsibility, knowledge areas and process groups. Knowledge areas are Integration, Scope, Time, Cost, Quality, Human Resources, Communications, Risk and Procurement. Process groups follow the process of project management: Initiating Process Group, Planning Process Group, Executing Process Group, Monitoring and Controlling Process Group, Closing Process Group.

The answer to "What is project management?" is described throughout this book. It can involve technical terms and processes, but it also involves roles and responsibilities and authority level. Do you know what project management is? Chances are, there are some key aspects of project management that have slipped by you and will be on the exam. Many people with advanced degrees in project management fail this exam because they do not know what project management really is. Be careful to discover the answer as you read this entire book. If you are reading this for the second time, have you already discovered that project management might be more than you thought?

What Is a Program (page 16) A program is a group of projects. Their management is coordinated because they may use the same resources, the results of one project feed into another, or they are parts of a larger "project" that has been broken down to smaller projects.

This coordination provides decreased risk, economies of scale and improved management that could not be achieved if the projects were not managed as parts of a program.

When you discover that you have more than one project, you can manage them as separate projects or, if there is a benefit to it, you can manage all the projects as a program. This should be done, as the definition says, only when there is a value to it.

Project Management Office (PMO or Program Office) (pages 17, 32) A
department that centralizes the management of projects. A PMO usually takes one of three roles:
- Providing the policies, methodologies and templates for managing projects within the organization
- Providing support and guidance to others in the organization on how to manage projects, training others in project management or project management software, and assisting with specific project management tools
- Providing project managers for different projects, and being responsible for the results of those projects (All projects, or projects of a certain size, type or influence, are managed by this office)

Be careful to understand the authority of the PMO and how it is different from the other players on a project. The PMO is an organizational structure, not a person. The role of the project manager is described throughout this book. The roles of the sponsor and other people involved in a project are described in the Human Resources chapter. The PMO may:
- Manage the interdependencies between projects
- Help provide resources
- Terminate projects
- Help gather lessons learned and make them available to other projects
- Provide templates (i.e., for work breakdown structures)
- Provide guidance
- Provide enterprise project management software
- Be more heavily involved during project initiating than later in the project
- Be part of the change control board

There is a strong trend to start PMOs. But realize the risk. If they do poorly, they generate a negative feeling towards professional project management that can set your company back years. To make them work, you should remember these key concepts:
- The role of the PMO must be clearly defined
- Pick one of the three roles, as previously defined, and stick to it without trying to do everything
- All those who are in the PMO must be PMP certified
- The commitment of executive management is required
- The PMO will not improve your project performance without the use of proper project management processes and techniques, so professional project management must be encouraged

Objectives There can be lots of different types of objectives mentioned on the exam, from project objectives (the most important type) to product objectives, cost objectives and stakeholder objectives. Make sure you read each question that mentions objectives carefully.

Project objectives are critical on a project as illustrated by the following summary. Read carefully to better understand this focus.
- Project objectives are contained in the preliminary project scope statement and project scope statement

- Projects are considered complete when the objectives have been met
- A reason for terminating a project before completion is that the project objectives cannot be met
- A more complete understanding of the objectives is achieved over the length of the project
- It is the project manager's role to accomplish the project objectives
- Objectives should be clear and achievable
- The reason for quality activities is to make sure the project meets its objectives
- The reason for the risk process group is to enhance opportunities and reduce threats to the project objectives
- Things that could negatively impact the project objectives, such as risk and stakeholders' influence should be watched and tracked
- Projects often require tradeoffs between the project requirements and the project objectives
- Project objectives are determined in the initiating process group and refined in the planning process group
- One of the purposes of the develop project management plan process is to determine how work will be accomplished to meet project objectives

Management by Objectives (MBO) A management philosophy that says an organization should be managed by objectives. It has three steps:

1. Establish unambiguous and realistic objectives
2. Periodically evaluate if objectives are being met
3. Implement corrective action

You should understand what this means for the project manager. If the project is not in line with or does not support the corporate objectives, the project is likely to lose resources, assistance and attention. You should also understand that MBO works only if management supports it.

Constraints or "Triple Constraint" (page 8) It is often said that a project manager must handle or juggle many things to accomplish a project. Project constraints are time, cost, risk, scope, or any other factors that limit options. Such factors may include the date a milestone or the project must be completed, or the maximum allowable risk a project may have. The "triple constraint" is used to help evaluate competing demands. Triple constraint is an old term that originally included cost, time and scope. A more advanced, expanded definition also includes quality, risk and customer satisfaction (or stakeholder satisfaction). The exam and this book will use the term "triple constraint" to refer to the expanded definition.

Management directly or indirectly sets the priority of each of the components of the "triple constraint." This prioritization is used throughout the project by the project manager to properly plan the project, evaluate the impact of changes and prove successful project completion. It is important to realize that a change to one component of the "triple constraint" should be evaluated for an effect on the other components. In other words, it is unlikely that you can shorten the schedule without causing a negative impact on cost, risk, etc.

It is understood that stakeholders, managers and others will try to get something changed or added to the project. It is the project manager's responsibility to analyze these change requests and identify the impacts to all components of the "triple constraint" through integrated change control. You will see the concept of the "triple constraint" used in many areas of this book. Take time to really understand the integrated change control discussion in the Integration chapter and how it relates to the "triple constraint." Whenever you see the term here, remember that we are using the broader definition.

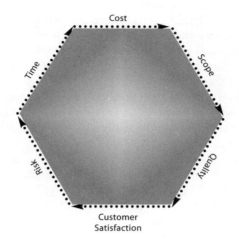

OPM3 PMI's organizational maturity model for project management is called OPM3. This model is designed to help organizations determine their level of maturity in project management. You need only know it exists for the exam.

Areas of Expertise (page 12) It is important to realize that a project manager can successfully manage a project whether or not he has relevant technical knowledge. A nurse can manage a construction project. An engineer can manage a graphic design project. (Obviously, technical knowledge is preferred.) Project managers must have people-managing and interpersonal skills and general management skills such as negotiation, leadership and mentoring. A key area of expertise for a project manager is understanding the project environment. This can involve knowing who the stakeholders are, why the project is being done and what is the strategic plan of the performing organization (the company or division of the company doing the project).

Stakeholder, Stakeholder Management (page 24) You should think of stakeholders as more than the project manager, customer, sponsor and team. A stakeholder is someone whose interests may be positively or negatively impacted by the project. Key stakeholders include: the project manager, customer, performing organization, project team, project management team, sponsor, and the project management office. They may also include those who may exert influence over the project, but would not otherwise be considered stakeholders.

You will see the topic of stakeholders repeated and expanded as you read this book, as their needs are analyzed and managed throughout the project. For example, in creating the preliminary project scope statement, the project manager analyzes the needs of the sponsor, who is also a stakeholder. Interestingly, when you pass your exam and receive your score sheet, you will only see stakeholder analysis specifically mentioned under the Initiating process group, although it is done throughout the project.

Many people score poorly here, so read the next area very carefully. See also the section on roles and responsibilities in the Human Resources chapter.

What should we do with stakeholders?

- **Identify ALL of them.** Ask yourself, "Why would this be so important?" Get the answer right and you will get two more answers correct on the exam. Any stakeholders who are missed will likely be found later. When they are uncovered, they will make changes and could cause delays. Changes made later in the project are much more costly and harder to integrate than those made earlier. Identifying all the stakeholders helps create a better organized project that meets all the stakeholders' interests. A list of stakeholders is included in the project team directory.

- **Determine ALL of their requirements.** This is neither easy nor fast, but the project manager must make every effort to obtain all the requirements before the work begins. Do you try to do this? How hard do you really try? Most project managers do not make the attempt.

  To realize why this is important, think about the effects of starting a project without all the requirements. Those effects would likely include changes, delay and possible failure. How would it look if you had to say to your manager, "I did not know Kerry was a stakeholder on this project. Now that I know this, I need to extend the schedule to accommodate her needs, or to cut out of the project another stakeholder's needs." This is just bad project management.

  Some people have said to me, "The nature of my project is that we will not know what we need for the second part until the first part is done." People will use any excuse to not do the right thing. You can imagine their faces when I say, "Well then of course you realize that you likely have two or more projects, not one, and you should be managing them that way."

  There are many ways to make sure you have all the requirements; from just asking if you do, to requirements reviews, to telling people the negative consequences to the company and to the project of a requirement found later.

- **Determine their expectations.** These are things the stakeholders expect to happen to them, their department and the company as a whole. They tend to be much more ambiguous than stated requirements, or may be undefined requirements. They may be intentionally or unintentionally hidden. Expectations include such things as, "I expect that this project will not interrupt my department's work" or "I expect that the system will be dramatically improved as a result of the project." Naturally, expectations that go unidentified will have major impacts across all components of the "triple constraint." Expectations can be converted to requirements. A great project manager will make sure they identify expectations.

- **Communicate with them.** Stakeholders' communications requirements must be determined early. Their information needs are analyzed and considered throughout the project. They are included in project presentations and receive project information including progress reports, updates and changes to the project management plan.

- **Manage their influence** in relation to the requirements to ensure a successful project. Stakeholders have greater influence over the requirements early in the project, but changes to the project requirements can have negative overall consequences to the project throughout the project's life.

This is one of the few parts of the *PMBOK® Guide* that actually uses the word success. A key to your success is how you handle stakeholders. Stakeholders must be involved and their involvement must be managed by the project manager. That involvement can be either extensive or minor depending on the needs of the project and the performing organization. Therefore, the list of where the stakeholders can be involved can also be extensive. The following are the areas the exam focuses on. If you miss two or more of the following answers, you should spend more time researching stakeholders in the *PMBOK® Guide*. Use a CD-ROM version of the *PMBOK® Guide* to search for the term stakeholders.

How the Project Manager Should Involve Stakeholders on the Project	Place ✔ Here If You Do It, Study Areas Unchecked
1. Determine all the stakeholders by name	
2. Determine all of their requirements	
3. Determine stakeholder expectations and turn them into requirements	
4. Manage and influence the stakeholders' involvement	
5. Get them to sign off that the requirements are finalized	
6. Assess their knowledge and skills	
7. Analyze the project to make sure their needs will be met	
8. Let them know what requirements will and what requirements will not be met and why	
9. Get and keep them involved in the project through assigning them project work such as the role of risk response owners	
10. Use them as experts	
11. Make sure the project communicates to them what they need to know, when they need to know it	
12. Involve them, as necessary, in change management and approval	
13. Involve them in the creation of lessons learned	
14. Get their sign-off and formal acceptance during project or project phase closing	

What if there is a difference between the requirements or other interests of the stakeholders? Such differences should generally be resolved in favor of the customer—the individual or organization that will use the product. Please see more about promoting interaction among stakeholders in the Human Resources, and Professional and Social Responsibility chapters.

Organizational Structure (page 32) A project does not operate in a vacuum. Projects are impacted by, and have impact on, the culture, management policies and procedures of the organizations they are part of. The best project managers look for these influences and manage them for the benefit of the project and the organization.

One of the main forms of influence is how the company is organized. This will dictate who the project manager goes to for help with resources, how communications must be handled and many other components of project management. So important is this that an answer to a question on the exam will change depending on the form of organization.

TRICKS OF THE TRADE The exam makes a habit of not telling you what form of organization you are in. When it does not say, assume matrix. If you remember this, you will get a few more questions right.

Organizational structures can be defined in terms of the project manager's level of authority. Many people have commented that they wished they had spent more time studying this topic. Questions on the exam related to organizational theory include:

- Who has the power in each type of organization—the project manager or the functional manager?
- Advantages of each type of organization
- Disadvantages of each type of organization

Functional This is the most common form of organization. The organization is grouped by areas of specialization within different functional areas (e.g., accounting, marketing and manufacturing). When you see the functional form of organization on the exam, think "silo." Projects generally occur within a single department. If information or project work is needed from another department, the request is transmitted up to the department head, who communicates the request to the other department head. Otherwise, communication stays within the project. Team members complete project work in addition to normal departmental work.

Projectized In a projectized organization, the entire company is organized by projects. The project manager has control of projects. Personnel are assigned and report to a project manager. When you see projectized on the exam, remember "no home." Team members complete only project work and when the project is over they do not have a department to go back to. They need to be assigned to another project or get another job with another employer. Communication generally occurs only within the project.

Matrix This form is an attempt to maximize the strengths and weaknesses of both the functional and projectized forms. When you see matrix forms of organization on the exam, think "two bosses." The team members report to **two bosses**: the project manager and the functional manager (e.g., VP Engineering, etc.). Communication goes from team members to both bosses. Team members do project work in addition to normal departmental work.

In a strong matrix, power rests with the project manager. In a weak matrix, power rests with the functional manager. The power of the project manager is comparable to that of a coordinator or expediter. In a balanced matrix, the power is shared between the functional manager and the project manager.

In a weak matrix, the project manager's role might be more of a:
- **Project Expediter** The project expediter acts primarily as a staff assistant and communications coordinator. The expediter cannot personally make or enforce decisions.
- **Project Coordinator** Similar to the project expediter except the coordinator has some power to make decisions, some authority, and reports to a higher-level manager.

TRICKS OF THE TRADE: A tight matrix has nothing to do with a matrix organization. It simply refers to locating the offices for the project team in the same room. Because it sounds similar to the other forms of organization, it is often used as a fourth choice for these questions.

Exercise Test yourself! You can expect questions about the advantages and disadvantages of each organizational form. Practice by listing your answers in the spaces below.

Functional

Advantages	Disadvantages
• Teams are formed based skill sets	• Information sharing b/w teams is slower
• Communication within team is fast	• Overall the company may be weak but individual teams are stronger
• centralization of expertise	
	• Little authority for PM

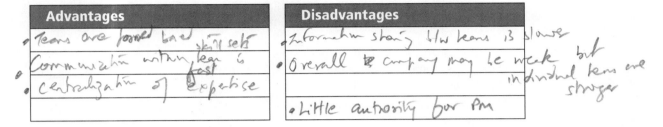

Projectized

Advantages	Disadvantages
• project teams are well formed	• Redundancy of job profiles
• good communication	• When workers are between projects they may not be productive
	• Conflicts ... possible

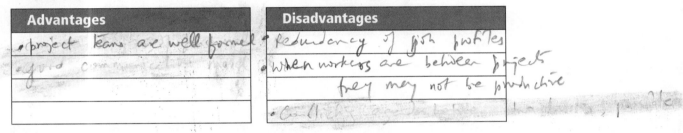

Matrix

Advantages	Disadvantages
• combines strengths of functional & projectized	• Possible conflicts between two bosses
• good overall communication	

Answer Several potential answers are listed on the next page. When reading this list you might wonder "advantages or disadvantages compared to what?" Compare everything to functional. But remember, that you are assuming that you work in a matrix organization on the exam. In this type of question, they are asking you to compare to functional without saying "as compared to functional."

Functional

Advantages	Disadvantages
Easier management of specialists	People place more emphasis on their functional specialty to the detriment of the project
Team members report to only one supervisor	No career path in project management
Similar resources are centralized, the company is grouped by specialties	Project manager has little or no authority
Clearly defined career paths in areas of work specialization	

Projectized

Advantages	Disadvantages
Efficient project organization	No "home" when project is completed
Loyalty to the project	Lack of professionalism in disciplines
More effective communications than functional	Duplication of facilities and job functions
	Less efficient use of resources

Matrix

Advantages	Disadvantages
Highly visible project objectives	Extra administration required
Improved project manager control over resources	More than one boss for project teams
More support from functional organizations	More complex to monitor and control
Maximum utilization of scarce resources	Tougher problems with resource allocation
Better coordination	Need extensive policies and procedures
Better horizontal and vertical dissemination of information than functional	Functional managers may have different priorities than project managers
Team members maintain a "home"	Higher potential for conflict

Life Cycle (page 23) A life cycle is a progression through a series of differing stages of development. There are two life cycles and one process you must know for the exam.

Product Life Cycle (page 23) This life cycle lasts from the conception of a new product to its withdrawal. A product can require or spawn many projects over its life. A project during conception might be to determine the customer's needs; a project during maturity might be to analyze the competition.

Product Life Cycle

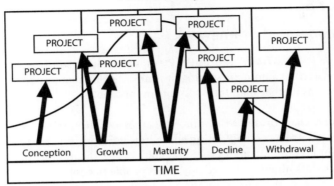

Project Life Cycle (page 19) You need two methodologies to complete a project; the first a project life cycle for what you need to do to *do* the work and the second a project management methodology or project management process for *managing* the project.

There are many different types of project life cycles depending on the industry you work in or the company's preferences. Some example life cycles are:

- **Construction** Feasibility, planning, design, production, turnover and startup
- **Information systems** Requirements analysis, high-level design, detailed design, coding, testing, installation, conversion and turnover to operations

The life cycle is sometimes referred to as the performing organization or department's methodology for projects. You need to know that this life cycle exists and you will see the phrase "project life cycle" on the exam but you should not expect detailed questions on project life cycles.

Project Management Process The project management process includes the initiating, planning, executing, monitoring and controlling, and closing process groups and is described in the next chapter.

PM framework items

- Project definition
- Stakeholder
- Organizational structures
- PMO & programs
- triple constraints
- Doing v/s managing L I, P, E, c/m, cl
L Life cycle

Practice Exam

Project Management Framework

NOTE: If you have *PM FASTrack*®, RMC's PMP exam simulation software, you will save time, learn more, and get automatic scoring of your tests plus about 1,000 more questions by using that program rather than the questions in this book!

1. Four project managers are having lunch together and discussing their projects. Most of the time they are just complaining about how hard projects are to manage in their company. Some complain about the stakeholders and the number of changes they cause. Others talk about how hard it is to get people to cooperate and perform. One project manager wants to focus on the advantages of the matrix type organization they all work in for their projects. Which of the following would he mention?
   A. Improved project manager control over resources
   B. More than one boss for project teams
   C. Communications are easier
   D. Reporting is easier

2. Two project managers have just realized that they are in a weak matrix organization and that their power as project managers is quite limited. One figures out that he is really a project expediter and the other realizes he is really a project coordinator. How is a project expediter different from a project coordinator?
   A. The project expediter cannot make decisions.
   B. The project expediter can make more decisions.
   C. The project expediter reports to a higher-level manager.
   D. The project expediter has some authority.

3. In a projectized organization the project team:
   A. reports to many bosses.
   B. has no loyalty to the project.
   C. reports to the functional manager.
   D. will not always have a "home."

4. A project manager is trying to complete a software development project, but cannot get enough attention for the project. Resources are focused on completing process-related work and the project manager has little authority to properly assign resources. What form of organization must the project manager be working in?
   A. Functional
   B. Matrix
   C. Expediter
   D. Coordinator

5. A project manager has very little project experience, but he has been assigned as the project manager of a new project. Because he will be working in a matrix organization to complete his project, he can expect communications to be:
   A. simple.
   B. open and accurate.
   C. complex.
   D. hard to automate.

Ⓑ □ △ 6. **A project team member is talking to another team member and complaining that so many people are asking him to do things. If he works in a functional organization, who has the power to give direction to the team member?**
A. The project manager
B. The functional manager
C. The team
D. Tight matrix

Ⓐ □ △ 7. **Who has the MOST power in a projectized organization?**
A. The project manager
B. The functional manager
C. The team
D. They all share power

Ⓓ □ △ 8. **All of the following are characteristics of a project EXCEPT:**
A. Temporary
B. Definite beginning and end
C. Interrelated activities
D. Repeats itself every month

Ⓐ □ △ 9. **All of the following are parts of the team's stakeholder management effort EXCEPT?**
A. Giving stakeholders extras
B. Identifying stakeholders
C. Determining stakeholders' needs
D. Managing stakeholders' expectations

Ⓓ □ △ 10. **A manager and the head of engineering discuss a change to a major work package. After the meeting, the manager contacts you and tells you to complete the paperwork to make the change. This is an example of:**
A. management attention to scope management.
B. management planning.
C. a project expediter position.
D. a change control system.

Ⓒ □ △ 11. **The project is in the planning process group when three stakeholders come to the project manager asking for information on the company's new project management methodology, where it came from and why it is different from how they manage projects. These stakeholders are also friends of the project manager and the entire group has worked together for years. The project is using some new terms like "corrective action" that are making some stakeholders nervous as they are unsure if the way the project will be managed is going to change along with new terms. What should the project manager do?**
A. Advise the stakeholders that he will keep them in the communication loop for the project.
B. Supply a list of new terms and their definitions.
C. Notify the project management office.
D. Make sure he maintains his authority as the project manager even though they are friends.

12. **A project manager is managing his second project. It started one month after the first and both are ongoing. Though his first project is small, this one seems to be growing in**

size every day. As each day passes, the project manager is beginning to feel more and more in need of help. The project manager has recently heard that there was another project in the company last year that is similar to his second project. What should he do?

A. Contact the other project manager and ask for assistance.
B. Obtain historical records and guidance from the PMO.
C. Wait to see if the project is impacted by the growth in scope.
D. Make sure the scope for the project is agreed to by all the stakeholders.

13. The project has been going well, except for the number of changes being made. The project is being installed into seven different departments within the company and will greatly improve departmental performance when operational. There are 14 project management processes selected for use on this project. The project manager is a technical expert as well as having been trained in communications and managing people. Which of the following is the MOST likely cause of the project problems?

A. The project manager was not trained in understanding the company environment.
B. The project should have more management oversight since it will result in such great benefits to the company.
C. The project should have used more of the project management processes.
D. Some stakeholders were not identified.

14. The project life cycle differs from the product life cycle in that the project life cycle:

A. does not incorporate a methodology.
B. is different for each industry.
C. can spawn many projects.
D. describes project management activities.

15. Stakeholders can be identified in which project management process groups?

A. Initiating, planning, executing, monitoring and controlling, and closing
B. Initiating and planning
C. Planning and monitoring and controlling
D. Monitoring and controlling and closing

16. Management by objectives works only if:

A. it is supported by management.
B. the rules are written down.
C. the project does not impact the objectives.
D. the project includes the objectives in the project charter.

17. Your management has decided that all orders will be treated as "projects" and that project managers will be used to update orders daily, resolving issues and ensuring that the customer formally accepts the product within 30 days of completion. Revenue from the individual orders can vary from U.S. $100 to U.S. $150,000. The project manager will not be required to perform planning or provide documentation other than daily status. How would you define this situation?

A. Because each individual order is a "temporary endeavor," each order is a project.
B. This is program management since there are multiple projects involved.
C. This is a recurring process.
D. Orders incurring revenue over $100,000 would be considered projects and would involve project management.

Project Management Framework Answers

1. **Answer** A
   Explanation Remember that if the question doesn't state what it is comparing to, it is comparing to a functional organization.

2. **Answer** A
   Explanation The project coordinator reports to a higher-level manager and has authority to make some decisions. The project expediter has no authority to make decisions.

3. **Answer** D
   Explanation The main drawback of the projectized organization is that at the end of the project, the team is dispersed but they do not have a functional department (home) to which to return.

4. **Answer** A
   Explanation In a functional organization, the project manager has the least support for the project and has little authority to assign resources. Choices C and D are forms of weak matrix.

5. **Answer** C
   Explanation Because a project done in a matrix organization involves people from across the organization, communications are more complex.

6. **Answer** B
   Explanation In a functional organization, the functional manager is the team member's boss and probably also the project manager's boss.

7. **Answer** A
   Explanation In a projectized organization, the entire company is organized by projects, giving the project manager the most power.

8. **Answer** D
   Explanation Choice D implies that the whole project repeats every month. Generally, the only things that might repeat in a project are some activities. The whole project does not repeat.

9. **Answer** A
   Explanation Giving stakeholders extras is gold plating (see the Quality chapter). This is not effective stakeholder or quality management.

10. **Answer** C
    Explanation This is an example of a project expediter position because you are not evaluating the change, looking for impacts, etc. You are merely implementing others' requests. In this case, you are acting as the project expediter and the manager is acting as the project manager.

11. **Answer** C
    Explanation This is one of the first times you are seeing a question which can be thought of having more than one right answer. It does not. There are many things

that the project manager can do, but what should be done? The company policies are managed by the project management office and the project manager should make sure the stakeholders have clear information and send them right to the authority on company policies for project management.

12. **Answer** B

Explanation Here again, there are many things the project manager could do. Choice A is not the best choice, as the other project manager might not be an experienced mentor. His advice might not be adequate to help this project manager. Choice C is reactive, while a project manager should be proactive. Choice D is not the best choice. It would be helpful, but does not specifically address the issues in this situation. If the PMO is contacted, the project manager can receive the knowledge of many project managers, historical information from many projects and have the assistance of someone whose job it is to help.

13. **Answer** D

Explanation Once again, it is important here to look for the choice that would solve the real problem. There is no reason to think that training (choice A), management oversight (choice B), or a need for more processes (choice C) are factors contributing to the number of changes. The root cause would be that stakeholders were missed and therefore their requirements were not found. Those stakeholders are now causing changes to accommodate their needs. The best choice is D.

14. **Answer** B

Explanation The project life cycle does incorporate a methodology—for doing the work—so choice A cannot be best. It is the product life cycle that spawns many projects, so choice C cannot be best. Project management activities are described in the project management process, so choice D cannot be best. The project life cycle is different for each industry and so choice B is the best answer.

15. **Answer** A

Explanation Stakeholders can be identified throughout the project management process groups. However, the earlier stakeholders are identified, the better for the project. If all of the stakeholders' needs and requirements are taken into account before plans are finalized and project work is begun, fewer changes will be needed later in the project, when they will be more costly.

16. **Answer** A

Explanation The best answer is the need for management to support the objectives.

17. **Answer** C

Explanation Because orders are numerous and of short duration, this situation is a process, not a project.

First Try: 3 wrong

Project Management Processes

Whereas the project life cycle describes what you need to *do* the work, the project management process describes what you need to do to *manage* the project. It includes:

- Initiating
- Planning
- Executing
- Monitoring and Controlling
- Closing

For small projects this might be exactly the process you need to use to manage your projects. For large projects, this process may be repeated for each phase of the project life cycle (page 69, Figure 3-12). The processes frequently overlap during the life of the project (page 68, Figure 3-11).

Many quality experts follow the Plan-Do-Check-Act cycle to improve the quality of processes. This cycle can be correlated to the project management processes as follows:

- Initiating = Start the cycle
- Planning = Plan
- Executing = Do
- Monitoring and Controlling = Check and act
- Closing = Ends the cycle

You know a lot about project management already. Want to make sure you do not waste hours of studying? This chapter cuts to the chase by summarizing huge volumes of information about project management. Sound good? It may be this chapter that gets you past the exam.

Take this chapter extremely seriously and look for gaps in your knowledge as you complete the chapter. It is also important to write in the book as you go. For reasons that cannot be explained here, it is not smart to use a separate piece of paper. Write in the book.

To pass the PMP Exam, you must understand the project management process groups and knowledge areas. On the next pages, you will find several ways to help you understand the overall project management process, as well as the relationship between process groups and knowledge areas. Go though them now and come back to them as you study.

Rita's Process Chart Since the first groundbreaking edition of this book in 1998, the following exercise has been one of the key things helping people pass the exam. There are over 50 questions on the exam about the process of project management; yet answering these questions can be very confusing. This exercise is designed to put it all into perspective.

NOTE: The chart is a trick for getting more questions right on the exam. It is a shortcut to help you gain a better understanding of project management, with little memorization. The chart is a consolidated version of the exercises you will complete in the rest of this chapter. It will help you to focus on the key items you need to know for the exam. Know this chart for the exam as follows:

- Understand the overall project management process (a PMI-ism)
- Find terms you do not know and learn what they are by looking them up in this book
- UNDERSTAND the project management process groups, when each should be done, and possible looping between the process groups
- Complete the Rita's Process Game that follows at least three times
- Understand what each item is
- Understand what column each item goes in
- MEMORIZE the specific order of the planning process. Knowing the planning column IN THIS ORDER can get you a large number of questions right on the exam.

Be prepared for questions that describe situations and ask you to pick the next thing to do or to name the project management process group you are in.

Rita's Process Chart

Initiating	Planning	Executing	Monitoring & Controlling	Closing
Select project manager	Determine how you will do planning—part of management plans	Acquire final team	Measure against the performance measurement baselines	Develop closure procedures
Determine company culture and existing systems	Create project scope statement	Execute the PM plan	Measure according to the management plans	Complete contract closure
Collect processes, procedures and historical information	Determine team	Work to produce product scope	Determine variances and if they warrant corrective action or a change	Confirm work is done to requirements
Divide large projects into phases	Create WBS and WBS dictionary	Recommend changes and corrective actions	Scope verification	Gain formal acceptance of the product
Identify stakeholders	Create activity list	Send and receive information	Configuration management	Final performance reporting
Document business need	Create network diagram	Implement approved changes, defect repair, preventive and corrective actions	Recommend changes, defect repair, preventive and corrective actions	Index and archive records
Determine project objectives	Estimate resource requirements	Continuous improvement	Integrated change control	Update lessons learned knowledge base
Document assumptions and constraints	Estimate time and cost	Follow processes	Approve changes, defect repair, preventive and corrective actions	Hand off completed product
Develop project charter	Determine critical path	Team building	Risk audits	Release resources
Develop preliminary project scope statement	Develop schedule	Give recognition and rewards	Manage reserves	
	Develop budget	Hold progress meetings	Use issue logs	
	Determine quality standards, processes and metrics	Use work authorization system	Facilitate conflict resolution	
	Determine roles and responsibilities	Request seller responses	Measure team member performance	
	Determine communications requirements	Select sellers	Report on performance	
	Risk identification, qualitative and quantitative risk analysis and response planning		Create forecasts	
	Iterations—go back		Administer contracts	
	Determine what to purchase			
	Prepare procurement documents			
	Finalize the "how to execute and control" aspects of all management plans			
	Create process improvement plan			
	Develop final PM plan and performance measurement baselines			
	Gain formal approval for plan			
	Hold kickoff meeting			

* → People management

✗ → Performance management

TRICKS OF THE TRADE **Notes on the Chart** Notice in the planning column of the Process Chart the word "iterations." This is an important concept. One creates a WBS, and the other items listed on the table above "iterations," to the best of his ability. As the project evolves, many of the initial plans will need to be modified or added to. For example, it is only after completing risk management that the WBS and the other items can be finalized. A risk response strategy (see the Risk chapter) might be to hire a contractor. That work is then added to the WBS. One might work with discretionary dependencies (see the Time chapter) in order to decrease some risk and thereby change the network diagram. The important thing to remember is that planning should lead to a realistic, bought into, and approved project management plan. Iterations help you get there.

Planning is the only project management process group that has a specific order of activities. However, you should also know that release resources is the last activity in the closing process group.

Team building, risk identification, risk response planning and integrated change control are focused on where they are placed in the chart. These activities can start in project initiating and do not end until project closing.

Notice that corrective actions (not preventive actions) and changes can be recommended or requested in both the executing and monitoring and controlling process groups. The processes of quality assurance, information distribution, select sellers in project executing, and scope, schedule, quality and cost control in monitoring and controlling result in requested changes. The changes are then evaluated and approved or rejected as part of integrated change control.

Rita's Process Game
The following pages contain the pieces of the Rita's Process Game. Cut them out and practice putting them into the correct process groups at least three times, on your own or in a group. This will help test your knowledge of what will be discussed throughout this chapter. When you think they are all in the correct process groups, put the planning processes in order. Lastly, check your answers using the chart on the previous page.

I have said that you must understand project management to pass the test. If you do not understand many of the items or you do not agree with the order in planning, you are lacking a basic understanding of project management. In that case, you might want to consider additional project management training before taking the exam.

Select Project Manager	Determine How You Will Do Planning— Part of Management Plans	Acquire Final Team
Measure Against the Performance Measurement Baselines	Develop Closure Procedures	Complete Contract Closure
Measure According to the Management Plans	Execute the Project Management Plan	Identify Stakeholders
Collect Processes, Procedures, and Historical Information	Divide Large Projects into Phases	Release Resources
Document Business Need	Determine Project Objectives	Document Assumptions and Constraints

Intentionally
left
blank

Determine Team	Develop Project Charter	Develop Preliminary Project Scope Statement
Create Project Scope Statement	Create WBS and WBS Dictionary	Create Activity List
Create Network Diagram	Estimate Resource Requirements	Estimate Time and Cost
Determine Critical Path	Develop Schedule	Develop Budget
Determine Quality Standards, Processes and Metrics	Determine Roles and Responsibilities	Determine Communications Requirements

Intentionally
left
blank

Risk Identification, Qualitative and Quantitative Risk Analysis and Risk Response Planning	Iterations—Go Back	Determine What to Purchase
Prepare Procurement Documents	Finalize the "How to Execute and Control" Aspects of All Management Plans	Create Process Improvement Plan
Develop Final Project Management Plan and Performance Measurement Baselines	Gain Formal Approval	Hold Kickoff Meeting
Complete Product Scope	Recommend Changes and Corrective Actions	Send and Receive Information
Implement Approved Changes, Defect Repair, Preventive and Corrective Actions	Continuous Improvement	Follow Processes

Intentionally
left
blank

Team Building	Give Recognition and Rewards	Hold Progress Meetings
Use Work Authorization System	Request Seller Responses	Select Sellers
Determine Variances and Whether They Warrant Corrective Action or a Change	Scope Verification	Configuration Management
Recommend Changes, Defect Repair, Preventive and Corrective Actions	Integrated Change Control	Approve Changes, Defect Repair, Preventive and Corrective Actions
Risk Audits	Manage Reserves	Use Issue Logs

Intentionally
left
blank

Facilitate Conflict Resolution	Measure Team Member Performance	Report on Performance
Create Forecasts	Administer Contracts	Confirm Work Is Done to Requirements
Gain Formal Acceptance of the Product	Final Performance Reporting	Index and Archive Records
Update Lessons Learned Knowledge Base	Hand Off Completed Product	Determine Company Culture and Existing Systems

Intentionally
left
blank

The What-Comes-Before Game Here is another game to see if you really have it. Only do this game after you have completed Rita's Process Game at least three times. Then you will really be able to judge if you know this.

Instructions Name the project planning process that comes before each of the following items.

Planning	What Comes Before?
Create network diagram	
Prepare procurement documents	
Create project scope statement	
Create work breakdown structure (WBS) and WBS dictionary	
Determine critical path	
Develop budget	
Estimate time and cost	
Gain formal approval for plan	
Hold kickoff meeting	
Determine quality standards, processes and metrics	
Determine what to purchase	
Determine communications requirements	
Iterations	
Create process improvement plan	
Determine roles and responsibilities	
Risk identification, qualitative and quantitative risk analysis and risk response planning	
Estimate resource requirements	
Create activity list	

Answer to the What-Comes-Before Game

Planning	What Comes Before?	
Create network diagram	Create activity list	
Prepare procurement documents	Determine what to purchase	
Create project scope statement	Determine how you will do planning	
Create work breakdown structure (WBS) and WBS dictionary	Determine team	
Determine critical path	Estimate time and cost	
Develop budget	Develop schedule	
Estimate time and cost	Estimate resource requirements	
Gain formal approval for plan	Develop final PM plan and performance measurement baselines	
Hold kickoff meeting	Gain formal approval for plan	
Determine quality standards, processes and metrics	Develop budget	
Determine what to purchase	Iterations	
Determine communications requirements	Determine roles and responsibilities	
Iterations	Risk identification, qualitative and quantitative risk analysis, and risk response planning	
Create process improvement plan	Finalize the "how you will execute and control" aspects of all management plans	
Determine roles and responsibilities	Determine quality standards, processes and metrics	
Risk identification, qualitative and quantitative risk analysis and risk response planning	Determine communications requirements	
Estimate resource requirements	Create network diagram	
Create activity list	Create work breakdown structure (WBS) and WBS dictionary	

How to Use the Rest of This Chapter
For many, this is the hardest chapter in the book and uncovers the most gaps in their knowledge. As you read this chapter, you will see many exercises. They are designed to help you explore what needs to be done as a project manager during each of the project management process groups. Spend about two to five minutes trying to answer each exercise and about five to fifteen minutes reviewing the answers to each exercise. The point of the exercises is to help you discover gaps in your project management knowledge. It is NOT to have you regurgitate long lists of data. The lists do not require memorization (unless indicated), but rather they require an understanding of what a project manager should be doing in the real world. Take these exercises seriously, as the exam includes common project management errors as choices and will focus on things most people don't know they should be doing. Any gaps in your knowledge should be thought through and researched.

You should read each chapter in this book more than once. On your second time through this chapter, don't try to recreate the complete lists in each answer. Just make sure you fill in the gaps you discover the first time through.

▬▬Initiating Process Group
Essentially, the initiating processes formally start a new project or project phase by incorporating all the needs of the organization into the project charter and preliminary project scope statement.

The initiating processes can begin with the project in varying states. Sometimes feasibility studies have been completed, and sometimes not. Sometimes the projects are selected from a list of possible projects before project initiation, and sometimes this is done within the initiating process group. In any case, the project charter and the preliminary project scope statement are the major outputs of this process group.

Inputs to the Initiating Process Group
You do not have to memorize inputs. Let me help prove it. Here is another trick. Try this exercise.

Exercise What do you think you would need to know or have before you initiate a project?

TRICKS OF THE TRADE **Answer** Note: You may wish the answers to exercises were not listed right after the questions. If this bothers you, simply keep a blank piece of paper available to cover the answer as you complete each exercise. My analysis shows that having the answers right after the questions helps you more than it hurts.

If you know what the initiating processes are, watch how easy the inputs are to guess.

- Business need
- Product description or product scope description describes the product requirements as they are known up to this point. In other words, what is the project being asked to do?
- How the project fits into or supports the company's strategic plan
- Who are likely to be stakeholders
- Contracts, if the work is done under a contract
- Industry standards
- Company change process
- How the company does business; defined processes and procedures
- Past relationships with the sponsor of the project, likely stakeholders and team
- Templates from past projects
- Historical WBSs
- Historical estimates
- What is going on in the company today? What are the major projects? What might their impact be on this project?
- The company's future
- The company's culture
- People who may be good team members

How many of the items on this list were also on yours? I think you had a lot of them. Now let's move further and consider what should be done during the initiating processes, by completing the next exercise.

Exercise What are the specific ACTIONS required to complete the project initiating processes?

Answer If you are thinking only in terms of the *PMBOK® Guide*, you come up with the following:

- Develop project charter (Integration chapter)
- Create preliminary project scope statement (Integration chapter)

This will not be enough to help you pass the exam. You need a more detailed understanding of what really needs to be done in the initiating process group (actions), and to find out if there are any of these you do not know, or have never done. Then you can fill in your gaps and pass the exam.

As you check your answers with the following list, remember, what needs to be done depends on the specific project and the industry. Make sure you understand the following as being done during the initiating process group.

Action	Place ✔ Here If You Do It, Study Areas Unchecked
1. Select a project from a list of possible projects	
2. Select the project manager	
3. Determine the authority of the project manager	
4. Collect historical information	
5. Divide large projects into phases	
6. Identify high-level stakeholders, their influences and their risk tolerances	
7. Turn stakeholder needs, wants and expectations into requirements	
8. Make sure business needs have been documented	
9. Document assumptions	
10. Document constraints (e.g., resources, schedule, cost)	
11. Ensure the product scope is as final as practical	
12. Understand how the project fits into the organization's strategic objectives	
13. Determine project objectives and product objectives	
14. Facilitate the resolution of conflicting objectives	
15. Get familiar with the company culture and structure as it relates to the project	
16. Find existing processes and standards	
17. Understand how the organization does business and what procedures and policies are already in place to use on the project	
18. Do planning using the project planning process on a high-level basis	
19. Complete order of magnitude estimating of the project schedule and budget	
20. Determine what form the project charter will take, why, etc.	
21. Coordinate project initiating efforts with stakeholders and the customer	
22. Work with the customer and others to determine acceptance criteria and what is and is not in the project	
23. Determine the initial project organization	
24. Document any risks already known	
25. Determine any milestones needed	
26. Determine how scope will be controlled	
27. Finalize the project charter	
28. Obtain formal approval of the project charter	
29. Create the preliminary project scope statement	

You may notice that many of the items in the previous table (e.g., estimates, assumptions, constraints, product scope, etc.) are begun in the initiating process group and refined later in the project management process. Here are some other items needing further clarification.

Project Manager Assigned You should notice in the previous exercise that the project manager is assigned early in the process. This means that the project manager is involved in the project initiating processes. Are you? Assume you are involved and make sure you understand what is going on during the initiating processes.

Business Need Do you know why your project was started? Does it matter? The reason the project was started will be taken into account throughout the project. It will influence how the project is planned, what changes are allowed, and the design of the scope of the project. Projects are initiated for many reasons. You need to know your reasons.

High-Level Planning Is Done During the Initiating Processes The other important thing to notice in the previous exercise is that high-level planning may be done during the initiating processes. Such planning may include creating a high-level WBS, order of magnitude estimating, preliminary project scope statement and high-level risk identification. How else can you come up with project objectives of schedule, cost, scope, etc.?

More discussion of unrealistic schedules is available on the Free Tips page of the RMC Web site.

The following diagram shows reasons the project initiating process is begun.

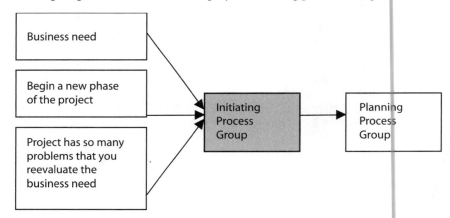

━━━Planning Process Group How much better would your last project be if you could magically do it over again? This is the power of planning, because it entails walking through the project and getting it organized before it is actually done. It is during project planning, in addition to when the work is being done, that resources, time and money can be saved.

Project planning determines if the project charter can or cannot be done, as well as how the project will be accomplished; addressing all appropriate project management processes and knowledge areas. This means that the project manager and the project team will determine what processes in the *PMBOK® Guide* are appropriate for the needs of the project, to avoid wasting project resources on activities that are not relevant to the particular project.

Exercise What are the specific ACTIONS required to complete the project planning process group?

Answer If you are thinking only in terms of the *PMBOK® Guide*, you come up with the following:

- Develop project management plan (Integration chapter)
- Scope planning (Scope chapter)
- Scope definition (Scope chapter)
- Create WBS (Scope chapter)
- Activity definition (Time chapter)

This will not be enough to help you pass the exam. (Heard this before?) You need a more detailed understanding of what really needs to be done in the planning process group (actions), and to find out if there are any of these you do not know, or have never done.

As you check your answers with the following list, note which items you do in the real world. Make sure you understand the following as being done during the planning process group.

NOTE: Do not fall into the trap of losing focus when you are working through these long lists. The lists purposely jump around and are intended to contain a lot of information to save you the time of reading hundreds of pages of boring text. Each list should take you about 15 minutes to think through.

Action	Place ✔ Here If You Do It, Study Areas Unchecked
1. Determine how you will plan scope, time, cost, risk, quality, process improvement and procurement and put that into beginnings of management plans for each knowledge area	
2. Refine requirements from project initiating so they are more specific	
3. Create a description of the project deliverables and the work required to complete those deliverables (project scope statement)	

Action	Place ✔ Here If You Do It, Study Areas Unchecked
4. Use the project scope statement to gain approval of the "final" scope from the stakeholders before further planning is done	
5. Determine team	
6. Break down the work into smaller, more manageable pieces (WBS)	
7. Create descriptions of each work package in a WBS dictionary so that the work can be understood by those assigned, with little gold plating	
8. Break down the work packages from the WBS into lists of activities, if necessary	
9. Sequence activities and determine predecessors and successors	
10. Estimate resource requirements	
11. Meet with managers to gain resource commitments	
12. Decide what level of accuracy is needed for estimates	
13. Have those working on the activities estimate time and cost	
14. Determine how long the project will take without compressing the schedule	
15. Develop preliminary schedule model	
16. Develop preliminary budget	
17. Determine quality standards and what metrics will be used to measure quality performance	
18. Determine what processes should be followed on the project to reduce the need to supervise work, to improve quality and to make use of standards	
19. Clearly determine roles and responsibilities so all team members and stakeholders know what their roles are on the project; what work they will need to do	
20. Determine what information you will need from other projects and what information you can send to other projects	
21. Work with all the stakeholders to understand their communications requirements	
22. Complete risk identification, qualitative and quantitative risk analysis and risk response planning	
23. Iterations—go back, in order to work toward a project management plan that is bought into, approved, realistic and formal	
24. Determine what to purchase	
25. Prepare procurement documents	
26. Look for positive and negative interactions from and to other projects that can affect this project	
27. Finalize how you will execute and control aspects of all management plans	
28. Plan ways to measure project performance, measurements to be used, when they will be used and how they will be interpreted	
29. Determine what meetings, reports and other activities you will use to control the project to the project management plan	

Action	Place ✔ Here If You Do It, Study Areas Unchecked
30. Determine how you will improve the processes in use on the project	
31. Develop final project management plan and performance measurement baselines by performing schedule network analysis, looking for options and confirming that project objectives can be met	
32. Gain formal approval of the project management plan from the sponsor, team and managers of resources	
33. Hold kickoff meeting with all the key stakeholders, team, team members' managers and the customer to make sure everyone is on the same page and to gain buy-in	

The result of the planning processes is a project management plan. Project planning is iterative. Each process above may use the results of the previous process, and each process may affect or cause changes to the previous processes. The idea, in the real world, is to follow these processes in the planning process group, attempting to complete each one as fully as possible. Then, after risk identification, qualitative and quantitative risk analysis and risk response planning, go back to finalize all the components of the project management plan. This process of planning saves time and is efficient. Can you guess why iterations start after risk management? Because it is only after risk management is completed that the final cost and schedule can be determined. Risk management could also result in changes to the resources, when they are used, in what sequence activities are performed, and almost all other parts of the planning process group.

Did the last two sentences make sense? If so, you are in excellent shape. If not, you will need to read the Risk chapter of this book carefully to find out what I mean and why those sentences should make sense.

Notice also the use of management plans in the previous list. Do you remember that these are PMI-isms? So many times project managers jump right into whatever they are doing without thinking about it beforehand. Such actions lead to inefficiencies, rework, mistakes, conflict, needless overtime and just plain bad project management. Better project managers think about things before they do them. Take a more formal approach to considering "How will I do this?" before doing the work. The answer to this question is a management plan.

There are many components to management plans but generally they consist of a "How will I go about planning scope, schedule, etc.?" and "How will I manage and control scope, schedule, etc., now that I have planned what needs to be done?" Both answers are determined in the planning process group. For clarity, the previous exercise groups management plans together instead of listing each management plan. It also lists the iterations of the management plans by separating them into the planning, management and control pieces. See more about management plans in the Integration chapter.

Another important aspect of planning is that the amount of time spent in the planning process group should be related to the needs of the project. A project where the schedule needs to have a high level of confidence will require more planning. A project with a low priority will require less planning.

Imagine that you have chosen to organize the project by phases (test phase, install phase, etc.) It might not be possible to plan each phase to a detailed degree until the phase before is almost completed. This is called "rolling wave planning." Even though each part of the "project" is called a phase, each phase could be, and maybe should be, planned as a project with its own charter, scope statement, WBS, etc.

It also needs to be decided what level of detail the project should be planned to. Many projects have enough information to plan to the activity level right away, others can only be planned to a work package level or even some higher level until more is known about the project. Projects that require more control to meet the project objectives of time or cost may need to be planned to a more detailed level. Those that do not need so much control can be planned to a lesser degree of detail.

Who is involved in the planning processes? Everyone! The project management plan is compiled by the project manager with input from stakeholders. Historical records from previous projects, company policies, magazine articles about projects and other such information may also be utilized in planning the project.

When are we in the planning process group? Project planning does not just occur when the project is beginning. We enter project planning for various reasons illustrated by the diagram below.

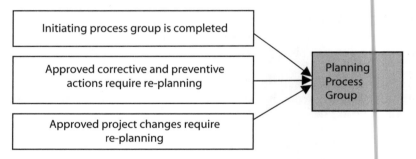

See the rest of the book for descriptions of each of the processes in the planning process group, particularly the Integration chapter for the project manager's role in creating a project management plan.

▬▬▬ Executing Process Group
The purpose of the executing processes is to complete work in the project management plan and to meet the project objectives. This is the "do" step of the plan-do-check-act cycle. The focus is on managing people, following processes and distributing information. It is essentially a guiding, proactive role accomplished by constant referral back to the project management plan.

Think about project planning again. Do you create a project management plan that is realistic and approved? Does your project management plan contain the same things that were previously described, such as management plans? Probably not. Therefore, the questions in this area can be impossibly hard and tricky as they will be asking about managing a project assuming proper project management planning was done. For the exam, get your mind around the critical difference planning provides and assume you have properly planned your projects in the real world.

Exercise Imagine you are about to begin the project executing process group. What type of ACTIONS must be taken?

Answer If you are thinking only in *PMBOK® Guide* terms, you come up with the following as part of the executing process group:

- Direct and manage project execution (Integration chapter)
- Perform quality assurance (Quality chapter)
- Acquire project team (Human Resources chapter)
- Develop project team (Human Resources chapter)
- Information distribution (Communications chapter)
- Request seller responses (Procurement chapter)
- Select sellers (Procurement chapter)

In order to pass the exam, you need an extremely good understanding of what it takes to manage a project. You also need to understand what management is like, assuming you have a project management plan that is bought into, approved, realistic and formal. Since many people do not have such project management plans, questions relating to the executing process group (as well as the monitoring and controlling process group which follows) are the worst scoring areas.

As you check your answers with the following list, note which items you do in the real world. Then you can fill in your gaps and pass the exam.

NOTE: Here is another long list. Keep focused and spend at least five to 15 minutes thinking this through.

Action	Place ✔ Here If You Do It, Study Areas Unchecked
1. Set and manage the expectations of all stakeholders	
2. Ensure common understanding of the work	
3. Implement the original project management plan or the project management plan that was revised as a result of control activities	

Action	Place ✔ Here If You Do It, Study Areas Unchecked
4. Complete work packages	
5. Collect and document lessons learned	
6. Establish and manage communication channels	
7. Evaluate the team's effectiveness as a team	
8. Implement approved changes, corrective actions, preventive actions and defect repair	
9. Implement quality assurance procedures	
10. Produce project reports	
11. Hold team building activities	
12. Follow ground rules at team meetings	
13. Obtain needed training for team members	
14. Distribute information	
15. Remove roadblocks	
16. Achieve work results that meet requirements	
17. Meet with managers to reconfirm resource commitments	
18. Keep managers apprised of when their resources will be needed on the project	
19. Commit project resources in accordance with the project management plan	
20. Manage project progress	
21. Guide, assist, communicate, lead, negotiate, help, coach	
22. Utilize your technical knowledge	
23. Authorize when work on work packages should be done using a work authorization system	
24. Hold progress meetings	
25. Send and receive information	
26. Focus on preventing problems rather than just dealing with them as they arise	
27. Make sure all team members have the skills, information and equipment needed to complete their work	
28. Focus on looking for exceptions to the approved project management plan rather than checking up on every team members' work or babysitting	
29. Recommend changes and corrective actions to be handled in integrated change control	
30. Follow organizational policies, processes and procedures	
31. Increase the effectiveness of processes	
32. Recommend actions to increase the effectiveness of the performing organization	
33. Determine if project activities comply with processes, policies and procedures	
34. Ensure continued agreement to the project management plan	

Action	Place ✔ Here If You Do It, Study Areas Unchecked
35. Keep everyone focused on completing the project to the charter, requirements or product scope, project scope, business case and project management plan	
36. Reevaluate the project's business case when a severe problem occurs	
37. Solve problems	
38. Implement the recognition and reward system created during the planning processes	
39. Determine team members who could not be named during the planning processes	
40. Implement approved process improvements	
41. Implement contingency plans (created in project planning), or workarounds as required	
42. Request seller responses to procurement documents	
43. Review bids and quotes, and select sellers	
44. Expend and monitor project funds	

Did you include such items as asking for percent complete and dealing with problems? Haven't you realized that percent complete may not be worthwhile, that it is too subjective, and that a project manager should be spending more time preventing problems than dealing with them?

Did you list meetings? I hope you were not thinking about "go around the room and report what you have done" type meetings. If so, you might not be able to pass the exam, because you have not realized that status can be collected through other means. Occasions when the team gets together are too important to just collect status. How about reviewing risks or upcoming contingency plans? Status meetings can cause you to lose buy-in from your team for wasting their time. If you need more on this, I encourage you to visit the Free Tips area of our Web site.

 Keep the phrases "Work to the project management plan," "Be proactive," "Adjust," and "Guide" in mind as you take the exam to make sure you are thinking like PMI.

The processes of project management are not always performed in the same sequence. Executing means executing the project management plan or the latest revised project management plan. The following diagram will illustrate when you enter project execution.

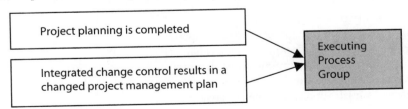

Therefore, you are always executing to the project management plan, but the plan might have changed over time.

▬▬**Monitoring and Controlling Process Group** Monitoring and controlling means measuring the performance of the project to the project management plan, approving change requests, preventive actions and defect repair, and managing changes. Here is a reason that project monitoring and controlling is among the worst scoring process groups on the exam. You are expected to know how to control a project that has a real project management plan. If you spend most of your time having meetings where people go around the room and report on how their work is going, asking for percent complete, not sure if the project will meet its performance baselines and thinking that an unrealistic schedule should be blamed on management, you will have such difficulty on the exam that you might not even pass. These actions are indications of a project manager who is not managing appropriately.

The following exercise should help you get your mind around what you should be doing to monitor and control a project. Be very careful NOT to jump right to the answers. The value is in doing these exercises and finding gaps in your knowledge and experience, not just memorizing the answers. The result is that you will be a better project manager, not just pass an exam!

Exercise What are the specific ACTIONS required to complete the project monitoring and controlling process group?

Answer If you are thinking only in *PMBOK® Guide* terms, you come up with the following:
- Monitor and control project work (Integration chapter)
- Integrated change control (Integration chapter)
- Scope verification (Scope chapter)
- Scope control (Scope chapter)
- Schedule control (Time chapter)
- Cost control (Cost chapter)
- Perform quality control (Quality chapter)
- Manage project team (Human Resources chapter)
- Performance reporting (Communications chapter)
- Manage stakeholders (Communications chapter)
- Risk monitoring and control (Risk chapter)
- Contract administration (Procurement chapter)

The above listed items are described in the chapters of this book as referenced. They will not, however, be enough to help you pass the exam. You need a more detailed understanding of what really needs to be done in the monitoring and controlling process (actions), and to find out if there are any of these you do not know, or have never done. Once again, read over the following list looking for gaps in your knowledge.

NOTE: **Because this is one of the worst scoring knowledge areas, you should spend considerable time here.** Do not lose focus as you read. Take a break in the middle of the list if you need to, and remember the list intentionally jumps around.

Action	Place ✔ Here If You Do It, Study Areas Unchecked
1. Measure project performance according to the measures in the management plans	
2. Measure against the performance measurement baselines	
3. Determine variances and if they warrant recommending a corrective action or change	
4. Exercise judgment to determine what variances are important	
5. Recommend changes, defect repair, preventive and corrective actions	
6. Approve changes, defect repair, preventive and corrective actions in integrated change control	
7. Facilitate conflict resolution using conflict resolution techniques	
8. Create forecasts	
9. Manage configuration	
10. Control schedule, cost and quality to their baselines	
11. Use issue logs	
12. Refine control limits	
13. Hold meetings regarding controlling the project	
14. Identify the root causes of problems	
15. Recommend updates to the project management plan	
16. Obtain formal acceptance of deliverables from the customer	
17. Identify the need for re-planning	
18. Manage the time and cost reserves	
19. Recalculate how much the project will cost and how long it will take	
20. Obtain additional funding when needed	
21. Hold periodic inspections	
22. Make decisions to accept or reject work	
23. Evaluate the effectiveness of implemented corrective actions	
24. Reassess the effectiveness of project control systems	
25. Spend time trying to improve quality	
26. Get information from stakeholders to determine if project controls need to be updated	
27. Identify and analyze trends	
28. Evaluate the effectiveness of risk responses in a risk audit	
29. Look for newly arising risks	

Action	Place ✔ Here If You Do It, Study Areas Unchecked
30. Reanalyze existing risks	
31. Use milestones as a project control feature	
32. Observe	
33. Measure individual team member performance	
34. Report on performance to all stakeholders	
35. Use variance reports to help correct small problems before they become serious	
36. Calculate estimate to complete	
37. Use and interpret earned value calculations	
38. Use quality control tools—inspection, Pareto charts, fishbone diagrams	
39. Do project performance appraisals	
40. Identify variances from the project management plan	
41. Control changes	
42. Ensure that only approved changes are implemented	
43. Work with the change control board	
44. Manage stakeholders	
45. Contract administration	
46. Hold status review meetings	

How have you been doing so far with the exercises in this chapter? Please keep in mind that the PMP exam is a test of experienced project managers. Chances are you know enough about project management if you checked most of the boxes in the previous exercises.

For the exam, assume:
- You have a real project management plan
- You have metrics for all project objectives already in place
- Your metrics cover all the objectives and are reasonable measures of how the project is performing
- You measure and the measurement gives you information on the status of the project

A project manager spends time and focused effort controlling scope, time, communications, risks, etc. Do you? Read over the following in order to get a better sense of what is control. Since these concepts overlap and repeat themselves, I am including them all here, to provide a better understanding of the overall monitoring and controlling process group. Control processes are also discussed in the other chapters of this book.

Scope Verification
- Inspect a deliverable
- Obtain formal acceptance of a deliverable from the customer
- Request changes
- Recommend corrective actions

Scope Control
- Manage actual changes

- Control impact of scope changes
- Recommend corrective actions
- Analyze variances
- Re-plan
- Recommend changes
- Adjust the scope baseline
- Document lessons learned

Schedule Control
- Follow change control system
- Measure schedule performance against the performance measurement baseline
- Manage actual changes
- Control impact of schedule changes
- Recommend corrective actions
- Request changes
- Analyze variances
- Document lessons learned
- Update project management plan
- Manage the time reserve
- Use earned value

Cost Control
- Follow change control system
- Measure cost performance against the performance measurement baseline
- Manage actual changes
- Control impact of cost changes
- Recommend corrective actions
- Request changes
- Analyze variances
- Document lessons learned
- Update project management plan
- Update the cost baseline
- Recalculate the estimate at completion
- Obtain additional funding when needed
- Manage the budget reserve
- Use earned value

Perform Quality Control
- Hold periodic inspections
- Ensure authorized approaches and processes are followed
- Recommend corrective actions
- Make changes or improvements to work and processes
- Complete rework as needed to meet requirements
- Make decisions to accept or reject work
- Evaluate the effectiveness of implemented corrective actions
- Reassess the effectiveness of project control systems
- Improve quality

Manage Project Team
- Track and report individual performance
- Resolve issues

- Manage and resolve conflict
- Update staffing management plan
- Maintain issue log

Manage Stakeholders
- Communicate to satisfy needs and resolve issues with stakeholders
- Maintain issue log
- Update communications management plan

Performance Reporting
- Continually measure project performance using variance or trend analysis, earned value
- Distribute information
- Hold performance reviews
- Identify and analyze trends and variances
- Issue change requests

Risk Monitoring and Control
- Respond to risk triggers
- Create and implement workarounds
- Implement risk response plans
- Evaluate the effectiveness of risk response plans
- Implement corrective actions
- Work in accordance with the risk management plan
- Update lists of risks and risk response plans
- Use risk management procedures
- Issue change requests

Contract Administration
- Monitor to make sure both parties to the contract meet contractual obligations
- Protect your legal rights
- Authorize work
- Performance reporting
- Inspect and verify product
- Manage changes
- Make payments

The process of project management is not sequential. The following diagram will illustrate when you might enter the monitoring and controlling process group.

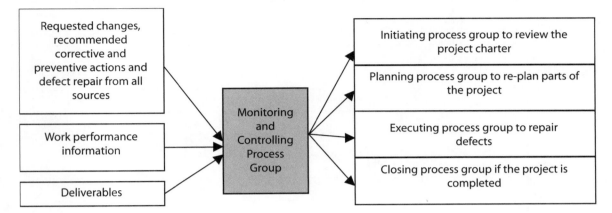

■■■■**Closing Process Group**   You have completed all the product scope. Is the project now done? No, work remains to be done. The closing process group is where the project is finished. This is one of the most ignored parts of the project management process. Get these important concepts down and the 14 questions about closing are generally easy.

Remember that a project is not completed when the final product scope is done, it is completed only when closure is completed. This effort will include administrative activities such as collecting and finalizing all the paperwork needed to complete the project, and technical work to verify that that product of the project is acceptable. It will also include any work needed to transfer the completed project to those who will use it and to return all resources back to the performing organization and/or the customer.

In many real-world situations, projects never seem to officially finish. Sometimes the project manager just goes on to do other things, sometimes the project just stops being worked on, sometimes the project decreases in priority. There are no official titles for the ways projects can end, because they should all be completed using the closing processes.

In any situation, ignoring project closing is a real mistake, as the work to be done during closure is extremely important to the performing organization and to the customer. The exam has many questions in this area to see if you know what the valuable activities are and when a project is really done. Try this!

Exercise Here is your last chance to score well on the exercises in this chapter. You can do it! What are the specific ACTIONS required to complete the project closing process group?

Answer If you are thinking only in *PMBOK® Guide* terms, you come up with the following:
- Close project (Integration chapter)
- Contract closure (Procurement chapter)

This will not be enough to help you pass the exam. You need a more detailed understanding of what really needs to be done in the closing process (actions), and to find out if there are any of these you do not know, or have never done. Once again, read over the following list looking for gaps in your knowledge.

Action	Place ✔ Here If You Do It, Study Areas Unchecked
1. Confirm that all the requirements in the project have been met	
2. Verify and document that the project, or project phase, meets completion or exit criteria set in place during the planning process group	
3. Obtain formal (legal) sign-off of the product of the project from the customer	
4. Document the reasons for early termination	
5. Make final payments and complete cost records	
6. Gather lessons learned	
7. Update project records	
8. Ensure all the project management processes are complete	
9. Update corporate processes, procedures and templates based on lessons learned	
10. Add new skills acquired to team members' human resource records	
11. Perform procurement audits	
12. Develop closure procedure	

Action	Place ✔ Here If You Do It, Study Areas Unchecked
13. Complete contract closure and administrative closure	
14. Analyze and document the success and effectiveness of the project	
15. Create and distribute final report of project performance	
16. Index and archive project records	
17. Measure customer satisfaction	
18. Hand off the completed project deliverables to operations and maintenance	
19. Release resources	
20. Celebrate	

Did you notice something very valuable in the list above? To some people, celebration and reporting final project performance seem like unimportant parts of the project, but not the best project managers! This is why you will see them on the exam. Having some form of celebration and a final report that shows, beyond a shadow of a doubt, that you were successful and sends a strong message to all stakeholders that your team finished a project. Isn't that a good thing? Would you sign your name to the last few projects you completed? Why not? What about having a party where the entire team autographs the project?

Remember that we talked about historical records as a PMI-ism? It is during project closing that the team compiles the final version of the lessons learned and makes them available to other projects and the project management office. In addition, a concerted effort must be made to index and put all files, letters, correspondence and other records of the project into an organized archive which is stored for use on future projects.

Formal sign-off is important because it indicates the customer considers the project completed and accepts the whole project. Formal sign-off in a contracting situation constitutes legal acceptance. Without that acceptance, one cannot be sure the project was successful. Imagine that the team never gains formal acceptance, they move on to other projects. Then the customer calls for additional scope to be added to the project. How difficult would it be to regroup the team to perform the new work? Gaining formal acceptance helps ensure this is not necessary.

In addition to obtaining formal acceptance, another important part of project closing is measuring customer satisfaction. Have you ever had a customer accept your work although they were not happy with the project? This is such a common occurrence that smart project managers will also measure the customer's satisfaction level during project closing.

Just like lessons learned, measuring customer satisfaction should be ongoing throughout the project, but MUST occur during all parts of project closing.

What about handing off the completed project deliverables to operations and maintenance? Did you realize there is work to be done as part of the project to complete such a transfer? The work could include meetings to explain the project nuances, training and other activities as needed by the project.

Confirming that all the requirements have been met also seems unimportant to many project managers. Most studies show that many requirements are not met on projects, especially on projects with numerous pages of requirements.

Once administrative closure is completed and formal sign-off that the products of the project are acceptable is received from the customer, other stakeholders and/or the sponsor, the project is closed.

Release resources is not just releasing team members. Make sure you realize that resources are used to close a project or project phase. To complete the closing process group, all human resources are released back to their functional areas and other resources (computers, supplies, etc.) are transferred to appropriate departments.

The following diagram illustrates when we might enter the closing process group.

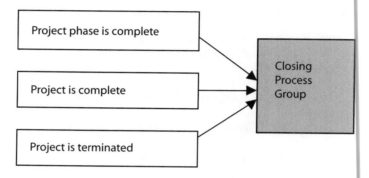

Inputs and Outputs
Why worry about inputs and outputs? Here is yet another trick to help you gain confidence in your understanding of the project management processes.

An input means:
- "What do I need before I can ..."

An output means:
- "What will I have when I am done with ..."
- Or, "What am I trying to achieve when I am doing ..."

These are logical. If you really know project management, they should not require memorization. What is an input to a WBS? If you cannot answer right now, you need more basic training before training for the exam.

Do not expect all the inputs tested on the exam to be clearly listed in the *PMBOK® Guide*. For example, you know that you need a team (or at least an initial team) to create a work breakdown structure, yet acquire team is not specifically listed as an input to create the work breakdown structure. You should rely on this book to understand inputs and outputs, but also be able to see the logic behind the inputs and outputs in the *PMBOK® Guide*.

TRICKS OF THE TRADE **Exercise** The following are the most important project management processes for which you should know the inputs and outputs. Make sure you add in this exercise real-world inputs and outputs that are not in the *PMBOK® Guide*. When you are finished, check your answers with *PMBOK® Guide* and the rest of this book.

Project Management Process	Key Inputs	Key Outputs
Activity Definition		
Activity Sequencing		
Close Project		
Plan Purchases and Acquisitions		
Develop Project Management Plan		
Direct and Manage Project Execution		
Activity Resource Estimating		
Schedule Development		
Scope Planning		

Project Management Process	Key Inputs	Key Outputs
Scope Definition		
Scope Verification		
Request Seller Responses		
Plan Contracting		
Select Sellers		

Exercise Here is one more TRICK to getting more familiar with the inputs and outputs. Try this exercise AFTER you have read the rest of this book. For each of the project management processes listed, fill in the rest of the columns.

Project Management Process	Knowledge Area	Process Group	What Does It Mean?	What Knowledge Area Process Comes Before?	What Knowledge Area Process Comes After?
Activity Definition					
Activity Sequencing					
Plan Purchases and Acquisitions					

Project Management Process	Knowledge Area	Process Group	What Does It Mean?	What Knowledge Area Process Comes Before?	What Knowledge Area Process Comes After?
Develop Project Management Plan					
Direct and Manage Project Execution					
Schedule Development					
Scope Definition					
Scope Planning					
Scope Verification					
Request Seller Responses					
Plan Contracting					
Select Sellers					
Develop Preliminary Project Scope Statement					
Monitor and Control Project Work					
Integrated Change Control					

TRICKS OF THE TRADE. **Answer** As you read the answers to this exercise, notice the words, "Whatever needs to be done." They repeat often and are meant to hint at all the soft, interpersonal activity needed, as well as the project management and technical activity needed. Using the phrase "whatever needs to be done" is a TRICK to understanding the full range of activity to which each topic relates.

Project Management Process	Knowledge Area	Process Group	What Does It Mean?	What Knowledge Area Process Comes Before?	What Knowledge Area Process Comes After?
Activity Definition	Time	Planning	Whatever needs to be done to create an activity list from each work package	None	Activity Sequencing
Activity Sequencing	Time	Planning	Whatever needs to be done to create a network diagram	Activity Definition	Activity Resource Estimating
Plan Purchases and Acquisitions	Procurement	Planning	Whatever needs to be done to create the contract statement of work and the procurement management plan	None	Plan Contracting
Develop Project Management Plan	Integration	Planning	Whatever needs to be done to create a project management plan that is bought into, achievable and realistic	Develop Preliminary Project Scope Statement	Direct and Manage Project Execution
Direct and Manage Project Execution	Integration	Executing	Producing work according to the project management plan	Develop Project Management Plan	Monitor and Control Project Work

Project Manage-ment Process	Knowledge Area	Process Group	What Does It Mean?	What Knowledge Area Process Comes Before?	What Knowledge Area Process Comes After?
Schedule Develop-ment	Time	Planning	Whatever needs to be done to create a bought into, achievable and realistic schedule, schedule baseline and final schedule management plan	Activity Duration Estimating	Schedule Control
Scope Definition	Scope	Planning	Whatever needs to be done to create the project scope statement	Scope Planning	Create WBS
Scope Planning	Scope	Planning	Whatever needs to be done to create a project scope management plan	None	Scope Definition
Scope Verification	Scope	Monitoring and Controlling	Inspecting project work and meeting with the customer to gain formal acceptance at the end of each project or phase	Create WBS	Scope Control
Request Seller Responses	Procurement	Executing	Whatever occurs after the procurement documents are ready and before the proposals are received	Plan Contracting	Select Sellers

Project Manage-ment Process	Knowledge Area	Process Group	What Does It Mean?	What Knowledge Area Process Comes Before?	What Knowledge Area Process Comes After?
Plan Contracting	Procurement	Planning	Whatever needs to be done after the statement of work is ready and before the procurement documents are finished	Plan Purchases and Acquisitions	Request Seller Responses
Select Sellers	Procurement	Executing	Whatever needs to be done after the proposal is received to obtain a signed contract and create a contract management plan	Request Seller Responses	Contract Administration
Develop Preliminary Project Scope Statement	Integration	Initiating	Whatever needs to be done to come up with the preliminary project scope statement for the project	Develop Project Charter	Develop Project Management Plan
Monitor and Control Project Work	Integration	Monitoring and Controlling	Whatever needs to be done to measure performance against the project management plan and recommend corrective and preventive actions, defect repair and request changes	Direct and Manage Project Execution	Integrated Change Control

Project Manage- ment Process	Knowledge Area	Process Group	What Does It Mean?	What Knowledge Area Pro- cess Comes Before?	What Knowledge Area Pro- cess Comes After?
Integrated Change Control	Integration	Monitoring and Controlling	Whatever needs to be done to evaluate the impact to all components of the "triple constraint" and approve or reject corrective and preventive actions, defect repair and changes	Monitor and Control Project Work	Close Project

Practice Exam

Project Management Processes

1. In which project management process group is the detailed project budget created?
   A. Initiating
   B. Before the project management process
   C. Planning
   D. Executing

2. The project charter is created in which project management process group?
   A. Executing
   B. Planning
   C. Closing
   D. Initiating

3. The project team has just completed the initial project schedule and budget. The NEXT thing to do is:
   A. begin risk identification.
   B. begin iterations.
   C. determine communications requirements.
   D. create a bar (Gantt) chart.

4. A detailed project schedule can be created only after creating the:
   A. project budget.
   B. work breakdown structure.
   C. project management plan.
   D. detailed risk assessment.

5. The person who should be in control of the project during project management planning is the:
   A. project manager.
   B. team member.
   C. functional manager.
   D. sponsor.

6. Which of the following is NOT an input to the initiating process group?
   A. Company processes
   B. The company culture
   C. Historical WBSs
   D. Project scope statement

7. The project sponsor has just provided the preliminary project scope statement. What is the NEXT thing to do?
   A. Begin to complete work packages
   B. Complete scope verification
   C. Start integrated change control
   D. Start to create management plans

8. The high-level project schedule constraints have just been determined. What project management process group are you in?
   A. Initiating
   B. Planning
   C. Executing
   D. Monitoring and controlling

9. The WBS and WBS dictionary are completed. The project team has begun working on identifying risks. The sponsor contacts the project manager, requesting that the responsibility assignment matrix be issued. The project has a budget of U.S. $100,000 and is taking place in three countries using 14 human resources. There is little risk expected for the project and the project manager has managed many projects similar to this one. What is the next thing to do?
   A. Understand the experience of the sponsor on similar projects.
   B. Create an activity list.
   C. Make sure the project scope is defined.
   D. Complete risk management and issue the responsibility assignment matrix.

10. A project manager does not have much time to spend planning before the mandatory start date arrives. He therefore wants to move through planning as effectively as possible. Which of the following would you recommend?
    A. Make sure you have a completed preliminary project scope statement and then start the WBS.
    B. Create an activity list before creating a network diagram.
    C. Document all the known risks before you document the high-level assumptions.
    D. Finalize the quality management plan before you determine quality metrics.

11. The project manager is making sure that the product of the project has been completed according to the project management plan. What part of the project management process is he in?
    A. Planning
    B. Executing
    C. Monitoring and controlling
    D. Closing

12. A project manager gets a call from a team member notifying the project manager that there is a variance between the speed of a system on the project and the desired or planned speed. The project manager is surprised because that performance measurement was not identified in planning. If the project manager then evaluates whether the variance warrants a response, the project manager is in what project management process?
    A. Initiating
    B. Executing
    C. Monitoring and controlling
    D. Closing

13. A team member notifies the project manager that the activities comprising a work package are no longer appropriate. It would be BEST for the project manager to be in what part of the project management process?
    A. Corrective action
    B. Integrated change control
    C. Monitoring and controlling
    D. Project closing

14. During a team meeting, a team member asks about the measurements that will be used on the project to judge performance. The team member feels that some of the measures related to activities assigned him are not valid measurements. The project is BEST considered in what part of the project management process?
    A. Closing
    B. Monitoring and controlling
    C. Executing
    D. Initiating

15. During the completion of project work, the sponsor asks the project manager to report on how the project is going. In order to prepare the report, the project manager asks all the team members what percent complete their work is. There is one team member who has been hard to manage from the beginning. In response to being asked what percent complete he is, the team member asks, "Percent complete of what?" Being tired of such comments, the project manager reports to the team member's boss that the team member is not cooperating. Which of the following is likely to be the real problem?
    A. The project manager did not get buy-in from the manager for the resources on the project.
    B. The project manager did not create an adequate reward system for team members to improve their cooperation.
    C. The project manager should have had a meeting with the team member's boss the first time the team member caused trouble.
    D. The project manager does not have work packages.

Project Management Processes Answers

1. **Answer** C
   Explanation Notice the use of the word "detailed." Such a budget is created during the planning process group.

2. **Answer** D
   Explanation The project charter is needed before planning and execution of the work can begin.

3. **Answer** C
   Explanation Iterations (choice B) cannot begin until the risks are identified, qualified, quantified and responses developed. These then create the need to revise the WBS and other parts of the project management plan. A bar chart (choice D) would have been done during the creation of the schedule, so it cannot be the next thing. Communications requirements and quality standards are needed before risks (especially risks relating to communications and quality) can be determined (choice A).

4. **Answer** B
   Explanation In the project management process, the project budget (choice A), project management plan (choice C) and detailed risk assessment (choice D) come after the schedule. The only answer that could be an input is the WBS.

5. **Answer** A
   Explanation The project manager should be named early in the project, during project initiating if possible.

6. **Answer** D
   Explanation Notice the question asks which is NOT an input to the initiating process group. Did you read it correctly? The project scope statement (choice D) is an output of the planning process group. Did you select choice A? Companies should have processes in place for hiring resources, reporting and managing risks on projects (to name only a few). Does yours?

7. **Answer** D
   Explanation The preliminary project scope statement is created during the initiating process group. Therefore the question is asking what is done next in either the initiating process group or the planning process group. For this type of question, you should look at the choice that occurs closest to the process group you are in. Choice A is done during the executing process group. Choices B and C are done during the monitoring and controlling process group. Choice D is the best choice, as it is part of the planning process group.

8. **Answer** A
   Explanation High-level project constraints are determined during the initiating process group.

9. **Answer** B
   Explanation Look at the order of planning the project the team has chosen. Though understanding the sponsor (choice A) might sound like a good idea, the sponsor is a stakeholder and understanding them is part of stakeholder analysis. That should have

occurred before the creation of a WBS. In planning the project, the project scope is defined (choice C is another name for finalize the project scope statement) and would come before creating a WBS. Choice D cannot be best, as that work does not come next in the process. Other work, like creating a network diagram, should be completed before risk can effectively be done. Only activity list (choice B) comes after the WBS and WBS dictionary.

10. **Answer** B
    Explanation This question is asking which of the choices is the most effective way to move through the planning process. Choice A skips the important steps of finalizing the scope and other activities. High-level assumptions are determined during the initiating processes and all the risks are documented during the planning processes, making choice C incorrect. Metrics are part of the quality management plan, making choice D incorrect. Choice B is best, as the activity list is created immediately before the network diagram.

11. **Answer** D
    Explanation Notice that this question asks about product verification, not scope verification. Scope verification is done during project monitoring and controlling, and product verification is done during project closing.

12. **Answer** C
    Explanation Even though the measurement was not identified in planning, the project manager would still have to investigate the variance and determine if it is important. Therefore, the project manager is in the project monitoring and controlling process group.

13. **Answer** C
    Explanation If you chose another part of the project management process, you probably forgot that the situation needs to be evaluated by the project manager before recommending a change or entering integrated change control.

14. **Answer** C
    Explanation This situation does not describe an actual measurement (a monitoring and controlling activity) but rather a meeting occurring during project executing talking about control issues.

15. **Answer** D
    Explanation Is this a hard question? The whole discussion of the team member and his actions is a distracter. The real problem is not that the team member is being uncooperative. He is asking a question that many team members want to ask in the real world. How can I tell you how things are going if I do not know what work I am being asked to do? The real problem is the lack of a WBS and work packages, otherwise the team member would not have to ask such a question. Choice A cannot be the answer because the project manager is not losing resources (what is implied by getting the manager's buy-in). Though a reward system (choice B) would help with cooperation, the real problem here is not cooperation. Choice C cannot be the answer because it does not solve the problem at hand (not knowing what the team member is to do). It solves another problem. If you chose C, be very careful! You can get 10 to 20 questions wrong on the exam simply because you do not see the real problem!

Integration Management

If you were asked, "What is the main role of the project manager?" what would you say? The answer is to perform integration. While the work of the project is being done, it is the team members' role to concentrate on completing the work packages. The project sponsor should be protecting the project from changes and loss of resources. It is the project manager's role to put all the pieces of the project together into one cohesive whole that gets the project done faster, cheaper and with fewer resources while meeting the project objectives.

The project management processes do not happen independently. A cost estimate needs to take into account risk reserves. A new resource added to the project may require changes in cost or schedule. In dealing with each situation the project manager is integrating the processes of project management.

This chapter, then, is about a key function of project managers. Integration could be said to cover the high-level work a project manager needs to do. The other knowledge areas in this book are the detailed work.

Read this chapter carefully as there is an embarrassing problem; many project managers do not know what project management is. You might find lots of things listed here that you do not know. Be careful, Integration is among the hardest areas on the exam!

Expect up to 14 questions on the exam! Many of the topics covered in this chapter relate to those in other knowledge areas. Therefore, I suggest that you read this chapter lightly the first time through the book. Return to it after reading the rest of the book and it will make more sense.

Rita's Process Chart—Integration Management
Where are we in the project management process?

To pass this exam you must understand both process groups and knowledge areas. This section of each chapter will remind you of Rita's Process Chart and where you are in the process as you go through each knowledge area. The areas that are bolded apply to the knowledge area being discussed. The rest of the chapter will provide more details and additional topics you will also need to know for the exam.

Initiating	Planning	Executing	Monitoring & Controlling	Closing
Select project manager	Determine how you will do planning—part of management plans	Acquire final team	Measure against the performance measurement baselines	**Develop closure procedures**
Determine company culture and existing systems	Create project scope statement	**Execute the PM plan**	Measure according to the management plans	**Complete contract closure**
Collect processes, procedures and historical information	**Determine team**	**Work to produce product scope**	**Determine variances and if they warrant corrective action or a change**	**Confirm work is done to requirements**
	Create WBS and WBS dictionary	**Recommend changes and corrective actions**		**Gain formal acceptance of the product**
Divide large projects into phases	Create activity list	Send and receive information	Scope verification	**Final performance reporting**
Identify stakeholders	Create network diagram	**Implement approved changes, defect repair, preventive and corrective actions**	**Configuration management**	**Index and archive records**
Document business need	Estimate resource requirements		**Recommend changes, defect repair, preventive and corrective actions**	**Update lessons learned knowledge base**
Determine project objectives	Estimate time and cost	Continuous improvement		
	Determine critical path	Follow processes	**Integrated change control**	**Hand off completed product**
Document assumptions and constraints	Develop schedule	Team building	**Approve changes, defect repair, preventive and corrective actions**	**Release resources**
	Develop budget	Give recognition and rewards		
Develop project charter	Determine quality standards, processes and metrics	Hold progress meetings	Risk audits	
Develop preliminary project scope statement	Determine roles and responsibilities	**Use work authorization system**	Manage reserves	
	Determine communications requirements	Request seller responses	Use issue logs	
	Risk identification, qualitative and quantitative risk analysis and response planning	Select sellers	Facilitate conflict resolution	
	Iterations—go back		Measure team member performance	
	Determine what to purchase		Report on performance	
	Prepare procurement documents		**Create forecasts**	
	Finalize the "how to execute and control" aspects of all management plans		Administer contracts	
	Create process improvement plan			
	Develop final PM plan and performance measurement baselines			
	Gain formal approval for plan			
	Hold kickoff meeting			

© 2005 Rita Mulcahy, PMP • Phone: (952) 846-4484 • E-mail: info@rmcproject.com • Web: www.rmcproject.com

The following should help you understand how each part of Integration Management fits into the project management process.

The Integration Management Process

The Integration Management Process	Done During
Develop project charter	Initiating process group
Develop preliminary project scope statement	Initiating process group
Develop project management plan	Planning process group
Direct and manage project execution	Executing process group
Monitor and control project work	Monitoring and controlling process group
Integrated change control	Monitoring and controlling process group
Close project	Closing process group

—**Develop Project Charter** (page 81) The exam could include up to eight questions that reference a project charter. You should understand what a project charter is and why it is important to the project manager.

Exercise Test yourself! Answer the question below.

What Is Included in a Project Charter?

Answer Unfortunately, many companies' project charters require information such as a detailed schedule and a full risk analysis that are not available at this stage of the project management process. A project charter is not a project management plan! The following is a brief example of what a project charter includes. It should help you to understand the elements of a project charter.

Project Charter

Project Title and Description (What is the project?) Customer Satisfaction Fix-It Project

Over the last few months the quality assurance department has discovered many of our customers' orders for our XYZ equipment have taken the customer ten times longer to place through our computer network than our competitors' networks. The purpose of this project is to investigate the reasons for the problem and propose a solution. The solution will be authorized as a subsequent project. Quality Control has detailed records of their findings that can be used to speed up this project.

Project Manager Assigned and Authority Level (Who is given authority to lead the project, and can he/she determine, manage and approve changes to budget, schedule, staffing, etc.?)

Alexis Sherman shall be the project manager for this project and have authority to select team members and determine the final project budget.

Business Need (Why is the project being done?)

This project is being completed in order to prevent a further breakdown of customer satisfaction.

Project Justification (Business case—On what financial or other basis can we justify doing this project?)

We expect that improved customer satisfaction will increase revenue to the company in the first year by at least $200,000 due to a decrease in service calls. As a side benefit, we hope that the project will generate ideas on improving customer satisfaction while fixing this problem.

Resources Pre-assigned (How many or what resources will be provided?)

Morgan Kolb and Danny Levins are already dedicated to the project because of their expertise in computer networks of this type. Other resources will be determined by the project manager.

Stakeholders (Who will affect, or be affected by, the project (influence the project), as known to date?)

Stakeholders include Connor representing Quality Control, Ruth in Customer Service and Mary in Marketing. These resources are available to assist the project as needed by the project manager.

Stakeholder Requirements As Known (Requirements related to both project and product scope)

Attached to this document are the detailed specifications for the existing system, the requirements that the existing system was designed to meet. It is expected that this project will not change how the system affects the existing requirements. The project must include utilizing the data available from Quality Control.

Product Description/Deliverables (What specific product deliverables are wanted and what will be the end result of the project?)

1. *A report that outlines what can be changed, how much each change will cost and the expected decrease in the time it takes to place an order resulting from each change. Few words are necessary in the report, but it must be created electronically and be agreed to by the heads of Quality Control, Customer Service and Marketing in addition to the project team.*
2. *A list of the interactions with our customers necessary to complete the changes. A work breakdown structure, due within two weeks, that outlines the plan for accomplishing the project, followed one week later by a list of risks in completing the project.*

Constraints and Assumptions (A constraint is any limiting factor and an assumption is something taken to be true, but which may not be true.)

Complete the project no later than September 1, 20XX. Spend no more than U.S. $5,000. We have assumed that Kerry will be available to assist the project and that testing can be done on the seller's computer.

Project Sponsor Approval:

_____   _____
Samantha Levins, *Executive Vice President*   Kerry Mulcahy, *Vice President*

Exercise Test yourself! Answer the question below.

What Does the Project Charter Do for the Project Manager?

Answer Do not underestimate the value of the project charter! The project charter is such an important document that a project cannot be started without one. If the project charter is your target for the project, and a definition of how success will be measured, then without a project charter, the project and project manager cannot be successful! Know the following for the exam:

A project charter provides, at a minimum, the following benefits:
- Formally recognizes (authorizes) the existence of the project, or establishes the project. This means that a project does not exist without a project charter.
- Gives the project manager authority to spend money and commit corporate resources. On the exam, this is the most commonly described benefit or use of the project charter. In most project situations, the project team does not report to the project manager in the corporate structure. This leads to issues of "how to gain cooperation and performance."
- Provides the high-level requirements for the project.
- Links the project to the ongoing work of the organization.

The project charter is also:
- Issued by a sponsor, not the project manager
- Created in the initiating process group
- Broad enough so it does not NEED to change as the project changes

Any change to the project charter should call into question whether or not the project should continue.

Constraints and Assumptions (throughout) Constraints are factors that limit the team's options such as limits on resources, budget, schedule and scope (e.g., management saying the project must be completed with only five resources). Assumptions are things that are assumed to be true which may not be true (e.g., it is assumed that we will not need engineering department approval before we start the activity). Constraints and assumptions are inputs to many project management processes.

Constraints and assumptions are identified and then managed. The sponsor, the team and other stakeholders can identify constraints and assumptions in the initiating process group and throughout the project. Constraints and assumptions are also reviewed for validity throughout the life of the project. If the constraints change or the assumptions are proven wrong, the project management plan may need to change. Assumptions analysis is part of the risk management process.

Project Statement of Work (page 82) The project statement of work is created by the customer/sponsor and describes their needs, product scope and how the project fits into their strategic plan. If you have worked with contracts, think of this as the long wordy document the buyer sends the seller. This document may not be complete when received as an input to develop project charter. It is further defined in the preliminary project scope statement and project scope statement in the initiating process group and planning process group. Please see the diagram later in this chapter to help you further.

TRICKS OF THE TRADE **Enterprise Environmental Factors** (page 83 and throughout) Since the beginning of time, project managers have had to deal with and make use of company culture and existing systems. The *PMBOK® Guide* calls these enterprise environmental factors. They are inputs to develop project charter and many other processes. The trick is to think of them as what they really are: "company culture and existing systems that the project will have to deal with or can make use of." They could also be thought of as the company "baggage" that comes with the project. With this trick, you can more easily understand the meaning of questions or the choices on the exam no matter how it uses the term enterprise environmental factors.

TRICKS OF THE TRADE **Organizational Process Assets** (page 84 and throughout) Since the beginning of time, project managers have also been dealing with existing processes, procedures and historical information. These help the project benefit from past company experience. The *PMBOK® Guide* calls these organizational process assets. The trick is to think of organizational process assets as what they really are, "processes, procedures and historical information."

Processes, Procedures and Policies Why reinvent the wheel? Over time, organizations develop processes, procedures and policies that have been tested to be best practices. Such information is a key part of organizational process assets.

Corporate Knowledge Base This concept can be important for you on the exam. Assume that your company has information such as historical records and lessons learned from previous projects and that the company has incorporated them into a corporate knowledge base that is available to all.

Many project managers do not even have their own historical databases from previous projects and so each project is essentially planned, estimated and scheduled from scratch. The creation of a corporate knowledge database of historical information and lessons learned is an organizational responsibility that can result in continuous improvement. Assume you have such historical information from all company projects readily accessible for the exam.

Historical Information Historical information (or data) is a record of past projects. It is used to plan and manage future projects, thereby improving the process of project management. Historical information can include:

- Activities
- WBS
- Reports
- Estimates
- Project management plans

- Lessons learned
- Benchmarks
- Risks
- Resources needed
- Correspondence

© 2005 Rita Mulcahy, PMP • Phone: (952) 846-4484 • E-mail: info@rmcproject.com • Web: www.rmcproject.com

Lessons Learned Project initiating involves looking up past lessons learned for use on the current project. But there is more to lessons learned than that. A detailed discussion of lessons learned is included in the Communications chapter of this book since lessons learned is a communications function.

Project Selection Methods There are many ways to select a project to be initiated from among many possible projects. What projects were considered before yours was picked and what the process was for selecting your project will influence how the project is planned and managed. There should be a formal process for selecting projects in all companies in order to make the best use of limited corporate resources. Without such a formal method, projects are often selected not for their value, but for less quantitative reasons such as personal relationships. You should know that such efforts occur and that the project manager may be involved, even if you are not involved in them in your real world. Two project selection methods frequently on the exam are:

1. **Benefit measurement methods** (Comparative approach)
   - Murder board—a panel of people who try to shoot down a new project idea
   - Peer review
   - Scoring models
   - Economic models
   - Benefit compared to cost

2. **Constrained optimization methods** (Mathematical approach)
   - Linear programming
   - Integer programming
   - Dynamic programming
   - Multi-objective programming

What type of project selection technique is linear programming? The answer is constrained optimization. The exam does not require you to know what each constrained optimization method means.

Although the project manager may not be involved in the selection of one project over another, you need to understand that such a process occurs, as well as the two methods of project selection that can be used.

TRICKS OF THE TRADE **Project Management Methodology** (page 85) Many companies refer to a project management methodology, or just methodology, and take these words to mean "how they will do the work." As explained in previous chapters, what they are referring to, in *PMBOK® Guide* terms, is called the project life cycle. In the *PMBOK® Guide*, the term project management methodology relates to "How you will use project management on the project," or "What parts of the *PMBOK® Guide* you will use on your project." You will see the project management methodology listed as an input or tool of many processes. The methodology will influence the content of the project charter as part of the develop project charter process.

TRICKS OF THE TRADE **Project Management Information System** (PMIS, page 86) Think of a PMIS as all the software (automated tools) available in your company that can be used to help manage a project. It can include commercial and privately created computer software, Worldwide Web access and any other computer related tools. It is used to help submit and track changes, monitor and control project activities and other efforts from project initiating to project closing. As in all computerized systems, there are usually some manual components.

This term frequently shows up on the exam as a choice, as it is used in all parts of project management. Be prepared to see it often. Because there are an infinite variety of possible PMISs, you should keep this general description in mind.

Management Plans (throughout) Most people are not familiar with management plans, nor have they created them. Why are management plans so important?

Separate management plans are created for scope, schedule, cost, quality, process improvement, staffing, communications, risk and procurement. They are a key part of project planning and could be said to be the reason you exist as a project manager. Management plans are your strategy for managing the project. Someone needs to put the whole thing together.

A management plan means, "How will I plan, manage and control scope, time, cost, etc. for the project?" Think about this for a minute. A project manager must make sure that all the project management work that needs to get done is done. Instead of just planning how you will manage a project, the management plan focuses your thoughts and planning toward how you will manage each individual knowledge area.

Management plans are customized to the needs of the project, the style of the project manager and organizational influences. For example, a project scope management plan might address such topics as who will be involved in figuring out what the final scope will be, how you will do it (what meetings, expert opinions, etc.), how you will make sure that all the scope is completed and how you will control the work to the plan for scope.

Management plans, when completed, become part of the project management plan.

Remember that I just said that a management plan covers how you will define, plan, manage and control. Note the inclusion of control. While in project planning, the project manager must determine how scope, risk etc, will be measured to the risk management and project scope management plans, variances found and corrective actions, preventive actions or changes recommended, approved and implemented. Do you do this? If not, spend some time thinking about management plans. Once you understand what they are, questions are generally easy on the exam.

▬▬Develop Preliminary Project Scope Statement (page
86) The preliminary project scope statement is the first attempt to determine the project scope—what must be done to accomplish the project objectives. It is developed based on information from the sponsor.

TRICKS OF THE TRADE: Think of the purpose of the preliminary project scope statement as making sure the project manager and the sponsor have a similar understanding or a meeting of the minds about project scope before planning begins. This preliminary project scope statement will be further developed into the project scope statement during the planning process group, covered in the Scope chapter.

TRICKS OF THE TRADE: You can also think of the preliminary project scope statement as the effort during the initiating processes to obtain all the information needed in order to plan the project. This includes interviewing the sponsor, for the purposes of obtaining a clearer understanding of what needs to be done to accomplish the requirements. What would you want to know? Wouldn't you want more detail on the requirements, how success will be measured, and any information from the sponsor regarding risks, budgets and schedules? The preliminary project scope statement provides input into the planning process group by creating a high-level (or initial) WBS, cost estimates, and additional schedule milestones, as well as identifying initial risks, project organization, what is and what is not in the project, acceptance criteria, and project requirements.

Let's see how everything so far connects by looking at the following picture.

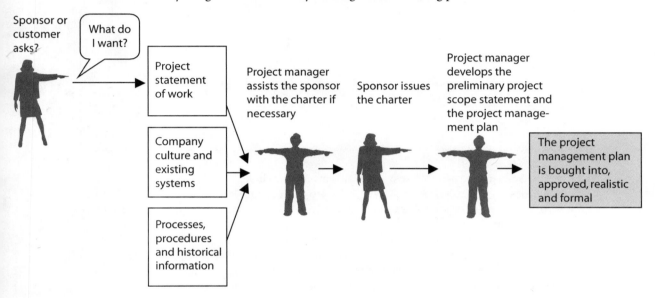

▬▬Develop Project Management Plan (page 88) First, let's talk about

what you now think of as a project management plan. The exam is especially designed to weed out those who do not know project management, including those who think a project management plan is a bar chart. If you are one of those people, it is likely that your knowledge of project management is too weak to pass the exam.

Knowing that a project management plan is more than just a bar chart, what do you think it contains? A project management plan is a multi-page document based on input from the team and other stakeholders. It contains all the management plans and the performance measurement baselines. It is these baselines that will be used to measure the progress and completion of the project. Once completed, a project management plan is used as a day-to-day tool to help manage the project. It is not just a document created for management.

Though it may evolve and change over the life of the project, a project management plan is designed to be as complete as possible when the project executing process group begins.

Develop project management plan is the process of creating a project management plan that is bought into, approved, realistic and formal. A project management plan is agreed to (bought into) by everyone, formally approved, everyone believes it can be done according to plan (realistic) and remains a formal document that is controlled and used throughout the project. You should spend time here thinking about how to accomplish B.A.R.F. in the real world. (Yes, I did just say barf!)

Exercise Test yourself! Make a list of the specific ACTIONS required to create a project management plan that is bought into, approved, realistic and formal.

Answer Some of the possible answers to this exercise include:
- Determine a methodology for creating the project management plan
- Work through iterations of the plan (e.g., change the work breakdown structure after risk analysis)
- Meet with resource managers to get the best resources possible
- Get resource managers to approve the schedule and when their resources will be used
- Apply risk reserves to the project schedule and budget
- Analyze the skills and knowledge of all the stakeholders and determine how you will use them on the project
- Meet with stakeholders to define their roles on the project
- Look for the impact on your project from other projects
- Agree on reporting formats and communications plans
- Agree on processes to report, control and incorporate change
- Give team members a chance to approve the final schedule that converts the team's activity estimates into a calendar schedule
- Hold meetings or presentations to let the sponsor know what project requirements, outlined in the project charter, cannot be met
- Crash, fast track and present options to the sponsor

If you got most of the answers correct, you are in good shape. It is absolutely imperative that you realize that a project management plan must be realistic. This means that everyone must believe it can be done. Why? Later in the project management process, you will need to constantly measure progress against the project management plan to see how the project is going. The end date, end cost and other constraints in the project MUST be met. There is no excuse. You will use the project management plan as the measurement tool to make sure the project meets these constraints.

So, when you think of the project management plan, think of all the meetings, sign-offs, interactions with other projects, negotiations, compressing, juggling, begging, crying, etc. that will be required to bring the plan to be bought into, approved, realistic and formal.

Configuration Management System (page 90 and throughout) With all the documents that are part of the project management plan and all the changes to them that will occur throughout the life of the project, wouldn't it be wise to have a plan for making sure everyone knows what version of the scope, the schedule and other components of the project management plan are the latest version?

The configuration management system may include a change control system and is part of the project management information system. It is designed in the planning process group and used in the integrated change control process.

Change Control System (page 90) A collection of formal, documented procedures, paperwork, tracking systems and approval levels for authorizing changes. There can be a change control system for each knowledge area in project management (scope, schedule, risk etc.) These systems are described in the management plan for each knowledge area (project scope management plan, schedule management plan, etc.) and are implemented in integrated change control as part of the overall effort to control change.

The collected change control system may include:
- A change control plan included in the project management plan outlining how changes will be managed
- Creation of a change control board to approve all changes (described later in this chapter)
- Change control procedures (how, who)
- Performance statistics (e.g., time/system, time/drawing)
- Reports (e.g., software output, milestone charts, resource usage)
- Change forms

The project scope management plan may add the following in order to control changes to scope:
- Specification reviews
- Demonstrations
- Testing
- Meetings to review scope to identify changes

Work Authorization System If you think of a larger project with team members from various locations, you might think it would be worthwhile to create a system for authorizing work—notifying team members or contractors that they may begin work on a project work package. In many cases this system for authorizing work is a companywide system used on the project, not created just for the project. Expect to see one question about this on the exam, but expect the term to be included frequently as a choice.

Baseline (Performance measurement baseline) To illustrate further why it is so important to have a B.A.R.F project management plan, the plan also contains baselines (performance measurement baselines) that will be used to measure performance against. Needless to say, the project management plan must be realistic and the project team must be willing to be measured to it.

There can be scope, schedule, cost and quality baselines, but many projects will also include a resource baseline or technical performance baselines. The scope baseline on a project includes the WBS, project scope statement and WBS dictionary.

Baselines are used during project executing to measure performance and to help control the project. Forecasts of final cost and schedule should be compared to the baselines. Projects that deviate far from their baselines should have their risk management process reviewed. Project baselines may be changed by formally approved changes, but the evolution of the baselines should be documented.

Baselines are mentioned a lot on the exam. They are only described in detail in this chapter of this book.

Project Management Plan Approval Since the project management plan is a formal document that will be used to manage the execution of the project and includes items like project completion dates, milestones and costs, etc., it must receive formal approval by management, the sponsor the project team and other stakeholders. Formal approval means sign-off (signatures). If the project manager has identified all the stakeholders and their needs and objectives, included those needs and objectives in the plan, and dealt with conflicting priorities in advance, project management plan approval will be less difficult. A project or project phase cannot effectively start without formal approval of the project management plan.

Kickoff Meeting A meeting of all parties to the project (customers, sellers, project team, senior management, agencies, functional management, sponsor). It is held at the end of the planning process group just before beginning work on the project. This is a communications and coordination meeting to make certain everyone is familiar with the details of the project and the people working on the project. Topics can include introductions, a review of the project risks, communications management plan and meeting schedule.

━━ Direct and Manage Project Execution (page 91) This is the integration part of the executing process group where the project manager integrates all the processes of the executing processes into one coordinated effort to accomplish the project management plan.

Approved corrective actions, preventive actions and defect repair (requests to correct product defects found in the quality process) are implemented as part of this process.

TRICKS OF THE TRADE Please note the confusing terms. If the exam talks about direct and manage project execution, it is NOT talking about the entire executing process group, just one of the processes in that group.

The work of direct and manage project execution can be illustrated as follows:

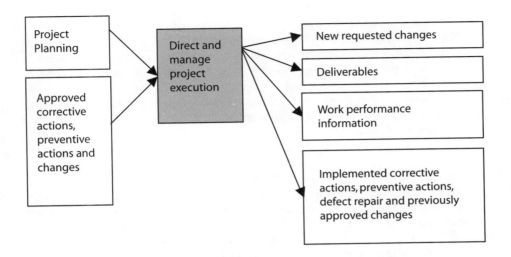

Monitor and Control Project Work (page 94) Monitoring and controlling project work is a control function that is done from project initiating through project closing. Think of a large project and it makes sense that the project manager might need to monitor and control how the planning processes are going, because he would not necessarily be involved in performing all the planning processes himself. The results of monitoring and controlling are recommended changes to the project, as well as recommended corrective actions, preventive actions and defect repair. These recommendations, and those from other processes, are evaluated and approved or rejected in integrated change control, described later in this chapter.

TRICKS OF THE TRADE: Please note the confusing terms. If the exam talks about monitoring and controlling project work, it is NOT talking about the entire monitoring and controlling process group, just one of the processes in that group.

Corrective Action (recommended corrective actions, page 96, approved corrective actions, implemented corrective actions throughout) Corrective action is described here in its entirety in order to make sure you understand the whole concept.

Corrective action is any action taken to bring expected future project performance in line with the project management plan. Stop! Do not read on until you read the last sentence again. Now think about how you do this in your real world. Most project managers have serious problems with this in the real world and thus on the exam.

If I can be direct with you, projects MUST meet their performance measurement baselines. Not meeting those baselines is a sign of poor project management. The only way to make sure they meet those baselines is to constantly measure while the project is going on, to see if they will be met. But ask yourself what you do now. Do you have predetermined areas to measure and acceptable measurements in place to determine if the project is going according to schedule?

One cannot jump in and start implementing corrective action. To implement corrective action, you need:
- A focused attention rather than random attention
- To look for problems rather than just waiting for them to be brought to your attention

- Metrics created in the planning process group that cover all aspects of the project
- A realistic project management plan to measure against
- Continued measurement throughout the project
- The ability to know when the project is off track and the ability to identify the need for recommending corrective action
- The ability to find the root cause of the deviation rather than the surface cause
- Measurement of project performance after corrective action is implemented to evaluate the effectiveness of the corrective action
- A determination of the need for recommending further corrective action

As you can see, a large portion of the project manager's time while the work is being done is spent measuring and implementing corrective actions. Therefore you can expect a very large number of questions on this topic on the exam. Do not expect all of these questions to even use the words corrective action. Many will just describe a situation and ask you, "What is the BEST thing to do?" In order to answer those questions, you need to discover the need to recommend corrective actions. See how well you do on the next exercise.

Exercise When in the project management process would you identify the need for recommending corrective actions?

Answer A general answer to this question would say that recommended corrective actions are determined during (are outputs of):
- Monitor and control project work (Integration chapter)
- Scope verification (Scope chapter)
- Scope control (Scope chapter)
- Schedule control (Time chapter)
- Cost control (Cost chapter)
- Perform quality assurance (NOTE: the only one in the executing process group, Quality chapter)
- Perform quality control (Quality chapter)
- Manage project team (Human Resources chapter)
- Performance reporting (Communications chapter)
- Risk monitoring and control (Risk chapter)
- Contract administration (Procurement chapter)

A more specific way to answer the question would be to think about specific situations. Some of the possible answers are listed below. Think about these as you read them.

When	*PMBOK® Guide* Title
When meeting with the customer to obtain acceptance of deliverables	Scope verification
When measuring project performance against performance measurement baselines	Scope, schedule, cost, perform quality control
When making sure people are using the correct processes	Perform quality assurance
When creating performance reports	Performance reporting
When working with the project team	Manage project team
When you notice that there are many unidentified risks occurring	Risk monitoring and control
When you discover that the seller's performance is not meeting expectations	Contract administration
When you discover that a team member is not performing	Manage project team

You must understand the process for identifying, recommending and approving corrective actions. Read the following diagram and make sure it makes sense to you. Also note that recommended corrective actions result in the creation of change requests which are approved or rejected in the integrated change control process and are implemented in the direct and manage project execution process.

Corrective Action Process

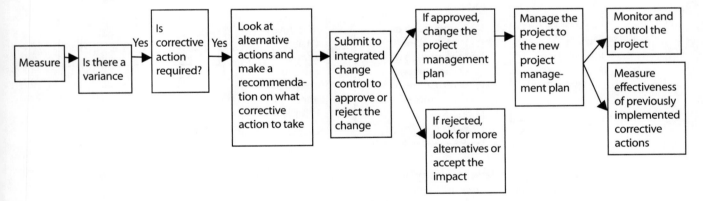

 Because this topic is so important, I have a trick for you. Make sure you have the CD-ROM version of the *PMBOK® Guide* and search for the term "corrective action." Seeing how it is used will improve your understanding of the topic.

Preventive Action (page 96 and throughout) Whereas corrective action involves implementing actions to deal with *actual* deviations from the performance baselines, preventive action deals with *anticipated or possible* deviations from the performance baselines. The process for this is not as clear as it is for corrective action. Knowing when preventive action is needed requires more experience than calculation. Examples of preventive actions include:

- Action to prevent the same problem from occurring again later in the project
- Changing a resource because the resource's last activity nearly failed to meet its acceptance criteria
- Arranging for team members to gain training in a certain area because there is no one with the necessary skills to back up a team member who may unexpectedly get sick.

You will see preventive action mentioned throughout the *PMBOK® Guide*, though not as frequently as corrective action. This topic is also described only in this chapter of this book rather than in every chapter. Preventive action can be implemented at any time for any project management process, but recommended preventive action is only specifically mentioned in the *PMBOK® Guide* as being an output of:

- Monitor and control project work (Integration chapter)
- Perform quality control (Quality chapter)
- Manage project team (Human Resources chapter)
- Risk monitoring and control (Risk chapter)

Like corrective actions, preventive actions result in the creation of recommended change requests which are approved or rejected in the integrated change control process and implemented during the direct and manage project execution process.

Defect Repair (page 96 and throughout) This is another word for rework and is necessary when a component of the project does not meet its specifications. Discovered during the quality management process, and formed into a change request during the monitor and control project work process, these changes are approved or rejected in the integrated change control process.

The process is as follows:

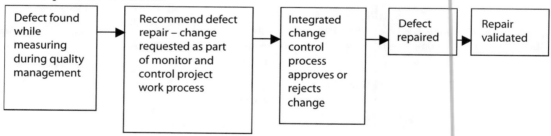

Defect repair relates to quality, so recommended defect repair is only specifically mentioned in the *PMBOK® Guide* as being an output of:

- Monitor and control project work (Integration chapter)
- Perform quality control (Quality chapter)

▬▬**Integrated Change Control** (page 96) The integrated change control process is a control function that is done from project initiating through project closing. This is where all the recommendations for changes, corrective actions, preventive actions and defect repairs are evaluated across all the knowledge areas and either approved or rejected. Changes to any part of the project management plan or the product of the project are handled in the integrated change control process.

A stakeholder wants to add scope to the project. You estimate that the change will add two weeks to the project duration. What do you do next?

Do not read on, try to answer the question. The integrated change control process is very important, and can cover up to 20 questions on the exam. What did you answer? How about: Look for ways to save time so that the change can be accommodated? Get the sponsor to approve the change? Ask for an extension of time to accommodate the change?

Answer any of the above and you are in trouble. The best project managers know that the NEXT thing to do would be to see how the proposed change impacts cost, quality, risk and possibly customer satisfaction. A change in any component of the "triple constraint" should be evaluated for impacts on all the other components!

In order to complete such an evaluation it is necessary to have:
- A realistic project management plan to measure against
- A complete product scope and project scope (see the definitions in the Scope chapter)

Do you do any of this? Looking for impacts of change on all components of the "triple constraint" is the concept behind integrated change control.

Exercise Let's get into more detail. What ACTIONS do you think need to be taken as part of the integrated change control process?

Answer

Action	Place ✔ Here If You Do It, Study Areas Unchecked
1. Let stakeholders know how the change will impact cost, time, risk, quality and any other project objectives	
2. Review for approval all recommended corrective and preventive actions	
3. Reject some changes	
4. Make sure proposed changes fit within the reason the project was initiated	

Action	Place ✔ Here If You Do It, Study Areas Unchecked
5. Recommend changes, do not just wait for others to recommend them	
6. Stop during the project to see where changes are coming from and what you can do to eliminate the root cause of the need for change	
7. Validate defect repair	
8. Review and approve requested changes	
9. Update the project baselines	
10. Update the project management plan	
11. Make sure the correct versions of all the components of the project management plan and product of the project are being used and updated as needed in a controlled fashion—configuration management	
12. Work with a change control board	
13. Expand change control efforts when overall project risk increases	
14. Review all changes to deliverables	

Are changes bad? This can be a controversial question in many industries. The function of each process within the monitoring and controlling process group is to control changes. Changes can have negative effects. In fact, changes can be very expensive. Some studies show that changes made late in the project can be up to 100 times more expensive than if they were made early in the project. Also, it can become impossible for a project manager to coordinate work that is constantly changing.

All changes are not bad, but the project manager should make sure to:
- Work to obtain final requirements as soon as possible
- Spend enough time in risk management identifying the risks
- Come up with time and cost reserves
- Have a process in place to control changes
- Follow the process to control changes
- Have a process and templates in place for creating change requests
- Have clear roles and responsibilities for approving changes
- Reevaluate the business case (in the project charter) if the number of changes becomes excessive
- Consider terminating a project that has excessive changes and starting a new project with a more complete set of requirements
- Allow only approved changes to be added to the project baselines

The exam has many situational questions, dealing with how to make changes. For example:

> *A functional manager wants to make a change to the project. What is the first thing a project manager should do? Or, someone wants to make a change to the project scope. What is the best thing to do first?*

The answers are the same in either case. Generally, the project manager should follow these steps:

1. **Evaluate impact** Evaluate (assess) the impact of the change to the project. (e.g., this change will add three weeks to the project length, require $20,000 additional funding and have no effect on resources).
2. **Create options** This can include cutting other activities, crashing, fast tracking, etc., as described in the Time chapter. (e.g., we can decrease the effect of the change on the project by spending more time decreasing project risk, or by adding one more technician to the project team).
3. **Get internal buy-in**
4. **Get customer buy-in (if required)**

The process of handling changes is often tested on the exam. I suggest you go back and reread the last paragraph and make sure you understand that changes are always evaluated first. In most cases, "evaluate" involves considering all components of the "triple constraint." "Options" are created based on crashing, fast tracking, re-estimating and playing "what if" using project management software. See the Time chapter for questions about crashing, fast tracking and re-estimating and the Human Resources chapter for questions about roles and responsibilities.

 Just a few paragraphs ago, I asked the question:

> *A stakeholder wants to add scope to the project. You estimate that the change will add two weeks to the project duration. What do you do next?*

Notice how the following question is different.

> *A change in scope has been determined to have no effect on the components of the "triple constraint." What is the BEST thing to do?*

Be careful when reading these questions. Expect the right answer to "What is the best thing to do?" about a change to depend on how the question is written and the situation involved. Sometimes evaluation has been done, so the best thing to do is to look for options. Sometimes evaluation AND looking for options have been done and the best thing to do is to meet with the sponsor. In the question above, evaluation has been done. The answer would be to look for options and then meet with the sponsor to let them know about the change and that there will not be any impact. After sponsor has been informed, the customer may be informed according to the communications management plan.

Process for Making Changes Now let's get into more tricks for handling questions about changes on the exam. The most important one is to make sure you understand the following process for handling changes in a more detailed form than the steps 1 to 4 listed above.

1. **Prevent the root cause of change** The project manager should not just focus on managing changes, but proactively eliminate the need for changes.
2. **Identify change** Changes can come from the project manager, as a result of measuring against performance measurement baselines, from the sponsor, management, the customer or from stakeholders. The project manager should actively be looking for changes from all these sources. Discovering a change earlier will decrease the impact of the change.

3. **Create a change request** Changes can be made to the project scope, product scope, project management plan or even the performance measurement baselines. A change request follows the four step process outlined in the previous section.

4. **Assess the change** Does the change fall within the project charter? If not, it should not be a change to your project, but may be an entirely different project. Re-read this one. Many project managers have never really thought about this. Is the change beneficial to the project? Is it needed? If the answer to any of these questions is no, the change should not be approved. However, any change that already had a reserve created for it (a previously identified risk event) should be handled as part of risk management.

5. **Look at the impact of the change** If it is a scope change, how will it affect the scope of the project? If it is a time change, how will it affect the schedule for the project?

6. **Perform integrated change control** How will the change affect all other components of the "triple constraint?"

7. **Look for options** Options include actions to decrease threats further, increase opportunities, compress the schedule through crashing, fast tracking, changing how the work is performed, adjusting quality or cutting scope so that the effect of the change will be minimized. Be careful, it is not wise to decrease the impact of every change. In doing so, the project manager could decrease the overall probability of success on the project as a whole. Sometimes an additional two weeks worth of scope added to the project should receive a two week extension of time to the project, if the work occurs on the critical path. (Notice that I am assuming you know what a critical path is.)

8. **Change is approved or rejected** Have you noticed that all the recommended corrective actions, preventive actions and requested changes feed into integrated change control, but nowhere in the *PMBOK® Guide* does it describe who approves changes? This is extremely important on the exam!

    There is a general rule you should assume on the exam. UNLESS THE QUESTION SAYS OTHERWISE, if there is a change to the project charter, the sponsor who signed or approved the project charter has to make the final decision. The project manager may provide options.

    If the change affects or changes the performance measurement baselines or any project constraints, the change control board or sponsor needs to be involved. The project manager should analyze the project to see if the baselines or constraints can be met. If not, then come up with options, including crashing and fast tracking. Also see the situations described in the Human Resources chapter, and fast tracking and crashing discussed in the Time chapter.

    If the change is within the project management plan, or the project manager can adjust the project to accommodate the change, the project manager can make the decision. He may, under certain circumstances, get the sponsor involved to help protect the project from changes. So, although a formal change request must be created for all changes to the project, the project manager could be the one to create and approve certain change requests without getting anyone else's approval.

    It is important to realize the project manager is often given the authority to approve most changes in emergency situations.

9. **Adjust the project management plan and baselines** Approved changes need to be incorporated into the project baselines. The changes could affect other parts of the project management plan or affect the way the project manager will manage the project, so changes could be made to management plans (e.g., schedule management plan) and the project management plan as a whole.

10. **Notify stakeholders affected by the change** How often do you remember to do this? This could be thought of as configuration management, a form of version control or a way to make sure everyone is working off the same project management plan.

11. **Manage the project to the new project management plan**

The integrated change control process is listed in the monitoring and controlling process group, but it really occurs during all the project management processes. For example, various management plans are created in project planning. Integrated change control should be done during project planning to approve or reject requested changes to the planning portion of management plans.

Exercise Test yourself! Describe common changes on projects and determine what you would do to handle each. Because of the wide variety of possible changes, this exercise does not have an "answer," but it will help you prepare for questions related to change on the exam.

Common Change	How to Handle It
Customer wants to add scope	Make sure you know what the specific scope is and why it is necessary, make sure all the data needed in the change request is filled out, assess the change including determining if the added scope was already included in the reserves, look at the impact of the change, look for options, have the change reviewed by the change control board.

Common Change	How to Handle It

Corrective Action and Integrated Change Control Processes The following diagram combines the corrective action process and the change process to show how these merge into integrated change control. Not shown are defect repair and preventive actions because they are similar to the other processes and could also result in a new project management plan.

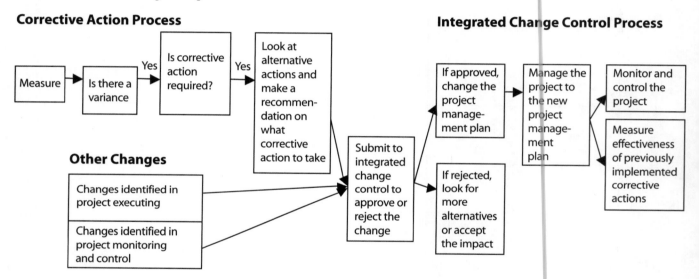

Corrective Action Process

Other Changes

Integrated Change Control Process

Change Control Board (page 98) Why should the project manager always have to be the one to deny a change request? The project manager alone might not even have the knowledge or expertise to analyze a change request. The project manager's role might be to facilitate a decision about a change, rather than to make it herself. For these reasons, it might be wise to form a change control board. The board would have the responsibility to review change requests to determine if additional analysis is warranted. They also approve or reject project changes. The board may include the project manager, customer, experts, sponsor and others. For the exam, assume that all projects have change control boards. See the change control process and other areas of this book for the roles and responsibilities of the change control board.

Close Project (page 100, see also the Project Management Processes chapter of this book for a discussion on the closing process group) Is your project really done when the technical work is done? Not if you do not close it out! The close project process is one part of the closing process group. The other is the contract closure process described in the Procurement chapter. Together, these topics are addressed in about 14 questions on the exam. Should you be worried? Not really, as long as you become familiar with what should be done to close a project, and why the closing processes are so critical, and identify what you miss in your real world.

Many of the high-level concepts of closing have already been discussed in the Project Management Processes chapter. What remains is to realize that this process finalizes all activities across all process groups to formally close out the project or project phase. It also has an unusual aspect to it; it includes planning how the project will be closed out and the creation of two procedures.
- Administrative closure procedure
- Contract closure procedure

The difference between these procedures is focus, frequency and formality. Administrative closure focuses on closing the project or project phase. Contract closure focuses on closing a contract that is part of a project.

 Be sure to remember for the exam that "You always close out a project no matter the circumstances under which it stops, is terminated, or completed!"

Practice Exam

Integration Management

1. Effective project integration usually requires an emphasis on:
   A. the personal careers of the team members.
   B. timely updates to the project management plan.
   C. effective communications at key interface points.
   D. product control.

2. The need for _____ is one of the major driving forces for communication in a project.
   A. optimization
   B. integrity
   C. integration
   D. differentiation

3. Which of the following describes the BEST use of historical records from previous projects:
   A. Estimating, life cycle costing and project planning
   B. Risk management, estimating and creating lessons learned
   C. Project management planning, estimating and creating a status report
   D. Estimating, risk management and project planning

4. When it comes to changes, the project manager's attention is BEST spent on:
   A. making changes.
   B. tracking and recording changes.
   C. informing the sponsor of changes.
   D. preventing unnecessary changes.

5. The sponsor's role on a project is BEST described as:
   A. helping to plan activities.
   B. helping to prevent unnecessary changes to project objectives.
   C. identifying unnecessary project constraints.
   D. helping to put the project management plan together.

6. All of the following are parts of an effective change control system EXCEPT?
   A. Procedures
   B. Standards for reports
   C. Meetings
   D. Lessons learned

7. A work authorization system can be used to:
   A. manage who does each activity.
   B. manage what time and in what sequence work is done.
   C. manage when each activity is done.
   D. manage who does each activity and when it is done.

8. **A project is plagued by changes to the project charter. Who has the primary responsibility to decide if these changes are necessary?**
   A. Project manager
   B. Project team
   C. Sponsor
   D. Stakeholders

9. **Integration is done by the:**
   A. project manager.
   B. team.
   C. sponsor.
   D. stakeholders.

10. **Which of the following BEST describes the project manager's role as an integrator?**
    A. Help team members become familiar with the project.
    B. Put all the pieces of a project into a cohesive whole.
    C. Put all the pieces of a project into a program.
    D. Get all team members together into a cohesive whole.

11. **Approved corrective action is an input to:**
    A. scope verification.
    B. direct and manage project execution.
    C. develop project charter.
    D. schedule development.

12. **A particular stakeholder has a reputation for making many changes on projects. What is the BEST approach a project manager can take at the beginning of the project to manage this situation?**
    A. Say "No" to the stakeholder a few times to dissuade him from submitting more changes.
    B. Get the stakeholder involved in the project as early as possible.
    C. Talk to the stakeholder's boss to find ways to direct the stakeholder's activities to another project.
    D. Ask that the stakeholder not be included in the stakeholder listing.

13. **You are a new project manager who has never managed a project before. You have been asked to plan a new project. It would be BEST in this situation to rely on _____ during planning in order to improve your chance of success.**
    A. your intuition and training
    B. stakeholder analysis
    C. historical information
    D. configuration management

14. **Which of the following BEST describes a project management plan?**
    A. A printout from project management software
    B. A bar chart
    C. Risk, management, staffing, process improvement and other management plans
    D. The project scope

15. **You are taking over a project and determine the following: Activity B has an early finish (EF) of day 3, a late finish (LF) of day 6, and an early start (ES) of day 2.**

Activity L is being done by a hard-to-get resource. The cost performance index (CPI) is 1.1 and the schedule performance index (SPI) is 0.8. Based on this information what would you be more concerned about?

A. Float
B. Resources
C. Cost
D. Schedule

16. The previous project manager for your project managed it without much project organization. There is a lack of management control and no clearly defined project deliverables. Which of the following would be the BEST choice for getting your project better organized?

A. Adopt a life cycle approach to the project.
B. Develop lessons learned for each phase.
C. Develop specific work plans for each work package.
D. Develop a description of the product of the project.

17. You are taking over a project during the planning process group and discover that six individuals have signed the project charter. Which of the following should MOST concern you?

A. Who will be a member of the change control board
B. Spending more time on configuration management
C. Getting a single project sponsor
D. Determining the reporting structure

18. The project charter for a project was approved for planning and you have just been assigned as project manager. Realizing that project planning is an ongoing effort throughout the project, which processes are you MOST likely to combine?

A. Create WBS and activity definition
B. Activity duration estimating and schedule development
C. Human resource planning and cost estimating
D. Cost estimating and cost budgeting

19. All of the following are parts of direct and manage project execution except?

A. Identifying changes
B. Using a work breakdown structure
C. Implementing corrective actions
D. Setting up a project control system

20. A project manager is appointed to head a highly technical project in an area with which this person has limited familiarity. The project manager delegates schedule development, cost estimating, selection of activities, and assignments of activities

to various project team members, and basically serves as an occasional referee and coordinator of activities. The results of this approach are likely to be:

A. a team functioning throughout the project at a very high level, demonstrating creativity and commitment.

B. a team that initially experiences some amounts of confusion, but that after a period of time becomes a cohesive and effective unit.

C. a team that is not highly productive, but that stays together because of the work environment created by the project manager.

D. a team that is characterized by poor performance, low morale, high levels of conflict and high turnover.

21. **You are in the middle of executing a major modification to an existing product when you learn that the resources promised at the beginning of the project are not available. The BEST thing to do is to:**

A. show how the resources were originally promised to your project.

B. re-plan the project without the resources.

C. explain the impact if the promised resources are not made available.

D. crash the project.

22. **You have been assigned to manage the development of an organization's first Web site. The site will be highly complex and interactive, and neither your project team nor the client has much experience with Web site development.**

The timeline is extremely aggressive. Any delay will be costly for both your firm and the client. You have a project sponsor and have achieved agreement and sign-off on both the project charter and the project management plan. Client personnel have been kept fully informed of the project's progress through status reports and regular meetings. The project is on schedule, within the budget, and a final perfunctory review has been scheduled.

Suddenly you hear that the entire effort may be cancelled because the product developed is totally unacceptable. What is the MOST likely cause of this situation?

A. A key stakeholder was not adequately involved in the project.

B. The project charter and project management plan were not thoroughly explained or adequately reviewed by the client.

C. Communications arrangements were inadequate and did not provide the required information to interested parties.

D. The project sponsor failed to provide adequate support for the project.

23. **The project manager has just received a change from the customer that does not affect the project schedule and is easy to complete. What should the project manager do FIRST?**

A. Make the change happen as soon as possible.

B. Contact the project sponsor for permission.

C. Go to the change control board.

D. Evaluate the other components of the "triple constraint."

24. Your company just won a major new project. It will begin in three months and is valued at $2,000,000. You are the project manager for an existing project. What is the FIRST thing you should do once you hear of the new project?
    A. Ask management how the new project will use resources.
    B. Resource level your project.
    C. Crash your project.
    D. Ask management how the new project will affect your project.

25. You are a project manager who was just assigned to take over a project from another project manager who is leaving the company. The previous project manager tells you that the project is on schedule, but only because he has constantly pushed the team to perform. What is the FIRST thing you should do as the new project manager?
    A. Check risk status.
    B. Check cost performance.
    C. Determine a management strategy.
    D. Tell the team your objectives.

26. You are assigned as the project manager in the middle of the project. The project is within the baselines, but the customer is not happy with the performance of the project. What is the FIRST thing you should do?
    A. Discuss it with the project team.
    B. Recalculate baselines.
    C. Renegotiate the contract.
    D. Meet with the customer.

27. A project manager learns that corrective action was implemented by a team member, but not documented. What should the project manager do NEXT?
    A. Report the violation to the functional manager.
    B. Clarify the reasoning behind the team member's action.
    C. Add the implemented corrective action to the historical record.
    D. Find out who caused the problem.

28. The client demands changes to the product specification that will add only two weeks to the critical path. Which of the following is the best thing for the project manager to do?
    A. Compress the schedule to recover the two weeks.
    B. Cut scope to recover the two weeks.
    C. Consult with the sponsor before taking any action.
    D. Advise the client of the impact of the change.

29. During project executing, the project manager determines that a change is needed to material purchased for the project. The project manager calls a meeting of the team to plan how to make the change. This is an example of:
    A. management by objectives.
    B. lack of a change control system.
    C. good team relations.
    D. lack of a clear work breakdown structure.

30. The project was going well when all of a sudden there were changes to the project coming from multiple stakeholders. After all the changes were determined, the

project manager spent time with all the stakeholders to find out why there were changes and to discover any more.

The project work has quieted down when a team member casually mentions to the project manager that the team member added functionality to a product of the project. Do not worry they say, "I did not impact time, cost or quality!" What should a project manager do FIRST?

A. Ask the team member how the need for the functionality was determined.

B. Hold a meeting to review the team member's completed work.

C. Look for other added functionality.

D. Ask the team member how he knows there is no time, cost or quality impact.

31. A project manager is managing a fixed price (FP) contract. She thinks that a large customer-requested change might impact the schedule of the project. What should she do FIRST?

A. Meet with the stakeholders.

B. Meet with the team.

C. Renegotiate the remainder of the contract.

D. Follow the change control system.

32. While completing a project, a project manager realizes he needs to decrease project costs. After researching his options, he comes up with the following choices. Which choice would DECREASE project costs?

A. Change to component A from component B. Component A costs more to purchase, but has a lower life cycle cost than B.

B. Change activity A to be completed by resource B instead of resource C. Resource B is a more experienced worker.

C. Move activities B and H to occur concurrently, and accept a 30 percent increase in the risk that five more resources will be needed later.

D. Remove a test from the project management plan.

33. This project is chartered to determine new ways to extend the product life of one of the company's medium-producing products. The project manager comes from the engineering department and the team comes from product management and marketing departments.

The preliminary project scope statement and project planning are completed when a stakeholder notifies the team that there is a better way to complete one of the work packages. They even supply a technical review letter from their department proving that the new way to complete the work package will actually be faster than the old way.

The project manager has had similar experiences with this department on other projects, and was expecting this to happen on this project. What is the FIRST thing the project manager should do?

A. Contact the department and complain again about their missing the deadline for submission of scope.

B. Look for how this schedule change will impact the cost to complete the work package and the quality of the product of the work package.

C. See if there is a way to change from a matrix environment to a functional organization so as to eliminate all the interference from other departments.

D. Ask the department if they have any other changes.

34. **Contract closure is similar to administrative closure in that they both involve:**
    A. product verification.
    B. kickoff meetings.
    C. quality assurance activities.
    D. creation of the scope verification plan.

35. **An output of administrative closure is the creation of:**
    A. project archives.
    B. a project charter.
    C. a project management plan.
    D. a risk analysis plan.

36. **All of the following would occur during the closure of the project EXCEPT:**
    A. creating lessons learned.
    B. formal acceptance
    C. reducing resource spending.
    D. performing benefit cost analysis.

37. **The project is not completed until:**
    A. the project scope is completed, administrative closure is completed and payment is received.
    B. formal acceptance is received, and any other requirements for project closure as stated in the contract are met.
    C. the customer is satisfied and final payment is received.
    D. lessons learned are completed.

38. **You have been working on a very large software development project that has made use of over 230 people. Finally, all the scope is completed. It would be BEST to:**
    A. throw a party for the team members.
    B. make sure the project is integrated with other projects.
    C. begin to focus on your other projects.
    D. analyze project success or failure.

39. **Which of the following is included in a project charter?**
    A. Identification of risks
    B. Work package estimates
    C. Detailed resource estimates
    D. The business need for the project

40. **A project manager is trying to convince management to use project management and has decided to start improving the company's project management by obtaining a project charter. Which of the following BEST describes why the project charter would help the project manager?**
    A. It describes the details of what needs to be done.
    B. It lists the names of all team members.
    C. It gives the project manager authority.
    D. It describes the project's history.

41. **Linear programming is an example of what type of project selection criteria?**
    A. Constrained optimization
    B. Comparative approach
    C. Benefit measurement
    D. Impact analysis

42. **You have created the project charter, but could not get it approved. Your manager and his boss have asked that the project begin immediately. Which of the following is the BEST thing to do?**
    A. Set up an integrated change control process.
    B. Show your manager the impact of proceeding without approval.
    C. Focus on completing projects that have signed project charters.
    D. Start work on only the critical path activities.

43. **The engineering department has uncovered a problem with the cost accounting system and has asked the systems department to analyze what is wrong and fix the problem. You are a project manager working with the cost accounting programs on another project. Management has issued a change request to the change control board to add the new work to your project.**

    Your existing project has a cost performance index (CPI) of 1.2 and a schedule performance index (SPI) of 1.3 so you have some room to add work without delaying your existing project or going over budget. However, you cannot see how the new work fits within the project charter for your existing project. After some analysis, you determine that the new work and existing work do not overlap and can be done concurrently. They also require different skill sets. Which of the following is the BEST thing to do?
    A. Create the project objectives and develop the preliminary project scope statement.
    B. Re-estimate the project schedule with input from the engineering department.
    C. Perform scope verification on the new work with the help of the stakeholders.
    D. Identify specific changes to the existing work.

44. **All technical work is completed on the project. Which of the following remains to be done?**
    A. Scope verification
    B. Risk response plan
    C. Staffing management plan
    D. Lessons learned

Integration Management Answers

1. **Answer** C
   Explanation This question is asking for the most important of the choices. Think about what is involved in integration – project management plan development, project management plan execution and integrated change control. In order to integrate the project components into a cohesive whole (integration), communication is key when one activity will interface with another, one team member will interface with another, and any other form of interfacing. Choices B and D are only parts of the monitoring and controlling process group, while integration includes more than control. Choice A falls under project management plan execution.

2. **Answer** C
   Explanation The project manager is an integrator. This is a question about your role as an integrator and communicator.

3. **Answer** D
   Explanation Historical records are not generally used for life cycle costing (choice A) lessons learned (choice B) or creating status reports (choice C).

4. **Answer** D
   Explanation Project managers should be proactive. The only proactive answer here is preventing unnecessary changes.

5. **Answer** B
   Explanation Though the sponsor may help with some of the activities (choice A) it is not his exclusive duty. Some project constraints (choice C) come from the sponsor, but they should be considered necessary. The project management plan (choice D) is created by the team and approved by the sponsor and other management. Since the project objectives are stated in the project charter and it is the sponsor who issues the project charter, choice B is the correct answer.

6. **Answer** D
   Explanation A change control system consists of the processes and procedures that allow smooth evaluation and tracking of changes. Lessons learned (choice D) are reviews of the processes and procedures to improve them; they are not part of the system.

7. **Answer** B
   Explanation Who does each activity (choices A and D) is managed with the schedule and responsibility assignment matrixes. When each activity is done (choice C) is managed with the project schedule. A work authorization system is used to coordinate when and in what order the work is performed so that work and people may properly interface with other work and other people.

8. **Answer** C
   Explanation The sponsor issues the project charter and so he should help the project manager control changes to the charter. The primary responsibility lies with the sponsor.

9. **Answer** A
   Explanation Integration is a key responsibility of the project manager, so choice A is the best answer.

10. **Answer** B

    Explanation Integration refers to combining activities, not team members (choice D). Could the project manager smash two team members together and create one big team member? (I just wanted to see if you are still laughing about this PMP thing!)

11. **Answer** B

    Explanation Choice B is the only correct response.

12. **Answer** B

    Explanation We cannot avoid the stakeholder (choices C and D) because he has a stake in the project. A project manager can say "No" (choice A), but this does not solve the root cause. There may be some good ideas within those changes. The only choice that deals with the problem is choice B.

    Changes are not bad! Changes normally come from lack of input at the beginning of the project. If we begin effective communication with this stakeholder early (choice B), we stand a much better chance of discovering his changes during the planning process, when they will have less of an impact on the project.

13. **Answer** C

    Explanation Because you have no experience, you will have to look at the experience of others. This information is captured in the historical records from previous projects.

14. **Answer** C

    Explanation The project management plan contains more than just a bar or Gantt chart and the project manager's plan for completing the work. It includes all the documentation that went into creating and planning the project, approved by the stakeholders.

15. **Answer** D

    Explanation You may not understand this question until you review the rest of the book. Come back to it. This question tries to integrate a lot of information and test your ability to discern what information is relevant to the question. Though some figures to calculate float are provided (choice A), there is no information to say that the float is a problem. Most projects have hard-to-get resources (choice B). The question does not give an indication that having hard-to-get resources is a problem. CPI (choice C) is greater than one, so cost is not something to worry about. SPI is less than one, so choice D is the best answer.

16. **Answer** A

    Explanation Choice B would help improve subsequent phases but would do nothing for control and deliverables. Choice C would help control each phase but would not control the integration of the phases into a cohesive whole. Choice D would help, but not help both control and deliverables for each phase. Effective project management requires a life cycle approach to running the project. Choice A is the only answer that covers both control and deliverables.

17. **Answer** B

    Explanation This situation implies that there are six areas concerned with this project. In addition to added communications requirements, you should be concerned with competing needs and requirements impacting your efforts on configuration management.

18. **Answer** A

   Explanation Create WBS consists of subdividing major product deliverables (scope) into smaller, more manageable work packages. Activity definition defines the activities that must take place to produce those deliverables.

19. **Answer** D

   Explanation A project control system (choice D) is set up during the planning process group, not during project executing. Did choice B confuse you? A WBS is created in project planning, but can be used to help manage the project during project executing. The wording here was not "creating the WBS" but "using the WBS."

20. **Answer** D

   Explanation A project manager must manage a project. If all activities are delegated, chaos ensues and team members will spend more time jockeying for position than completing activities.

21. **Answer** C

   Explanation Choices B and D are essentially delaying the situation. Instead, the project manager should try to prevent the situation by showing the consequences if the resources are not available (choice C). This is a more effective strategy than saying "but you gave them to me," as in choice A.

22. **Answer** A

   Explanation A single high-level executive can end an entire project if he or she is not satisfied with the results, even if that person has, by choice, been only tangentially involved in the project. It is critical to ensure that all of the final decision makers have been identified early in a project in order to ensure that their concerns are addressed.

23. **Answer** D

   Explanation The other impacts to the project should be evaluated first. Such impacts include cost, quality, scope, risk and customer satisfaction. Once these are evaluated, the change control board, if one exists, can approve or deny the change.

24. **Answer** D

   Explanation As you work on a project, you need to constantly reevaluate the project objectives and how the project relates to other concurrent projects. Is your project still in line with corporate objectives? If the other project will impact yours, you need to be proactive and work on options now.

25. **Answer** C

   Explanation Before you can do anything else, you have to know what YOU are going to do. Developing the management strategy will provide the framework for all the rest of the choices presented and the other activities that need to be done.

26. **Answer** D

   Explanation First, you need to find out why the customer is not happy. Then meet with the team and determine options.

27. **Answer** C

   Explanation Such actions should be documented. Since such documents become part of the historical records database, choice C is correct.

28. **Answer** C
Explanation Do you remember what to do when there is a change? Evaluate first. The use of the word "only" shows that evaluation was done. The words "what options are chosen" show that compressing the schedule (choice A) and cutting scope (choice B) have also been done. The next step is to consult with the sponsor before the client (choice D).

29. **Answer** B
Explanation The project manager is asking how to make a change. The procedures, forms, sign-offs and other similar requirements for handling changes should have already been determined in the change control system (choice B). Because they weren't, the project manager will waste valuable work time trying to figure it out after the fact.

30. **Answer** D
Explanation Notice that the first paragraph is extraneous. Also notice that the question states that the change has already been made. Your actions will be different than if the change had not been made. It is the project manager's job to investigate impacts, as the project manager is the only one who can tell how a change impacts the project as a whole. Choices A, B and C could all be done, but they do not address the immediate concern. Choice D is the best answer since it begins the project manager's analysis of the impacts to the project as a whole by finding out what analysis has already been done. He can then determine how he must finalize the analysis as it applies to the entire project. Can you see that?

31. **Answer** D
Explanation Ideally, there is a change control system in place that should be followed to make changes in the project.

32. **Answer** D
Explanation Getting tired yet? Get used to answering questions for four hours before you take the exam. Choice A will not decrease project costs, just costs over the life of the project. It will not solve the problem. Choice B will almost always lead to higher costs and choice C could affect costs later, due to the increased risk. Though it may not be the first choice to think of, deleting a test would decrease costs, so it is the best answer. It may also decrease quality, but this is not the question.

33. **Answer** B
Explanation Choice A could be done, but notice that it is not proactive? It would be helpful to get to the root cause of why this department always comes up with such ideas or changes after the project begins. However, this is not the immediate problem, the change is, and therefore choice A is not best. The type of project organization described is a matrix organization. There is not anything inherently wrong with such an organization, nor is there anything wrong in this particular situation that would require it to be changed, so choice C cannot be best. The department's history makes choice D something that should definitely be done, but the proposed change needs more immediate attention. Only choice B begins integrated change control by looking at the impact of one change on other components of the "triple constraint."

34. **Answer** A

    Explanation Kickoff meetings (choice B) occur during project planning. Quality assurance (choice C) occurs during project executing. A scope verification plan (choice D) is created earlier in the project and used during project monitoring and controlling, not closing. All types of closure must make sure that the actual product of the project meets the requirements for the product. Therefore choice A is the best answer.

35. **Answer** A

    Explanation The project management plan and project charter (choices B and C) are products of earlier steps in the project management process. You have not seen the term risk analysis plan (choice D) in this book so it is unlikely to be the best answer.

36. **Answer** D

    Explanation Benefit cost analysis (choice D) is done earlier in the project to help select between alternatives. All the other choices are done during closing. Therefore choice D must be the best answer.

37. **Answer** B

    Explanation Look at the wording of the choices and you will see that this question is talking about a contract situation. To find the best answer, think about the rules for contract closure. Choice A seems like a good choice until you remember the importance of getting acceptance in writing (formal acceptance). Making sure the customer is satisfied is certainly a good thing, but that satisfaction must turn into formal acceptance in order for a contract to be closed out. Therefore choice C cannot be best. Choice D cannot be the best choice as it does not include formal acceptance required to close a contract. Each project is different and may have different requirements for closure. Lien waivers, export certificates, warranty and guarantee information might need to be received before the contract can be closed. These unique needs of the project would be included in the contract, making B the best choice.

38. **Answer** D

    Explanation Though all the choices seem like good ideas, there is only one best. Usually these questions can be reworded to, "What do you do next?" Integrating (choice B) is a great idea, but not all projects have another project with which to integrate. The project manager cannot move on (choice C) until the project is actually completed. That means that administrative closure must occur. The only choice that relates to administrative closure is choice D. Once administrative closure is done, then throw a party!

39. **Answer** D

    Explanation This question may seem simple, but it is really testing if you know what is a correct project charter. Choices A and B do not come until project management planning, after the project charter. A project charter may include the names of some resources (the project manager, for example), but not detailed resources (choice C).

40. **Answer** C

    Explanation The exam will ask questions like this to make sure you know the benefits you should be getting out of the process and tools of project management. The details of what needs to be done (choice A) are found in the WBS dictionary. The names of team members (choice B) are included in responsibility assignment matrix and other documents. Project history (choice D) is found in the lessons learned and other project documents.

41. **Answer** A
Explanation Constrained optimization uses mathematical models. Linear programming is a mathematical model.

42. **Answer** B
Explanation The best thing to do would be to show the impact. This is the only choice that prevents future problems—always the best choice. The other choices just pretend the problem does not exist.

43. **Answer** A
Explanation How long did it take you to read this question? Expect long-winded questions on the exam. Take another look at the choices before you continue reading. Did you notice that each of the choices occurs during a different part of the project management process?

This question is essentially asking if the new work should be added to the existing project. There may be many business reasons to try to do this, but from a project management perspective, major additions to the project are generally discouraged. In this case, the question is trying to imply that the new work is a self-contained unit of work, has no overlap with the existing work and needs a different skill set. Therefore, it is generally best to make it a new project. The first step to answering this question is to realize that the work should be a separate project. The second step is to look at the choices and see which relates to initiating a new project. Choice D is done during project executing. Choice C is done during project monitoring and controlling. Choice B sounds like the best choice but only if you did not realize that the new work should be a separate project. The key words are "develop the preliminary project scope statement." Such work is only done during project initiating.

44. **Answer** D
Explanation Did you pick choice A? Then you may have forgotten that scope verification is done during the monitoring and controlling process group, not the closing process group. The other plans (choices B and C) are created earlier in the project. The lessons learned (choice D) can only be completed after the work is completed.

Scope Management

How many times have you added scope to a project? How many times have your team members added extra functionality? Scope management is the process of defining what work is required and then making sure that all of that work and only that work is done. Since all projects have difficulty with controlling scope, I recommend you read this chapter carefully.

Though it is not technically true, to many people it seems there are more scope questions than any other topic on the exam. It would be worthwhile to review the project scope management process in the *PMBOK® Guide*. The process includes scope planning, scope definition, create WBS, scope verification and scope control. Make certain that you understand the outputs of each.

Scope Management (page 103) Scope management means:

- Constantly checking to make sure you are completing all the work
- Not letting people randomly add to the scope of the project without a structured change control system
- Making sure all changes fit within the project charter
- Defining and controlling what is and is not included in the project
- Preventing extra work or gold plating

You should give the customer what they asked for; no more and no less. Giving any extras is a waste of time and adds no benefit to the project, especially since only 34 percent of projects are successful. Make sure you understand this approach and why it is a good idea.

Scope management involves managing both product and project scope. Be very careful here to notice which word is used in a question. The answer to a question about product scope is different than the answer to a question about project scope. Many people have gotten questions wrong in this area needlessly because of misreading the question.

Rita's Process Chart—Scope Management
Where are we in the project management process?

Initiating	Planning	Executing	Monitoring & Controlling	Closing
Select project manager	**Determine how you will do planning—part of management plans**	Acquire final team	**Measure against the performance measurement baselines**	Develop closure procedures
Determine company culture and existing systems	**Create project scope statement**	Execute the PM plan	**Measure according to the management plans**	Complete contract closure
Collect processes, procedures and historical information	Determine team	Work to produce product scope	**Determine variances and if they warrant corrective action or a change**	Confirm work is done to requirements
Divide large projects into phases	**Create WBS and WBS dictionary**	Recommend changes and corrective actions		Gain formal acceptance of the product
Identify stakeholders	Create activity list	Send and receive information	**Scope verification**	Final performance reporting
Document business need	Create network diagram	Implement approved changes, defect repair, preventive and corrective actions	**Configuration management**	Index and archive records
Determine project objectives	Estimate resource requirements		**Recommend changes, defect repair, preventive and corrective actions**	Update lessons learned knowledge base
Document assumptions and constraints	Estimate time and cost	Continuous improvement	Integrated change control	Hand off completed product
Develop project charter	Determine critical path	Follow processes	Approve changes, defect repair, preventive and corrective actions	Release resources
Develop preliminary project scope statement	Develop schedule	Team building		
	Develop budget	Give recognition and rewards	Risk audits	
	Determine quality standards, processes and metrics	Hold progress meetings	Manage reserves	
	Determine roles and responsibilities	Use work authorization system	Use issue logs	
	Determine communications requirements	Request seller responses	Facilitate conflict resolution	
	Risk identification, qualitative and quantitative risk analysis and response planning	Select sellers	Measure team member performance	
	Iterations—go back		Report on performance	
	Determine what to purchase		Create forecasts	
	Prepare procurement documents		Administer contracts	
	Finalize the "how to execute and control" aspects of all management plans			
	Create process improvement plan			
	Develop final PM plan and performance measurement baselines			
	Gain formal approval for plan			
	Hold kickoff meeting			

The following should help you understand how each part of Scope Management fits into the project management process.

The Scope Management Process

The Scope Management Process	Done During
Scope planning	Planning process group
Scope definition	Planning process group
Create WBS	Planning process group
Scope verification	Monitoring and controlling process group
Scope control	Monitoring and controlling process group

Product Scope (page 104) Product scope is another way to say "requirements that relate to the product of the project." What do they want you to do? Product scope may be supplied as a result of a previous project to determine requirements, or may be created as part of the project.

Project Scope (page 104) The work you need to do to deliver the product of the project. This includes the meetings, reports, analysis and all the other parts of project management that become part of the project scope management plan.

Scope Baseline (page 117) Measurements of success on the project include whether the requirements have been met and whether the scope baseline has been met. The scope baseline is the project scope statement, the work breakdown structure and the work breakdown structure dictionary.

▬▬Scope Planning (page 107) Scope planning is focused on thinking ahead to determine, "How will I do this?" before doing the work, and turning the answer into a project scope management plan.

Project Scope Management Plan Most knowledge areas have management plans. For scope it means, "How will I do scope? What tools should I use to plan how the project will accomplish the scope on this project? What enterprise environmental factors and organizational process assets (described in the Integration chapter) come into play?" The process then goes on to cover such topics as managing the scope and controlling the scope to the project management plan. Therefore, the project scope management plan could be thought of as containing three parts: how will scope be planned, executed and controlled.

Almost no companies have templates, forms and standards for scope management, but they should. The output of scope planning is the project scope management plan. The project scope management plan for each project will be unique but may cover topics that for the company or the type of project can be standardized. Once completed, the project scope management plan becomes part of the project management plan and is used to guide and measure the project until the closing process group.

The project scope management plan may not be created in one sitting, but can be formulated in stages, or iterated during project planning. First comes the part of the project scope management plan that describes how the scope will be planned. Once the project is planned, the project manager will have enough information to decide how the scope will be executed and controlled, and thereby add those components to the project scope management plan. Another aspect of iterations is that later parts of project planning, such as risk response planning, can add new scope to the project, thereby changing the project scope management plan.

Stop. Do not just read on. Read this section over again. Notice that scope planning is not hard to understand, but it requires a good understanding of the project scope in order to complete. The idea behind the creation of this and all management plans is: if you cannot plan it, you cannot do it. So for those projects where scope planning is hard, perhaps more work needs to be done in project planning before moving into project executing. Management plans are a PMI-ism!

▬▬Scope Definition (page 109) Scope definition is primarily concerned with what is and is not included in the project. It involves taking the preliminary project scope statement created during the initiating process group and fleshing it out to include all the

needs of the stakeholders. Scope definition takes into account constraints and assumptions. The result, or output, is the project scope statement which is used to manage and measure project performance against.

Stakeholder Analysis This process makes sure that the stakeholders' needs, wants and expectations are turned into requirements. I strongly suggest that you look again at the stakeholder management section in the Framework chapter of this book. Much of what you need to know about stakeholders is described there.

Product Analysis The purpose of product analysis is to analyze the objectives stated by the customer or sponsor and turn them into tangible requirements. For example, the project team is asked to "improve" the product. In product analysis, the project team might come up with specific requirements that meet the need to "improve," and then look at ways to accomplish this.

This is a project life cycle term rather than a project management term and thus will not be on the exam much at all. Just realize that effort may need to be expended to determine and define requirements as part of the project, rather than just receiving complete requirements from the customer.

Project Scope Statement See the discussion in the Integration chapter on this topic. The preliminary project scope statement is expanded into the "final" project scope statement to be used on the project. It is expanded from that received during project initiating by analyzing the product of the project and translating objectives into deliverables. Expert opinion on what should be done may be used. Different approaches to performing the work and incorporating the needs of the stakeholders into the project are considered.

Scope definition will be included on your exam score sheet as part of Define and Record Requirements, Constraints and Assumptions.

▬▬ Create the Work Breakdown Structure (WBS) (page 112 and throughout) Before you go any further, ask yourself, "What is a WBS?" You cannot afford to misunderstand this important project management tool.

Exercise 1 Test yourself! What is a WBS?

Answer 1 This question should be easy as, of course, you already create WBSs. You will be in serious trouble on the exam if you do not create these in the real world. Why? The WBS is a required element in project management. Without it, the project will take longer, elements will slip through the cracks and the project will be negatively impacted. So there is no choice. All projects, even small ones, need a WBS. Be wary, questions on the exam are designed to weed out those who know what WBSs are, but who do not use them in the real world. What if a question described details of a project to you and then asked, "You are in

the middle of planning this project and creating a WBS. Which of the following would you most likely need to worry about?" You cannot answer such questions with only academic knowledge. You need to have been there! You need experience.

A WBS is deliverable-oriented. This does not mean that only customer deliverables are included in the WBS. All deliverables are included.

Smart project managers understand that they cannot plan, organize, manage and control a project. It is too big. The WBS breaks the project into smaller and more manageable pieces. This is a top-down effort to decompose the work into smaller pieces called work packages.

TRICKS OF THE TRADE Please note that PMI does not make extensive use of the word "task." Cut that word from your vocabulary. Instead replace it with the word "work package." Work packages are divided further into schedule activities; activities for short, with the help of the WBS dictionary described later in this chapter.

Exercise 2 Test yourself! The chart on the right is a segment of a list of work packages on a bar chart. The one on the left shows the format of a real, but blank, WBS. Many people think the list in a bar chart is the WBS. That is not correct. What is the difference between making a list and completing a real WBS?

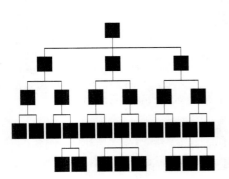

Work Package Name
Custom Vendor Selection
• Agenda for visits
• Evaluation criteria
• Team preparation
• Visit schedule
• Report on visits
• Vendor scores
• Finalist list
Vendor Reference Checks
• Reference format
• Vendor reference requests
• Reference evaluation forms

Answer 2 The image on the right side of the previous page:
- Represents a summary of the WBS, not the WBS itself
- Does not break down the project into small enough pieces. May include work packages that are greater than the eight to 80-hour rule of thumb
- May not include all the work (In contrast, the construction of the WBS chart on the left helps to ensure that nothing slips through the cracks)
- Does not allow the team to walk through the project
- Is usually not created by the team
- Does not help to get your mind around the project
- Does not help get team and other stakeholders' buy-in to the project
- Does not easily show a complete hierarchy of the project, even with indentation
- Does not result in a clear understanding of the project by all the stakeholders

A WBS (on a Summary Level) for a Hardware/Software Creation and Installation Project

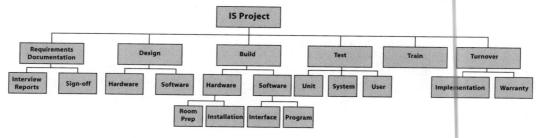

Although the WBS may look like a corporate organizational chart, it is not! Understand that there are few set rules for creating a WBS. WBSs created by two people for the same project will look different. That is fine as long as the following rules are followed:
- It is created with the help of the team
- The first level is completed before the project is broken down further
- Each level of the WBS is a smaller piece of the level above
- The entire project is included in each of the highest levels of the WBS. Eventually some levels will be broken down further than others.
- Includes only work needed to create deliverables
- Work not in the WBS is not part of the project
- Continues breaking down the project until you reach what are called work packages; pieces that:
  - Can be realistically and confidently estimated
  - Cannot be logically subdivided further
  - Can be completed quickly
  - Have a meaningful conclusion and deliverable
  - Can be completed without interruption (without the need for more information)
  - Will be outsourced or contracted out

Most commonly, the top level of the WBS is the project title. The first level is most commonly the same as the project life cycle (for a software project—requirement analysis, design, coding, testing, conversion or operation). The second and later levels break the project into smaller pieces. Such decomposition continues until the project manager reaches the level appropriate to manage the project, following the rules listed in the previous bullets (e.g., can be realistically estimated, etc.).

The levels in the WBS are often numbered for ease of location later. When the WBS is completed, code numbers are assigned to help distinguish where a work package is in the WBS. There are many different numbering schemes one can use. One is shown below.

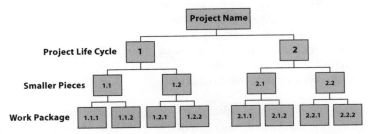

On some small projects, the WBS may be broken down into work packages that are very small (four to 40 hours long) and therefore not needing to be broken down to the activity level. On large projects, the work packages may be large (there is no rule of thumb for how large these are, but they could be 300 hours in size), leaving the work packages to be broken into activities by the team members. Some projects require a branch of the WBS for project management efforts, some only require the WBS to include the work necessary to complete deliverables, and exclude the project management-related work.

If your company works on many similar projects, it is important to realize that the WBS from one project may be used as the basis for the next. Therefore, the project management office should collect WBS examples and encourage the creation of templates.

Great project managers realize that it is not only having the WBS that will be valuable, but that the creation of the WBS will add value to the project. If you really know what a WBS is, and you know that it is more than an academic exercise, you will easily be able to complete the next exercise. If you get many wrong, you must rethink your knowledge of WBSs in order to pass the exam.

Exercise Test yourself! What are the benefits of using a WBS?

Answer The benefits of using a WBS are:
- Helps prevent work from slipping through the cracks
- Provides the project team with an understanding of where their pieces fit into the overall project management plan and gives them an indication of the impact of their work on the project as a whole

- Facilitates communication and cooperation between and among the project team and other stakeholders
- Helps prevent changes
- Focuses the team's experience on what needs to be done, resulting in higher quality and a project that is easier to manage
- Provides a basis for estimating staff, cost and time
- Provides PROOF of need for staff, cost and time
- Gets team buy-in and builds the team
- Helps people get their minds around the project

The WBS is the foundation of the project. This means almost everything that occurs in the planning process group after the creation of the WBS is directly related to the WBS. For example, project costs and time are estimated by work package, not for the project as a whole. Risks are identified by work package, not just for the project as a whole. Work packages are assigned to individuals or parts of the performing organization, depending on the size of the project. Note the following diagram and make sure this makes sense to you. Are you getting the value of the WBS for your projects?

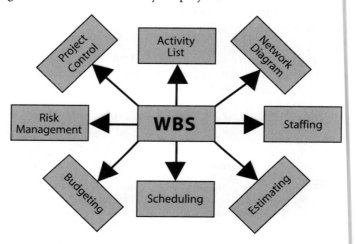

You may see a term on the exam called control account (previously called cost account). Can you imagine that in a large project one might not want to estimate costs to the same level of detail as a work package? This level, higher in the WBS than a work package, is called the control account.

Exercise Let's look again at project control. How would you use a WBS while the work is being done?

| |
| |
| |
| |
| |

Answer This may be a more important exercise than you think. If you were going to test someone's knowledge, would you test the basics like what is a WBS, or would you test knowledge about how a WBS helps you to be a better project manager? This exam strongly weighs toward the latter.

When completed, the WBS can be used any time the project needs to reevaluate the scope of the project. For example:
- When there is a scope change to the project
- As part of integrated change control to evaluate any impacts of other changes on scope
- As a way to control scope creep by reminding everyone what work is to be done
- As a communications tool
- To help new team members see their roles

TRICKS OF THE TRADE: There can be many references to the WBS on the exam. In short, remember the following. A WBS:
- Is a graphical picture of the hierarchy of the project
- Identifies all the work to be performed—if it is not in the WBS, it is not part of the project
- Is the foundation upon which the project is built
- Is VERY important
- Should exist for every project
- Forces you to think through all aspects of the project
- Can be reused for other projects
- Shows hierarchy or is the foundation of the project
- Does NOT show dependencies

TRICKS OF THE TRADE: Now that you know the above and are going to get a few more tricky questions right, would you like to get one more right? Many people confuse the terms WBS and decomposition. The best way to think of decomposition is that decomposition is *what* you are doing, and the WBS is the *tool* to do it. One can decompose the project using a WBS. You will thank me when this helps you on the real exam!

TRICKS OF THE TRADE Like tricks? This whole book is one big trick. Here is another one. Use the following diagram to keep the relationships straight in your mind.

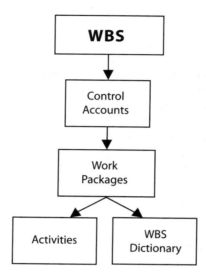

WBS Dictionary (page 117) Want to hear of a really great idea you will not want to do, yet will wish you had? Imagine the work package in a WBS. It usually takes the form of one to three words such as "casing design" or "module XYZ code." Assigning such a brief description to a team member allows for too much variation from what may be needed; it allows for scope creep. The WBS dictionary provides a description of the work to be done for each WBS work package and helps make sure the resulting work better matches what is needed. Therefore, a project manager uses this tool of project management to prevent scope creep, rather than using just management skills and constant inspection.

The WBS dictionary contains:
- A number identifier
- Related control account (for cost)
- A statement of the work to be done
- Who is responsible for doing the work
- Any schedule milestones

The WBS dictionary can be used as part of a work authorization system to inform team members of when their work package is going to start, schedule milestones and other information. It can then be used to control what work is done when, to prevent scope creep and to increase understanding of the effort for each work package. The WBS dictionary helps the project by putting boundaries on what is included in the work package and what is not. NOTE: Some of the entries in the WBS dictionary are filled in during iterations, not when it is first drafted (e.g., duration, interdependencies, etc.).

A WBS dictionary may contain information similar to the following:

WBS Dictionary			
Control Account ID #	Work Package #	Date of Update	Responsible Organization/ Individual
Work Package Description			
Acceptance Criteria (How to know if the work is acceptable)			
Deliverables			
Assumptions			
Resources Assigned			
Duration			
Schedule Milestones			
Cost			
Due Date			
Interdependencies	Before this work package _____ After this work package _____		
Approved by: Project manager _____			Date: _____

——Scope Verification (page 118) Have you heard people tell you that you must
memorize inputs and outputs? Let me prove to you why you purchased the best way to get
ready for the exam, and save you over 20 hours of study.

 First, let's think about this term. If I did not point it out to you, you might think it
means making sure you have the right scope during project planning. That would
be incorrect and cause you to get several questions wrong on the exam. Scope verification
is actually checking the work against the project management plan and the project scope
management plan, WBS and WBS dictionary, and then meeting with the customer to gain
formal acceptance of deliverables. Big difference, right?

Let's look at inputs. Try this out.

Exercise What do you expect the inputs to scope verification would be? Remember that the
word input means, "What do I need before I can ..."

Answer
- Deliverables
- Project scope statement
- Project scope management plan
- WBS dictionary

Bet you got them all right. Now try the dreaded outputs.

Exercise Name the outputs of scope verification. Remember that output means, "What will I have when I am done with …"

Answer
- Accepted deliverables
- Customer satisfaction
- Requested changes
- Recommended corrective actions

OK, maybe you might not have added the word "requested" before changes. But I bet you got most of them right and you did not have to study them!

TRICKS OF THE TRADE The exam will describe situations rather than definitions. It may describe situations that relate to scope verification without using the term. Look for any of the following phrases as alternative ways to describe scope verification:
- Reviewing work products and results to ensure that all are completed according to specifications
- Conducting inspections, reviews, audits
- Determining whether results conform to requirements
- Determining whether work products are completed correctly
- Documenting completion of deliverables
- Gaining formal sign-off

There are a couple more tricky aspects of scope verification. First, scope verification can be done at the end of each project phase in the project life cycle (to verify the phase deliverables along the way) and during the monitoring and controlling process group in the project management process.

The second tricky area is how scope verification relates to quality control. Although quality control is generally done first (to make sure the work meets the quality requirements before meeting with the customer), scope verification and quality control can overlap. The two topics are very similar in that both involve checking for the correctness of work. The difference is focus. The primary focus of scope verification is customer *acceptance* of the deliverables while quality control involves meeting the quality requirements specified for the deliverables and analysis of the *correctness* of the work.

Scope verification is also done whenever a project is terminated, to verify the level of completion. It is an entire step, not just an output, of the scope management process. There can be five questions on the exam that deal with scope verification.

━━ Scope Control (page 119)

To control a project, one needs to focus on controlling scope as well as looking for the impact of scope changes on other knowledge areas and the impact of other changes on scope (integrated change control). Remember that scope control is extremely proactive.

Scope control might involve thinking about where changes to scope are coming from on the project, and what you can do to limit the effects. Can you imagine having time to do such things? If you cannot, then you are farther away from being a great project manager than you might wish. Great project managers will not let the project control them, but will try to control the project by spending the time to go through such a thought process.

Scope control involves following the change control process set up in the project scope management plan. To control scope, one first needs to have a clear definition of what is the scope on the project; the project scope statement, WBS and WBS dictionary. One then has to measure scope performance against the scope baseline. Once that information is known, the next step is to determine if any updates to the project management plan or the components of the scope baseline are needed, and what corrective and preventive actions should be recommended.

There is a connection between scope control and integrated change control, shown below:

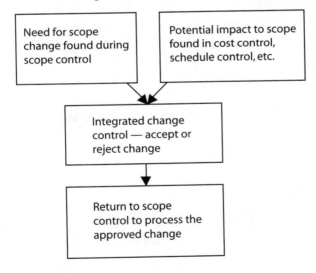

Practice Exam

Scope Management

1. **A work breakdown structure numbering system allows project staff to:**
   A. systematically estimate costs of work breakdown structure elements.
   B. provide project justification.
   C. identify the level at which individual elements are found.
   D. use it in project management software.

2. **The work breakdown structure can BEST be thought of as an effective aid for _____ communications.**
   A. team
   B. project manager
   C. customer
   D. stakeholder

3. **Which of the following is a KEY output of scope verification?**
   A. More complete project scope management plan
   B. Customer acceptance of project deliverables
   C. Improved schedule estimates
   D. An improved project management information system

4. **During project executing, a team member comes to the project manager because he is not sure of what work he needs to accomplish on the project. Which of the following documents contain detailed descriptions of work packages?**
   A. Work breakdown structure (WBS) dictionary
   B. Activity list
   C. Preliminary project scope statement
   D. Project scope management plan

5. **During what part of the project management process is the project scope statement created?**
   A. Initiating
   B. Planning
   C. Executing
   D. Monitoring and controlling

6. **The program was planned years ago before there was a massive introduction of new technology. While planning the next project to start in this program, the project manager has expanded the project scope management plan because as a project becomes more complex, the level of uncertainty in the scope:**
   A. remains the same.
   B. decreases.
   C. decreases then increases.
   D. increases.

7. A project management plan should be realistic in order to be used to manage the project. Which of the following is the BEST method to achieve a realistic project management plan?
   A. Sponsor creates the project management plan based on input from the project manager.
   B. Functional manager creates the project management plan based on input from the project manager.
   C. Project manager creates the project management plan based on input from senior management.
   D. Project manager creates the project management plan based on input from the team.

8. A new project manager is being mentored by a more experienced certified project management professional (PMP). The new project manager is finding it difficult to find enough time to manage the project because the product and project scope are being progressively elaborated. The PMP mentions that the basic tools for project management, such as a work breakdown structure, can be used during project executing to assist the project.
   For which of the following can a work breakdown structure be used?
   A. Communicating with the customer
   B. Showing calendar dates for each work package
   C. Showing the functional managers for each team member
   D. Showing the business need for the project

9. During a project team meeting, a team member suggests an enhancement to the scope that is beyond the scope of the project charter. The project manager points out that the team needs to concentrate on completing all the work and only the work required. This is an example of:
   A. change management process.
   B. scope management.
   C. quality analysis.
   D. scope decomposition.

10. When should scope verification be done?
    A. At the end of the project
    B. At the beginning of the project
    C. At the end of each phase of the project
    D. During the planning processes

11. The project is mostly complete. The project has a schedule variance of 300 and a cost variance of -900. All but one of the quality control inspections have been completed and all have met the quality requirements. All items in the issue log have been resolved. Many of the resources have been released. The sponsor is about to call a meeting to obtain product verification when the customer notifies the project manager that they want to make a major change to the scope. The project manager should:
    A. meet with the project team to determine if this change can be made.
    B. ask the customer for a description of the change.
    C. explain that the change cannot be made at this point in the process.
    D. inform management.

12. You have just joined the project management office after five years of working on projects. One of the things you want to introduce to your company is the need to do

WBSs. Some of the project managers are angry that you are asking them to do "extra work." Which of the following would be the BEST thing you could tell the project managers to convince them to use WBSs?

A. Tell them it will prevent work from slipping through the cracks.
B. Tell them that it is not needed.
C. Tell them it is required if the project involves contracts.
D. Tell them it is the only way to identify risks.

13. A new project manager has asked you for advice on creating a work breakdown structure. After you explain the process to him, he asks you what software he should use to create the WBS and what should he do with it when he is finished creating it. You might respond that it is not the picture that is the most valuable result of creating a WBS. It is:

A. a bar chart.
B. team buy-in.
C. activities.
D. a list of risks.

14. To manage a project effectively, work should be broken down into small pieces. Which of the following does NOT describe how far to decompose the work?

A. Until it has a meaningful conclusion
B. Until it cannot be logically subdivided further
C. Until it can be done by one person
D. Until it can be realistically estimated

15. A project manager may use _____ to make sure the team clearly knows what work is included in each of their work packages.

A. the project scope statement
B. the product scope
C. a WBS dictionary
D. a schedule

16. A project manager has just been assigned to a new project and has been given the preliminary project scope statement and the project charter. The FIRST thing the project manager must do is:

A. create a project scope statement.
B. confirm that all the stakeholders have had input into the scope.
C. analyze project risk.
D. begin work on a project management plan.

17. The construction phase of a new software product is near completion. The next phase is testing and implementation. The project is two weeks ahead of schedule. What should the project manager be MOST concerned with before moving on to the final phase?

A. Scope verification
B. Quality control
C. Performance reports
D. Cost control

18. You are managing a six-month project and have held bi-weekly meetings with your project stakeholders. After five and a half months of work, the project is on schedule and budget, but the stakeholders are not satisfied with the deliverables. This situation

will delay the project completion by one month. The MOST important process that could have prevented this situation is:

A. risk monitoring and control.

B. schedule control.

C. scope planning.

D. scope control.

19. All of the following are part of the scope baseline EXCEPT the:

A. project scope management plan.

B. project scope statement.

C. work breakdown structure.

D. work breakdown structure dictionary.

20. One of the stakeholders on the project contacts the project manager to discuss some additional scope they would like to add to the project. The project manager asks for details in writing and then works through the scope control process. What should the project manager do NEXT when the evaluation of the requested scope is completed?

A. Ask the stakeholder if there are any more changes expected.

B. Complete integrated change control.

C. Make sure the impact of the change is understood by the stakeholder.

D. Find out the root cause of why the scope was not discovered during project planning.

Scope Management Answers

1. **Answer** C
   Explanation The numbering system allows you to quickly identify the level in the work breakdown structure where the specific element is found. It also helps to locate the element in the WBS dictionary.

2. **Answer** D
   Explanation The term stakeholder encompasses all the other choices. In this case, it is the best answer since the WBS can be used (but does not need to be used) as a communications tool for all stakeholders to "see" what is included in the project.

3. **Answer** B
   Explanation The output of scope verification is customer acceptance of project deliverables. The other choices all happen during project planning, well before the time that scope verification takes place.

4. **Answer** A
   Explanation Activity lists (choice B) may list the work package they relate to, but they do not contain detailed descriptions of work packages. The preliminary project scope statement (choice C) may contain project scope, but does not describe the work a team member is assigned. The project scope management plan (choice D) describes how scope will be planned, managed and controlled. It does not include a description of each work package. The WBS dictionary defines each element in the WBS. Therefore, descriptions of the work packages are in the WBS dictionary.

5. **Answer** B
   Explanation Did you say project initiating? If so, you did not read the question. It did not refer to the preliminary project scope statement, just the project scope statement. Tricky I know. Do you hate me yet? And you were worried about long wordy questions!

6. **Answer** D
   Explanation Not all questions will be difficult. The level of uncertainty in scope increases based on the scale of effort required to identify all the scope. For larger projects it is more difficult to "catch" everything.

7. **Answer** D
   Explanation If we were to rephrase the question, it is asking, "Who creates the project management plan?" The best answer is that project management plans are created by the project manager but require input from the team.

8. **Answer** A
   Explanation A WBS does not show dates or responsibility assignments (choices B and C). Those are included on the bar chart and possibly in the communications management plan. The business need (choice D) is shown in the project charter. Never thought that a WBS could be shown to the customer? Made you think! Of course it could be used for that purpose. In this situation, the product and project scope are being fine tuned. It would save the project manager time to effectively manage progressive elaboration if the WBS were used to assist. The WBS helps ensure everyone understands the scope of the work.

9. **Answer** B
   Explanation The team member is suggesting an enhancement that is outside the project charter. Scope management involves focusing on doing the work and only the work in the project management plan that meets the needs of the project charter. The project manager is performing scope management.

10. **Answer** C
    Explanation It is product verification that occurs at the end of the project (choice A). Scope verification is done during the monitoring and controlling process group, so choices B and D cannot be correct. The description of scope verification defines it as being done at the end of each phase (the end of design, implementation) making choice C the best answer.

11. **Answer** B
    Explanation Do not jump into the problem without thinking. The customer only notified the project manager that "they want to make a change." They did not describe the change. The project manager would need to understand the nature of the change and have time to evaluate the impact of the change before doing anything else. Of these choices, the first thing to do is to determine what is the change (choice B) and then meet with the team (choice A), but only if their input is required. The project manager should not just say no (choice C) until he knows more about the possible change. He also should not go to management (choice D) without more information.

12. **Answer** A
    Explanation Choice C is not generally true. The WBS is not only needed in order to have a contract, every project must have a WBS. Risks can be identified using various methods. Therefore, choice D is an incorrect statement and not the best answer. Choice A, preventing work from being forgotten (slipping through the cracks) is ONE of the reasons the tool is used.

13. **Answer** B
    Explanation The WBS is an input to all of these choices. However, team buy-in (choice B) is a direct result of the WBS creation process, while the other choices use the WBS to assist in their completion. The best answer is B.

14. **Answer** C
    Explanation The lowest level of the WBS is a work package, which can be performed by more than one person.

15. **Answer** C
    Explanation The project scope statement (choice A) describes work on a high-level basis. Work packages need to be specific to enable team members to complete their work with less gold plating. The product scope (choice B) would not tell the team members what work is assigned to them. The team should have a copy of the schedule (choice D) but a schedule will not show them what work is included in each of their work packages. Work packages are described in the WBS dictionary (choice C). NOTE: Do not think of the WBS dictionary as a dictionary of terms.

16. **Answer** B
    Explanation This question can be tricky, especially if you have spent so much time studying that you have forgotten some good project management practices. A quick

look at Rita's Process Charts in this book might draw you to conclude that the FIRST thing would be to start planning. Wouldn't it be smart to make sure what you have in the preliminary project scope statement and project charter are clear and complete before moving on? This is why choice B is the best choice.

17. **Answer** A

    Explanation Scope verification deals with acceptance by the customer. Without this acceptance, you will not be able to move into the next project phase.

18. **Answer** C

    Explanation Choices A, B and D are processes in the monitoring and controlling process group. This situation asks how to prevent the problem. This would have been done during the planning processes (choice C), as the project deliverables are defined in scope planning. Good planning reduces the likelihood of a similar situation by including the right people, and spending adequate time in clarifying the project scope.

19. **Answer** A

    Explanation The project scope management plan is not part of the scope baseline.

20. **Answer** B

    Explanation Notice that there are many things that the project manager could do listed in the choices. The question asks what is the BEST thing to do NEXT. Though they are great things to do, choices A and D are not next. Choice C would be done as part of integrated change control. Management of the change is not complete when scope control is completed. It is important to look at the impact of the change on other parts of the project such as time and cost. Therefore, choice B is the best thing to do next, probably followed by C and then D and A.

Time Management

This chapter might be hard for you if you do not know how to manually create network diagrams, but you can easily get over that. The chapter will be very hard for you if you have never realized that an unrealistic schedule is the project manager's fault! Yes, it's true. One of the key reasons for the project manager's existence is to see if the needed end date can be met and create options to make it happen, all BEFORE project executing starts. If you know the many options for compressing a project schedule, and that a project schedule must be realistic before project executing starts, you will probably be fine.

In order to answer time management questions correctly, you need a thorough understanding of the process of scheduling a project. Though most project managers use some type of software to assist with scheduling, you will need to manually draw network diagrams and answer questions about network diagrams and scheduling. As a result, you will need to know some things that normally go on behind the scenes when using software for project management.

Watch out! Make sure you realize there is no such thing as project management software. The "project management" software available can be extremely helpful for scheduling, "what if" scenarios and status reporting functions, but it does not tell you how to manage a project. You cannot follow software; you must make it conform to your needs.

Many existing software programs suggest planning a project in ways that do not conform to proper project management methods; first make a list of the activities, then assign them to calendar dates and the project management plan is finished. They do not address all aspects of project management and may have changed some of the basic components of the tools of project management (such as what is in a bar chart) in ways that could cause you to get questions wrong on the exam. Read this chapter carefully and check your knowledge as you go.

Rita's Process Chart—Time Management
Where are we in the project management process?

Initiating	Planning	Executing	Monitoring & Controlling	Closing
Select project manager	**Determine how you will do planning—part of management plans**	Acquire final team	**Measure against the performance measurement baselines**	Develop closure procedures
Determine company culture and existing systems	Create project scope statement	Execute the PM plan	**Measure according to the management plans**	Complete contract closure
Collect processes, procedures and historical information	Determine team	Work to produce product scope	**Determine variances and if they warrant corrective action or a change**	Confirm work is done to requirements
Divide large projects into phases	Create WBS and WBS dictionary	Recommend changes and corrective actions	Scope verification	Gain formal acceptance of the product
Identify stakeholders	**Create activity list**	Send and receive information	Configuration management	Final performance reporting
Document business need	**Create network diagram**	Implement approved changes, defect repair, preventive and corrective actions	**Recommend changes, defect repair, preventive and corrective actions**	Index and archive records
Determine project objectives	**Estimate resource requirements**	Continuous improvement	Integrated change control	Update lessons learned knowledge base
Document assumptions and constraints	**Estimate time and cost**	Follow processes	Approve changes, defect repair, preventive and corrective actions	Hand off completed product
Develop project charter	**Determine critical path**	Team building	Risk audits	Release resources
Develop preliminary project scope statement	**Develop schedule**	Give recognition and rewards	Manage reserves	
	Develop budget	Hold progress meetings	Use issue logs	
	Determine quality standards, processes and metrics	Use work authorization system	Facilitate conflict resolution	
	Determine roles and responsibilities	Request seller responses	Measure team member performance	
	Determine communications requirements	Select sellers	Report on performance	
	Risk identification, qualitative and quantitative risk analysis and response planning		Create forecasts	
	Iterations—go back		Administer contracts	
	Determine what to purchase			
	Prepare procurement documents			
	Finalize the "how to execute and control" aspects of all management plans			
	Create process improvement plan			
	Develop final PM plan and performance measurement baselines			
	Gain formal approval for plan			
	Hold kickoff meeting			

The following should help you understand how each part of Time Management fits into the project management process.

The Time Management Process

The Time Management Process	Done During
Activity definition	Planning process group
Activity sequencing	Planning process group
Activity resource estimating	Planning process group
Activity duration estimating	Planning process group
Schedule development	Planning process group
Schedule control	Monitoring and controlling process group

TRICKS OF THE TRADE **Things About Estimating to Know for the Exam** (This is repeated in the Cost chapter as it also relates to cost.)
- Estimating should be based on a WBS to improve accuracy
- Estimating should be done by the person doing the work whenever possible
- Historical information from past projects (part of organizational process assets) is a key to improving estimates
- A schedule baseline (and cost, scope, quality and resource baselines) should be kept and not changed except for approved project changes
- The schedule should be managed to the schedule baseline for the project
- Changes are approved in integrated change control
- Estimates are more accurate if smaller sized work components are estimated
- Corrective actions and preventive actions should be recommended when schedule problems (and cost, scope, quality and resource problems) occur
- A project manager should never just accept requirements from management, but rather analyze the needs of the project, come up with her own estimates and reconcile any differences to produce realistic objectives. Yes, this should be true in the real world!
- A project manager may continually calculate the estimate to complete for the project in order to make sure there is adequate time (and cost, etc.) available for the project
- Plans should be revised, as necessary, during completion of the work
- How to get a good estimate
- Padding is not an acceptable project management practice
- The project manager must meet any agreed upon estimates
- What to do with the estimates when received
- How to keep the estimates realistic

Think about these! Remember that incorrect project management practices will be listed as choices on the exam. If you do not adequately understand and manage your projects this way, you will have difficulty on the exam and not even know why.

The exam focuses on the role of the project manager in producing good estimates. It does not focus on calculations. NOTE: You will frequently see one-time estimate per activity used on the exam, as shown in the series of exercises later in this chapter. This method is not always best, but it is an easier way to improve your understanding of finding critical paths and drawing network diagrams. Using one-time estimates also allows for a quick calculation and proof that you understand those concepts.

Schedule Management Plan (page 124) Though specifically listed in other chapters, the management plan for schedule is not listed as a separate part of the scheduling process. Imagine it exists for the exam. Therefore, the first process in time management is planning, which answers the questions, "How will I go about planning the schedule for the project?" and then, "How will I effectively manage and control the project to the schedule baseline, and manage schedule variances?" Once again, you can see that such a plan requires thinking in advance about how you will manage. This is a concept that many project managers miss.

This plan includes:
- Establishment of a schedule baseline for measuring against during the monitoring and controlling process group
- Identification of performance measures, to identify variances early
- Planning for how schedule variances will be managed
- Identification of schedule change control procedures

Does this list make you think? Do you currently do any of this for your projects? Notice the identification of performance measures. Most project managers just work on the project and hope they meet the deadline. A schedule management plan requires that progress be measured along the way. Measures of performance are determined in advance so you can plan to capture the data you need to measure. How will you measure schedule performance during the project? The schedule management plan can be formal or informal, but is part of the project management plan.

The schedule management plan will help make the schedule estimating process faster by providing guidelines on how estimates should be made (e.g., stating that estimates must be in hours or days). During the direct and manage project execution process, the schedule management plan can help determine if a variance is over the allowable threshold and therefore must be acted upon. The schedule management plan can also help determine the types of reports required on the project relating to schedule.

━━━Activity Definition (page 127) This process involves taking the work packages created in the WBS and breaking them down further (decomposing) in order to reach the activity level; a level small enough to estimate, schedule, monitor and manage. These activities are then sequenced in the next process; activity sequencing.

TRICKS OF THE TRADE This is not always done in the real world. Many project managers skip activity definition because they take their WBS down to the activity level rather than the work package level. Other project managers say that they cannot work with a network diagram created at the activity level because it would be too large. They create the network diagram to the work package level instead of the activity level. Neither of these practices is wrong, just know this for the exam: the *PMBOK® Guide* states that in activity definition, the WBS is decomposed into activities (schedule activities) and in activity sequencing (described next) those activities are sequenced into the network diagram.

Have you ever felt that the project had too many unknown components to adequately break down the work and schedule it? Be careful, you might really have more than one project! Please see the earlier discussion on this in the Framework chapter. You might also just have found it better not to plan to the lowest detail in advance, but plan at a higher level and then wait until the project work has begun and the work is more clear to plan the lower levels. This is called rolling wave planning. Summary activities are not planned to the detail needed to manage the work until you start the project management process for that phase of the project life cycle.

Watch out! The existence of rolling wave planning and planning to a higher level than a work package are not excuses for not properly planning a project or making sure all the scope that can be known is known before starting work!

When completed, activity definition will also result in an activity list and the details of the activities (activity attributes) being completed. No part of project management exists alone. Activity definition can lead to a discovery that the WBS or some other part of the project management plan under development needs to be changed. This will result in requested changes to the developing project management plan.

━━Activity Sequencing (page 130) The next process is to take the activities and start to sequence them into how the work will be performed. The result is a network diagram (or project schedule network diagram) which can look like the following picture.

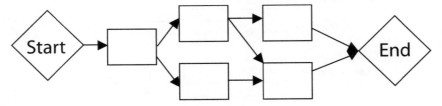

Some people incorrectly call a network diagram a PERT chart. There are extensive exercises to help you draw network diagrams later in this chapter.

For the exam, know that, in its pure form, the network diagram shows just dependencies. If activity duration estimates (estimates) are added, the network diagram could also show the critical path.

If plotted out against time (or placed against a calendar-based scale), the network diagram would be a time-scaled schedule network diagram.

✋ Methods to Draw Network Diagrams There are two ways to draw network diagrams, Precedence Diagramming Method and Arrow Diagramming Method. (GERT is a minor item, but it occasionally shows up on the exam.) Today most network diagrams are created using PDM, described below. You should, however, understand both methods for the exam and MEMORIZE the following attributes of the two methods.

Precedence Diagramming Method (PDM) or Activity-on-Node (AON) In this method, nodes (or boxes) are used to represent activities, and arrows show activity dependencies as follows:

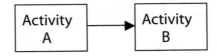

 This type of drawing can have four types of relationships between activities:

- **Finish-to-start** An activity must finish before the successor can start (most common)
- **Start-to-start** An activity must start before the successor can start
- **Finish-to-finish** An activity must finish before the successor can finish
- **Start-to-finish** An activity must start before the successor can finish (rarely used)

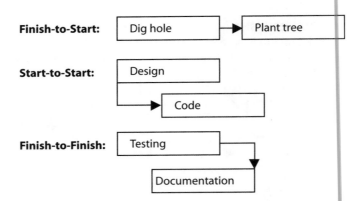

- **Finish-to-start** You must finish digging a hole before you can start the next activity, planting a tree
- **Start-to-start** You must start design and wait for two weeks lag before you can start coding
- **Finish-to-finish** You must finish testing before you can finish documentation
- **Start-to-finish** Start-to-finish relationships are rarely used

Arrow Diagramming Method (ADM) or Activity-on-Arrow (AOA)

In this method of drawing a network diagram, the arrows are used to represent activities. The nodes (in this case circles) represent activity dependencies. Any activity (arrow) coming into a node is a predecessor to any activity leaving the node. This method:

- Uses only finish-to-start relationships between activities.
- May use dummy activities. Dummies are usually represented by a dotted line and are inserted simply to show dependencies between activities. They do not require work or take time.

There are two ways to denote an activity-on-arrow activity. Either the name will be on the arrow, as shown at left, below, or the activity will be named as shown on the right, below. This therefore requires two-letter identifiers to name a single activity (e.g., A-B). You will see an example of this in one of the upcoming exercises.

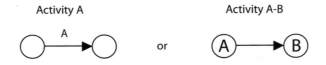

Review the following to reduce your confusion. If activity D is "determine requirements," activity E is "research," activity C is "determine acceptance criteria" and activity K is "initial design," then you need a dummy to show that the "initial design" activity is dependent upon the "determine requirements" activity. However, no work needs to be done between the two activities. An activity-on-arrow diagram with a dummy is shown opposite.

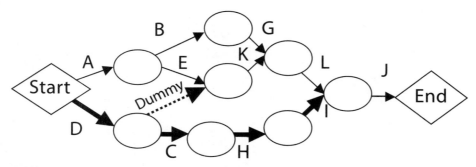

GERT A network diagram drawing method that allows loops between activities. The easiest example is when you have an activity to design a component and then test it. After testing, it may or may not need to be redesigned. GERT is only rarely on the exam and when it does appear, it is most often just a choice on the multiple choice questions.

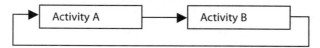

Types of Dependencies The sequence of activities is determined based on the following dependencies:

- **Mandatory Dependency (Hard Logic)** Inherent in the nature of the work being done or required by the contract (e.g., you must design before you can construct).
- **Discretionary Dependency (Preferred, Preferential or Soft Logic)** The way the project manager prefers to set dependencies. These dependencies can be changed if needed, while the others cannot easily be changed.
- **External Dependency** Based on the needs or desires of a party outside the project (e.g., government or suppliers).

Milestones Milestones are significant events within the project schedule. Some examples include: the design is completed, or a deliverable due date from the customer. Milestones can be imposed by the sponsor in the project charter and preliminary project scope statement. What many project managers miss is that additional milestones can be imposed by the project manager during activity sequencing or schedule development, as checkpoints to help control the project. If the checkpoint in the schedule arrives and all the work planned has been completed, then the project manger has a measure that the project may be progressing as planned. A list of milestones becomes part of the project management plan and is included in the project scope statement and WBS dictionary.

Leads and Lags (page 134) A lead may be added to start an activity before the predecessor activity is completed. Coding might be able to start five days before the design is finished. A lag is inserted waiting time between activities. For example, you must wait three days after pouring concrete before you can construct the frame for the house.

Requested Changes Watch for changes throughout the planning processes. The creation of a network diagram could easily reveal an additional WBS element. These changes are proposed and addressed as part of integrated change control.

TRICKS OF THE TRADE Instead of just asking what is a network diagram, the exam will ask the harder question, "How can the network diagram help you?" Only those who have worked with network diagrams can answer such questions. See how you do with the next exercise.

Exercise Describe how the network diagram can help you on the project.

Answer You should know that network diagrams can be used to:
- Show interdependencies of all activities
- Show workflow so the team will know what activities need to happen in a specific sequence
- Aid in effectively planning, organizing and controlling the project
- Compress the schedule in planning and throughout the life of the project (defined later)
- Show project progress if used for schedule control and reporting
- Help justify your time estimate for the project

Activity Resource Estimating (page 135) Once the activities are sequenced, the type and quantity of needed resources is determined. Remember that resources include equipment and materials, as well as people. Resources must be planned and coordinated in order to avoid common problems such as lack of resources and resources being taken away from the project.

Exercise Which of the following do you think is involved in activity resource estimating? Simply put a yes or no in the right hand column.

Action	Is It Part of Resource Estimating?
Review resource pool availability	
Get one time estimate per activity	
Complete an analysis of the reserves needed on the project	
Create a company calendar identifying working and non-working days	
Create milestones	
Review WBS	
Develop a risk register	
Identify potentially available resources	
Review historical information about the use of resources on past or similar projects	
Review organizational policies on resource use	
See how leads and lags affect the time estimate	
Solicit expert judgment on what resources are needed and available	
Analyze alternative ways of completing the work and whether those ways help to better utilize resources	
Show network dependencies per activity	
Make-or-buy decisions	

Action	Is It Part of Resource Estimating?
Crash the project	
Break the activity down further if activity is too complex to resource estimate (bottom-up estimating)	
Quantify resource requirements by activity	
Create a hierarchical structure of the identified resources by resource category and type (a resource breakdown structure [RBS])	
Fast track	
Schedule development	
Develop a plan as to what types of resources will be used	

Answer Activity resource estimating involves:

Action	Is It Part of Resource Estimating?
Review resource pool availability	Yes
Get one time estimate per activity	No
Complete an analysis of the reserves needed on the project	No
Create a company calendar identifying working and non-working days	No
Create milestones	No
Review WBS	Yes
Develop a risk register	No
Identify potentially available resources	Yes
Review historical information about the use of resources on past or similar projects	Yes
Review organizational policies on resource use	Yes
See how leads and lags affect the time estimate	No
Solicit expert judgment on what resources are needed and available	Yes
Analyze alternative ways of completing the work and whether those ways help to better utilize resources	Yes
Show network dependencies per activity	No
Make-or-buy decisions	Yes
Crash the project	No
Break the activity down further if activity is too complex to resource estimate (bottom-up estimating)	Yes
Quantify resource requirements by activity	Yes
Create a hierarchical structure of the identified resources by resource category and type (a resource breakdown structure [RBS])	Yes
Fast track	No
Schedule development	No
Develop a plan as to what types of resources will be used	Yes

Activity Duration Estimating (page 139) Once the previous time management processes are completed, the amount of time each activity is expected to take is needed. In order to estimate well, the estimator (the person doing the work, when possible) will need to know resource requirements, resource calendars, organizational process assets (processes, procedures and historical information) and enterprise environmental factors (company culture and existing systems that the project will have to deal with or can make use of, such as estimating software). The estimator might also make use of time estimates and any other information gathered during estimating while creating the risk register (risk management).

How Is the Estimating Done? Activities can be estimated using the following techniques:

One-Time Estimate When estimating using a one-time estimate, one estimate per activity is received. For example, the person doing the estimating says that the activity will take five weeks. The time estimate can be made based on expert judgment, by looking at historical information, or even by just guessing.

Let's think about estimating in your real world for a moment. Does your team feel like this?

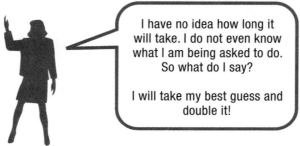

I have no idea how long it will take. I do not even know what I am being asked to do. So what do I say?

I will take my best guess and double it!

A pad is adding some time to the project estimate. A pad added to an activity is merely unidentified uncertainties and risks. These uncertainties should not remain hidden, but should be identified and managed in the risk management process. Someone has to tell you this; padding is a sign of poor project management! After all, achieving the project schedule baseline date created during the time management process will be a measure of project success.

One-time estimate per activity has the following negative effects on the project:
- Can force people into padding their estimates
- Hides important information about risks and uncertainties from the project manager, which are needed to better plan and control the project
- Creates a schedule that no one believes in, thus losing buy-in to the project management process
- When a person estimates that an activity will take 20 days and it is completed in 15 days, it can make the person who provided the estimate look untruthful and untrustworthy
- Has the estimators working against the project manager to protect themselves, rather than with the project manager, to help all

In real project management, the estimators have a WBS and may even have helped create it. They also have a description for each work package (the WBS dictionary) and may have helped create that also. They may even have helped create the activity list from the work package, and know there will be time reserves on the project. With that information, they should not need to pad their estimates!

One-time estimates should only be used for projects that do not require a detailed, highly probable schedule. If one-time estimates are used, it is critical that the project manager provide the estimator with as much information as possible, including the WBS, WBS dictionary and the activity list, or the estimate will likely be unreliable.

If the people doing the work are the ones who estimate, what is the project manager doing? The role of the project manager in estimating is to:
- Provide the team with enough information to properly estimate each activity
- Let those doing the estimating know how refined their estimates must be
- Complete a sanity check of the estimates
- Prevent padding
- Formulate a reserve (more on this later)
- Make sure assumptions made during estimating are recorded for later review

Analogous Estimating (Top-down, page 141) Analogous estimating can be done for a project (The last five projects similar to this one each took five months, so this one should also.) or an activity (The last two times this activity was completed each took three days. Since we have no other information to go on, we will use three days as the estimate for this activity and review the estimate when more details become available.). However, the exam seems to take an analogous estimate to mean only the overall project estimate given to the project manager from management or the sponsor. Take care to interpret these questions correctly. Analogous estimating is a form of expert judgment.

Parametric Estimating (page 142) Parametric estimating is used if you do not have detailed information on which to base time estimates. It uses a mathematical model to calculate projected times for an activity based on historical records from previous projects and other information. The result is an activity estimate based on such measures as time per line of code, time per linear meter or time per installation. There are two ways to create parametric estimates:

- **Regression analysis (scatter diagram)** This diagram tracks two variables to see if they are related and creates a mathematical formula to use in future parametric estimating.
- **Learning curve** The 100th room painted will take less time than the first room because of improved efficiency.

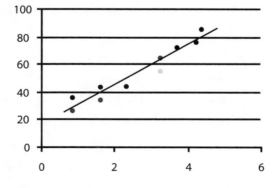

Heuristics A heuristic means a rule of thumb. An example of a heuristic is the 80/20 rule that, in quality, suggests that 80 percent of quality problems are caused by 20 percent of potential sources of problems. The results of parametric estimates can become heuristics.

Three-Point Estimates It is important to understand that statistically there is a very small probability of completing a project on any one date. Therefore, time estimates for an activity or a project must be in a range. Three time (or cost) estimates per activity is superior to one time (or cost) estimate because a weighted average is used instead of the most likely estimate.

In this form of estimating, the person estimating the activity provides an optimistic (O), pessimistic (P) and most likely (M) estimate for each activity. The final activity duration estimate could be calculated based on an average of the three estimates, or by using a formula. (See three-point estimates described in schedule development next.)

The resulting estimates for an activity will be stated as seven days plus or minus two days, which means that the activity will take anywhere from five to nine days.

Reserve Analysis It is required project management to accommodate the time and cost risk in a project through the use of reserves. As described in the Risk chapter, there can be two types of reserve added: contingency reserve and management reserve. Contingency reserve is for the risks remaining after risk response planning. Management reserve is any extra amount of funds to be set aside to cover unforeseen risks. The cost baseline will include the contingency reserve, and the cost budget will include the management reserve. Please see the Risk chapter to learn how these are calculated. The work should include making sure individual activity estimates are not padded.

▬ Schedule Development (page 143) Once a network diagram and estimates are completed, it is time to put the information into a schedule. The difference between a time estimate and a schedule is that the schedule is calendar-based.

Exercise 1 Let's start at the beginning. What do you need before you try to develop a schedule for your project?

Answer 1 In order to develop a schedule, you need to have:
- An understanding of the work required on the project (project scope statement)
- Defined activities (WBS, WBS dictionary and activity list)
- The order of how the work will be done (activity sequencing)
- An estimate of the resources needed (activity resource estimating)
- An estimate of the duration of each activity (activity duration estimating)

Let's get more specific. You should also have:
- A company calendar identifying what are working and non-working days
- Imposed dates
- Milestones
- Assumptions
- Constraints
- Activity list
- Risk management plan—because it includes a schedule and budget for performing risk identification, qualitative risk analysis and other risk management activities
- Risk register—because it includes risks known to date
- Leads and lags

Exercise 2 Think about the real world. You need to create a schedule that you will be able to stake your reputation on meeting. What would you need to do in order to take the estimating data and create such a finalized schedule?

| |
| |
| |
| |
| |
| |
| |
| |
| |
| |

Answer 2 Let's go way beyond the *PMBOK® Guide*. Schedule development really means everything you need to do to develop a finalized schedule that is bought into, approved, realistic and formal. This is what schedule development is all about. What is done to get it to that level?
- Work with stakeholders' priorities
- Look for alternative ways to complete the work
- Look for impacts on other projects
- Meet with managers to negotiate for resource availability
- Give the team a chance to approve the final schedule. They might have estimated an activity, but should also look at the calendar allocation of their estimates to see if they are feasible
- Compress the schedule by crashing, fast tracking and re-estimating

- Adjust all the components of the project management plan (e.g., change the WBS because of risk responses planned)
- Simulate the project using Monte Carlo analysis
- Level resources
- Conduct meetings and conversations to gain stakeholder and management formal approval

Think about this carefully before you continue. Then refer to the list of actions for develop project management plan in the Integration chapter. Many of those apply to schedule development as well.

The data available so far is put into a schedule, called the schedule model, and the project manager then performs various calculations and alternative what-if analysis to determine the optimum schedule. Schedule development is iterative and will occur many times over the life of the project (at least once per project life cycle phase). Schedule development is another large source of problems on the exam for many project managers. Read this entire section over carefully! For the exam, you will be expected to be an expert at handling schedule development during project planning and whenever there are changes!

Schedule Network Analysis Once the schedule model is completed, schedule network analysis can begin and may take the form of one or all of the following techniques:
- PERT
- Critical path method
- Schedule compression
- What-if scenario analysis
- Resource leveling
- Critical chain method

PERT Please read carefully. The formulas listed below have been called PERT formulas (short for the Program Evaluation and Review Technique). You might see them referenced up to three times on the exam.

 You must MEMORIZE these formulas and know that they can also be used for cost estimates.

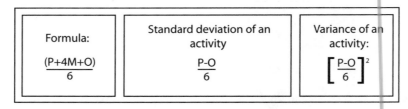

Formula:	Standard deviation of an activity	Variance of an activity:
$\dfrac{(P+4M+O)}{6}$	$\dfrac{P-O}{6}$	$\left[\dfrac{P-O}{6}\right]^2$

Notice that the formulas relate to activities. To find the duration and standard deviation for a project, one would add the PERT estimates for each activity on the critical path. Statistically, however, it is not correct to add standard deviations. One must calculate the variances for the activities, add those and then take the square root to obtain the project standard deviation. This is why there is a formula for the standard deviation and variance.

Did you get lost in the last paragraph? Do not worry, it is further explained in Exercise 2 that follows. For the exam, you need to be able to do simple calculations using the formulas, have a general understanding that estimates of time (or cost) should be in a range, and know the concept of three time (or cost) estimates per activity.

Time Management

 TRICKS OF THE TRADE® Know the formula for variance as simply, "Standard deviation squared."

Exercise 1 Complete the chart using the formulas from the previous page. All estimates are in hours. It is best to calculate to three decimal places and round to two decimal places when you are ready to check your answers on the real exam.

Activity	O	M	P	(PERT or) Expected Duration	Activity Standard Deviation	Activity Variance	Range of the Estimate
A	14	27	47				
B	41	60	89				
C	39	44	48				
D	29	37	42				

Answer 1 Remember that square is not times two, but a number times itself.

	O	M	P	(PERT or) Expected Duration	Activity Standard Deviation	Activity Variance	Range of the Estimate
A	14	27	47	28.167	5.500	30.250	22.667 to 33.667 *or* 28.167 +/- 5.500
B	41	60	89	61.667	8.000	64.000	53.667 to 69.667 *or* 61.667 +/- 8.000
C	39	44	48	43.833	1.500	2.250	42.333 to 45.333 *or* 43.833 +/- 1.500
D	29	37	42	36.500	2.167	4.694	34.333 to 38.667 *or* 36.500 +/- 2.167

Exercise 2 Assuming that the activities listed in Exercise 1 make up the entire critical path for the project, how long should the project take?

Answer 2 This question is provided for understanding and does not represent the complexity of questions on the exam! Most of the questions on the exam relating to PERT are as simple as the ones at the end of this chapter.

The following table summarizes the answer and is explained below.

Project	O	M	P	(PERT or) Expected Duration	Project Standard Deviation	Project Variance	Range of the Estimate
Project				170.167	10.060	101.194	160.107 to 180.227 *or* 170.167 +/- 10.060

The answer is 170.167 hours +/- 10.06 hours at one standard deviation.

The expected duration of the project, 170.167, is found by adding the PERT estimates for each of the critical path activities (in this case all the activities listed). The +/- 10.06 represents the standard deviation of the estimate (the range of the estimate) and is found by adding the variances of the critical path activities, total of 101.194, and taking the square root to get 10.060.

In order to find the standard deviation of a series of items, remember the rule. You cannot add standard deviations; you must convert standard deviations into variances, add the variances and then take the square root of the total to convert back into standard deviation. This calculation means adding 30.250 + 64.000 + 2.250 + 4.694 and taking the square root to find 10.06. Therefore, if we add one standard deviation to the PERT total (for a 68.26 percent confidence level, see the Quality chapter) the project would not be estimated to take 170.167 hours, but between 160.107 hours and 180.227 hours. If we add two standard deviations (for a 95.46 percent confidence level) the project would be estimated to take between 150.047 hours and 190.287 hours (170.167 +/- 20.12).

Critical Path Method The critical path method includes determining the longest path in the network diagram (the critical path) and the earliest and latest an activity can start and the earliest and latest it can be completed. This method requires the understanding of some basic concepts. These are described first.

Critical Path The critical path is the longest duration path through a network diagram and determines the shortest time to complete the project.

Exercise Test yourself! How does the critical path help the project manager?

Answer The critical path:
- Helps prove how long the project will take
- Helps the project manager determine where best to focus her project management efforts
- Helps determine if an issue needs immediate attention
- Provides a vehicle to compress the schedule during project planning and whenever there are changes
- Provides a vehicle to determine which activities have float and can therefore be delayed without delaying the project

TRICKS OF THE TRADE The easiest way to find the critical path is to identify all paths through the network and add the activity durations along each path. The path with the longest duration is the critical path.

Near-Critical Path In addition to the critical path, a smart project manager should be familiar with the concept of a near-critical path. This path is close in duration to the critical path. Something could happen so the critical path is shortened, or the near-critical path lengthened so the near-critical path becomes critical. The closer the near-critical and critical paths are, the more risk the project has. The project manager should spend more time and effort monitoring and controlling critical and near-critical path activities so they don't delay the project completion.

Float (Slack) You must be able to understand float and to calculate it manually for the exam. There are three types of float to know and understand for the exam. They are:
- **Total float (slack)** The amount of time an *activity* can be delayed without delaying the project end date or an intermediary milestone. This is the key type of float, but there are others. Please note that the terms float and slack mean the same thing. You may see either or both on your exam.
- **Free float (slack)** The amount of time an *activity* can be delayed without delaying the early start date of its successor(s).
- **Project float (slack)** The amount of time a *project* can be delayed without delaying the externally imposed project completion date required by the customer, management, or previously committed to by the project manager.

Activities on the critical path almost always have zero float. Critical path activities that are delayed or have dictated dates can result in negative float.

Float is an asset and is extremely useful for a project manager to understand. Most project managers know where they have float and use it to help manage a project. Do you? If not, study this carefully, as float may be a major problem for you!

How is float an asset? Once you know the critical path and any near-critical paths, you can use float as a way to focus your management of a project. It allows for better allocation of resources. For example, let's say you have a resource who is not very experienced and you must make use of him. You can assign him, assuming he has the skill set, to work on the activity with the most float. This gives you some safety that even if his activity takes longer, the project will not be delayed.

Float also helps team members juggle multiple projects by telling them how much time flexibility they have on each activity they are working on, of course with their project manager's approval for any delays from the plan.

Float is computed using either the equation Float = LS – ES, or the equation Float = LF – EF. Notice the formulas again. Either formula gets you the same answer. Want to remember them without any further study? Just remember the following:

TRICKS OF THE TRADE® "There is a start formula and a finish formula and we always begin late." Notice that the formula uses either two starts or two finishes and each begins with late.

Using the appropriate formula based on the situation provided will help you get many questions right. For example, you have a LS of 30, an ES of 18 and a LF of 34. What is the float? Since you remember the trick above you will know to subtract the two starts or the two finishes. Since you do not have two finishes, you would subtract 30 – 18 to get 12.

There are many ways to calculate float, the one shown above or others that you might have learned. Which method to use to calculate float will depend on the way the question is presented. Sometimes the information is such that you can just see the amount of float, sometimes you will have to be able to calculate it in order to answer the questions. The following will give you a few examples.

When drawing network diagrams manually, many people have been taught to draw them with each node or activity having boxes in the corners as shown below.

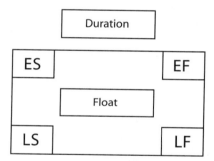

To review, the critical path method includes determining the earliest and latest each activity can start and the earliest and latest each activity can be completed. Remember the float formulas? What was that trick again? "There is a start formula and a finish formula and we always begin late." Therefore the formulas must be LS – ES or LF – EF. The "early" figures are found by calculating from the beginning of the project to the end of the project, following the dependencies in the network diagram—a forward pass through the network diagram. The "late" figures are found by moving from the end of the project following the dependencies to the beginning of the project—a "backward" pass. See the diagram below.

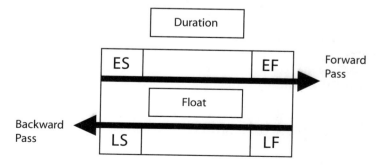

The first node in a diagram normally has an early start of zero. Some people, however, use one as the ES for the first activity. There is no right way to start calculating through network diagrams for the early and late starts, but do not worry. Either method will get you the right answer. Just pick one method and use it consistently.

To calculate float and the critical path using a forward and backward pass, first work through the network diagram doing the forward pass moving through the activities from the start until the end is reached, as illustrated below.

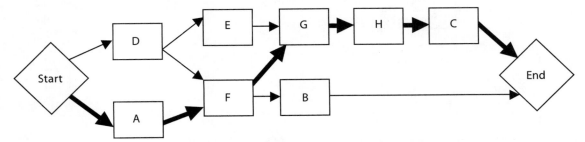

It is important to look at where paths converge (path convergence) in order to correctly perform a forward and backward pass. To compute the ES and the EF in a forward pass, you have to take into account all the paths that lead into that activity. In the backward pass, to compute the LF and LS you need to consider all the paths that flow backward into the activity. In the diagram above, paths converge during the forward pass at activities F and G. You should do the forward pass on both paths leading up to activity F, calculating EF for activities D and A. You select the latest EF to use as the ES for activity F, since activity F cannot start until both activities D and A are complete. Use the same process for calculating the EF of activities E and F before calculating the ES of activity G.

Once you have completed the forward pass, you will begin the backward pass. A backward pass computes the LF and LS for each activity. The backward pass uses the duration of the critical path as the EF of the last activities in the network. You move through the network, being careful at points of convergence. Using the diagram above, you have convergence at activities F and D. You work from the end back to these by computing the LS of activities B and G, selecting the earliest LS to use for the LF of activity F, since activity F must be finished before either activity B or G can start. This same process would be used on activities E and F before calculating the LF for activity D.

Now that you have the data required to calculate float, simply use the float formulas (LS – ES or LF – EF) for each activity. Those activities that have zero float are on the critical path.

The next few exercises should help you understand this better. As you do them, think about how knowing float might help you better manage your real-world projects. Remember that there are many more questions like this in *PM FASTrack*®.

Exam questions could be substantially similar to the following exercises, or more situational and wordy rather than requiring the drawing of network diagrams. Be prepared for both types. Please note that the exam may have the picture of a network diagram in a separate window, available at the click of a button.

Exercise 1 Let's start with an exercise that uses the AOA type diagram. You can complete these exercises without using a forward and backward pass. Using the table below, draw the network diagram and answer the questions.

Activity	Estimate In Weeks	
Start -A	3	
Start -B	9	
A-C	3	
B-C	Dummy	
B-E	2	
C-D	2	
C-E	1	
E-End	4	
D-End	2	

NOTE: What did you notice first in this exercise? I hope you saw the activities defined by two letters and there was a dummy activity. These are indicators you need to use the arrow diagramming method.

1. What is the critical path? _____

2. If the duration of Activity C–E changes to 2, what is the effect on the project?

   _____

3. What activity (activities) must be completed before Activity C–D begins?

   _____

4. If management tells you to complete the project two weeks early, what is the project float? Does the critical path change?

   _____

Answer 1 Did you read the questions carefully? Are you reading more into the questions than was asked? Are you thinking about what you would do to fix the situation if it were a real project, and not just answering the question presented? These are all problems for people taking this exam.

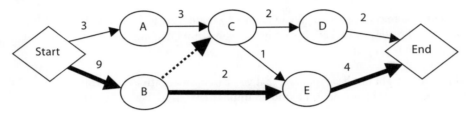

1. The critical path is Start–B, B–E, and E–End. (Sometimes the exam asks for the path, other times for its length.) Use the easy way to figure this out; list all the paths and make sure you see them all. In this instance there are five paths as shown below. Did you see them all? Do not forget the dummy activity represents a depencency and must be included in your paths.

Paths	Duration
Start–A, A–C, C–D, D–End	10
Start–A, A–C, C–E, E–End	11
Start–B, B–C, C–E, E–End	14
Start–B, B–C, C–D, D–End	13
Start–B, B–E, E–End	15

2. If C–E changes from 1 to 2, the critical path would be:

Paths	Duration
Start–B, B–E, E–End	15
Start–B, B–C, C–E, E–End	15

   Yes, you can have more than one critical path. What is the effect on the project? The project is riskier. Make sure you can see the five paths through this network diagram, and be able to analyze the diagram completely.

    Always check for a second or more critical path when you answer questions that change the critical path.

3. Start–A, A–C, and Start–B. The question is really trying to get you to answer Start–B because that is what the dummy is for, to show that dependency. Remember there are no one-letter activity names (e.g., not activity C, but activity A–C). B–C is a dummy, not an activity.

4. The project float is -2 and the critical path would not change. This question is about *project* float. Remember project float compares the project length to an external due date. Your difficulty with this question may have been in one of three areas:

First, you might not realize there is always an assumption on the exam that the project was on time before the situation described. At that time, there was a zero project float. Asking for a due date two weeks sooner makes the project two weeks late, so you now have a -2 weeks float.

Second, you may have assumed you had to do something to fix the problem. This is not what the question asked. It simply said something had happened and asked the status of your project.

Third, you might not have realized that you can have negative float. You can have negative float if the project is behind an imposed external date, when an activity is late, etc.

Exercise 2 Using the table below, draw the network diagram and answer the questions.

Activity	Estimate In Weeks		
Start-A	8		
Start-B	2		
A-C	Dummy		
B-C	4		
A-F	5		
C-F	6		
C-E	7		
E-End	5		
F-End	7		

1. What is the critical path? _____

2. What is the near-critical path and what does knowing this information about this project tell you?

   _____

3. If the duration of activity Start-B changes to 4, what is the effect on the project?

   _____

Answer 2 Using the trick described previously, there are five paths found in this diagram.

Paths	Duration
Start–A, A–F, F–End	20
Start–A, A–C, C–F, F–End	21
Start–A, A–C, C–E, E–End	20
Start–B, B–C, C–F, F–End	19
Start–B, B–C, C–E, E–End	18

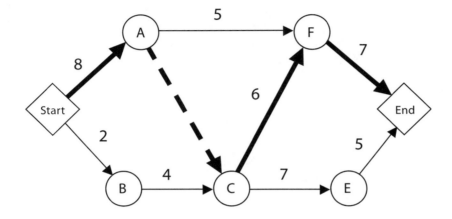

1. Start–A, A–C, C–F, F–End. It has a duration of 21 weeks.

2. There are two near-critical paths, each with a duration of 20. This tells you that the project has more risk than a project with only one near-critical path with a wider difference in length between the critical and near-critical paths.

3. There will be two critical paths:

Paths	Duration
Start–A, A–C, C–F, F–End	21
Start–B, B–C, C–F, F–End	21

Exercise 3 Test yourself. Draw a network diagram and answer the questions below.

You are the project manager for a new project and have figured out the following dependencies.
- Activity 1 can start immediately and has an estimated duration of three weeks.
- Activity 2 can start after activity 1 is completed and has an estimated duration of three weeks.
- Activity 3 can start after activity 1 is completed and has an estimated duration of six weeks.
- Activity 4 can start after activity 2 is completed and has an estimated duration of eight weeks.
- Activity 5 can start after activity 4 is completed and after activity 3 is completed. This activity takes four weeks.

1. What is the duration of the critical path? _____

2. What is the float of activity 3? _____

3. What is the float of activity 2? _____

4. What is the float of the path with the longest float? _____

5. The resource working on activity 3 is replaced with another resource who is less experienced. The activity will now take 10 weeks. How will this affect the project?

_____

6. Using the original information, after some arguing between stakeholders, a new activity 6 is added to the project. It will take 11 weeks to complete and must be completed before activity 5 and after activity 3. Management is concerned that adding the activity will add 11 weeks to the project. Another stakeholder argues the time will be less than 11 weeks. Who is correct?

_____

7. Based on the information in number 6 above, how much longer will the project take?

_____

Answer 3 There are many ways to answer these questions. If you learned another way in your project management training, use it. Here is a simple way to compute the answers.

1. The length of the critical path is 18. There are two paths here:

Paths	Duration
Start, 1, 2, 4, 5, End	18
Start, 1, 3, 5, End	13

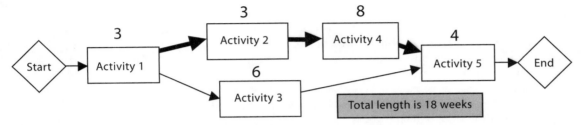

Start, 1, 2, 4, 5, End (shown with the dark line above) is the longest duration path and is therefore the critical path. The durations of the activities add up to 18, so the critical path is 18 weeks long. Follow the dark line in the diagram.

2. Five weeks per the diagram below. The following illustration shows how to calculate float using the forward and backward pass.

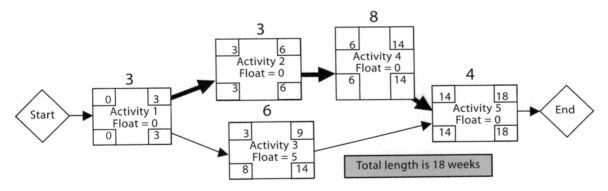

Key for the diagram above:

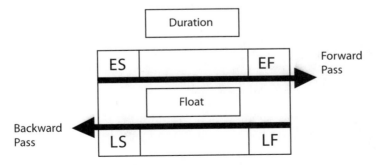

You can use either float formula to compute float. LF – EF = 14 – 9 = 5 or
LS – ES = 8 – 3 = 5.

How about a shorter way to find the float? Since there are only two paths and the difference between the two paths is 5, any activity on the non-critical path would have a float of 5.

3. Zero, it is on the critical path. An activity on the critical path almost always has no float.

4. Five weeks. There are only two paths in this example; Start, 1, 2, 4, 5, End and Start, 1, 3, 5, End. The length of the non-critical path (Start, 1, 3, 5, End) is 13. The length of the project is 18 and 18 – 13 is 5. The total float of the path with the longest float is 5.

5. It will have no effect. The length of path activities 1, 3, 5 is 13. Adding four more weeks to the length of activity 3 will make that path 17. Since it is shorter than the critical path, the critical path does not change. The length is still 18 weeks because activity 3 is not on the critical path.

6. The stakeholder. This new activity will be added to a non-critical path that has float of five weeks. Therefore, adding 11 weeks will make this path the new critical path. The overall effect will be that adding an activity that takes 11 weeks will only delay the project by six weeks.

7. Six weeks longer. (NOTE: if you answered 24, it means you did not read the question correctly!) Follow the dark line in the diagram below.

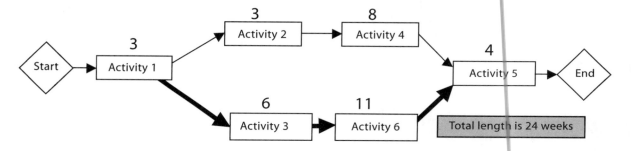

Time Management

Exercise 4 Considering the following data:

Activity	Preceding Activity	Estimate In Months
Start		0
D	Start	4
A	Start	6
F	D, A	7
E	D	8
G	F, E	5
B	F	5
H	G	7
C	H	8
End	C, B	0

1. What is the duration of the critical path? _____

2. To shorten the length of the project, the sponsor has offered to remove the work of activity E from the project, making activity D the predecessor to activities G and F. What will be the effect?

    _____

3. What is the float of activity B? _____

4. What is the float of activity E? _____

5. What is the float of activity D? _____

Answer 4

1. The critical path (project duration) is 33 months.

Paths	Duration
Start, D, E, G, H, C, End	32
Start, D, F, G, H, C, End	31
Start, D, F, B, End	16
Start, A, F, G, H, C, End	33
Start, A, F, B, End	18

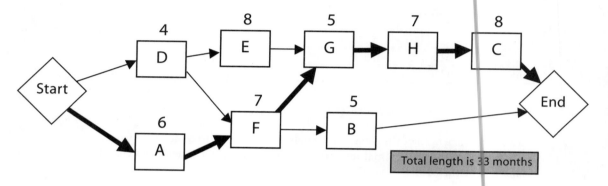

Total length is 33 months

2. No effect on the critical path. The paths are now:

Paths	Duration
Start, D, G, H, C, End	24
Start, D, F, G, H, C, End	31
Start, D, F, B, End	16
Start, A, F, G, H, C, End	33
Start, A, F, B, End	18

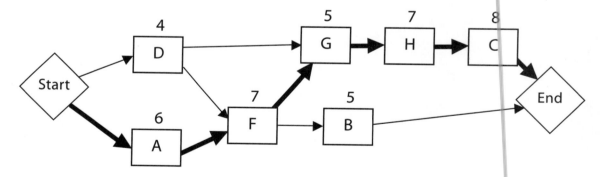

3. Fifteen months per the diagram below.

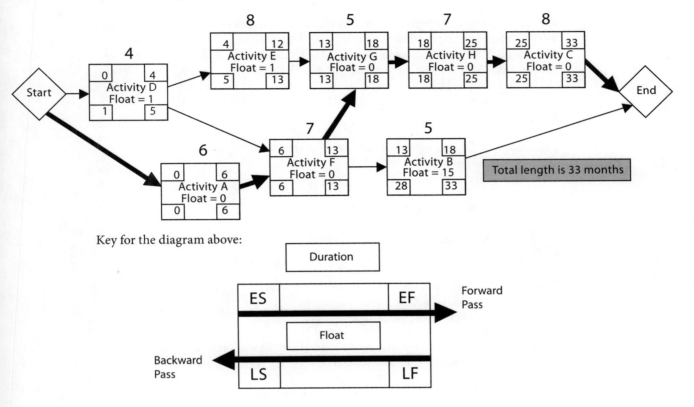

Key for the diagram above:

Depending on how the questions are asked and the flow of the network diagram, you may be able to calculate float using a quicker method, however, you must know the method shown in the diagram above.

Try another fast way to find float. The project must be completed by month 33 and activity B takes five months. So LF = 33. Activities A and F must occur before activity B can start and they will finish no sooner than the end of month 13. Activity B takes five months so the earliest activity B can finish is the end of month 18. So EF = 18. Float = 33 − 18 = 15.

4. One month. Once you have finished calculating using the long way, all the other answers are quick. Just look at the diagram to see the float of any activity.

The float for activity E is not so easy to calculate using a quick way! The project must be completed by the end of month 33. Activity E must be completed before activities G, H and C can start. So LF for E is, 33 − 8 − 7 − 5 or 13.

Activity E must be completed after Activity D. So EF is 4 + 8 or 12.

Float = LF − EF (or 13 − 12) = 1

5. One month, just look on the network diagram.

Calculating float for activity D using any quick method gets even harder! The project must be completed by the end of month 33. Activity D must be completed before activities E, F, G, H, C and B can start. Looking backward through the dependencies, the LF is 33 – 8 – 7 – 5, but then we run into a problem. Normally we would go along the critical path, but look at activities E and F. Activity E is longer than activity F so we must go along the longest duration path, from activity G to activity E, making LF 33 – 8 –7 – 5 – 8, or 5.

EF is easier. There are no predecessors, so EF is the end of month four.

Float = 5 – 4 or 1 month.

You survived!! See it was not that hard. Or was it?

TRICKS OF THE TRADE The following are good questions to test your knowledge about critical paths, float, etc.:

- Can there be more than one critical path? Yes, you can have two, three or many critical paths.
- Do you want there to be? No, it increases risk.
- Can a critical path run over a dummy? Yes.
- Why is a dummy included in a network diagram? To show interdependencies of activities on an activity-on-arrow diagram.
- Can a critical path change? Yes.
- How much float does the critical path have? Generally the critical path should have zero float.
- Can there be negative float? Yes, it shows you are behind.
- Does the network diagram change when the end date changes? No, not automatically, but the project manager should investigate options such as fast tracking and crashing the schedule to meet the new date and then, with approved changes, change the network diagram accordingly.
- Would you leave the project with a negative float? No, you would compress the schedule.

TRICKS OF THE TRADE When you take the exam, there is a good chance you will be able to reuse the same network diagram to answer more than one network diagram question. Look to see if this is true before you spend time redrawing the diagram.

Schedule Compression (page 145, see also resource leveling, page 146) One of the most common problems projects have is an unrealistic timeframe. This can occur during project planning when the customer requires a completion date that cannot be met, or during project executing when the project manager needs to bring the project back in line with the schedule baseline or to adjust the project for changes. As I have said before, many project managers think an unrealistic schedule is their boss' fault when it is really a lack of good project management; it is the project manager's fault!

Schedule compression is done during project planning to see if the desired completion date can be met, and what will have to change to make that date. It is also done during integrated change control to look at the schedule impacts of changes to time, cost, scope and risk. The objective is to try to compress the schedule without changing project scope. Here are two techniques:

Fast Tracking Doing critical path activities in parallel that were originally planned in series. Fast tracking often results in rework, usually increases risk and requires more attention to communications.

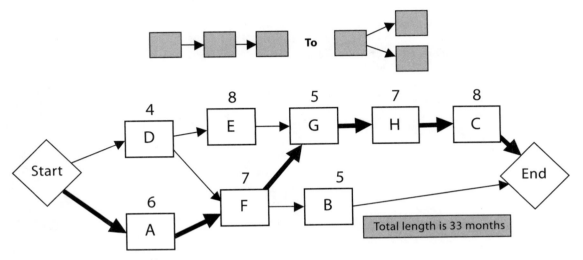

For example, using the network diagram above, what activity would you fast track to shorten the project length? Activity H could be fast tracked by making it occur at the same time, or in parallel with, activity G. Activities C and H (or any other pair of activities on the critical path) could also be fast tracked by having part of activity C done concurrently with activity H.

Crashing Making cost and schedule tradeoffs to determine how to obtain the greatest amount of schedule compression for the least incremental cost while maintaining project scope. (If time must change, what option will cause the least impact on cost?) Crashing, by definition, almost always results in increased costs.

For example, using the diagram shown in the previous fast tracking discussion, resources could be added to activity G or any other activity on the critical path (assuming that this was logical based on the nature of the work). These resources could be acquired from activity B or from outside the project.

In crashing or fast tracking, it is best to see all potential choices and then select the choice or choices that have the least impact on the project. If you have negative project float (the estimated completion date is after the desired date) would your first choice be to tell the customer the date could not be met or to ask for more time? No, the first choice would be to analyze what could be done about it by compressing the schedule.

If you have to choose between crashing and fast tracking, what would you do? Adding resources to the project would *generally* cost more than fast tracking. However, crashing can also mean *moving* resources around within the project. If making such moves does not add cost, then crashing would be preferable to fast tracking. Think about this! In the real world, many project managers use the network diagram to manage the day-to-day operations of the project and to make adjustments when changes occur. You should expect this to be reflected in the exam by the number of questions on network diagrams, calculations and "What do you do in this situation?" type of questions.

Let's make sure you are prepared to deal with unrealistic schedules on the exam. So important is this issue that you should expect to see over 10 questions on the exam. Most project managers are not completely knowledgeable in this area and it shows on their score sheets. To prevent this, let's try an exercise.

Exercise During project planning, the project duration is estimated to be 33 months. However, you have been given a completion date of 30 months. Using the network diagram below, and the limited information available, describe as many options as possible for shortening the schedule to 30 months. This is a general exercise with little detail. Make any assumptions you need to make in order to come up with as many options as possible.

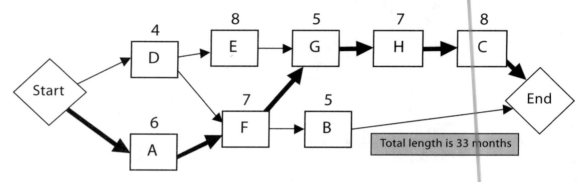

Total length is 33 months

Option	How to Achieve It	Explanation	

Option	How to Achieve It	Explanation

Answer Did this situation make sense? If it did, you are in good shape. If not, a little more study is required. Notice how this effort allows the project manager to proactively deal with reality and take action during the project. The project manager should know whether the project completion date can be met! The following options and methods are explained in the next few pages.

Option	How to Achieve It	Explanation
Re-estimate	Review risks	Now it is time to look at the estimates and see which contain hidden risks. By reducing the risks, the estimate can be lowered and the project finished faster. It is never an option to just cut 10 percent off of the estimate.
Execute activities H and C in parallel	Fast track (schedule compression)	We assume that the dependency between activities H and C is a discretionary one.
Move resources from activity B to activity G	Crash (schedule compression)	We do not have a lot of detail about resources, but assuming that the resources in activity B have the skills to complete activity G, crashing is an option.
Cut activity H	Reduce scope	Though not the first choice, as it likely will affect the customer, reducing scope should be considered an option.
Hire consultants to assist on activity G, H or C	Crash (schedule compression)	We assume that adding resources to these activities would, in fact, be practical and that there are resources available.
Move more experienced people to activities on the critical path, e.g., activities G, H or C	Crash (schedule compression)	We assume that some of the critical path activities are being done by less experienced people.
Cut time	Lower quality standards (schedule compression)	Do not get excited. Quality is a component of the "triple constraint" and is an option. In this case it would probably be easier and thus faster to complete.

Option	How to Achieve It	Explanation
Say no, the project must have 33 months	Stand your ground	This is not a viable option until other alternatives are exhausted.
Get more work done with the same amount of resources	Work overtime	Not an option during project planning. There are too many other ways to compress the schedule that do not have the negative effects of overtime. Save it for a last resort.

Which of the options listed is the best? To answer the question, think of the impacts to the project of each one. Is it option 7? Why not cut quality? Is there another option? Why not do what many project managers do, ask for more resources? But adding resources may also add cost. Why not work overtime? If you have not realized overtime should be one of the last choices, you have a large gap in your knowledge. Most organizations are working at close to 100 percent capacity. Your project working overtime removes the possibility of resources working on emergencies for any other project they are working on, thereby putting other projects at risk. Besides, how much overtime can one take? Overtime is not always free. Why not do something that does not add cost to your project?

The first, and possibly the best, choice is to look at risks. Once it is known the schedule (or budget) must be reduced, a project manager can investigate the activity estimates that contain the most unknowns, eliminate or reduce these "risks" and thus decrease the estimate. Eliminate risks in the risk management process and everyone wins!

Let's try this again with another exercise.

Exercise 1 What are the impacts of different schedule shortening options?

Option	General Impacts to the Project
Fast track	
Crash	
Reduce scope	
Cut quality	

Answer 1

Option	General Impacts to the Project
Fast track	• Adds risk • May add management time for the project manager
Crash	• Almost always adds cost • May add management time for the project manager
Reduce scope	• Could save cost and time • May negatively impact customer satisfaction
Cut quality	• Could save cost and resources • May increase risk • Requires good metrics

Exercise 2 Here is another chance to test yourself on schedule compression!

Activity	Original Duration (In Months)	Crash Duration (In Months)	Time Savings	Original Cost in Dollars	Crash Cost	Extra Cost	Cost per Month
F	14	12	2	10,000	14,000	4,000	2,000
A	9	8	1	17,000	27,000	10,000	10,000
H	3	2	1	25,000	26,000	1,000	1,000
G	7	5	2	14,000	20,000	6,000	3,000
C	11	8	3	27,000	36,000	9,000	3,000

1. Imagine that this project has a project float of -3 months. Which activity or activities presented above would you crash to save three months on the project, assuming that the activities listed above represent critical path activities?

2. How much would it cost to crash this project?

Answer 2

1. The options to save three months are:

Activities	Cost
F and H	$5,000
F and A	$14,000
G and H	$7,000
A and G	$16,000
C	$9,000

Activities F and H is the least expensive and there is nothing in the question to eliminate it, so activities F and H is the best answer. Any time you have negative project float, it means that the project is not going to meet its external deliverable date. The answer, depending on how the question is worded, involves crashing or fast tracking the project and coming up with options, or telling the customer that the date cannot be met.

2. Crashing activities F and H would result in the least added cost, only $5,000.

Exercise 3 Consider: Management has told you to get the project completed two weeks early. What is the BEST thing for you to do?
A. Consult the project sponsor
B. Crash
C. Fast track
D. Advise the customer (management) of the impact of the change

Answer 3 Did you get fooled by this question? Did you think you had to choose between crashing and fast tracking? There is no information in the first part of this exercise to help you determine which one is better. Therefore, the best choice presented is D, inform the customer of the impact of the change.

The exam will ask many such questions requiring you to know that you analyze first and then let management, the sponsor, the customer or other parties know the impact of their requests. A project manager does NOT just say yes! She could say, for example, "Yes, I would be happy to make the change, BUT the project will be delayed two weeks, I will need two more resources or the project will cost $25,000 more."

Exercise 4 To handle the situation described in exercise 3, you could assign a more experienced resource to activity Start–B in order to get the activity done in seven weeks, but it would cost an additional $20,000 to do so. You could eliminate part of Activity C–D or E–End and save $5,000 and one week of work. You could move work from Activity A–C to Activity B–E and save $2,000 and two weeks. What is the cost of compressing this project?

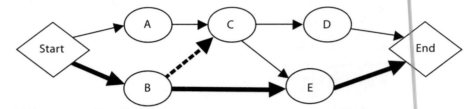

Activity	Estimate (In Weeks)
Start–A	3
Start–B	9
A–C	3
B–C	Dummy
B–E	2
C–D	2
C-E	1
E-End	4
D-End	2

Answer 4 There is only one viable solution presented that would save the two weeks. That is to assign a more experienced resource to Start-B. Therefore, the crash cost is $20,000.

Eliminating activity C–D is not an option as it is not on the critical path. Eliminating activity E–End would only save one week, not two weeks. Moving work from activity A–C to activity B–E moves more work to the critical path thus lengthening it, rather than decreasing it. If you read move "resources" instead of "work" you will get it wrong! On the exam, you need to take the time to read and understand every word in each question.

Common errors on the exam relating to schedule compression include the use of overtime or telling the team, "cut 10 percent off your estimates." Project management does not involve having the team work overtime to complete the project on time because the project manager did not control and adjust along the way. Cutting 10 percent is just delaying the inevitable, a late project. These are both inappropriate project management techniques because more effective choices exist, as discussed previously.

WARNING: In questions about changes to the network diagram, make sure you look for shifts to new critical paths caused by the changes to the network diagram.

What-if Scenario Analysis (page 146) In creating a finalized, realistic schedule, it is helpful to ask "What if a particular thing changed on the project, would that produce a shorter schedule?" The assumptions for each activity can change and therefore their durations also change. One of the ways to calculate the effect of these changes is through a Monte Carlo analysis.

Monte Carlo Analysis (page 146, 258) This method of estimating uses a computer to simulate the outcome of a project making use of the three time estimates (optimistic, pessimistic and most likely) for each activity and the network diagram. The simulation can tell you:
- The probability of completing the project on any specific day
- The probability of completing the project for any specific amount of cost
- The probability of any activity actually being on the critical path
- The overall project risk

Monte Carlo analysis is another way of putting together the details of a three-point estimate into a project estimate that is more accurate than other methods because it simulates the actual details of the project and takes into account probability.

Monte Carlo Analysis can also help deal with "path convergence," places in the network diagram where multiple paths converge into one or more activities, thus adding risk to the project.

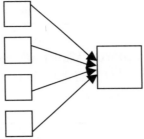

Resource Leveling (page 146) Resource leveling is used to produce a resource-limited schedule. Leveling lets schedule slip and cost increase in order to deal with a limited amount of resources, resource availability and other resource constraints. A little-used tool in project management software, leveling allows you to level the peaks and valleys of resource use from one month to another resulting in a more stable number of resources used on your project.

You would level the resources if your project utilized five resources one month, 15 the next and three the next, or some other up and down pattern that was not an acceptable use of resources. It could also be used if you do not have fifteen resources available and would prefer to lengthen the project, a result of leveling, instead of hiring more resources.

Critical Chain Method (page 147) The critical chain method is another way to develop a bought into, approved, realistic and formal schedule. It is said to go beyond the others because it takes into account, directly, both activity and resource dependencies. There are many variations of this method, so be careful here.

A network diagram is developed using the most likely estimates. The schedule is then developed by scheduling each activity to occur as late as possible to still meet the end date. Resource dependencies are added and the critical chain calculated. Starting at the end date, you build into the chain at critical milestones, duration buffers (think of this as your time reserves from risk response planning). These reserves, spread throughout the project, will provide cushions for delays in the scheduled activities. You manage these buffers so that you meet each individual milestone date and thus the project milestone completion date as well.

Do not get carried away with studying this technique, it should not be mentioned on the exam more than three times. Remember, mentioning does not necessarily mean three questions, it means it could be a question or a choice.

Milestone Charts These are similar to bar charts, but only show major events. Remember that milestones have no duration; they are simply the completion of activities. Milestones may include "requirements are complete" or "design is finished" and are part of the inputs to activity sequencing. Milestone charts are good tools for reporting to management and the customer.

ID	Milestone	December	January	February	March	April
1	Start	◆ 12/14				
2	Requirements gathered		◆ 12/31			
3	Design complete		◆ 1/17			
4	Coding complete			◆ 2/15		
5	Testing complete				◆ 3/15	
6	Implementation complete					◆ 4/4
7	End					◆ 4/15

Bar Charts (also called Gantt Charts) Weak planning tools, but effective tools for progress reporting and control. Bar charts are not project management plans.

A bar chart looks like the following:

ID	Task Name	Duration	Start	Finish	September 8/18	8/25	9/1	9/8	9/15	9/22	9/29	October 10/8
1	Start	0 days	Mon 8/26/02	Mon 8/26/02		◆ 8/26						
2	D	4 days	Mon 8/26/02	Thu 8/29/02		▬						
3	A	6 days	Mon 8/26/02	Mon 9/2/02		▬▬						
4	F	7 days	Mon 9/2/02	Tue 9/29/02			▬▬					
5	E	8 days	Fri 8/30/02	Tue 9/10/02		▬▬▬						
6	G	5 days	Wed 9/12/02	Wed 9/17/02				▬▬				
7	B	5 days	Wed 9/12/02	Wed 9/17/02				▬▬				
8	H	7 days	Wed 9/18/02	Thu 9/26/02					▬▬			
9	C	8 days	Fri 9/27/02	Tue 10/8/02						▬▬▬		
10	Finish	0 days	Tue 10/8/02	Tue 10/8/02								◆

Notice that there are no lines between activities to show interdependencies, nor are assigned resources shown.

Bar charts do not help organize the project as effectively as a WBS or network diagram do. They are completed after a WBS and a network diagram in the project management process.

Project Schedule The project schedule is the result of schedule network analysis (in schedule development) and the previous planning processes. Therefore, risk and other parts of project planning will affect the project schedule until it is iterated into the schedule that becomes part of the project management plan as the schedule baseline (described below).

The schedule can be shown with or without dependencies (logical relationships) and can be shown in any of the following formats, depending on the needs of the project:
- Bar chart
- Network diagram
- Milestone chart

Scheduling Tools and Their Benefits No matter how much you know about project management, there are always questions on the exam that will be tricky if you have never thought of them before. Here is one of those areas. Be careful to work though this exercise slowly. Make sure you discover anything you did not know and also make sure you organize your knowledge according to the following answers. You can get quite a few questions right if you know what each of the tools listed above is used for.

Exercise Test yourself! Answer the following questions in the spaces provided.

Under what circumstances would you use a network diagram instead of a bar chart?	
Under what circumstances would you use a milestone chart instead of a bar chart?	
Under what circumstances would you use a bar chart instead of a network diagram?	

 Answer I assume that you already know what these tools are, and this is just a review.

Under what circumstances would you use a network diagram instead of a bar chart?	To show interdependencies between activities
Under what circumstances would you use a milestone chart instead of a bar chart?	To report to senior management
Under what circumstances would you use a bar chart instead of a network diagram?	To track progress To report to the team

Schedule Baseline (page 151) The schedule baseline is the final schedule. Remember that the baseline can only be changed by formally approved changes. Meeting the schedule baseline is one of the measures of project success.

Requested Changes (page 152) The process of creating a final schedule could cause changes to the WBS, project scope statement and other parts of the developing project management plan. For example, the scheduling process determines that the desired project completion date cannot be met. The best option for that particular project is to cut scope. That scope change would likely affect the WBS.

Schedule Control (page 152) This topic was discussed in the Project Management Processes chapter. It is important to realize that the project manager will be held to the schedule baseline. The project manager must measure how the project is going, and be able to recommend and implement corrective and preventive actions to adjust the project along the way to make sure the baseline is met.

Status will be reported as part of project monitoring and controlling, earned value calculations done (described in the Cost chapter) and the schedule change control system followed. Variances will be analyzed and actual schedules compared to planned schedules.

Issues to be addressed in schedule control include:
- Adjusting future parts of the project for delays, rather than asking for a time extension
- Adjusting metrics that are not giving the project manager the information needed to properly manage the project
- Adjusting progress reports and reporting
- Utilizing the change control processes
- Identifying requested changes and recommended corrective actions

Progress Reporting (page 153) A progress report is a useful method to control schedule and costs. Many project managers determine how much work has been accomplished by asking team members for an estimate of *percent complete* for each work package or activity. On projects where work cannot be measured, this estimate is simply a guess. This is time consuming and almost always a complete waste of time because a guess does not provide a confident estimate of the actual percent complete.

If a project has been planned using a WBS, and work packages require about 80 hours of work, there are alternatives to percent complete. Because work packages will be completed faster and more frequently, we can forget percent complete and use one of the following:

50/50 Rule An activity is considered 50 percent complete when it begins and gets credit for the last 50 percent only when it is completed.

20/80 Rule An activity is considered 20 percent complete when it begins and gets credit for the last 80 percent only when it is completed.

0/100 Rule An activity does not get credit for partial completion, only full completion.

Practice Exam

Time Management

1. To control the schedule, a project manager is reanalyzing the project to predict project duration. She does this by analyzing the sequence of activities with the least amount of scheduling flexibility. What technique is she using?
   A. Critical path method
   B. Flowchart
   C. Precedence diagramming
   D. Work breakdown structure

2. A dependency requiring that design be completed before manufacturing can start is an example of a:
   A. discretionary dependency.
   B. external dependency.
   C. mandatory dependency.
   D. scope dependency.

3. Which of the following are GENERALLY illustrated BETTER by bar charts than network diagrams?
   A. Logical relationships
   B. Critical paths
   C. Resource trade-offs
   D. Progress or status

4. If the optimistic estimate for an activity is 12 days, and the pessimistic estimate is 18 days, what is the standard deviation of this activity?
   A. 1
   B. 1.3
   C. 6
   D. 3

5. A heuristic is best described as a:
   A. control tool.
   B. scheduling method.
   C. planning tool.
   D. rule of thumb.

6. Lag means:
   A. the amount of time an activity can be delayed without delaying the project finish date.
   B. the amount of time an activity can be delayed without delaying the early start date of its successor.
   C. waiting time.
   D. the product of a forward and backward pass.

7. **Which of the following is the BEST project management tool to use to determine the longest time the project will take?**
   A. WBS
   B. Network diagram
   C. Bar chart
   D. Project charter

8. **Which of the following is CORRECT?**
   A. A critical path can run over a dummy.
   B. There can be only one critical path.
   C. The network diagram will change every time the end date changes.
   D. A project can never have negative float.

9. **What is the duration of a milestone?**
   A. Shorter than the duration of the longest activity
   B. Shorter than the activity it represents
   C. There is no duration
   D. Same length as the activity it represents

10. **Which of the following BEST describes the relationship between standard deviation and risk?**
    A. Nothing
    B. Standard deviation tells you if the estimate is accurate.
    C. Standard deviation tells you how unsure the estimate is.
    D. Standard deviation tells you if the estimate includes a pad.

11. **Monte Carlo analysis is used to:**
    A. get an indication of the risk involved in the project.
    B. estimate an activity's length.
    C. simulate the order in which activities occur.
    D. prove to management that extra staff is needed.

12. **The float of an activity is determined by:**
    A. performing a Monte Carlo analysis.
    B. the waiting time between activities.
    C. determining lag.
    D. determining the amount of time the activity can be delayed before it delays the critical path.

13. **A project has three critical paths. Which of the following BEST describes how this affects the project?**
    A. It makes it easier to manage.
    B. It increases the project risk.
    C. It requires more people.
    D. It makes it more expensive.

14. **If project time and cost are not as important as the number of resources used each month, which of the following is the BEST thing to do?**
    A. Perform a Monte Carlo analysis.
    B. Fast track the project.
    C. Perform resource leveling.
    D. Analyze the life cycle costs.

15. **When would a milestone chart be used instead of a bar chart?**
    A. Project planning
    B. Reporting to team members
    C. Reporting to management
    D. Risk analysis

16. **Your project management plan results in a project schedule that is too long. If the project network diagram cannot change but you have extra personnel resources, what is the BEST thing to do?**
    A. Fast track the project.
    B. Level the resources.
    C. Crash the project.
    D. Monte Carlo analysis.

17. **The precedence diagramming method (activity-on-node) is different from the arrow diagramming method (activity-on-arrow) because a precedence diagram:**
    A. can use PERT.
    B. has four relationships among activities.
    C. has only finish-to-finish relationships.
    D. may use dummy activities.

18. **Which of the following is the BEST thing to do to try to complete a project two days earlier?**
    A. Tell senior management that the project's critical path does not allow the project to be finished earlier.
    B. Tell your boss.
    C. Meet with the team and look for options for crashing or fast tracking the critical path.
    D. Work hard and see what the project status is next month.

19. **In attempting to complete the project faster, the project manager looks at the cost associated with crashing each activity. The BEST approach to crashing would also include looking at the:**
    A. risk impact of crashing each activity.
    B. customer's opinion of which activities to crash.
    C. boss's opinion of which activities to crash and in which order.
    D. project life cycle phase in which the activity is due to occur.

20. **A project manager is trying to coordinate all the activities on the project and has determined the following:**
    Activity 1 can start immediately and has an estimated duration of one week.
    Activity 2 can start after activity 1 is completed and has an estimated duration of four weeks. Activity 3 can start after activity 2 is completed and has an estimated duration of five weeks. Activity 4 can start after activity 1 is completed and has an estimated

duration of eight weeks. Both activities 3 and 4 must be completed before the end of the project. What is the duration of the critical path for this project?
A. 10
B. 11
C. 14
D. 8

21. Based on the data in the question above, if activity 4 takes 10 weeks, what is the duration of the critical path?
A. 10
B. 11
C. 14
D. 8

22. Which of the following includes asking team members about the time estimates for their activities and reaching agreement on the calendar date for each activity?
A. Activity sequencing
B. Schedule development
C. Scope definition
D. Creating a project charter

23. A project manager is in the middle of the executing process of a very large construction project when he discovers that the time needed to complete the project is longer than the time available. What is the BEST thing to do?
A. Cut product scope.
B. Meet with management and tell them that the required date cannot be met.
C. Work overtime.
D. Determine options for schedule compression and present management with your recommended option.

24. During project planning, you estimate the time needed for each activity and then add the estimates to create the project estimate. You commit to completing the project by this date. What is WRONG with this scenario?
A. The team did not create the estimate and estimating takes too long using that method.
B. The team did not create the estimate and a network diagram was not used.
C. The estimate is too long and should be created by management.
D. The project estimate should be the same as the customer's required completion date.

25. During activity definition, a team member identifies an activity that needs to be accomplished. However, another team member believes that the activity is not part of the project as he interprets the project scope statement. What is the BEST thing for the project manager to do?
A. Try to build a consensus of the team.
B. Make the decision herself.
C. Ask the sponsor for clarification.
D. Ask senior management for clarification.

26. You are a project manager on a U.S. $5,000,000 software development project. While working with your project team to develop a network diagram, you notice a series of

© 2005 Rita Mulcahy, PMP • Phone: (952) 846-4484 • E-mail: info@rmcproject.com • Web: www.rmcproject.com

activities that can be worked in parallel but must finish in a specific sequence. What type of activity sequencing method is required for these activities?

A. Precedence diagramming method
B. Arrow diagramming method
C. Critical path method
D. Operational diagramming method

27. You are a project manager on a U.S. $5,000,000 software development project. While working with your project team to develop a network diagram, your data architects suggest that quality could be improved if the data model is approved by senior management before moving on to other design elements. They support this suggestion with an article from a leading software development journal. Which of the following BEST describes what this type of input is called?

A. Mandatory dependency
B. Discretionary dependency
C. External dependency
D. Heuristic

28. Based on the following, if you needed to shorten the duration of the project, what activity would you try to shorten?

Activity	Estimate (In Weeks)
Start–A	1
Start–B	2
Start–C	6
A–D	10
B–E	1
C–E	Dummy
C–F	2
F–End	3
E–End	9
D–End	1

A. Activity Start-B
B. Activity A-D
C. Activity E-End
D. Activity C-E

29. You have a project with the following activities: Activity A takes 40 hours and can start after the project starts. Activity B takes 25 hours and should happen after the project starts. Activity C must happen after activity A and takes 35 hours. Activity D must happen after activities B and C and takes 30 hours. Activity E must take place after activity C and takes 10 hours. Activity F takes place after Activity E and takes 22 hours. Activities F and D are the last activities of the project. Which of the following is TRUE if activity B actually takes 37 hours?

A. The critical path is 67 hours.
B. The critical path changes to Start, B, D, End.
C. The critical path is Start, A, C, E, F, End.
D. The critical path increases by 12 hours.

30. A project manager has received activity duration estimates from his team. Which of the following does he need in order to complete schedule development?
    A. Change requests
    B. Schedule change control system
    C. Recommended corrective actions
    D. Reserves

31. A project manager is taking over a project from another project manager during the planning process group. If the new project manager wants to see what the previous project manager planned for managing changes to the schedule, it would be BEST to look at the:
    A. communications management plan.
    B. project management plan.
    C. staffing management plan
    D. schedule management plan.

32. A project manager is using weighted average duration estimates to perform schedule network analysis. Which type of mathematical analysis is being used?
    A. Critical path method
    B. PERT
    C. Monte Carlo
    D. Resource leveling

33. The WBS, estimates for each work package, and the network diagram are completed. Which of the following would be the NEXT thing for the project manager to do?
    A. Sequence the activities.
    B. Verify that they have the correct scope.
    C. Create a preliminary schedule and get the team's approval.
    D. Complete risk management.

34. A new product development project has four levels in the work breakdown structure and has been sequenced using the arrow diagramming method. The activity duration estimates have been received. What should be done NEXT?
    A. Create an activity list.
    B. Begin the work breakdown structure.
    C. Finalize the schedule.
    D. Compress the schedule.

35. You are a project manager for a new product development project that has four levels in the work breakdown structure, and has been sequenced using the arrow diagramming method. The duration estimates have been compressed and a schedule created. What time management activity should you do NEXT?
    A. Begin schedule control.
    B. Begin activity resource estimating.
    C. Analogously estimate the schedule.
    D. Gain approval.

36. A team member from research and development tells you that her work is too creative to provide you with a fixed single estimate for the activity. You both decide to use the

labor hours from past projects to predict the future. This is an example of which of the following?

A. Parametric estimating
B. Three-point estimating
C. Analogous estimating
D. Monte Carlo analysis

37. An activity has an early start (ES) of day 3, a late start (LS) of day 13, an early finish (EF) of day 9, and a late finish (LF) of day 19. The activity:

A. is on the critical path.
B. has a lag.
C. is progressing well.
D. is not on the critical path.

38. The project is calculated to be completed four days after the desired completion date. You do not have access to additional resources. The project is low risk, the benefit cost ratio (BCR) is expected to be 1.6, and the dependencies are preferential. Under these circumstances, what would be the BEST thing to do?

A. Cut resources from an activity.
B. Make more activities concurrent.
C. Move resources from the preferential dependencies to the external dependencies.
D. Remove an activity from the project.

39. A project manager for a small construction company has a project that was budgeted for U.S. $130,000 over a six week period. According to her schedule, the project should have cost U.S. $60,000 to date. However, it has cost U.S. $90,000 to date. The project is also behind schedule, because the original estimates were not accurate. Who has the PRIMARY responsibility to solve this problem?

A. Project manager
B. Senior management
C. Project sponsor
D. Manager of the project management office

40. Your organization is having a difficult time managing all of its projects. You have been asked to help senior management understand this. Which of the following types of reports would help provide summary information to senior management?

A. Detailed cost estimates
B. Project management plans
C. Bar charts
D. Milestone reports

41. Rearranging resources so that a constant number of resources is used each month is called:

A. crashing.
B. floating.
C. leveling.
D. fast tracking.

42. **Which of the following is a benefit of an analogous project estimate?**
    A. Estimate will be closer to what the work will actually require.
    B. It is based on a detailed understanding of what the work requires.
    C. It gives the project team an understanding of management's expectations.
    D. It helps the project manager determine if the project will meet the schedule.

43. **During project executing, a large number of changes are made to the project. The project manager should:**
    A. wait until all changes are known and print out a new schedule.
    B. make approved changes as needed, but retain the schedule baseline.
    C. make only the changes approved by management.
    D. talk to management before any changes are made.

Time Management Answers

1. **Answer** A
   Explanation There are only two choices related to scheduling: A and C. Choice C, however, is a diagramming technique that deals with the relationship between activities, not schedule flexibility.

2. **Answer** C
   Explanation Since the dependency is required, it could not be discretionary (choice A) and therefore must be mandatory. No mention is made that the dependency comes from a source outside the project, so external (choice B) is not correct. Scope dependency (choice D) is not a defined term. The key word in this question is "requires." The question defines a mandatory dependency.

3. **Answer** D
   Explanation The bar chart (or Gantt chart) is designed to show a relationship of activities to time. This is best used when demonstrating progress or status as a factor of time.

4. **Answer** A
   Explanation The standard deviation is computed by (P - O)/6. Therefore, the answer is $(18 - 12)/6 = 6/6 = 1$.

5. **Answer** D
   Explanation A heuristic is a rule of thumb. Examples are cost per line of code, cost per square foot of floor space, etc.

6. **Answer** C
   Explanation Total float and free float (choices A and B) are the time an activity can be delayed without impacting the entire project or the next activity. CPM (choice D) is a schedule network analysis technique, not waiting time. Choice C is the correct answer.

7. **Answer** B
   Explanation The bar chart (choice C) may show an end date, but it is not used to determine dates and show progress. The project charter (choice D) may include any required end dates, but not a logical determination of how long the project will take. The network diagram (choice B) takes the work packages from the work breakdown structure (choice A) and adds dependencies. The dependencies allow us to look at the various paths through the diagram. The longest duration path is the critical path. Choice B is the best answer.

8. **Answer** A
   Explanation This question tests your knowledge about a number of topics. There can often be more than one critical path (choice B) but you might adjust to decrease risk resulting in only one critical path. Choice C uses the word "will." The network diagram may change or it may not, depending on the amount of schedule reserve and the reason for the change to the schedule. You can have negative float (choice D) if you are behind schedule. Only choice A is correct.

9. **Answer** C

    Explanation A milestone shows the completion of a series of activities or work packages. Therefore it takes no time of its own. With this in mind, choice C is the best answer.

10. **Answer** C

    Explanation Choice A is not best, as the standard deviation tells you the amount of uncertainty or risk involved in the estimate for the activity. An estimate can have a wide range (choice B) and still be accurate if the item estimated includes risks. Choice D cannot be the best answer since there is no such thing as a pad in project management. An estimate might be inflated, but it is because of risks, not padding.

11. **Answer** A

    Explanation Notice how many choices are half right? Monte Carlo could help you know that an estimate for an activity needs to change, but not what the activity estimate should be (choice B). Monte Carlo is a simulation (choice C) but it simulates time, not order of activities. Monte Carlo can be used to prove things to management (choice D) but its main focus deals with time, not staff. Risk can be assessed using Monte Carlo analysis (choice A). By considering the inputs to the PERT estimates and the network diagram, you can obtain a better overview of the overall project risk.

12. **Answer** D

    Explanation This question does not specify what type of float. Total float is the amount of time an activity can be delayed without impacting the end date of the project. Free float is the amount of time an activity can be delayed without impacting the early start of the next activity. The only choice matching either of these definitions is choice D.

13. **Answer** B

    Explanation Though having three critical paths COULD require more people (choice C) or cost more (choice D) the answer that is definitely and always true, is B. Because you need to manage three critical paths, there is more risk that something could happen to delay the project.

14. **Answer** C

    Explanation Fast tracking (choice B) would affect time and cost. Monte Carlo analysis and life cycle costs (choices A and D) do not directly deal with resources. Leveling (choice C) is the only one that will definitely affect resources.

15. **Answer** C

    Explanation Project planning (choice A) would use both types of charts. Team members (choice B) need to see details and so they need a bar chart rather than a milestone chart. Risk analysis (choice D) COULD make use of both charts. A milestone chart is used instead of a bar chart for any situation where you want to report in a less detailed way (choice C). Bar charts can scare people with their complexity and often show too much detail to be worthwhile on a management level. Milestone charts are more effective for reporting to management.

16. **Answer** C

    Explanation Leveling resources (choice B) generally extends the schedule. Monte Carlo Analysis (choice D) does not directly address the constraints of this situation.

© 2005 Rita Mulcahy, PMP • Phone: (952) 846-4484 • E-mail: info@rmcproject.com • Web: www.rmcproject.com

To compress the schedule, you could either crash or fast track. However, the situation says that the network diagram cannot change. This eliminates the fast tracking option (choice A), leaving choice C as the best answer.

17. **Answer** B

    Explanation Choices A, C, and D apply only to activity-on-arrow diagrams. B is the only correct answer.

18. **Answer** C

    Explanation This is another question that asks about problem solving. Only choice C relates to "evaluate." Choices B and D do not try to solve the real problem. Choice A is just an untrue statement.

19. **Answer** A

    Explanation You may or may not need your customer's (choice B) or your boss's (choice C) input but you will definitely need to include an analysis of risk. Choice A is broader than choice D and therefore is better.

20. **Answer** A

    Explanation You need to draw a network diagram for this question.

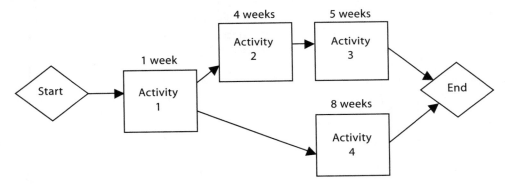

This diagram has two paths: Start, 1, 2, 3, End and Start, 1, 4, End. The length of the first path is 10 and the second is nine making the first path critical and the duration of the critical path 10. Notice that almost every other answer someone could pick is also listed.

21. **Answer** B

    Explanation If activity 4 now takes 10 weeks instead of eight, the critical path would change to Start, 1, 4, End and be 11 weeks long.

22. **Answer** B

    Explanation By the time this activity is taking place, activity sequencing (choice A) scope definition (choice C) and creating a project charter (choice D) would be completed.

23. **Answer** D

    Explanation This question tests whether you know how to solve problems, especially if you are one of those project managers who has not realized that an unrealistic schedule is something you should deal with before beginning work. Since cutting product scope affects the customer, choice A has a great negative effect and is therefore not best. A project manager's job is to determine options for meeting any end date or time, therefore choice B cannot be correct. Working overtime (choice C) is expensive and unnecessary when there are so many other choices that could be selected first. Choice D could have the least negative impact on the project.

24. **Answer** B
Explanation Time estimates for the activities should be created by the team and should not be added. Some activities may take place concurrently. Therefore, choice B must be the correct answer.

25. **Answer** C
Explanation The project scope statement is created based on the preliminary project scope statement and input from the sponsor. Therefore the answer is choice C, ask the sponsor.

26. **Answer** A
Explanation The question implies a finish-to-finish relationship between activities. The arrow diagramming method (choice B) does not support these types of relationships. Choice C is not a diagramming method and choice D is a made-up term.

27. **Answer** B
Explanation The situation is neither mandatory (choice A) nor driven by an external source (choice C). A rule of thumb (choice D) is something that can be used consistently. This situation is a unique occurrence. The situation is a suggestion or a preferred method, so choice B is the best answer.

28. **Answer** C
Explanation This is one of the two-stage questions you will find on the exam. First you need to draw the network diagram and find the critical path, then make a decision. The network diagram would be:

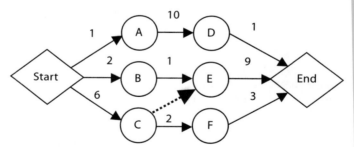

The diagram above has four paths:

Paths	Duration
Start–A, A–D, D–End	12
Start–B, B–E, E–End	12
Start–C, C–F, F–End	11
Start–C, C–E, E–End	15

The critical path is 15 (Start–C, C–E, E–End) and runs across the dummy (yes that can happen). Without any other information to suggest another alterative, it is best to try to shorten the longest activity on the critical path, activity E–End, (choice C).

You may have selected activity A-D (choice B) because it is the longest activity, but notice that shortening it will not change the length of the project. You may not have understood a dummy and tried to look for the longest path that does not include a dummy. If you did, you would have found that Start-B, B-E, E-End and Start-A, A-D, D-End are the same length.

29. **Answer** C
Explanation Did you notice how difficult this question was to read? Such wording is intentional, to prepare you for interpreting questions on the real exam. Looking at this situation, you see that there are three paths through the network. They are Start, A, C, E, F, End with a duration of 40 + 35 + 10 + 22 or 107, Start, A, C, D, End with a duration of 40 + 35 + 30 or 105, and Start, B, D, End with a duration of 25 + 30 or 55. If the duration of activity B changes from 25 to 37, the activity will take 12 hours longer. As the activity is only on the third path, it will only change the duration of that path from 55 to 55 + 12 or 67 hours. Since the duration of the critical path is 107 hours, the delay with activity B will have no impact on the project timeline or the current critical path.

30. **Answer** D
Explanation Schedule development includes all work and uses all inputs needed to come up with a finalized, realistic schedule. One would need time reserves (choice D) in order to complete a schedule. All of the other items are parts of schedule control and occur after schedule development.

31. **Answer** D
Explanation Answer D is the most correct answer. The schedule management plan is an output of schedule development and is the repository for plans for schedule changes.

32. **Answer** B
Explanation PERT uses a weighted average.

33. **Answer** C
Explanation Choice A is the same thing as create a network diagram. Choice B is another name for scope verification, and is done during the monitoring and controlling process group, not during project planning. Since a schedule is an input to risk management, choice D comes after choice C and so it is not the "next thing to do." The only remaining choice is C.

34. **Answer** D
Explanation The question is really asking, "What is done after activity duration estimating?" Choices A and B are done before activity duration estimating. Duration compression (choice D) occurs before finalizing the schedule (choice C) and is, therefore, the best answer.

35. **Answer** D
Explanation Notice how this question and the one previous seem very similar. This is intended to prepare you for similar questions on the exam. Choices B and C should have already been completed. The situation described is within the schedule development process of time management. Choice A is the next time process after schedule development, but schedule development is not finished. Final approval (choice D) of the schedule by the stakeholders is needed before one has a project schedule.

36. **Answer** A

    Explanation Past history is being used to calculate an estimate. Monte Carlo (choice D) relates to what-if analysis. Choice B uses three time estimates per activity. One could use past history to come up with the estimate (choice C) but the best answer is choice A because an estimate such as hours per installation is a chief characteristic of parametric estimates.

37. **Answer** D

    Explanation The activity described has float because there is a difference between the early start and late start. An activity that has float is probably not on the critical path. There is no information presented about lag (choice B) or progress (choice C) so choice D is the best answer.

38. **Answer** B

    Explanation Cutting resources from an activity (choice A) would not save time, nor would moving resources in the way described (choice C). Removing an activity from the project (choice D) is a possibility, but since the dependencies are preferential and the risk is low, the best choice would be to make more activities concurrent (choice B) as this would have less impact on the project.

39. **Answer** A

    Explanation Did you get lost looking at all the numbers presented in this question? Notice that there are no calculations required, simply an understanding of what the problem is. Many project managers try to solve problems that are not within their area of control. This question describes schedule management, which is a responsibililty of the project manager. This question relates to cost, integration, human resources and time.

40. **Answer** D

    Explanation Detailed estimates (choice A) have nothing to do with the situation described. Project management plans (choice B) will have more detail than is necessary for the situation described and may distract from the conversation if used in this situation. Bar charts (choice C) are usually only for the team. The best answer is choice D because milestone reports present the right level of detail for upper management.

41. **Answer** C

    Explanation The key to this question is the phrase "constant number used each month." Only leveling, choice C, has such an effect on the schedule.

42. **Answer** C

    Explanation Remember that analogous estimates are top-down, high-level estimates. Therefore, choices A and B cannot be correct. The project manager needs more than an analogous estimate to determine if the project will meet the schedule (choice D). It is a benefit to know management's expectations of how much the project will cost so that any differences between the analogous estimate and the detailed bottom-up estimate can be reconciled in the planning processes. The best choice is C.

43. **Answer** B

    Explanation A project manager must be more in control of the project than choices C and D reflect. Choice A is a common error many project managers make. Instead, the project manager should be controlling the project throughout the completion of the project.

Cost Management

Quicktest

- Cost management process
- Earned value analysis
  - PV
  - EV
  - AC
  - CPI, SPI
  - BAC
  - EAC
  - ETC
  - VAC
  - CV, SV
- Cost baseline
- Cost budget
- Three-point estimating
- Analogous estimating
- Bottom-up estimating
- Parametric estimating
- Inputs to estimating
- Cost management plan
- Rough order of magnitude estimate
- Definitive estimate
- Cost risk
- Benefit cost ratio
- Net present value
- Internal rate of return
- Variable/fixed costs
- Direct/indirect costs
- Payback period
- Opportunity cost
- Present value
- Sunk costs
- Law of diminishing returns
- Working capital
- Straight line/accelerated depreciation
- Life cycle cost
- Value analysis

Do you manage costs on your projects? If not, you should carefully read this chapter. Questions will be very difficult for you because you have not been in the situations described on the exam.

Many people are nervous about questions relating to earned value. To ease your mind, let me tell you that an average of only about twelve questions on earned value have been on the exam for the last four years. Only an average of six questions have required a calculation. Do you feel better yet? How about this? There are only about five questions that deal with all the accounting standards topics. Remember, you do not have to be an accountant to pass this exam. With a little study, this type of cost question should be easy.

There is a strong connection between cost and time on the exam. Some topics (including planning, estimating and monitoring and controlling) covered here in Cost also apply to the Time chapter. Do not assume that because a topic is listed here it cannot be used for time planning, estimating and controlling. Earned value is a good example.

TRICKS OF THE TRADE® The Time chapter talked about the creation of activities (or schedule activities) as smaller components of work packages. Generally, it is these that are cost estimated. However, imagine a larger project. Costs might be more practical to estimate and control at a higher level. This is called a control account and is one level higher than the work package in the WBS.

Rita's Process Chart—Cost Management
Where are we in the project management process?

Initiating	Planning	Executing	Monitoring & Controlling	Closing
Select project manager	**Determine how you will do planning—part of management plans**	Acquire final team	**Measure against the performance measurement baselines**	Develop closure procedures
Determine company culture and existing systems	Create project scope statement	Execute the PM plan	**Measure according to the management plans**	Complete contract closure
Collect processes, procedures and historical information	Determine team	Work to produce product scope	**Determine variances and if they warrant corrective action or a change**	Confirm work is done to requirements
Divide large projects into phases	Create WBS and WBS dictionary	Recommend changes and corrective actions	Scope verification	Gain formal acceptance of the product
Identify stakeholders	Create activity list	Send and receive information	Configuration management	Final performance reporting
Document business need	Create network diagram	Implement approved changes, defect repair, preventive and corrective actions	**Recommend changes, defect repair, preventive and corrective actions**	Index and archive records
Determine project objectives	Estimate resource requirements	Continuous improvement	Integrated change control	Update lessons learned knowledge base
Document assumptions and constraints	**Estimate time and cost**	Follow processes	Approve changes, defect repair, preventive and corrective actions	Hand off completed product
Develop project charter	Determine critical path	Team building	Risk audits	Release resources
Develop preliminary project scope statement	Develop schedule	Give recognition and rewards	Manage reserves	
	Develop budget	Hold progress meetings	Use issue logs	
	Determine quality standards, processes and metrics	Use work authorization system	Facilitate conflict resolution	
	Determine roles and responsibilities	Request seller responses	Measure team member performance	
	Determine communications requirements	Select sellers	Report on performance	
	Risk identification, qualitative and quantitative risk analysis and response planning		**Create forecasts**	
	Iterations—go back		Administer contracts	
	Determine what to purchase			
	Prepare procurement documents			
	Finalize the "how to execute and control" aspects of all management plans			
	Create process improvement plan			
	Develop final PM plan and performance measurement baselines			
	Gain formal approval for plan			
	Hold kickoff meeting			

The following should help you understand how each part of Cost Management fits into the project management process.

The Cost Management Process

The Cost Management Process	Done During
Cost estimating	Planning process group
Cost budgeting	Planning process group
Cost control	Monitoring and controlling process group

TRICKS OF THE TRADE **Things About Estimating to Know for the Exam** (This is repeated in the Time chapter, as it also relates to time.)

- Estimating should be based on a WBS to improve accuracy
- Estimating should be done by the person doing the work whenever possible
- Historical information from past projects (part of organizational process assets) is a key to improving estimates
- A cost baseline (and schedule, scope, quality and resource baselines) should be kept and not changed except for approved project changes
- The budget should be managed to the cost baseline for the project
- Changes are approved in integrated change control
- Estimates are more accurate if smaller sized work components are estimated
- Corrective actions and preventive actions should be recommended when cost problems (and time, scope, quality and resource problems) occur
- A project manager should never just accept requirements from management, but rather analyze the needs of the project, come up with her own estimates and reconcile any differences to produce realistic objectives. Yes, this should be true in the real world!
- A project manager may continually calculate the estimate to complete for the project in order to make sure there are adequate funds (and time, etc.) available for the project
- Plans should be revised, as necessary, during completion of the work
- How to get a good estimate
- Padding is not an acceptable project management practice
- The project manager must meet any agreed upon estimates
- What to do with the estimates when received
- How to keep the estimates realistic

Think about these! Remember that incorrect project management practices will be listed as choices on the exam. If you do not adequately understand and manage your projects this way, you will have difficulty on the exam and not even know why you scored low.

Inputs to Estimating (or What do you need before you estimate cost or time?) These inputs help you to create an estimate more quickly, and more accurately. Imagine having access to a file that contains all the previous WBSs for projects similar to yours and the estimates for each activity. Would that help you create a more accurate estimate? Interestingly, the professional estimators I have come across rarely know what a WBS is. Be careful not to skim over this list of inputs, but to think through why each might help the estimate.

In order to create a good estimate, you need the following before you begin estimating:
- **Project scope statement** Including any cost constraints
- **WBS and WBS dictionary** The work to be done
- **Network diagram** Costs cannot be estimated until it is known how the project will flow from beginning to end
- **Schedule management plan/Schedule** This is one of the key inputs to cost management as it contains the type and quantity of resources needed to complete the work. NOTE: This refers to an overall schedule, not a detailed final one. The final schedule is created after estimating.
- **Policies on estimating, templates, processes, procedures, lessons learned and historical information** (organizational process assets)
- **Company culture and existing systems** that the project will have to deal with or can make use of. For cost, this includes marketplace conditions and commercial cost databases (enterprise environmental factors)

- **Project management costs** Although project management efforts save money on projects overall, they do incur costs and should be included in the project cost estimates
- **Staffing management plan/Resource pool** This contains the available resources or the resources assigned and their rates of pay
- **Risk management plan** This is important because it includes a budget for risk
- **Risk register** A list of risks uncovered to date. Remember, a full risk analysis of the details of the project will not have been completed before costs are estimated

Exercise So you think you read it well! Try to recreate the list of inputs to estimating and see what you forgot. Then spend time thinking about what you forgot to make sure you do not forget it again.

━━━**Cost Management Plan** (page 158) Though specifically listed in other chapters, the management plan for cost is not listed as part of the cost process. Imagine it exists for the exam. Therefore, the first process in cost management is planning, which answers the questions, "How will I go about planning cost for the project?" and "How will I effectively manage the project to the cost baseline and manage cost variances?"

This plan is similar to other management plans (a PMI-ism). The cost management plan can be formal or informal, but is part of the project management plan. Once again, you can see that such a plan requires thinking in advance about how you will manage. This is a concept that many project managers miss.

The cost management plan will help make the cost estimating process faster by specifying how estimates should be stated (i.e., that estimates must be in hours or days, be rounded to the second decimal point) and to what level of the WBS estimates will be made (i.e., the control account described previously). During direct and manage project execution, the cost management plan can help determine if a variance is over the allowable threshold and therefore must be acted upon, the ways earned value can be calculated, and the types of reports required on the project relating to cost.

Other concepts to know include the following:

Life Cycle Costing Remember the product life cycle we talked about earlier? Would it be wise to design the project so that the project costs are low but the maintenance costs are higher than the project cost savings? For example, you plan the project to a lower level of quality and save $9,000. After the project is completed, the project needs maintenance and repair of $100,000 over its life instead of the $20,000 in maintenance and repair that it could have cost. Your $9,000 "saving" cost the company $80,000 (or $71,000 additional cost). This is the concept of life cycle costing; looking at the cost of the whole life of the product, not just the cost of the project.

Value Analysis (Sometimes referred to as value engineering in the real world.) Finding a less costly way to do the same work. It requires the systematic use of techniques to identify the required project functions, assign values to these functions and provide functions at the lowest overall cost without loss of performance. If a team is looking at decreasing project cost but maintaining the same scope, they are performing value analysis.

Cost Risk Sometimes a question on the exam will cross boundaries between risk, procurement and cost. Cost risk is best explained with an example question:

> *Who has the cost risk in a fixed price contract, the buyer or the seller?*
> **Answer** *The seller.*

▬▬Cost Estimating (page 161) This is the process where the estimates for each
activity are made. The next step, budgeting, is the process of combining all the estimates into one cost budget.

What is estimated? All the work needed to complete the project including:
- Quality efforts
- Risk efforts
- The project manager's time
- Costs of project management activities
- Costs directly associated with the project, including training for the project, paper, pencils, needed labor
- Office expenses for offices used directly for the project
- Profit, when applicable
- Overhead, such as management salaries, general office expenses

Types of Cost There are several ways to look at costs when creating an estimate. Expect only about three questions about this on the exam. The examples below should help you answer questions about types of costs.

A cost can be either variable or fixed:
- **Variable Costs** Costs that change with the amount of production or the amount of work. Examples include the cost of material, supplies and wages.
- **Fixed Costs** Costs that do not change as production changes. Examples include set-up, rental, etc.

A cost can be either direct or indirect:
- **Direct Costs** Costs that are directly attributable to the work on the project. Examples are team travel, team wages, recognition, and costs of material used on the project.
- **Indirect Costs** Overhead items or costs incurred for the benefit of more than one project. Examples include taxes, fringe benefits and janitorial services.

How Is the Estimating Done? Activities can be estimated using the same techniques as described in the Time chapter: One-cost, analogous, parametric or three-point estimates. An additional way of estimating cost is bottom-up estimating.

Bottom-up Estimating (page 165) Detailed estimating is done for each activity (if available) or work package (if activities are not defined) and the estimates are then rolled up into an overall project estimate.

The creation of estimates is assisted by the use of:

Project Management Software Remember there is no such thing as one software package to tell you how to manage a project. The software referred to here might be any software used for estimating. Imagine there are 30 activities and each will have similar cost components added, such as overhead. Software can speed up the calculations.

Determining Resource Cost Rates You may not have access to this on your projects, but detailed cost estimating requires the knowledge of the actual cost of labor. Remember that resources are not just human resources. This work might also involve getting pricing from consultants, vendors and suppliers. Work provided by sellers may also require bid analysis. Further cost estimating may be required in order to finalize agreement.

Reserve Analysis It is required project management to accommodate the cost and time risk in a project estimate through the use of reserves. Please see the Risk chapter to learn how these are calculated. The work should include making sure individual activity estimates are not padded.

Cost of Quality The work added to the project to accommodate quality planning should be added to the project estimate.

Exercise Answer the questions below in the spaces provided.

What Are the Advantages of Analogous Estimating?	What Are the Disadvantages of Analogous Estimating?

What Are the Advantages of Bottom-up Estimating?	What Are the Disadvantages of Bottom-up Estimating?

Answer There are many possible answers. The purpose is to get you thinking about the differences so that you can answer any questions on the topic, no matter how they may be worded.

Advantages of Analogous Estimating	Disadvantages of Analogous Estimating
Quick	Less accurate
Activities need not be identified	Estimates are prepared with a limited amount of detailed information and understanding of the project
Less costly to create	Requires considerable experience to do well
Gives the project manager an idea of the level of management's expectations (for a project analogous estimate)	Infighting to gain the biggest piece of the budget without being able to justify the need
Overall project costs will be capped (for a project analogous estimate)	Extremely difficult for projects with uncertainty
	Does not take into account the differences between projects

Advantages of Bottom-up Estimating	Disadvantages of Bottom-up Estimating
More accurate	Takes time and expense to do this form of estimating
Gains buy-in from the team because the team creates estimates they can live with	Tendency for the team to pad estimates unless taught about reserves
Based on a detailed analysis of the project	Requires that the project be defined and well understood before work begins
Provides a basis for monitoring and controlling, performance measurement and management	Requires time to break the project down into smaller pieces

Accuracy of Estimates Think about someone walking in to your office now and asking you to estimate the total cost of a new project. The first question you would probably ask is, "How accurate do you want me to be?" Estimates made in the early part of the project will be less accurate than those made later in the project. Estimates must be in a range (there is little possibility that an activity will be completed for exactly any particular amount of money) and be refined as the project progresses. Therefore, in the early part of the project, a wider range is all that can be provided. Over time, as more information is determined during planning, the estimate range can narrow.

Every company can have a different standard for different ranges, from preliminary to conceptual to feasibility to order of magnitude to definitive estimates. The standard ranges are only in the order of magnitude and definitive areas as shown below. Such ranges tell you how much time and effort needs to go into estimating to make sure that the actual cost is within the range of the estimate.

These ranges do show up on the exam. Make sure you memorize them.

- **Rough Order of Magnitude Estimate (ROM)** This type of estimate is usually made during the initiating process and is in the range of -50 percent to +100 percent from actual.
- **Definitive** Later during the project, the estimate could become more refined to a range of -5 percent to +10 percent from actual.

What should we have when we are finished with estimating cost? When completed, cost estimating should result in estimates and supporting detail on how the estimates were derived. It can also result in changes to resources, schedule and other parts of the project management plan in order to decrease the project costs.

──**Cost Budgeting** (page 167)

A budget is merely a compilation of the individual cost estimates. Remember that meeting the cost baseline will be a measure of project success, so budgeting should not be taken lightly. Activity costs are rolled up to work package costs. Work package costs are rolled up to control account costs and finally into project costs. This process is called cost aggregation.

The next step is to add reserves to the project (reserve analysis). As described in the Risk chapter, there can be two types of reserves added; management reserve and contingency reserve. Contingency reserve is for the risks remaining after risk response planning. Management reserve is any extra amount of funds to be set aside to cover unforeseen risks or changes to the project. The cost baseline will contain the contingency reserve and the cost budget will include the management reserve.

See the diagram below.

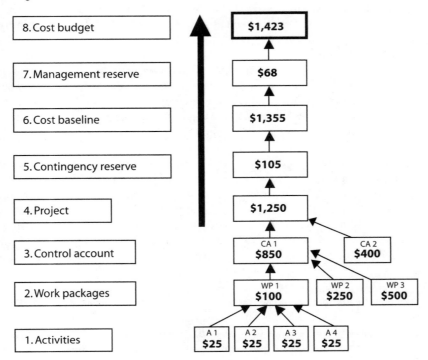

8. Cost budget	$1,423
7. Management reserve	$68
6. Cost baseline	$1,355
5. Contingency reserve	$105
4. Project	$1,250
3. Control account	CA 1 $850 — CA 2 $400
2. Work packages	WP 1 $100 — WP 2 $250 — WP 3 $500
1. Activities	A 1 $25 — A 2 $25 — A 3 $25 — A 4 $25

After the cost baseline and cost budget are completed, many estimators will compare these numbers to parametric estimates in order to do a sanity check of the detailed estimate and the high-level estimate. For example, a rule of thumb for a high-level parametric estimate in some industries is that the design should be 15 percent of the cost of construction. Other industries have design as 60 percent of the project budget. The detailed estimate is checked against these parametric estimates and any great differences are investigated and justified.

The next thing to be checked is cash flow (part of funding limit reconciliation). Funding may not be available when needed, causing changes to the other parts of the project and iterations of the project management plan (e.g., we will need $500,000 to purchase the equipment on June 1, but the money will not be available until July 1. We will have to move this activity to later in the schedule). The cost baseline therefore is time-phased and may be shown as an S-curve.

There is another obvious reconciliation needed before the proposed cost baseline and cost budget become final; reconciliation with any cost constraints in the preliminary project scope statement. You already know what this entails; meeting with management, justifying if their cost can be met, and proposing options to decrease costs. Read that last sentence again. An unrealistic budget is the project manager's fault! It is part of the project manager's responsibility to reconcile in this way. Such reconciliation is done as part of integration.

▬▬ Cost Control (page 171) Cost control is similar to the control part of any other knowledge area, with a focus on cost.

The cost management plan should have included your plan for controlling the costs of the project, such as meetings on cost, reports, measurements that will be made and their frequency. The control part of the management plan is customized to the needs of the project.

An important part of control is to measure, see if there are any variances, and then decide if those variances require the recommendation of corrective actions. Do you do this in the real world? How do you know when corrective action is needed if you do not have a realistic project management plan (that is always kept up-to-date) and if you have not pre-determined what areas are worth measuring? Most of the project manager's activities while the work is being done should be focused on controlling the project.

Earned Value Technique (page 173) The earned value technique is a method to measure project performance against the project baseline. Results from an earned value analysis indicate potential deviation of the project from cost and schedule baselines. Many project managers manage their project performance by comparing planned to actual results. With this method, you could easily be on time but overspend according to your plan. Using the earned value technique is a better method because it integrates cost, time and the work done (or scope) and can be used to forecast future performance and project completion dates and costs.

Earned value is also a large part of the reporting that should be done on a project. Earned value will lead to new forecasted completion costs, change requests and other items that will need to be communicated. Since the results of earned value analysis should be a major part of project reporting, you will also see earned value mentioned in the Communications chapter. Here are the earned value terms you need to know.

 Terms to Know

Acronym	Term	Interpretation (As of today ...)
PV	Planned Value	What is the estimated value of the work planned to be done?
EV	Earned Value	What is the estimated value of the work actually accomplished?
AC	Actual Cost	What is the actual cost incurred for the work accomplished?
BAC	Budget at Completion	How much did we BUDGET for the TOTAL project effort?
EAC	Estimate at Completion	What do we currently expect the TOTAL project to cost?
ETC	Estimate to Complete	From this point on, how much MORE do we expect it to cost to finish the project?
VAC	Variance at Completion	How much over or under budget do we expect to be at the end of the project?

Cost Management

Formulas and Interpretations to Memorize

 The exam focuses not just on calculations, but also on knowing what the numbers mean. Therefore you should know all the following:

Name	Formula	Interpretation (As of today ...)
Cost Variance (CV)	EV − AC	NEGATIVE is over budget, POSITIVE is under budget.
Schedule Variance (SV)	EV − PV	NEGATIVE is behind schedule, POSITIVE is ahead of schedule.
Cost Performance Index (CPI)	$\dfrac{EV}{AC}$	We are getting $_____ worth of work out of every $1 spent. Funds are or are not being used efficiently.
Schedule Performance Index (SPI)	$\dfrac{EV}{PV}$	We are (only) progressing at _____ percent of the rate originally planned.
Estimate at Completion (EAC) NOTE: There are many ways to calculate EAC, depending on the assumptions made. The first formula to the right is the one most often asked on the exam.	 $\dfrac{BAC}{CPI}$ AC + ETC AC + (BAC − EV) $AC + \dfrac{(BAC - EV)}{CPI}$	As of now, how much do we expect the total project to cost? $ _____. See formulas at the left. • Used if no variances from the BAC have occurred or you will continue at the same rate of spending. • Actual plus a new estimate for remaining work. Used when original estimate was fundamentally flawed. • Actual to date plus remaining budget. Used when current variances are thought to be atypical of the future. AC plus the remaining value of work to perform • Actual to date plus remaining budget modified by performance. Used when current variances are thought to be typical of the future.
Estimate to Complete (ETC)	EAC − AC	How much more will the project cost?
Variance at Completion (VAC)	BAC − EAC	How much over or under budget will we be at the end of the project?

The CPI above is a cumulative CPI because it is using costs to date. It could be written as $CPI^C = EV^C/AC^C$. with the superscript C standing for cumulative. This formula is the same as that above, but more clearly states that the data used is cumulative. CPI can also be calculated for a period of time rather than all the time to date.

 Make sure you understand and MEMORIZE the following.

 • Notice that EV comes first in every formula. Remembering this one fact alone should help you get about half the earned value questions right. (Aren't you glad you purchased this book?)
  • If it is a variance, the formula is EV minus something.

- If it is an index, it is EV divided by something.
- If the formula relates to cost, use AC.
- If the formula relates to schedule, use PV.
- For interpretation: negative is bad and positive is good. Thus a −200 cost variance means that you are behind (over budget).
- For interpretation: greater than one is good, less than one is bad.

One of the earned value questions people often answer incorrectly requires that you differentiate between EAC and ETC and the other terms. The following table may help.

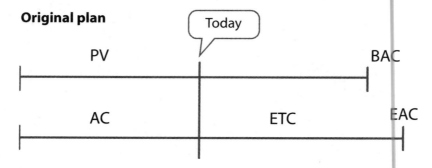

Many people learned earned value using terms which have since changed. Therefore you may see the old terms in parentheses on the exam next to the new ones, i.e., PV (BCWS). Just ignore the old terms. The old and new terms are shown below. Do not memorize them, just be prepared to see them on the exam.

Old Term	Old Acronym	New Term	New Acronym
Budgeted cost of work scheduled	BCWS	Planned value	PV
Budgeted cost of work performed	BCWP	Earned value	EV
Actual cost of work performed	ACWP	Actual cost	AC

Still worried about earned value? Not for long. Read the following pages, do the exercises and you might end up appreciating earned value questions over some of the more ambiguous, wordy and confusing questions on this exam.

Earned Value in Action   Earned value is an effective tool for measuring performance and determining the need to recommend corrective actions. Following is a sample team meeting conversation on this subject.

Danny, the project manager, calls a meeting of the team and says, "We are six months into this million dollar project and my latest analysis shows a CPI of 1.2 and an SPI of 0.89. This means that we are getting 1.2 dollars for every dollar we put into the project, but only progressing at 89 percent of the rate originally planned. Let's look for options to correct this problem."

"We could remove me from the project team and replace me with someone less expensive. I must be the most expensive team member," Samantha says.

"Not only would it sadden me to lose you, but your suggestion would improve costs, not schedule. You are the company's best network specialist. Someone else would not be as proficient as you in completing the work."

"We could remove the purchase of the new computers from the project," says Niki. "Or, we could just tell the customer the project will be two weeks late."

"Canceling the new computers would save us money, not time. We need to focus on time," Danny says. "Nor can we just change the project schedule baseline arbitrarily. That would be unethical."

"Since we are doing well on cost, why don't we bring in another programmer from the IT department to work on this project? We can get the next two activities completed faster," Jose suggests.

"That sounds like the most effective choice in this situation. Let's see if we can find someone who will improve performance, but not cost as much. Thanks for your help," Danny says.

The best way to learn this technique is to use it. These exercises are designed to give you a chance to practice calculations AND interpretation. Earned value questions on the exam will be in the multiple choice format and require less calculations for each one than these exercises.

Exercise Cost performance index (CPI) and schedule performance index (SPI) can be charted each month to show the project trends. Based on the following, what would you be more concerned about, cost or schedule, if you were taking over this project from another project manager?

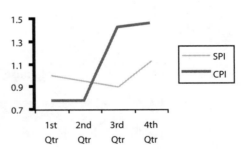

Answer The answer is schedule. As of today, SPI is closest to 1.

Exercise The Fence #1

You have a project to build a new fence. The fence is four sided as shown. Each side is to take one day to build and is budgeted for $1,000 per side. The sides are planned to be completed one after the other. Today is the end of day three.

Using the project status chart below, calculate EV, etc. When completed, check your answers on the answer sheet on the following page. Interpretation is also important on the exam. Can you interpret what each answer means?

Do the calculations to three decimal place accuracy on the exercises. Round to two decimal places when you are ready to check your answers on the real exam.

Activity	Day 1	Day 2	Day 3	Day 4	Status End of Day 3
Side 1	S---------F				Complete, spent $1,000
Side 2		S--------PF	----F		Complete, spent $1,200
Side 3			PS--S---PF		50% done, spent $600
Side 4				PS --------PF	Not yet started

Key S = Actual Start, F = Actual Finish, PS = Planned Start, and PF = Planned Finish

What Is:	Calculation	Answer	Interpretation of the Answer
PV			
EV			
AC			
BAC			
CV			
CPI			
SV			
SPI			
EAC			
ETC			
VAC			

Answer The Fence #1

What Is:	Calculation	Answer	Interpretation of the Answer
PV	1,000 plus 1,000 plus 1,000	3,000	We should have done $3,000 worth of work.
EV	Complete, complete, half done or 1,000 plus 1,000 plus 500	2,500	We have actually completed $2,500 worth of work.
AC	1,000 plus 1,200 plus 600	2,800	We have actually spent $2,800.
BAC	1,000 plus 1,000 plus 1,000 plus 1,000	4,000	Our project budget is $4,000.
CV	2,500 minus 2,800	-300	We are over budget by $300.
CPI	2,500 divided by 2,800	.893	We are only getting 89 cents out of every dollar we put into the project.
SV	2,500 minus 3,000	-500	We are behind schedule.
SPI	2,500 divided by 3,000	.833	We are only progressing at 83 percent of the rate planned.
EAC	4,000 divided by .893	4,479	We currently estimate that the total project will cost $4,479.
ETC	4,479 minus 2,800	1,679	We need to spend $1,679 to finish the project.
VAC	4,000 minus 4479	-479	We currently expect to be $479 over budget when the project is completed.

NOTE: If your answers differ, check your rounding. It is best to calculate to three decimal places and round to two decimal places when you are ready to check your answers on the real exam.

Exercise The Fence #2

You have a project to build a new fence. The fence is four sided as shown. Each side is to take one day to build and is budgeted for $1,000 per side. The sides are planned to be completed one after the other. IN THIS CASE, ASSUME THAT THE SIDES HAVE A FINISH-TO-FINISH RELATIONSHIP INSTEAD OF A FINISH-TO-START RELATIONSHIP! Today is the end of day three.

Using the project status chart below, fill in the blanks in the chart and check your answers on the answer sheet on the following page.

Activity	Day 1	Day 2	Day 3	Day 4	Status End of Day 3
Side 1	S----------F				Complete, spent $1,000
Side 2		S-----F----PF			Complete, spent $900
Side 3		S---	PS---------PF		50% done, spent $1,000
Side 4			S----	PS -------PF	75% done, spent $300

Key S = Actual Start, F = Actual Finish, PS = Planned Start, and PF = Planned Finish

What Is:	Calculation	Answer	Interpretation of the Answer
PV			
EV			
AC			
BAC			
CV			
CPI			
SV			
SPI			
EAC			
ETC			
VAC			

Answer The Fence #2

What Is:	Calculation	Answer	Interpretation of the Answer
PV	1,000 plus 1,000 plus 1,000	3,000	We should have done $3,000 worth of work.
EV	Complete, complete, half done, 75% done or 1,000 plus 1,000 plus 500, plus 750	3,250	We have actually completed $3,250 worth of work.
AC	1,000 plus 900, plus 1,000, plus 300	3,200	We have actually spent $3,200.
BAC	1,000 plus 1,000 plus 1,000 plus 1,000	4,000	Our project budget is $4,000.
CV	3,250 minus 3,200	50	We are under budget by $50.
CPI	3,250 divided by 3,200	1.016	We are getting 1.016 dollars out of every dollar we put into the project.
SV	3,250 minus 3,000	250	We are ahead of schedule.
SPI	3,250 divided by 3,000	1.083	We are progressing at 108 percent of the rate planned.
EAC	4,000 divided by 1.016	3,937	We currently estimate that the total project will cost $3,937.
ETC	3,937 minus 3,200	737	We need to spend $737 to finish the project.
VAC	4,000 minus 3,937	63	We currently expect to be $63 under budget when the project is completed.

In this example, you are looking for the value of the work that has actually been done. Since the value of each side is $1,000, we look at how much is complete of each side and apply that percent to the value. Here for sides one and two, they are completed and thus each receives a value of $1,000. (It doesn't matter what it actually cost, just the value). Side three is 50 percent done and receives a value of $500 (50 percent of $1,000). Side four is 75 percent done and receives a value of $750 (75 percent of $1,000). The total of the four sides is $3,250.

Understanding the meaning of each of the calculations' results is as important as knowing how to calculate them.

Expect many questions on the exam that say things like, "The CPI is 0.9 and the SPI is 0.92. What should you do?" You will need to interpret this and other data in the question and then be able to determine which choice would address the issue(s) described; in this example, both cost and schedule problems.

Accounting Standards Remember when you took an accounting class and they said some day you will need this? This is the day! Many people are confused by the use of accounting terms or standards on the exam, so I have included high-level explanations of terms you will need to know. I have also included details to help you understand. Remember, you do not have to be an accountant to pass this exam. You do NOT have to calculate using the following formulas or even remember these formulas for the exam. You will have to understand what the terms mean. You will see only about four references to these terms, so do not spend much time here.

Many of these accounting terms are used in project initiation questions when one is determining which project to select. Try the following exercise first. Get the answers right and you should spend time reading the rest of this chapter only once. Get any wrong and you will have to spend more time.

Exercise Test yourself! For each row on the following chart, enter the letter of the project you would select if the following information was provided.

	Project A	Project B	Which Project Would You Pick?	
Net present value	$95,000	$75,000		
IRR	13 percent	17 percent		
Payback period	16 months	21 months		
Benefit cost ratio	2.79	1.3		

Answer

	Project A	Project B	Which Project Would You Pick?	
Net present value	$95,000	$75,000		A
IRR	13 percent	17 percent		B
Payback period	16 months	21 months		A
Benefit cost ratio	2.79	1.3		A

Present Value PLEASE NOTE: Present value is only mentioned once or twice on the exam. You will not have to calculate it, nor know the formula, just understand the concept.

Present value means the value today of future cash flows and can be found by the formula:

$$PV = \frac{FV}{(1 + r)^n}$$

| FV = future value |
| r = interest rate |
| n = number of time periods |

In a simple example, without using the formula, see if you can guess at the following question.

> *What is the present value of $300,000 received three years from now if we expect the interest rate to be 10 percent? Should the answer be more or less than $300,000?*
> **Answer** *Less.*
> I can put an amount of money less than $300,000 in the bank and in three years have $300,000. To solve the problem, if you were inclined to do so: 300/(1 + 0.1) 3 equals, 300/1.331, equals $225,394.

Net Present Value (NPV) You will not have to calculate NPV, just know that it is the present value of the total benefits (income or revenue) less the costs over many time periods. NPV is useful because it allows for a comparison of many projects, to select the best project to initiate. Generally, if the NPV is positive, the investment is a good choice unless an even better investment opportunity exists. One selects the project with the greatest NPV.

© 2005 Rita Mulcahy, PMP • Phone: (952) 846-4484 • E-mail: info@rmcproject.com • Web: www.rmcproject.com

Let's see if you already have a good understanding of this topic by asking you a question.

You have two projects to choose from. Project A will take three years to complete and has an NPV of $45,000. Project B will take six years to complete and has an NPV of $85,000. Which one would you prefer?

> **Answer** Project B.

> The number of years is not relevant as it would have been taken into account in the calculation of the NPV. See the sample calculation below if you are confused. If you understand the concept of NPV already, skip the example.

To calculate NPV, you need to calculate the present value of both income and revenue figures using the PV formula and then add the present values as shown below.

Time Period	Income/ Revenue	Present Value of Income at 10% Interest Rate	Costs	Present Value of Cost at 10% Interest Rate
0	0	0	200	200
1	50	45	100	91
2	100	83	0	0
3	300	225	0	0
Total		353		291

$$NPV = 353 - 291 = 62$$

Internal Rate of Return (IRR) To explain this concept, think of a bank account. You put money in a bank account and expect to get a return of 2 percent. You can think of a project in the same way. If a company has more than one project in which to invest, the company may look at the projects' returns and then select the highest one.

IRR does get confusing when you give it a formal definition. DEFINITION: The rate (read it as interest rate) at which the project inflows (revenues) and project outflows (costs) are equal. Calculating IRR is complex and requires the aid of a computer. You will not have to perform any IRR calculations on the exam. You will need to understand the definition and be able to answer questions like the following:

> *You have two projects to choose from; Project A with an IRR of 21 percent or Project B with an IRR of 15 percent. Which one would you prefer?*

> **Answer** Project A.

Payback Period The number of time periods it takes to recover your investment in the project before you start accumulating profit. For example:

> *You have two projects to choose from; Project A with a payback period of six months or Project B with a payback period of 18 months. Which one would you prefer?*

> **Answer** Project A.

Benefit Cost Ratio This term and many others in this book are not in the PMBOK® Guide, but may be on the exam. Benefit cost ratio relates to costing projects and to determining what work should be done. This ratio compares the benefits to the costs of different options. (In this case benefits are the same as revenue. Remember that revenue is not the same as profit.)

A benefit cost ratio of >1 means the benefits are greater than the costs. A benefit cost ratio of <1 means the costs are greater than the benefits. A benefit cost ratio of 1 means the costs and benefits are the same. Benefit cost ratios can be expressed as decimals or ratios.

> *If the benefit cost ratio of project A is 2.3 and the benefit cost ratio of project B is 1.7, which project would you select?*
> **Answer** *A. The project with the higher benefit cost ratio.*

> *A benefit cost ratio of 1.7 means?*
> *A. The costs are greater than the benefits*
> *B. Payback is 1.7 times the costs*
> *C. Profit is 1.7 times the costs*
> *D. Costs are 1.7 times the profit*
> **Answer** *B. Benefit cost ratio is talking about revenue (payback) not just the smaller figure of profits.*

Opportunity Cost
The opportunity given up by selecting one project over another. NOTE: This does not require any calculation. See the example below.

> *You have two projects to choose from; Project A with an NPV of $45,000 or Project B with an NPV of $85,000. What is the opportunity cost of selecting project B?*
> **Answer** *$45,000.*

Sunk Costs
Expended costs. People unfamiliar with accounting standards might have trouble with the following question:

> *You have a project with an initial budget of $1,000,000. You are halfway through the project and have spent $2,000,000. Do you consider the $1,000,000 over budget when determining whether to continue with the project?*
> **Answer** *No!*

Be aware that accounting standards say that sunk costs should not be considered when deciding whether to continue with a troubled project.

Law of Diminishing Returns
The more you put into something, the less you get out of it. For example, adding twice as many resources to an activity may not get the activity done in half the time.

Working Capital
Current assets minus current liabilities, or the amount of money the company has available to invest, including investment in projects.

Project Selection Methods
The items just described are also considered techniques to help select which projects will be undertaken:
- Present Value
- Net Present Value
- Internal Rate of Return
- Payback Period
- Benefit Cost Ratio

Depreciation
Large assets (e.g., equipment) purchased by a company lose value over time. Accounting standards call this depreciation. Several methods are used to account

for depreciation. The exam asks you what they are. You do not have to perform any calculations. (See, I told you I could make this easy for you!) The following information is all you need to know.

There are two forms of depreciation:

1. **Straight Line Depreciation** The same amount of depreciation is taken each year.

> ### Example
> A $1,000 item with a 10-year useful life and no salvage value (how much the item is worth at the end of its life) would be depreciated at $100 per year.

2. **Accelerated Depreciation** For the exam you only need to know:
   - There are two forms of accelerated depreciation. You do not have to understand what these two forms mean or do any calculations.
     - Double Declining Balance
     - Sum of the Years Digits
   - Accelerated depreciation depreciates faster than straight line.

> ### Example
> A $1,000 item with a 10-year useful life and no salvage value (how much the item is worth at the end of its life) would be depreciated at $180 the first year, $150 the second, $130 the next, etc.

Practice Exam

Cost Management

1. **One common way to compute estimate at completion (EAC) is to take the budget at completion (BAC) and:**
   A. divide by SPI.
   B. multiply by SPI.
   C. multiply by CPI.
   D. divide by CPI.

2. **Estimate at completion (EAC) is a periodic evaluation of:**
   A. cost of work completed.
   B. value of work performed.
   C. anticipated total cost at project completion.
   D. what it will cost to finish the job.

3. **If earned value (EV) = 350, actual cost (AC) = 400, planned value (PV) = 325, what is cost variance (CV)?**
   A. 350
   B. -75
   C. 400
   D. -50

4. **Double declining balance is a form of:**
   A. decelerated depreciation.
   B. straight line depreciation.
   C. accelerated depreciation.
   D. life cycle costing.

5. **Analogous estimating:**
   A. uses bottom-up estimating techniques.
   B. is used most frequently during the executing processes of the project.
   C. uses top-down estimating techniques.
   D. uses actual detailed historical costs.

6. **The cost of choosing one project and giving up another is called:**
   A. fixed cost.
   B. sunk cost.
   C. net present value (NPV).
   D. opportunity cost.

7. **The main focus of life cycle costing is to:**
   A. estimate installation costs.
   B. estimate the cost of operations and maintenance.
   C. consider installation costs when planning the project costs.
   D. consider operations and maintenance costs in making project decisions.

8. **Cost performance measurement is BEST done through which of the following?**
   A. Asking for a percent complete from each team member and reporting that in the monthly progress report
   B. Calculating earned value and using the indexes and other calculations to report past performance and forecast future performance
   C. Using the 50/50 rule and making sure the life cycle cost is less than the project cost
   D. Focusing on the amount expended last month and what will be expended the following month

9. **A cost performance index (CPI) of 0.89 means:**
   A. at this time, we expect the total project to cost 89 percent more than planned.
   B. when the project is completed we will have spent 89 percent more than planned.
   C. the project is only progressing at 89 percent of that planned.
   D. the project is only getting 89 cents out of every dollar invested.

10. **A schedule performance index (SPI) of 0.76 means:**
    A. you are over budget.
    B. you are ahead of schedule.
    C. you are only progressing at 76 percent of the rate originally planned.
    D. you are only progressing at 24 percent of the rate originally planned.

11. **Which of the following is not needed in order to come up with a project estimate?**
    A. WBS
    B. Network diagram
    C. Risks
    D. Change control procedure

12. **Which of the following is an example of a parametric estimate?**
    A. Dollars per module
    B. Learning bend
    C. Bottom-up
    D. CPM

13. **A rough order of magnitude estimate is made during which project management process group?**
    A. Project planning
    B. Project closing
    C. Project executing
    D. Project initiating

14. **Which factor would NOT be considered when choosing between two projects to undertake?**
    A. Net present value (NPV)
    B. Benefit cost ratio (BCR)
    C. Payback period
    D. Law of diminishing returns

15. If project A has a net present value (NPV) of U.S. $30,000 and project B has an NPV of U.S. $50,000, what is the opportunity cost if project B is selected?
    A. $23,000
    B. $30,000
    C. $20,000
    D. $50,000

16. Which type of cost is team training?
    A. Direct
    B. NPV
    C. Indirect
    D. Fixed

17. Project setup costs are an example of:
    A. variable costs.
    B. fixed costs.
    C. overhead costs.
    D. opportunity costs.

18. Value analysis is performed to get:
    A. more value from the cost analysis.
    B. management to buy into the project.
    C. the team to buy into the project.
    D. a less costly way of doing the same work.

19. Who has the cost risk in a fixed price (FP) contract?
    A. Team
    B. Buyer
    C. Seller
    D. Management

20. Which of the following represents the estimated value of the work actually accomplished?
    A. Earned value (EV)
    B. Planned value (PV)
    C. Actual cost (AC)
    D. Cost variance (CV)

21. You have four projects from which to choose one. Project A is being done over a six year period and has a net present value (NPV) of U.S. $70,000. Project B is being done over a three year period and has an NPV of U.S. $30,000. Project C is being done over a five year period and has an NPV of U.S. $40,000. Project D is being done over a one year period and has an NPV of U.S. $60,000. Which project would you choose?
    A. Project A
    B. Project B
    C. Project C
    D. Project D

22. Project A has an internal rate of return (IRR) of 21 percent. Project B has an IRR of 7 percent. Project C has an IRR of 31 percent. Project D has an IRR of 19 percent. Which of these would be the BEST project?
    A. Project A
    B. Project B
    C. Project C
    D. Project D

23. As a project manager, you are presented with the following information on the net present value (NPV) of several potential projects. Which project is your BEST choice?
    A. Project A with an NPV of U.S. $95,000
    B. Project B with an NPV of U.S. $120,000
    C. Project C with an NPV of U.S. $20,000
    D. Project D with an NPV of U.S. -$30,000

24. Your company can accept one of three possible projects. Project A has a net present value (NPV) of U.S. $30,000 and will take six years to complete. Project B has an NPV of U.S. $60,000 and will take three years to complete. Project C has an NPV of U.S. $90,000 and will take four years to complete. Based on this information, which project would you pick?
    A. They all have the same value.
    B. Project A
    C. Project B
    D. Project C

25. The seller tells you that your activities have resulted in an increase in their costs. You should:
    A. recommend a change to the project costs.
    B. have a meeting with management to find out what to do.
    C. ask the seller for supporting information.
    D. deny any wrongdoing.

26. Your cost forecast shows that you will have a cost overrun at the end of the project. Which of the following should you do?
    A. Eliminate risks in estimates and re-estimate.
    B. Meet with the sponsor to find out what work can be done sooner.
    C. Cut quality.
    D. Decrease scope.

27. A new store development project requires the purchase of various equipment, machinery and furniture. The department responsible for the development recently centralized its external purchasing process and standardized its new order system. In which document can these new procedures be found?
    A. Project scope statement
    B. WBS
    C. Staffing management plan
    D. Organizational policies

28. Early in the life of your project, you are having a discussion with the sponsor about what estimating techniques should be used. You want a form of expert judgment, but the sponsor argues for analogous estimating. It would be BEST to:

A. agree to analogous estimating as it is a form of expert judgment.
B. suggest life cycle costing as a compromise.
C. determine why the sponsor wants such an accurate estimate.
D. try to convince the sponsor to allow expert judgment because it is typically more accurate.

29. You have just completed the initiating processes of a small project and are moving into the planning processes when a project stakeholder asks you for the project's budget and cost baseline. What should you tell her?

A. The project budget can be found in the project's charter, which has just been completed.
B. The project budget and baseline will not be finalized and accepted until the planning processes are completed.
C. The project management plan will not contain the project's budget and baseline; this is a small project.
D. It is impossible to complete an estimate before the project management plan is created.

30. The project manager is allocating overall cost estimates to individual activities to establish a baseline for measuring project performance. What process is this?

A. Cost management
B. Cost estimating
C. Cost budgeting
D. Cost control

31. You are asked to prepare a budget for completing a project that was started last year and then shelved for six months. All the following would be included in the budget EXCEPT?

A. Fixed costs
B. Sunk costs
C. Direct costs
D. Variable costs

32. To accommodate a new project in your department, you need to move resources from one project to another. Because your department is currently working at capacity, moving resources will inevitably delay the project from which you move the resources. It would cause the LEAST negative impact if you move resources from which of the following projects?

A. Project A with a benefit cost ratio of 0.8, no project charter, and four resources
B. Project B with a net present value of U.S. $60,000, 12 resources, and variable costs between U.S. $1,000 and U.S. $2,000 per month
C. Project C with an opportunity cost of U.S. $300,000, no project control system, and an internal rate of return of 12 percent
D. Project D with indirect costs of U.S. $20,000 and 13 resources

33. A manufacturing project has a schedule performance index (SPI) of 0.89 and a cost performance index (CPI) of 0.91. Generally, what is the BEST explanation for why this occurred?
    A. The scope was changed.
    B. A supplier went out of business and a new one needed to be found.
    C. Additional equipment needed to be purchased.
    D. A critical path activity took longer and needed more labor hours to complete.

34. Although the stakeholders thought there was enough money in the budget, halfway through the project the cost performance index (CPI) is 0.7. To determine the root cause, several stakeholders audit the project and discover the project cost budget was estimated analogously. Although the activity estimates add up to the project estimate, the stakeholders think something was missing in how the estimate was completed. Which of the following describes what was missing?
    A. Estimated costs should be used to measure CPI.
    B. SPI should be used, not CPI.
    C. Bottom-up estimating should have been used.
    D. Past history was not taken into account.

35. You are a project manager for a large consulting firm. Your superior has just asked for your input on a decision about which project your company should pursue. Project A has an internal rate of return (IRR) of 12 percent. Project B has a predicted benefit cost ratio (BCR) of 1.3. Project C has an opportunity cost of U.S. $75,000. Project D has a payback period of six months. If you had to choose based on this data, which project would you select?
    A. Project A
    B. Project B
    C. Project C
    D. Project D

36. You are about to take over a project from another project manager and find out the following information about the project. Activity Z has an early start (ES) of day 15 and a late start (LS) of day 20. Activity Z is a difficult activity. Cost performance index (CPI) is 1.1. Schedule performance index (SPI) is 0.8. There are 11 stakeholders on the project. Based on this information, which of the following would you be the MOST concerned about?
    A. Schedule
    B. Float
    C. Cost
    D. The number of available resources

37. The difference between the cost baseline and the cost budget can be BEST described as?
    A. The management reserve
    B. The contingency reserve
    C. The project cost estimate
    D. The cost account

38. You provide a project cost estimate to the project sponsor. He is unhappy with the estimate, because he thinks the price should be lower. He asks you to cut 15 percent off the project estimate. What should you do?
    A. Start the project and constantly look for cost savings.
    B. Tell all the team members to cut 15 percent from their estimates.
    C. Inform the sponsor of the activities to be cut.
    D. Add additional resources with low hourly rates.

Cost Management Answers

1. **Answer** D
   Explanation This question is asking for the formula for EAC, which is BAC/CPI. Notice how you will have to remember the formulas to get the answers correct.

2. **Answer** C
   Explanation When you look at earned value, many of the terms have similar definitions. This could get you into trouble. Since the EAC means the estimate at completion, choice C is the best answer. Choice D is the definition of ETC, estimate to complete.

3. **Answer** D
   Explanation CV = EV - AC

4. **Answer** C
   Explanation We need to know that double declining balance is a form of depreciation. That eliminates choice D. We also know that double declining balance is a form of accelerated depreciation, eliminating choices A and B. Therefore, C is the correct response.

5. **Answer** C
   Explanation Analogous estimating is used most frequently during the planning processes, not the executing processes (choice B). You do not need to use historical costs (choice D) for an analogous estimate. Therefore, choice C is the correct answer.

6. **Answer** D
   Explanation Choices A and B are types of costs and do not relate to "giving up another." Choice C is a way to determine today's value of a future cash flow and does not deal with the quoted phrase. The definition of opportunity cost includes the cost of choosing one project and giving up another, and thus it is the best answer.

7. **Answer** D
   Explanation Life cycle costing looks at operations and maintenance costs and balances them with the project costs to try to reduce the cost across its entire life.

8. **Answer** B
   Explanation Asking percent complete (choice A) is not a best practice since it is usually a guess. Often the easiest work is done first on a project, throwing off any percentage calculations of work remaining. It may be a good thing to use the 50/50 rule, as in choice C. However, the 50/50 rule is not necessarily included in the progress report, and the second part of the sentence is incorrect. The life cycle cost cannot be lower than the project cost as the life cycle cost includes the project cost. Choice D is often done by inexperienced project managers who know of nothing else. Not only does it provide little information, but also it cannot be used to predict the future. Choice B is the best answer since it looks at the past and uses this information to estimate future costs.

9. **Answer** D
   Explanation The CPI is less than one, so the situation is bad. Choice D is the best answer.

10. **Answer** C

    Explanation Earned value questions ask for a calculation or an interpretation of the results. See the tricks under this topic in this book.

11. **Answer** D

    Explanation A change control procedure is not required to obtain estimates, but without the other three choices, you cannot develop the estimates. You need the WBS to define the activities, the network diagram to see the dependencies and the risks to determine contingencies. NOTE: These are high-level risks, not the detailed risks we identify later in the planning process group.

12. **Answer** A

    Explanation Parametric estimates use a mathematical model to predict project cost or time.

13. **Answer** D

    Explanation This estimate has a wide range. It is done during project initiating, when very little is known about the project.

14. **Answer** D

    Explanation The law of diminishing returns has nothing to do with choosing between projects. Notice that this question requires you to understand that projects should be systematically selected and that the selection should be based on some formal evaluation of all projects available. Many project managers have little experience or knowledge of the activities such as this that go on during project initiation. Though there are not many questions on the exam on project initiation, a little study can help you get many of these questions right, even if you are not currently involved in initiating projects in your company.

15. **Answer** B

    Explanation The opportunity cost is the value of the project that was not selected; the lost opportunity.

16. **Answer** A

    Explanation You are training the team on skills required for the project. The cost is directly related to the project and thus a direct cost.

17. **Answer** B

    Explanation Setup costs do not change as production on the project changes. Therefore, they are fixed costs.

18. **Answer** D

    Explanation Notice that you need to know the definition of value analysis to answer this question. Also notice that the other choices could be considered correct by someone who does not know the definition.

19. **Answer** C

    Explanation If the costs are more than expected under a fixed price contract, the seller must pay those costs. As explained in the Procurement chapter, "cost risk" refers to the person who will have to pay for the added cost if costs escalate. Because the price is fixed, the seller will have to pay any increased costs out of their profit. Naturally, this

© 2005 Rita Mulcahy, PMP • Phone: (952) 846-4484 • E-mail: info@rmcproject.com • Web: www.rmcproject.com

does not include increased PRICE due to change orders. A fixed price contract and the PRICE could be changed with change orders.

20. **Answer** A
   Explanation It can be confusing to differentiate earned value terms from each other. The definition presented here is for EV or earned value, so choice A is the best choice.

21. **Answer** A
   Explanation The number of years is already included in the calculation of NPV. You simply pick the project with the highest NPV.

22. **Answer** C
   Explanation Remember, the internal rate of return is similar to the interest rate you get from the bank. The higher the rate is, the better the return.

23. **Answer** B
   Explanation You should pick the higher number.

24. **Answer** D
   Explanation Remember, project length is incorporated when computing NPV. You would choose the project that provides the most value, in this case the project with the highest NPV.

25. **Answer** C
   Explanation This is a professional and social responsibility/procurement/cost question. The situation described involves a claim. The best thing to do would be to get supporting information to find out what happened and take corrective action for the future. After choice C and negotiation, choice A would most likely occur. Choice D is unethical. Choice B is a meeting with YOUR management and should not occur until you have all the information.

26. **Answer** A
   Explanation Look for the choice which would have the least negative impact in this situation. You would not need to meet with the sponsor to do choice B. Choices C and D always have negative effects. The choice with the least negative impact is Choice A.

27. **Answer** D
   Explanation Procedures for the rental and purchase of supplies and equipment are found in the organizational policies.

28. **Answer** A
   Explanation This is a tricky question. In order to pick the best answer, you need to realize that analogous estimating is a form of expert judgment. Notice choice C, "determine why," sounds like a good idea, but look at the rest of the sentence. Analogous estimates are not accurate. Reading every word of this choice helps eliminate it.

29. **Answer** B
   Explanation The overall project budget (choice A) may be included in the project charter but not the detailed costs. Even small projects (choice C) should have a budget and schedule. It is not impossible to create a project budget before the project

management plan is created (choice D). It is just not wise, as the budget will not be accurate.

30. **Answer** C
Explanation Choice A is too general. The estimates are already created in this example, so the answer is not B. The answer is not D, cost control, because the baseline has not been created. The correct answer is C.

31. **Answer** B
Explanation Sunk costs (choice B) are expended costs. The rule is that they should not be considered when deciding whether to continue with a troubled project.

32. **Answer** A
Explanation A project without a charter is a project without support. The information provided for the other projects does not justify selecting them. Even the number of resources is not relevant since the number of resources for the new project is not supplied.

33. **Answer** D
Explanation To answer this question, you must look for a choice that would take longer and cost more. If you picked choice A, reread it. It says scope was changed, not necessarily added to. If the change was to reduce the scope, it might also have reduced cost. Though it would take time to handle the event described in choice B, the impacted activity might not be on the critical path, and thus might not affect time. Choice C would definitely add cost, but not necessarily time. Only choice D would negatively affect both time and cost.

34. **Answer** C
Explanation Actual costs are used to measure CPI, and there is no reason to use SPI in this situation, so choices A and B are not correct. Using past history (choice D) is another way of saying "analogous." The best way to estimate is bottom-up (choice C). Such estimating would have improved the overall quality of the estimate.

35. **Answer** A
Explanation This is a question about project selection and could easily be included in other chapters. In order to interpret the information, you need to know what each item is. A 12 percent IRR (choice A) is a more quantified benefit than a BCR of 1.3. You need more information to understand what the BCR of 1.3 will mean on the project. Thus, it is impossible to determine whether the BCR of 1.3 is better than an IRR of 12 percent. There is not enough information provided to support recommending or not recommending choices C or D. This leaves only choice A, with a 12 percent return, as providing a clear benefit.

36. **Answer** A
Explanation This is one of those questions that combines topics from various knowledge areas. Did you fall into the trap of calculating the float for Z? The amount of float for one activity and the number of stakeholders does not tell you anything in this case, so choices B and D cannot be the best answers. The CPI is greater than one and the SPI is less than one. Therefore, the thing to be most worried about would be schedule.

37. **Answer** A
Explanation The cost accounts are included in the project cost estimate, and the contingency reserve is added to that to come up with the cost baseline. Thereafter the

management reserve is added to come up with the cost budget. Therefore, only choice A is correct.

38. **Answer** C

    Explanation This question is full of choices that are not correct project management actions. If you picked the wrong answer, look again at the choices and try to determine what you are missing. Whatever it is, it will show up more than once on the real exam!

    To answer the question, you must first realize that it is never appropriate for a project manager to just cut estimates across the board (choice B). The project manager should have created an estimate with realistic work package estimates that do not include padding. Then, if costs must be decreased, the project manager can look to cut quality, decrease risk, cut scope or use cheaper resources (and at the same time closely monitoring the impact of changes on the project schedule).

    One of the worst things a project manager can do is to start a project while knowing that the time or cost for the project is unrealistic. Therefore, choice A cannot be best. Notice that choice D suggests adding additional resources. That would cost more. Choice C involves evaluating, looking for alternatives and then going to the sponsor to tell him the impact of the cost cutting.

Time and Cost Game

The following game is designed to improve your ability to correctly answer the difficult Time and Cost questions. It is best done verbally with more than one person. The second person can be a spouse, child or someone else studying for the PMP exam.

Cut out the cards along the lines provided. Try to answer as many questions as you can in 10 minutes. If you answer 10 questions correctly in ten minutes, this should prove to you that you will not have a time problem taking the exam. (The exam allows about 1¼ minutes per question.) GOOD LUCK!

- **For One Participant** Cover the answers.
- **For Two Participants** One person asks the questions and the other answers.
- **For More Than Two Participants** One person asks the questions and the others answer. One of those answering should also keep track of the number of correct answers.

Q: What is a formula for estimate at completion? A: BAC/CPI	Q: What estimating method would use optimistic time estimates? A: Three-point estimate	Q: "How much work should be done" has what earned value name? A: Planned value
Q: The critical path is? A: The longest duration path in the network The shortest time to complete the project	Q: The types and quantities of resources required are calculated in what part of time management? A: Activity resource estimating	Q: What does the schedule variance tell you? A: How far you are behind or ahead of schedule
Q: What schedule network analysis technique involves crashing? A: Schedule compression	Q: What does a finish-to-start relationship mean? A: One activity must finish before the next can start	Q: What does the estimate at completion tell you? A: What we now expect the total project to cost
Q: Why would you want to crash a project? A: To shorten the project duration	Q: The "what-if" scenario method of schedule network analysis primarily makes use of what technique? A: Monte Carlo analysis	Q: What are sunk costs? A: Expended costs
Q: What does a milestone chart show? A: Dates of significant events on the project	Q: What is the duration of a milestone? A: Zero	Q: What is analogous estimating? A: Top-down estimating

Intentionally
left
blank

Q: What are fixed costs?

A: Costs that do not change with project activity

Q: What are direct costs?

A: Costs incurred directly by the project

Q: What is the earned value name for "how much you have spent to date?"

A: Actual cost

Q: What is value analysis?

A: Finding a less costly way to complete the work without affecting quality

Q: What is a management reserve?

A: An amount of time or money set aside to cover unforeseen risks

Q: What is the cost variance formula?

A: EV - AC

Q: Cost risk is greater for the buyer in what type of contract?

A: Cost reimbursable

Q: What schedule network analysis technique uses buffers?

A: Critical chain

Q: What does present value mean?

A: The value today of future cash flows

Q: What is the formula for total float?

A: LS − ES, or LF − EF
The amount of time an activity can be delayed without delaying the project

Q: Why would a project manager want to use resource leveling?

A: To smooth the peaks and valleys of monthly resource usage consumed by the project

Q: What does a benefit cost ratio of 2.5 mean?

A: The benefits are 2½ times the costs

Q: A critical path activity will generally have how much float?

A: Zero

Q: What is parametric estimating?

A: Using mathematical relationships found in historical information to create estimates (e.g., dollars per foot)

Q: What is the range of accuracy with a definitive estimate?

A: -5 percent to +10 percent

Quality Management

Before you read this chapter, ask yourself, "Do I have a quality management plan on my projects?" If your answer is yes, this chapter probably needs only a brief review. If you do not have a quality management plan, please let me ask you why. Because you never thought about it? Because your company does not require it?

Honestly, there is no excuse. "But project managers do not have time to spend on quality," you might say. If you think about it, lack of attention to quality means more rework or defects. The more rework you need, the more time and money you are wasting and the less likely you are to meet the project time and cost baselines.

If asked, "Is it better to plan in quality, or inspect to find quality problems?" almost everyone will answer correctly that it is better to plan in quality. However, that is not how most of the quality-related questions are presented on the exam. Rather, they focus on situations relating to quality to see if you can properly handle the situation. For example:

The project manager finds that one of his team members has created her own process for installing hardware. What should the project manager do? Beginning project managers might choose a response that relates to thanking the team member for the effort. More experienced project managers might select a choice that relates to finding out if the process was a good one. The best project managers, and those worthy of PMP certification, will select the choice that relates to investigating the quality management plan to determine if they should have provided a standard process.

Those without quality experience will have a hard time with such questions. Thankfully, not all the quality questions are that difficult. Expect new terms. Expect to see questions that talk about manufacturing environments (e.g., you manufacture tables). Expect questions about the process of quality and how quality relates to the "triple constraint," as defined in this book.

Rita's Process Chart—Quality Management
Where are we in the project management process?

Initiating	Planning	Executing	Monitoring & Controlling	Closing
Select project manager	**Determine how you will do planning—part of management plans**	Acquire final team	**Measure against the performance measurement baselines**	Develop closure procedures
Determine company culture and existing systems	Create project scope statement	Execute the PM plan	**Measure according to the management plans**	Complete contract closure
Collect processes, procedures and historical information	Determine team	Work to produce product scope	**Determine variances and if they warrant corrective action or a change**	Confirm work is done to requirements
Divide large projects into phases	Create WBS and WBS dictionary	**Recommend changes and corrective actions**	Scope verification	Gain formal acceptance of the product
Identify stakeholders	Create activity list	Send and receive information	Configuration management	Final performance reporting
Document business need	Create network diagram	Implement approved changes, defect repair, preventive and corrective actions	**Recommend changes, defect repair, preventive and corrective actions**	Index and archive records
Determine project objectives	Estimate resource requirements	**Continuous improvement**	Integrated change control	Update lessons learned knowledge base
Document assumptions and constraints	Estimate time and cost	**Follow processes**	Approve changes, defect repair, preventive and corrective actions	Hand off completed product
Develop project charter	Determine critical path	Team building	Risk audits	Release resources
Develop preliminary project scope statement	Develop schedule	Give recognition and rewards	Manage reserves	
	Develop budget	Hold progress meetings	Use issue logs	
	Determine quality standards, processes and metrics	Use work authorization system	Facilitate conflict resolution	
	Determine roles and responsibilities	Request seller responses	Measure team member performance	
	Determine communications requirements	Select sellers	Report on performance	
	Risk identification, qualitative and quantitative risk analysis and response planning		Create forecasts	
	Iterations—go back		Administer contracts	
	Determine what to purchase			
	Prepare procurement documents			
	Finalize the "how to execute and control" aspects of all management plans			
	Create process improvement plan			
	Develop final PM plan and performance measurement baselines			
	Gain formal approval for plan			
	Hold kickoff meeting			

The following should help you understand how each part of Quality Management fits into the project management process.

The Quality Management Process

The Quality Management Process	Done During
Quality planning	Planning process group
Perform quality assurance	Executing process group
Perform quality control	Monitoring and controlling process group

Imagine a project to build a stadium that is mostly made of concrete. The concrete part of the stadium is two-thirds poured when the buyer arrives one day and tests the strength of the concrete. They find that it does not meet the clearly stated quality requirements for concrete strength in the contract. You can imagine the problems when the buyer says, "Rip out the concrete, it is not acceptable." Whose fault is this? Why did this occur?

Could we say it is the buyer's fault for not testing the concrete sooner? You might argue that case, but isn't the real fault with the sellers for not testing the quality themselves? Where was their quality plan? They should have noted the requirement and determined when and how they would confirm that they met it. Lack of attention to quality here needlessly added considerable risk to the project.

Here is another scenario to consider. Have any of your customers ever said one of your deliverables was not acceptable, although you were not provided in advance with a definition of what was acceptable from the customer? We need to know what is acceptable quality, how it will be measured and then determine what we will do to make sure we meet those requirements in order to avoid such unclear acceptance criteria as "the customer likes it."

Performing the quality process well avoids many issues that can arise later in the project.

Definition of Quality
What is quality? Know the short definition for the exam. Quality is defined as the degree to which the project fulfills requirements. MEMORIZE this phrase to help you answer about four questions.

Not too long ago I was teaching a class in New York City, N.Y., U.S.A. One of my students looked out the window and noticed someone painting the limestone of an old building white. She said, "That is not quality!" Why would such painting be quality? If the painting contract required the painter to use a certain kind of paint and follow painting standards, and he was doing so, the work was quality. The issue the student really had was that the wonderful old stone was being painted instead of cleaned. In other words, this was a disagreement with the requirements, not the quality of the work.

Go back and review the definition of quality again. Can you have quality if you do not have all the stated and unstated requirements defined in the project scope statement? Of course not. This makes the stakeholder analysis effort (from scope management) and the resulting project scope statement very important to quality.

Definition of Quality Management
(page 179) Quality management includes creating and following policies and procedures in order to ensure that a project meets the defined needs it was intended to meet. This can also mean the same thing as completing the project with no deviations from the project requirements. Quality management includes quality planning, perform quality assurance and perform quality control.

Quality Theorists
- **Joseph Juran** Developed the 80/20 principle, advocated top management involvement, defined quality as "fitness for use."
- **W. Edwards Deming** Developed *14 Steps to Total Quality Management*, advocated the Plan-Do-Check-Act cycle as the basis for quality improvement.
- **Philip Crosby** Popularized the concept of the cost of poor quality, advocated prevention over inspection and "zero defects." He believed that quality is "conformance to requirements."

TRICKS OF THE TRADE Quality-related questions can be confusing because many of the topics on the exam are not in the *PMBOK® Guide* and because PMI's quality philosophy may be different from that of your company. Some companies refer to what PMI calls perform quality assurance as quality planning. Some companies believe in giving the customer extras, while PMI wants us to focus on meeting the requirements.

TRICKS OF THE TRADE The following are PMI-isms related to quality.
- The project manager should recommend improvements to the performing organization's standards, policies and processes. Such recommendations are expected and welcomed by management.
- Quality should be considered whenever there is a change to any component of the "triple constraint."
- Quality should be checked before an activity or work package is completed.
- The project manager must spend time trying to improve quality.
- The project manager must determine metrics to be used to measure quality before the project work begins.
- The project manager must put in place a plan for continually improving processes.
- The project manager must make sure authorized approaches and processes are followed.
- Some of the quality activities could be done by a quality assurance or quality control department.

Exercise List the specific ACTIONS required to ensure quality on the project.

Answer There are lots of possible answers… Did you come up with these?
- Review the project charter and project scope statement
- Make sure you have asked the customer what his definition of quality is
- Identify any quality standards that are applicable to the project
- Identify the desired levels of performance in the product
- Identify what level you should control the project to
- Set standards to reach that level of performance
- Create other project standards and processes
- Decide what you will do to make sure the processes are followed and the standards met—your quality control system
- Meetings, reports, measurements, calculations
- Perform quality assurance

© 2005 Rita Mulcahy, PMP • Phone: (952) 846-4484 • E-mail: info@rmcproject.com • Web: www.rmcproject.com

- Perform quality control
- Evaluate the effectiveness of the quality control system

Gold Plating Gold plating refers to giving the customer extras (e.g., extra functionality, higher-quality components, and extra scope or better performance). This practice is not recommended, as gold plating adds no value to the project. Often, such additions are included based on the project team's impression of what the customer would like. This impression may not be accurate. Considering that as of 2004, only 34 percent of all projects succeed, project managers would be better off spending their time seeing that projects conform to requirements.

Prevention Over Inspection Prevention over inspection flows through many of the questions on the exam. Many years ago, the main focus of quality was on inspection (e.g., check production after items are produced). The cost of doing so (cost of nonconformance, discussed later) is so high that it is better to spend money on preventing problems. QUALITY MUST BE PLANNED IN, NOT INSPECTED IN! This frequently comes up on the exam.

Marginal Analysis Optimal quality is reached at the point where the incremental revenue from improvement equals the incremental cost to secure it.

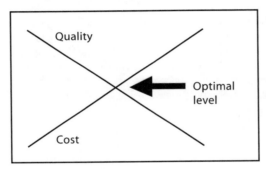

Continuous Improvement (or Kaizen) Small improvements in products or processes to reduce costs and ensure consistency of performance of products or services. These two words are taken to mean the same thing on the exam, however, in Japan this is just a word, not a quality movement. Kaizen means Kai (alter) and Zen (make better or improve). In the United States and most of Western Europe, improvements are thought of as BIG improvements. In Japan, improvements are thought of as small improvements.

Just in Time (JIT) Many companies are finding that holding goods in inventory is too expensive and unnecessary. Instead, they have their suppliers deliver materials just when they are needed or just before they are needed, thus decreasing inventory to close to zero. A company using JIT must have high quality, otherwise there will not be enough supplies or raw material to meet production requirements. A JIT system forces attention on quality.

Total Quality Management (TQM) A philosophy that encourages companies and their employees to focus on finding ways to continuously improve the quality of their business practices and products.

Responsibility for Quality The entire organization has responsibilities relating to quality. Therefore, read questions on this topic carefully. Determine to whom in the organization the question refers. The project manager has the ultimate responsibility for the quality of the product of the project, but each team member must check his or her work—self-inspection. Senior management has the ultimate responsibility for quality in the organization as a whole. W. Edwards Deming (an expounder of the quality philosophy) says that 85 percent of the costs of quality are the direct responsibility of management. It is not acceptable for a team member to simply complete the work and then turn it over to the project manager or their manager for checking. Work should meet the project requirements and testing should be done whenever appropriate before submission.

Impact of Poor Quality
You might get questions on this topic just to support that spending time on quality has value. If you have poor quality, you might also have:
- Increased costs
- Low morale
- Low customer satisfaction
- Increased risk
- Rework
- Schedule delays

Increases in quality can result in increased productivity and cost effectiveness and decreased cost risk.

Cost of Conformance and Cost of Nonconformance
Questions often ask, "Which are greater, costs of conformance to quality or costs of nonconformance to quality?" Obviously there are costs in both areas, but the costs of nonconformance must be greater. Otherwise, why spend time improving quality? Specifically, these costs are:

Cost of Conformance	Cost of Nonconformance	
Quality training	Rework	
Studies	Scrap	
Surveys	Inventory costs	
	Warranty costs	

TRICKS OF THE TRADE **For Understanding the Difference Between Quality Planning, Assurance, and Control** One of the major concerns people have while studying is how to understand the difference between quality planning, quality assurance and quality control. This can be due to the difference between what your company calls these activities and what the exam does. It can also be due to the confusing nature of the questions.

TRICKS OF THE TRADE It is easier to determine if something is part of quality control (e.g., relates to one of the quality control tools) than to determine if it is part of quality planning or quality assurance. Therefore, always eliminate quality control first when you see questions on the exam that require you to differentiate between quality planning, assurance and control.

The following chart and list of activities under each topic that follow the chart are a major trick for getting more questions of this type right. Be wary. Even if you study this a lot, you will still see confusing questions about the differences between the quality management processes on the exam. Be prepared to read such questions carefully! In addition to understanding these terms by reading this chapter, the following table will really help.

Quality Planning	Quality Assurance	Quality Control
Determine a plan for quality	Determine if the project is complying with organizational and project policies and processes	Measure specific project results against standards
• Find existing quality standards for product and project management • Create additional project-specific standards • Determine what work you will do to meet the standards • Determine how you will measure to make sure you meet the standards • Balance the needs of quality with scope, cost, time, risk and satisfaction • Create a quality management plan and add it to the project management plan	• Perform continuous improvement • Determine if project activities comply with organization and project policies, processes and procedures – quality audit • Correct deficiencies • Identify improvements the company needs to make • Recommend changes and corrective actions to integrated change control	• Measure specific project results against quality standards • Implement approved changes to the quality baseline • Identify quality improvements • Repair defects • Recommend changes, corrective and preventive actions and defect repair to integrated change control
Mostly done during project planning	Mostly done during project executing	Mostly done during project monitoring and controlling

Quality Planning (page 183) The project charter and project scope statement are needed before quality planning can begin. These serve as a guide to planning the entire project because they include the major project deliverables, project objectives, thresholds and acceptance criteria.

Quality planning results in the creation of a quality management plan, and includes the work described in the table above. One of the first things done in quality planning is to identify all relevant standards for the quality of the product of the project and for the quality of the project management efforts.

A standard is an agreed upon process to work or achieve a result. A standard is often strenuously tested before it is instituted, in order for it to become the recommended standard. Standards come from within the organization, or from government or professional associations.

These standards may be adopted by the performing organization or the project as they apply to the work of the project. Some available standards include:
• **The United Nations Convention on Contracts for International Sale of Goods (CISG)** The standard which governs international sales transactions.

- **ISO 9000** A family of standards created by the International Organization for Standardization (ISO) to help ensure that organizations have quality procedures and that they follow them. Many people think that ISO 9000 tells you what quality should be, or describes a recommended quality system. This is not correct.
- **Occupational Safety and Health Administration (OSHA)** United States standards for safety of American workers.

The project must comply with any applicable external standards (enterprise environmental factors) as well as organizational and departmental policies, standards and procedures (organizational process assets). Organizational process assets are the result of lessons learned on previous projects and the performing organization's idea of the best way to accomplish work. Standards are invaluable to prevent reinventing the wheel on the project, as they help get the work done faster and with higher quality.

In addition, the project manager must plan the project so it meets the customer's quality standards. These standards can include such measures as the number of software bugs per module that is acceptable, the strength of concrete, or average time per installation. Such measures of quality will help the project manager know when the project is out of control and to then recommend corrective action, as well as preventive action (to prevent the problem from reoccurring).

Once other standards are discovered, the project manager must create any standards needed by the project but not covered by any other standard. These may not violate other relevant standards. They could include processes for how the project management work of the project should be done.

When all standards have been found or created, quality planning involves determining what work will need to be done to meet those standards. Perhaps additional testing needs to be added to the project, resources moved around, or descriptions of products to be purchased changed.

Quality planning then continues by determining the specific measurements that will be made each week, month, or for each deliverable to ensure compliance with all standards.

Quality planning will result in additions or changes to the iterating project management plan to make sure the standards are met. Work can be added to the WBS, resources can be changed and extra actions by the project manager added to the project management plan.

Be careful not to negatively impact the project scope, time or cost if higher quality is not required on the project. Quality must be balanced with the other components of the "triple constraint," as described in this book. Sounds easy right? Maybe it is not! Remember all the times on your projects that team members delivered more than was needed? Remember how hard it can be to keep the project from producing the Taj Mahal when all you need is a garage? The project scope statement will help keep things in focus and help plan quality to the appropriate level. The resulting quality management plan becomes part of the project management plan.

In my own informal studies, only about 10 percent of projects have quality management plans. The hard part for those who do not have these already on their projects is to think of quality and quality planning as if you have worked with them on a regular basis.

The following is done to accomplish quality planning.

Cost-Benefit Analysis (page 185) Considering the benefits versus the costs of meeting quality requirements

Benchmarking (page 185) Looking at past projects to determine ideas for improvement on the current project and to provide a basis to use in measurement of quality performance.

Design of Experiments (DOE) (page 185) The use of experimentation to statistically determine what variables will improve quality. For example, people may try to improve quality by analyzing the effect on overall quality of using different processes for software development and leaving all other aspects the same, or changing the type of wood used on a desk but leaving all other variables the same. This is time consuming. DOE is a statistical method that allows you to systematically change all of the important factors in a process and see which combination has a lower impact on the project rather than the slower, less accurate way of changing them one at a time.

Cost of Quality (COQ) (page 186) Looking at how the costs of conformance and non-conformance to quality will cost the project and creating an appropriate balance. Costs of quality include prevention costs and appraisal costs. Failure costs are costs of poor quality.

Outputs of Quality Planning (page 186)
- **Quality Management Plan** There are many different examples of quality management plans. Most include the following:
  - What are the standards that apply to this project
  - Who will be involved in managing quality, when and what will their specific duties be
  - Review of earlier decisions to make sure they are correct
  - Meetings to be held addressing quality
  - Reports that will address quality
  - What metrics will be used to measure quality
  - What parts of the project or deliverables will be measured and when
- **Checklist** A list of items to inspect, or a picture of the item to be inspected with space to note any defects found. Imagine a sheet of paper with an image of a car. Any defect, dents or other damage on the car is marked on the image of the car. These quality-related checklists are created in quality planning and used in quality control.
- **Process Improvement Plan** Not only must the project manager manage the project, but he must also improve processes in use on the project to decrease the instances of defects and thus save time and money and increase satisfaction. The activities determined to be needed on the project to improve processes are included in the process improvement plan and such a plan becomes part of the project management plan.
- **Quality Baseline** Though most project managers do not like to think about it, their efforts as project managers are, and should be, measured. These areas of measurement are called baselines. Baselines do not exist just to be held against the project manager. They also exist so that the project manager can know what is expected of him and so that he can measure the project while the work is being done.
- **Quality Metrics** (page 186) Throughout this book is an underlying theme that the project manager must know how the project is going and be able to determine when to recommend corrective actions and preventive actions. The only way to do this is to have thought through the areas on the project which are important to measure and (in most cases) decide what measurement is acceptable. These are metrics. See also Control Limits.

───**Perform Quality Assurance** (page 187) Determining whether standards are being met, the work is continuously improved and deficiencies corrected are parts of quality assurance. A simple look at the quality assurance and quality control processes should help your understanding.

Not only is the project manager to manage the project, quality assurance includes identifying improvements that the organization needs to make. In the real world this might include such actions as recommending certain practices, equipment or other problems be fixed so as to not impact your project. In one recent example, a software installation project was having many problems and rework because one of the existing software programs already installed was old, patched together and constantly failed. The project manager, as part of the project's quality effort made sure management was aware of the issue, the impacts and the approximate cost of replacing the existing software program.

As quality assurance progresses, the process will result in recommended changes and corrective actions.

Perform quality assurance is primarily done during the executing process group of the project. In addition to the quality chart previously described, quality assurance (tools and techniques) include:

Quality Audits (page 189) Imagine a team of auditors walking into your office one day to check up on you and the project. Their job is to see if you are complying with company policies, standards and procedures and to determine whether the policies, standards and procedures being used are efficient and effective. This is called a quality audit and is an example of how seriously companies take their standards. It is not all negative. A good quality audit will look for new lessons learned that your project is able to contribute to the performing organization. Quality audits are usually done by the quality assurance department, but the project manager can do such work if the performing organization does not have a quality assurance department.

Process Analysis (page 189) Have you ever worked on a project where some of the activities or work packages were repeated? This often happens when projects have multiple installations; for example, in a software installation project onto hundreds of computers. Lessons learned on the first few installations are used to improve the process on the remaining ones. Though this often happens naturally, real process analysis is planned in at certain points in the project (e.g., after every 10 installations). Process analysis is a part of continuous improvement.

Quality Management

Outputs of Perform Quality Assurance (page 190) To sum up the value of perform quality assurance, it is important to know that it leads to the following outputs:
- **Changes requested to the project management plan**
- **Recommendations for corrective actions**
- **Updated standards and processes**
- **Updated project management plans**

Perform Quality Control (page 190)

Where quality assurance looks at whether standards and procedures are being followed, quality control looks at specific measurements to see if the project and its processes are in control. It is during quality control that the height of tables in a manufacturing process will be measured, where the number of bugs per module will be measured. Quality control helps answer the questions; "Is everything all right on the project?" "Do I have to spend any additional time or change my project management activities?" "Will the project succeed?" Quality control also involves taking action to eliminate the root causes of unsatisfactory project performance.

Quality control is done during the monitoring and controlling process group of the project and its focus is on the correctness of work. A major feature of quality control is inspection; checking the quality of work to see if it conforms to standards. Inspection can be done while the work is being done or after it is completed.

One of the key traits of the best project managers is making sure the plans are working. This shows up in the quality area as the need to evaluate the effectiveness of the quality control system. You might ask yourself whether you are measuring the right things. Are your measurements providing real, valuable information? Are you comfortable that your quality control efforts are telling you how the project is really doing? Stop here and read this again. A great project manager makes time to evaluate the effectiveness of his plans and processes. Do you?

Quality control results in recommended changes, corrective and preventive actions and defect repair to integrated change control. Once approved, such recommendations could lead to a changed quality baseline. It is also during quality control that defects are actually repaired after approval in integrated change control.

Let's think about the manufacturing industry again. Remember, many questions on the exam describe situations in one industry or another. Do not let that confuse you. A future PMP should easily understand the situation described in each question on the exam, no matter what 'industry' is described.

Population/Sample Let's say you make tables. Would each table be the same exact height? No, there would be some allowable variation. Even so, the tables must be checked to see if they meet quality standards on the project. What if inspecting each table would cause damage or take too much time? Then taking a statistically valid sample would be best. It is best to take a sample of a population if we believe there are not many defects, or if studying the entire population would:
- Take too long
- Cost too much
- Be too destructive

Mutual Exclusivity There can sometimes be statistical references on the exam. One that often confuses people is mutual exclusivity. Two events are said to be mutually exclusive if they cannot both occur in a single trial. For example, flipping a coin once cannot result in both a head and a tail.

Probability The likelihood that something will occur, usually expressed as a decimal or a fraction, on a scale of zero to one.

Normal Distribution A normal distribution is the most common probability density distribution chart. It is in the shape of a bell curve and is used to measure variations.

Statistical Independence Another confusing statistical term often showing up on the exam is statistical independence—the probability of one event occurring does not affect the probability of another event occurring (e.g., the probability of rolling a six on a die is statistically independent from the probability of rolling a five on the next roll).

Standard Deviation (or sigma) A measure of a range is its standard deviation. Also sometimes stated as a measure of how far you are from the mean (not the median). (Remember (P – O)/6 is the three-point estimate formula for standard deviation using optimistic, pessimistic and most likely estimates described in the Time chapter.)

3 or 6 Sigma Sigma is another name for standard deviation. 3 or 6 sigma represents the level of quality that a company has decided to try to achieve. At 6 sigma, less than 1.5 out of 1 million doors produced will have a problem. At 3 sigma, approximately 2,700 will have a problem. Therefore, 6 sigma represents a higher quality standard than 3 sigma. 3 or 6 sigma are also used to calculate the upper and lower control limits in a control chart, described later.

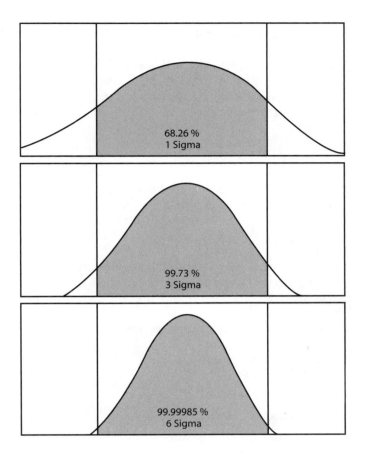

You should MEMORIZE:

- Sigma is taken on both sides of the mean. Half the curve is to the right of the mean, and half the curve is to the left of the mean.
- +/- 1 sigma is equal to 68.26% which is the percentage of occurances to fall between the two control limits
- +/- 2 sigma equals 95.46%
- +/- 3 sigma equals 99.73%
- +/- 6 sigma equals 99.99985%

Quality Control Tools In order to make sure you understand quality, the exam often describes a situation and asks what part of the quality management process you are in. A trick for these types of questions is to realize that if a situation is using one of these basic tools of quality, you are in quality control.

Seven Basic Tools of Quality (page 192) The following tools are the seven basic tools of quality. Each is used during quality control, as described on the following pages.

- Cause and effect diagram
- Flowchart
- Histogram
- Pareto chart
- Run chart
- Scatter diagram
- Control chart

Cause and Effect Diagram (Fishbone diagram, Ishikawa diagram) (page 192) Is it better to fix a defect or get to the root cause of the defect? Think before you answer. The best answer is to do both. But ask yourself if you really ever spend the time finding root causes. This is one of the benefits of a cause and effect diagram. Look at the example below. The chart lists the defect on the right; system will not install, and then lists the potential causes, such as hardware issues, software issues, etc. Various sub-causes of each potential cause are then listed in the hopes that the root cause of the defect will be found.

Cause and effect diagrams can be used in quality planning to look forward at what might contribute to the highest quality on the project. In quality control they are used to look backwards. The exam has used the following three phrases to describe this diagram.

1. A creative way to look at the causes or potential causes of a problem (as in quality control)
2. Helps stimulate thinking, organizes thoughts and generates discussion
3. Can be used to explore the factors that will result in a desired future outcome (as in quality planning)

The following is an illustration of a fishbone diagram.

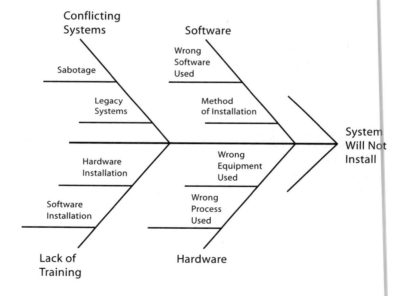

Flowchart A flowchart shows how a process or system flows from beginning to end and how the elements interrelate. It is used in quality control to analyze quality problems, but can also be used in quality planning to analyze potential future quality problems and determine quality standards. Imagine that work results are passed to four departments for approval. Might this lead to decreased quality? What about an unfinished fragile product in a manufacturing environment? Would the quality of the product be reduced if it needed to be passed by hand from person to person? Flowcharts graphically represent the process to help analyze how problems occur.

Pareto Chart (page 195) Imagine you have very little time to spend improving quality on the project. If you took all the problems you have had and stacked them into piles of like problems, which problem's root cause would you address; the large pile or the small pile? The answer is the large pile. Studies show that 80 percent of problems are due to 20 percent of the root causes. Addressing the root cause of the most frequent problems makes the greatest impact on quality.

A Pareto chart is a type of histogram. This means that the data is displayed in the form of bars or columns. The higher the bar, the more frequent the problem.

Understand the following phrases for the exam. The Pareto chart:
- Helps focus attention on the most critical issues
- Prioritizes potential "causes" of the problems
- Separates the critical few from the uncritical many

Run Chart To look at history and see a pattern of variation, you would use a run chart. If you have ever charted progress and looked for trends, then you have likely used run charts.

Scatter Diagram This diagram tracks two variables to see if they are related. If, in the manufacture of tables, the quality of the wood used has changed and so has the strength of the tables, a scatter diagram might be used to see if the two are related.

Control Chart (page 192) Never heard of these? Do not worry. They may be new to you, but it is generally easy to get these questions right. Read the following and then do the exercise. Control charts graphically help you to determine if a process is within acceptable limits. To better understand this, think of a manufacturer of doors. Would each door be the same exact height? Weight? Not likely. Rather there is a range, however small, that is acceptable. Each door should be within a range of normal and acceptable limits. A control chart can be used to monitor project performance figures such as cost and schedule variances. Most commonly, a control chart helps monitor production and other processes to see if the processes are within acceptable limits and if there are any actions required. A "special cause variation" means the process is out of control.

To create a control chart, samples are taken, variables measured, and attributes found. The attributes (size, for instance) are plotted on the chart (the small squares shown on the control chart exercise). The following can be found on a control chart:

> **Upper and Lower Control Limits** The acceptable range of variation of a process often shown as two dashed lines on a control chart. Every process is expected to have some variation—each door manufactured will not be exactly the same size. The acceptable range between the upper and lower control limit is determined by the organization's quality standard (e.g., 3 or 6 sigma). Data points within this range are generally thought of as "in control," excluding the rule of seven, and are an acceptable range of variation. Data points outside this range mean the process is out of control.
>
> The concept of control limits is also important outside of a control chart. A project manager can have control limits for many things. How about for a work package? Is one hour late in its delivery a problem? How about two hours? Control limits set here would help the project manager know whether to take action or not.

Mean (Average) A line in the middle of the control chart that shows the middle of the range of acceptable variation of the process.

Specification Limits While control limits represent the performing organization's standards for quality, specification limits represent the customer's expectations or contractual requirements for performance and quality on the project. Specification limits are characteristics of the measured process and are not inherent. In other words, specification limits are not calculated based on the control chart, but are inputs from the customer. Therefore, they can appear either inside or outside of the control limits. To meet the customer's specification limits, the performing organization's standards for quality (control limits) must be stricter than those of the customer. Accepting work when your process does not meet the customer's quality standards adds waste and extra management to the project to sort out acceptable items. Therefore, on the exam, assume that specification limits are outside the upper and lower control limits.

Out of Control The process is out of a state of statistical control under either of two circumstances:
- A data point falls outside of the upper or lower control limit
- Non-random data points that are still within the upper and lower control limits, such as the rule of seven

Think of "out of control" as a lack of consistency and predictability in the process.

Rule of Seven Is a rule of thumb or heuristic. It refers to non-random data points grouped together in a series that total seven on one side of the mean. The rule of seven tells you that although none of these points are outside of the control limits, they are not random and the process may be out of control. This type of situation should be investigated and a cause found.

Assignable Cause/Special Cause Variation A data point, or rule of seven, that requires investigation to determine the cause of the variation.

Exercise Much of what is tested on control charts is not in the *PMBOK® Guide*. Find all examples of each item listed on one or both of the control charts shown on the following page and place each item number next to its location on the chart. If you are unsure, take a guess and then review the control chart descriptions. These pictures represent two different control charts.

When you are able to pick out all the items in a control chart on the exercise, you should be ready to answer questions about control charts on the exam.

NOTE: The questions on the exam relating to control charts may ask questions that are easier to answer if you can picture a control chart in your mind. You do not have to draw one and it is unlikely one will be shown on the exam. Rather, the exam will use the terms in situational questions and you will need to know what they mean, i.e., a team member tells you that one sample is outside the lower control limit. What do you do? Because many people have excellent visual memory, this exercise is designed to make sure you understand control charts and can answer questions about them.

Find the following on the charts below:

1. Upper control limit
2. Lower control limit
3. Assignable cause/Special cause
4. The process is out of control
5. Normal and expected variation in the process

6. Rule of seven
7. Specification limits
8. Three sigma
9. Six sigma
10. Normal distribution curve

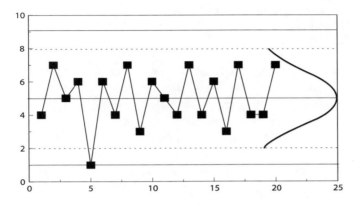

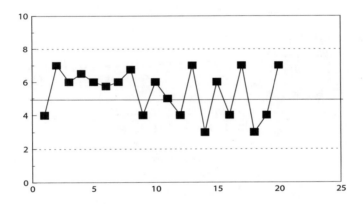

Answer

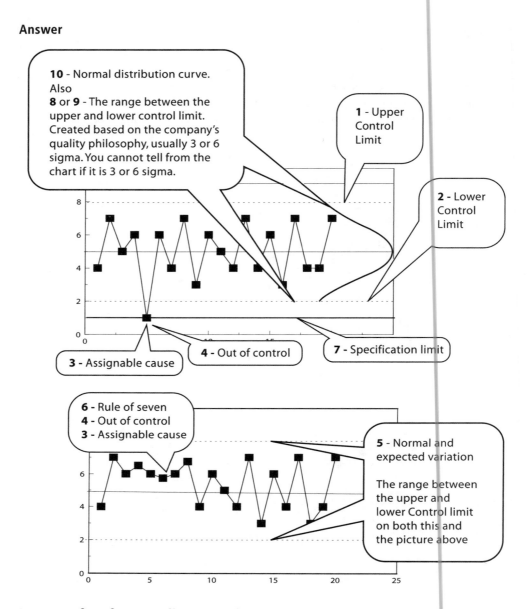

10 - Normal distribution curve. Also
8 or **9** - The range between the upper and lower control limit. Created based on the company's quality philosophy, usually 3 or 6 sigma. You cannot tell from the chart if it is 3 or 6 sigma.

1 - Upper Control Limit

2 - Lower Control Limit

3 - Assignable cause

4 - Out of control

7 - Specification limit

6 - Rule of seven
4 - Out of control
3 - Assignable cause

5 - Normal and expected variation

The range between the upper and lower Control limit on both this and the picture above

Outputs of Perform Quality Control (page 197) When you have completed the perform quality control process, you will have the following self-explanatory outputs:

- **Measurements**
- **Defects repaired**
- **Updates to quality baseline and the project management plan**
- **Recommended corrective actions and preventive actions**
- **Change requests**
- **Lessons learned**
- **Valid deliverables**

Perform quality control will be included on your exam score sheet as part of Ensure Project Deliverables Conform to Quality Standards.

Exercise Thought you were through with quality? After a few pages of other information let's see if you can recreate the quality chart previously described. When you are finished, check your answers with those on page 241.

Quality Planning	Quality Assurance	Quality Control

Practice Exam

Quality Management

1. When a product or service completely meets a customer's requirements:
   A. quality is achieved.
   B. the cost of quality is high.
   C. the cost of quality is low.
   D. the customer pays the minimum price.

2. To what does the following sentence refer? "The concept of optimal quality level is reached at the point where the incremental revenue from product improvement equals the incremental cost to secure it."
   A. Quality control analysis
   B. Marginal analysis
   C. Standard quality analysis
   D. Conformance analysis

3. Who is ultimately responsible for quality management on the project?
   A. Project engineer
   B. Project manager
   C. Quality manager
   D. Team member

4. A team is using a fishbone diagram to help determine what quality standards will be used on the project. What part of the quality management process are they in?
   A. Perform quality control
   B. Perform quality assurance
   C. Quality planning
   D. Variable analysis

5. A manager notices that a project manager is holding a meeting with some of the team and some stakeholders to discuss the quality of the project. The project schedule has been compressed and the CPI is 1.1. They have worked hard on the project, the team has been rewarded according to the reward system the project manager put in place and there is a strong sense of team. The manager suggests that the project manager does not have enough time to hold meetings about quality when the schedule is so compressed. Which of the following BEST describes why the manager is wrong?
   A. Improved quality leads to increased productivity, increased cost effectiveness and decreased cost risk.
   B. Improved quality leads to increased productivity, decreased cost effectiveness and increased cost risk.
   C. Improved quality leads to increased productivity, increased cost effectiveness and increased cost risk.
   D. Improved quality leads to increased productivity, decreased cost effectiveness and decreased cost risk.

© 2005 Rita Mulcahy, PMP • Phone: (952) 846-4484 • E-mail: info@rmcproject.com • Web: www.rmcproject.com

6. **From the project perspective, quality attributes:**
   A. determine how effectively the performing organization supports the project.
   B. provide the basis for judging the project's success or failure.
   C. are specific characteristics for which a product is designed and tested.
   D. are objective criteria that must be met.

7. **Quality is:**
   A. meeting and exceeding the customer's expectations.
   B. adding extras to make the customer happy.
   C. the degree to which the project meets requirements.
   D. conformance to management's objectives.

8. **All the following are NOT examples of quality assurance EXCEPT?**
   A. Inspection
   B. Process analysis
   C. Pareto chart
   D. Fishbone diagram

9. **Pareto charts help the project manager:**
   A. focus on the most critical issues to improve quality.
   B. focus on stimulating thinking.
   C. explore a desired future outcome.
   D. determine if a process is out of control.

10. **A control chart helps the project manager:**
    A. focus on the most critical issues to improve quality.
    B. focus on stimulating thinking.
    C. explore a desired future outcome.
    D. determine if a process is functioning within set limits.

11. **Testing the entire population would:**
    A. take too long.
    B. provide more information than wanted.
    C. be mutually exclusive.
    D. show many defects.

12. **All of the following are examples of the cost of nonconformance EXCEPT?**
    A. Rework
    B. Quality training
    C. Scrap
    D. Warranty costs

13. **Standard deviation is a measure of how:**
    A. far the estimate is from the highest estimate.
    B. far the measurement is from the mean.
    C. correct the sample is.
    D. much time remains in the project.

14. **What percentage of the total distribution are 3 sigma from the mean equal to?**
    A. 68.26%
    B. 99.99%
    C. 95.46%
    D. 99.73%

15. **All of the following are part of quality audits EXCEPT?**
    A. Determine whether project activities comply with organizational policies
    B. Determine inefficient and ineffective policies
    C. Validated defect repair
    D. Confirm the implementation of approved change requests

16. **A control chart shows seven data points in a row on one side of the mean. What should be done?**
    A. Perform a design of experiments.
    B. Adjust the chart to reflect the new mean.
    C. Find an assignable cause.
    D. Nothing. This is the rule of seven and can be ignored.

17. **You are managing a project in a just in time environment. This will require more attention, because the amount of inventory in such an environment is generally:**
    A. 45 percent.
    B. 10 percent.
    C. 12 percent.
    D. 0 percent.

18. **In planning your project, which would generally have the highest priority; quality, cost or schedule?**
    A. Cost is most important, quality next, and then schedule.
    B. Quality is more important than cost or schedule.
    C. Schedule is most important, quality next, and then cost.
    D. It should be decided for each project.

19. **A project manager is using a cause and effect diagram with the team to determine how various factors might be linked to potential problems. In what part of the quality management process is the project manager involved?**
    A. Quality analysis
    B. Perform quality assurance
    C. Perform quality control
    D. Quality planning

20. **A project manager and team from a firm that designs railroad equipment are tasked to design a machine to load stone onto railroad cars. The design allows for 2 percent spillage, amounting to over two tons of spilled rock per day. In which of the following does the project manager document quality control, quality assurance and quality improvements for this project?**
    A. Quality management plan
    B. Quality policy
    C. Control charts
    D. Project management plan

21. During a team meeting, the team adds a specific area of extra work to the project because they have determined it would benefit the customer. What is wrong in this situation?
    A. The team is gold plating.
    B. These efforts shouldn't be done in meetings.
    C. Nothing. This is how to meet or exceed customer expectations.
    D. Nothing. The project manager is in control of the situation.

22. The project team has created a plan describing how they will implement the quality policy. It addresses the organizational structure, responsibilities, procedures and other information about plans for quality. If this changes during the project, WHICH of the following plans will also change?
    A. Quality assurance
    B. Quality management
    C. Project management
    D. Quality control

23. You are a project manager for a major information systems project when someone from the quality department comes to see you about beginning a quality audit of your project. The team, already under pressure to complete the project as soon as possible, objects to the audit. You should explain to the team that the purpose of a quality audit is:
    A. part of an ISO 9000 investigation.
    B. to check if the customer is following its quality process.
    C. to identify inefficient and ineffective policies.
    D. to check the accuracy of costs submitted by the team.

24. You are in the middle of a major new facility construction project. The structural steel is in place and the heating conduits are going into place when senior management informs you that he is worried that the project will not meet the quality standards. What should you do in this situation?
    A. Assure senior management that during quality planning it was determined the project would meet the quality standards.
    B. Analogously estimate future results.
    C. Form a quality assurance team.
    D. Check the results from the last quality management plan.

25. You are asked to select tools and techniques to implement a quality assurance program to supplement existing quality control activities. Which of the following would you choose?
    A. Quality audits
    B. Statistical sampling
    C. Pareto charts
    D. Trend analysis

26. The new software installation project is in progress. The project manager is working with the quality assurance department to improve everyone's confidence that the project will satisfy the quality standards. Which of the following MUST they have before they start this process?
    A. Quality problems
    B. Quality improvement
    C. Quality control measurements
    D. Rework

27. The project you are working on has an increase in cost effectiveness, increased productivity and increased morale. What might be the reason for these changes?
    A. Project objectives are in line with those of the performing organization
    B. Increased quality
    C. Management's focus on cost containment
    D. Rewards presented for individual efforts

28. A project manager has just taken over the project from another project manager during the executing process group. The previous project manager created a project budget, determined communications requirements and went on to complete work packages. What should the new project manager do NEXT?
    A. Coordinate performance of work packages.
    B. Identify quality standards.
    C. Begin risk identification.
    D. Execute the project management plan.

29. A project is facing a major change to its project deliverables. If the project manager is involved in determining which quality standards are relevant to the change, the project manager must be involved in:
    A. quality management.
    B. perform quality assurance.
    C. quality planning.
    D. perform quality control.

30. At the end of a project, a project manager determines that the project has added four areas of functionality and three areas of performance. The customer has expressed satisfaction with the project. What does this mean in terms of success of the project?
    A. The project was an unqualified success.
    B. The project was unsuccessful because it was gold plated.
    C. The project was unsuccessful because the customer being happy means they would have paid more for the work.
    D. The project was successful because the team had a chance to learn new areas of functionality and the customer was satisfied.

31. During project executing, a project team member informs the project manager that a work package has not met the quality metric, and that she believes it is not possible to meet it. The project manager meets with all parties concerned to analyze

the situation. Which part of the quality management process is the project manager involved in?

A. Perform quality assurance
B. Project control
C. Perform quality control
D. Quality planning

32. The project manager notices that project activities being completed by one department are all taking slightly longer than planned. To date, none of the activities/work packages have been on the critical path, nor have they affected the critical chain planning that has occurred. The project manager is bothered by the problem, since four of the next five critical path activities are being completed by this department.

    After making three calls, the project manager is finally able to converse with the department manager to determine what is going on. The conversation is slow, because both speak different native languages and they are trying to converse in French, a shared language. To make communication easier, the project manager frequently asks the department manager to repeat back what has been said.

    The department manager communicates that his staff is following a company policy that requires two levels of testing. During the conversation, the department manager also makes a comment that leads the project manager to believe that the policy may include excessive work. This is the fourth time the project manager has heard such a comment. What is the BEST thing to do?

    A. Create a better communications management plan that requires only one language to be the universal language on the project and have translators readily available on a moment's notice.
    B. Contact someone else in the department who speaks the project manager's native language better to confirm the department manager's opinion.
    C. Find out if the upcoming activities should be re-estimated.
    D. Work on increasing the effectiveness of the performing organization by recommending continuous improvement of the policy in question.

33. A project manager has been overwhelmed with problems on his project. He would like to identify the root cause of the problems in order to determine where to focus his attention. Which of the following tools would be BEST for the project manager to use?

    A. Pareto chart
    B. Conflict resolution techniques
    C. Fishbone diagram
    D. Trend analysis

34. As the project manager, you are preparing your methods for quality management. You are looking for a method that can demonstrate the relationship between events and their resulting effects. You want to use a method to depict the events that cause a negative effect on quality. Which of the following is the BEST choice for accomplishing your objective?

    A. Histogram
    B. Pareto chart
    C. Ishikawa diagram
    D. Control chart

Quality Management Answers

1. **Answer** A

   Explanation As a general rule, one cannot say that quality (as defined in the question) is either of high or low cost (choices B and C) or that it provides the minimum price (choice D). It does give the customer what the customer wanted, which may not be the lowest or highest cost. Therefore, the best answer is A.

2. **Answer** B

   Explanation Know the term so you will be able to answer questions that deal with this concept. Choices A, C and D may sound good, but they are made-up terms.

3. **Answer** B

   Explanation Though each person working on the project should check their own work as part of any project, the project manager ultimately has the responsibility for quality on the project as a whole.

4. **Answer** C

   Explanation The key phrase here is "will be used." The team is looking to the future of what quality will be on the project and therefore must be in quality planning, choice C.

5. **Answer** A

   Explanation Notice in this question that there is a lot of data not relevant to answering the question? Expect these distracters to occur in almost every question on the exam. Quality should produce a decrease rather than an increase in cost risk as a result of less rework, so choices B and C can be eliminated. Quality should also provide increased cost effectiveness due to less rework. This eliminates Choice D leaving the best answer, choice A.

6. **Answer** C

   Explanation Quality attributes are the measurements that determine if the product is acceptable. They are based on the characteristics of the product for which they were designed.

7. **Answer** C

   Explanation Choices A and B cannot be the best, because there can be a cost impact (or time, risk etc,) of exceeding expectations or adding extras. Since a project should meet requirements, choice C is best.

8. **Answer** B

   Explanation Choice A is done as part of quality control. Choices C and D are done as part of quality planning or control (depending on how they are used). This leaves only choice B, which must be the best answer, as process analysis IS part of quality assurance. Watch out for "double-negative" questions like this on the exam!

9. **Answer** A

   Explanation Choices B and C relate to fishbone diagrams. Choice D relates to control charts. Only choice A relates to Pareto charts.

10. **Answer** D
    Explanation Choice A relates to Pareto charts. Choices B and C relate to fishbone diagrams. Only choice D relates to control charts.

11. **Answer** A
    Explanation The length of time it takes to test a whole population is one of the reasons to take a sample.

12. **Answer** B
    Explanation All the other choices are costs of nonconformance to quality.

13. **Answer** B
    Explanation Standard deviation is the measurement of a range around the mean. Therefore, choice B must be the best answer.

14. **Answer** D
    Explanation Memorize the numbers for 1-, 2-, 3- and 6-sigma.

15. **Answer** C
    Explanation Read this question, as "What is not part of quality audits?" Validated defect repair is done in quality control and so it is not part of quality audits, which are done during quality assurance.

16. **Answer** C
    Explanation The rule of seven applies here. If you have seven data points in a row on the same side of the mean, statistically, the mean has shifted, calling for action to correct the problem.

17. **Answer** D
    Explanation With just in time, supplies are delivered when you need them and not before. Therefore, you have little or no inventory.

18. **Answer** D
    Explanation This can be a tricky question, in that most project managers dismiss the need to focus on quality. Quality, cost and schedule should be considered of equal importance unless specific project objectives make any one of them most important. Quality, cost, schedule, scope, risk and other factors may be prioritized differently on each project.

19. **Answer** D
    Explanation The key words here are "potential problems." They are looking into the future and, therefore must be in quality planning.

20. **Answer** A
    Explanation Choices B and C are components of a quality management plan. The quality management plan is part of the project management plan. The best answer is choice A, the quality management plan.

21. **Answer** A

    Explanation This is an example of gold plating. You should provide ONLY what the customer asked for. The team does not know if their change will provide benefit to the customer. Focus efforts on fulfilling the requirements.

22. **Answer** C

    Explanation The plan described is the quality management plan. Since the quality management plan is part of the project management plan, changing the quality management plan will also change the project management plan.

23. **Answer** C

    Explanation Quality assurance, of which an audit is part, focuses on processes, procedures and standards. Though ISO may be thought of as a standard, audits are not required and so choice A cannot be best. The seller cannot generally control or review the customer's process, so choice B cannot be best. Choice D is more representative of a cost audit than a quality audit and so cannot be the best choice.

24. **Answer** C

    Explanation Choice A is not productive since it does not solve the problem. An analogous estimate (choice B) looks at past history of other projects. This would not be appropriate to determine how the current project is going. The quality management plan (choice D) does not provide results. Quality assurance (choice C) helps to determine if the project will satisfy the relevant quality standards.

25. **Answer** A

    Explanation Quality audits (choice A) are structured reviews of quality management activities performed to identify lessons learned that can be applied to this and other projects. Choices B, C and D are tools and techniques that apply to quality control rather than quality assurance.

26. **Answer** C

    Explanation This question is similar to others in this book, but not exactly the same. You may also see this occur on your exam. Carefully read the questions! Though quality problems (choice A) MAY lead to quality assurance efforts, they are not a MUST. Quality improvement (choice B) is a result of perform quality assurance, not an input. Rework (choice D) is an output of perform quality control. That leaves only quality control measurements (choice C) which are inputs to perform quality assurance.

27. **Answer** B

    Explanation As you increase quality, there will be associated benefits for the project. Some of these benefits are increased productivity, increased cost effectiveness, decreased cost risk and improved morale.

28. **Answer** B

    Explanation Performance of work packages (choice A) is done after project planning. Since the previous project manager did not finish planning, choice D should not be next. Risk identification (choice C) sounds like a good choice, however, identify quality standards (choice B) occurs before risk identification. The best answer is B.

29. **Answer** C
    Explanation Although quality planning usually occurs during project planning, it can occur during project execution when there is a change.

30. **Answer** B
    Explanation Gold plating a project wastes time and probably cost. It makes the project unsuccessful.

31. **Answer** C
    Explanation Measuring is part of the perform quality control process. Did you select choice B? The question asked what part of the quality process are you in, not what part of the project management process are you in.

32. **Answer** D
    Explanation "What?" you say. Yes, D is the best answer. Let's take a look, as this question could be said to have four right answers. Choice A might be a good idea, but has two problems. It may not be needed on the project, and it does not deal with the problem at hand, the policy that is slowing things down. Choice B is not the best choice as the project manager already has heard the opinion on many other occasions. It is already confirmed. Choice C is just being reactive. A good project manager will find the root cause and deal with that, even if it means attempting to improve the company's policies and processes. This is continuous improvement. Because there are several activities affected by the policy, it would serve the project better to get to the root cause of the problem and solve it.

33. **Answer** C
    Explanation A Pareto chart (choice A) might help the project manager decide which problems to focus on, but does little to find the root cause of problems. Though the project is troubled, there is nothing to use conflict resolution techniques with (choice B) because the real problem has not been identified. Trend analysis (choice D) does not deal with root causes, it deals more with predicting the future. The best choice is C.

34. **Answer** C
    Explanation All reports and diagrams are communications tools. This question asks you to pick the most appropriate quality tool to help communications. An Ishikawa diagram (choice C), also called a cause and effect diagram, is more appropriate than the Pareto chart (choice B) since you are trying to determine the causes. Once causes are known and you have data on occurrences, the data can be displayed in a Pareto chart.

Human Resource Management

Remember that I said to watch out for questions related to the executing and the monitoring and controlling process groups? Many of the questions in project execution deal with managing people and so are covered in this chapter.

PMI-isms for this chapter include:
- You are required to understand that people must be compensated for their work. (I am serious, this question has appeared on the exam.)
- A project manager creates a reward system during planning.
- You should spend time documenting who should do what.
- Since most projects are managed in a matrix environment, such seemingly easy topics as motivational theories and powers of the project manager become quite serious on the exam.

Human resources can be divided into administrative and behavioral management topics. Most of the answers to human resource questions should come from your everyday knowledge and work experience. But then again, many of us do not manage projects as well as we could and may have missed learning some of these topics.

Rita's Process Chart—Human Resource Management
Where are we in the project management process?

Initiating	Planning	Executing	Monitoring & Controlling	Closing
Select project manager	**Determine how you will do planning—part of management plans**	**Acquire final team**	Measure against the performance measurement baselines	Develop closure procedures
Determine company culture and existing systems	Create project scope statement	Execute the PM plan	**Measure according to the management plans**	Complete contract closure
Collect processes, procedures and historical information	Determine team	Work to produce product scope	**Determine variances and if they warrant corrective action or a change**	Confirm work is done to requirements
Divide large projects into phases	Create WBS and WBS dictionary	Recommend changes and corrective actions	Scope verification	Gain formal acceptance of the product
Identify stakeholders	Create activity list	Send and receive information	Configuration management	Final performance reporting
Document business need	Create network diagram	Implement approved changes, defect repair, preventive and corrective actions	**Recommend changes**, defect repair, **preventive and corrective actions**	Index and archive records
Determine project objectives	Estimate resource requirements	Continuous improvement	Integrated change control	Update lessons learned knowledge base
Document assumptions and constraints	Estimate time and cost	Follow processes	Approve changes, defect repair, preventive and corrective actions	Hand off completed product
Develop project charter	Determine critical path	**Team building**	Risk audits	Release resources
Develop preliminary project scope statement	Develop schedule	**Give recognition and rewards**	Manage reserves	
	Develop budget	Hold progress meetings	**Use issue logs**	
	Determine quality standards, processes and metrics	Use work authorization system	**Facilitate conflict resolution**	
	Determine roles and responsibilities	Request seller responses	**Measure team member performance**	
	Determine communications requirements	Select sellers	Report on performance	
	Risk identification, qualitative and quantitative risk analysis and response planning		Create forecasts	
	Iterations—go back		Administer contracts	
	Determine what to purchase			
	Prepare procurement documents			
	Finalize the "how to execute and control" aspects of all management plans			
	Create process improvement plan			
	Develop final PM plan and performance measurement baselines			
	Gain formal approval for plan			
	Hold kickoff meeting			

The Human Resource Management Process

The Human Resource Management Process	Done During
Human resource planning	Planning process group
Acquire project team	Executing process group
Develop project team	Executing process group
Manage project team	Monitoring and controlling process group

Roles and Responsibilities (page 207) A project manager must clearly show the roles and responsibilities of management, team members and other stakeholders, and may use a responsibility assignment matrix to do so. Roles and responsibilities are discussed throughout this book. There is an effort in this chapter to summarize all the roles from previous chapters because I have seen some people fail the exam solely because they did not know what a project manager was, at least not the kind of project manager the *PMBOK® Guide* defines. People also have problems differentiating between what the team, project manager and management should be doing.

Exercise 1 Test yourself! Describe the role of the project sponsor/initiator.

| |
| |
| |
| |
| |
| |
| |
| |
| |
| |
| |

Answer 1
The Role of the Project Sponsor/Initiator A basic definition of a sponsor is one who provides the financial resources for the project, but the exam will attribute more duties than just providing the financial resources to the sponsor. If the project is being done for an outside customer (you are the seller) the customer may fulfill the role of the sponsor as well as customer, and some of these functions would be taken over by senior management in the performing organization. (Management is anyone senior to the project manager in the organization(s).)

Think about your management as you read this. Do they know what their role is? Do you? How can you help them to better understand their role? Without having the sponsor or someone in management performing the following functions, the project will suffer, wasting time and resources. Management must serve as a protector of the project.

Read over the following list carefully to understand the role and characteristics of the sponsor and/or senior management in an organization.

Since the list is so long and since most project managers have large gaps in their knowledge here, I have organized this section by process groups.
- **During or prior to project initiating**
  - Has requirements that must be met
  - Is a project stakeholder
  - Provide funding
  - Provide statement of work
  - Provide information for preliminary project scope statement

- May dictate milestones, key events or project end date (along with customer)
- Issue the project charter
- Give the project manager authority as outlined in the project charter
- Help organize work into appropriate projects
- Set priorities between projects
- Determine the priorities between the "triple constraint" components
- Encourage the finalization of requirements and scope by the stakeholders
- **During project planning**
  - Provide the project team with time to plan
  - May review the WBS
  - Supply lists of risks
  - Determine the reports needed by management to oversee the project
  - Provide expert judgment
  - Help evaluate tradeoffs during crashing, fast tracking and re-estimating
  - Approve the final project management plan
- **During project executing and project monitoring and controlling**
  - Approve changes to the project charter
  - Protect the project from outside influences and changes
  - Enforce quality policies
  - Provide expert judgment
  - Help evaluate tradeoffs during crashing, fast tracking and re-estimating
  - Resolve conflicts that extend beyond the project manager's control
  - Approve or reject changes or authorize someone representing them to do so (change control board)
  - May direct that a quality assurance review be performed
  - Clarify scope questions
- **During project closing**
  - Provide formal acceptance of the deliverables (if he is the customer)
  - Support the collection of historical records from past projects

Exercise 2 Test yourself! Describe the role of the team.

Answer 2
The Role of the Team The team is a group of people who will complete work on the project. The team members can change throughout the project as people are added and removed from the project. Team members may have some project management responsibilities in addition to responsibilities for implementing the work.

See the role of the project manager.

Generally it is the team's role to help plan what needs to be done (WBS) and to create time estimates for their work packages or activities. During the project executing and monitoring and controlling process groups, the team members simply complete work packages or activities and help look for deviations from the project management plan. More specifically, the team may help:

- Identify and involve stakeholders
- Execute the project management plan to accomplish work defined in the project scope statement
- Attend project team meetings
- Process improvement
- Comply with quality and communications plans
- Enforce ground rules

Depending on the size and complexity of the project, the team role might also include helping the project manager do the following:

- Define the product of the project
- Identify and analyze constraints and assumptions
- Define requirements
- Determine the definition of quality on the project and how it will be met
- Create the work breakdown structure
- Decompose work packages they are responsible for into schedule activities
- Identify dependencies and create the network diagram
- Provide time and cost estimates
- Identify risks
- Perform qualitative and quantitative risk analysis and risk response planning
- Determine time and cost reserves for the project
- Produce project performance reports
- Measure project performance
- Determine the need for corrective action
- Close out phases of the project
- Select appropriate processes

Exercise 3 Test yourself! Describe the role of all the stakeholders combined.

| |
| |
| |
| |
| |

Answer 3
The Role of the Stakeholders As described in the Framework chapter, a stakeholder is anyone who can positively or negatively influence the project. The role of stakeholders and how they should be managed runs throughout the exam. As described in the Professional and Social Responsibility chapter, promoting interaction among stakeholders is one of the worst scoring areas of professional and social responsibility. Therefore, I suggest that you refer back to this section when reading the Professional and Social Responsibility chapter.

Stakeholders should be involved in planning the project and managing it more extensively than you might be doing on your projects. For example, stakeholders:

- May be involved in the creation of the project charter and the preliminary and project scope statements
- Are involved in:
  - Project management plan development
  - Approving project changes and being on the change control board
  - Scope verification
  - Identifying constraints
  - Risk management
- Become risk response owners

Exercise 4 Test yourself! Describe the role of the functional manager.

Answer 4

The Role of the Functional Manager
The individual who manages and "owns" the resources in a specific department such as IT, engineering, public relations, or marketing and generally directs the technical work of individuals from the functional area working on the project.

The amount of involvement of the functional manager depends on the form of organizational structure. In a matrix organization, the responsibility to direct the work of individuals is shared with the project manager. In a projectized organization, the project manager does all of the directing. The project manager does little directing in a functional organization. To avoid conflict, the project manager and functional manager must coordinate their respective needs regarding the use of resources to complete project work. It is generally the responsibility of the project manager to manage this relationship.

The specific activities performed by the functional manager vary greatly based on the type of organizational structure as well as the type of project. They MAY include:

- Assign specific individuals to the team and negotiate with the project manager regarding resources
- Let the project manager know of other projects that may impact the project
- Participate in the initial planning until work packages or activities are assigned
- Approve the final project management plan during project management plan development
- Approve the final schedule during schedule development
- Recommend corrective actions

- Assist with problems related to team member performance
- Improve staff utilization

Exercise 5 Test yourself! Describe the role of the project manager.

| |
| |

Answer 5
The Role of the Project Manager The project manager is responsible for managing the project to meet project objectives.

Some project management activities could be completed by team members. Whenever this is the case, the *PMBOK® Guide* refers to these people as the project management team. In order to assume this role, team members must have project management training. To avoid confusion, this book refers only to project manager or team.

People have failed the exam due to a lack of understanding of what is the project manager's role! Ask yourself whether you are able to do the things listed throughout this book. Do you have the knowledge, ability and authority? Do you really plan and control your projects? Are you the one person really in charge of the project?

In today's project environment, most people managing projects do not realize they are lacking knowledge of what good project management involves. Many companies also do not understand what project management is and why it is so important. Many people with the title of project manager are not really project managers at all, but some form of project coordinator (see the Framework chapter). It is important that you not only understand the project manager's role but also all the other roles on projects!

The project manager's role is described throughout this book. The project manager's level of authority can vary depending on the form of organization. On this exam, such authority generally means the project manager:
- Is assigned to the project no later than project initiating
- Is in charge of the project, but not necessarily the resources
- Does not have to be a technical expert
- Leads and directs the project planning efforts
- Must realize that an unrealistic schedule is his fault and know how to handle those situations
- Understands and enforces professional and social responsibility
- Determines and delivers required levels of quality

- Assists the team and other stakeholders during project executing
- Creates a change control system
- Maintains control over the project by measuring performance, determining if corrective action is needed, recommending corrective actions, preventive actions and defect repair
- Must have the authority and accountability necessary to accomplish the project management work
- Must say "no" when necessary
- Is the only one who can integrate the project components into a cohesive whole that meets the customer's needs
- Spends more time being proactive than in dealing with problems (reacting)
- Is accountable for project failure
- Performs or delegates most of the activities outlined in this book

Exercise Test yourself! This exercise is designed to cut down to the essence of the situational questions on the exam dealing with roles and responsibilities and to help you discover any incorrect procedures you may be following. You will probably disagree with a few of my answers, either because you read something into the question other than what was intended (a bad habit you should discover before you take the exam), or you have an error in your project management knowledge.

Considering the previous comments, write the initials of the key person responsible to solve each of the problems in the following chart. Since much of the confusion of roles is between team members (T), project manager (PM), Sponsor (SP), functional manager (FM), this exercise is limited to these people. HINT: Since most projects are managed in matrix forms of organizations, keep matrix organizations in mind when considering these situations.

Situation	Key Person
Two project team members are having a disagreement.	
There is a change to the overall project deliverable.	
A functional manager is trying to pull a team member off the project to do other work.	
The project manager does not have the authority to get things done.	
There are not enough resources to complete the project.	
The team is unsure of what needs to happen when.	
An activity needs more time and will cause the project to be delayed.	
An activity needs more time without causing the project to be delayed.	
A team member is not performing.	
The team is not sure who is in charge of the project.	
There is talk that the project may no longer be needed.	
Sponsor provides an unrealistic schedule objective.	
The team is in conflict over priorities between activities.	
The project is behind schedule.	
A team member determines that another method is needed to complete an activity.	
The project is running out of funds.	
Additional work is added to the project that will add cost and was not identified during the risk management process.	

© 2005 Rita Mulcahy, PMP • Phone: (952) 846-4484 • E-mail: info@rmcproject.com • Web: www.rmcproject.com

Answer

Situation	Key Person
Two project team members are having a disagreement. *The people involved in the conflict must solve it themselves.*	T
There is a change to the overall project deliverable. *This is a change to the project charter. Only the sponsor can approve changes to the project charter.*	SP
A functional manager is trying to pull a team member off the project to do other work. *The project manager must give team members enough information (e.g., bar chart, network diagram, project management plan, risks) so that they can manage their own workloads. Because the word "trying" is used, we know that this situation is occurring at the present time. If the question had used the words "has pulled," the answer would be project manager. Read situational questions carefully.*	T
The project manager does not have the authority to get things done. *It is the sponsor's role to give the project manager authority in the form of a project charter.*	SP
There are not enough resources to complete the project. *Sponsor and functional manager control resources.*	SP/FM
The team is unsure of what needs to happen when. *It is the project manager's role to take the individual estimates and combine them into the project schedule.*	PM
An activity needs more time and will cause the project to be delayed. *Notice the word "will." This means the evaluation by the team is completed and there is no available reserve since the project completion date is most likely included in the project charter. Any such changes are changes to the project charter and require sponsor involvement.*	SP
An activity needs more time without causing the project to be delayed. *Think about integrated change control here. It is the project manager's role to look for impacts to components of the "triple constraint."*	PM
A team member is not performing. *Functional management controls resources.*	FM
The team is not sure who is in charge of the project. *The sponsor designates the project manager in the project charter.*	SP
There is talk that the project may no longer be needed. *It is the sponsor's role to protect the project from changes, including such a large change.*	SP
Sponsor provides an unrealistic schedule objective. *Although it is often the sponsor's fault that this occurs, only they can make a change to the project charter (including schedule objectives). The project manager must provide evidence that the schedule is unrealistic.*	SP
The team is in conflict over priorities between activities. *It is the project manager's role to settle any such conflicts between activities and to provide a network diagram and critical path. It is the sponsor's role to set priorities between projects.*	PM
The project is behind schedule. *Only the project manager can control the overall project schedule.*	PM

Situation	Key Person
A team member determines that another method is needed to complete an activity. *The team member has control over his activities as long as he meets the time, quality, cost and scope objectives set up with the project manager. The team member must keep the project manager informed of these changes so the project manager can integrate them into the rest of the project and look for any impacts.*	T
The project is running out of funds. *It is the sponsor's role to provide funding for the project.*	SP
Additional work is added to the project that will add cost and was not identified during the risk management process. *The fact that the change was not identified in the risk management process and is additional work means it was not included in the original project budget (or the budget reserve). Therefore, the sponsor must be involved in providing additional funds.*	SP

If you got many of the answers wrong, you should reread the roles and responsibilities topic and the exact wording of the situations presented here. With such a brief description, you could easily have thought the question meant something different than I intended. This is planned to give you more experience interpreting questions on the exam. The exercise is meant to make you think. You may also have preferred the word "decide" or the words "make the final decision" in place of "solve" in some of these questions. Think!

Human Resource Responsibilities for Project Managers In the
Professional and Social Responsibility chapter, I talk about the proper way to treat team members. I suggest that you connect that section and this in your mind. That chapter is high-level and this one gets into more detail.

TRICKS OF THE TRADE The trick to getting questions right regarding this topic is to realize that you as a project manager have responsibilities to team members. Some of these are ethical ones described in the Professional and Social Responsibility chapter, but some are administrative. The best way to approach the administrative ones is to think of your team as if they were your own direct reporting employees. Project managers have some responsibilities similar to those of a manager or "owner" of the resources.

The following is a list of the responsibilities project managers most often do not know about before they get ready for this exam. Read the list carefully for PMI-isms!
- Create a project team directory
- Negotiate with resource managers for the best available resources
- Create project job descriptions for team members and other stakeholders
- Understand the team members' needs for training related to their work on the project and make sure they get the training
- Create a formal plan covering such topics as how the team will be involved in the project and what roles they will perform—a staffing management plan
- Insert reports of team members' performance into their official company employment record
- Send out letters of commendation to team members and their bosses
- Make sure team members' needs are taken care of
- Create reward systems—described in the staffing management plan section

▬▬Human Resource Planning (page 202)

In my own studies, team members commonly complain about the lack of defined roles and responsibilities on a project. Making sure roles and responsibilities are clear is called human resource planning. Project work often includes more than just completing work packages. For example, it may include assisting with risk and quality activities. Team members need to know what work packages and activities they are assigned to, when they are expected to report, what meetings they will be required to attend and any other "work" they will be asked to do on the project. This process includes all the following:

Enterprise Environmental Factors (page 203)

Before the project manager can complete human resource planning, he will need to understand what enterprise environmental factors can come into play. Remember that this term means "company culture and existing systems that the project will have to deal with or can make use of." In this instance, the company culture relates to such issues as: What organizations will be involved in the project? Are there hidden agendas? Is there anyone who does not want the project? For most experienced project managers, this is common sense. They are already experienced in this area, even if they did not call it analyzing enterprise environmental factors.

Organizational Process Assets (page 204)

Before the project manager can complete human resource planning, he should also consider organizational process assets or "processes, procedures and historical information." Wouldn't it be great to have a template that describes the common responsibilities on projects like yours so that you do not forget to assign those responsibilities? How about having lessons learned from past projects?

Project Organizational Charts and Position Descriptions (page 205, 206 with illustrations)

All roles and responsibilities on the project must be clearly assigned and closely linked to the project scope statement. Do you do so in your real-world projects? Does everyone know what activities they are assigned to and what project management work such as meeting attendance and other actions the project manager expects of them? If not, you might want to carefully think this through, as the lack of clear roles and responsibilities is a major complaint of team members. Project organizational charts are extremely valuable in communicating assigned responsibilities. These are PMI-isms. You can expect some simple questions as listed below. For the exam, you should understand what is shown on each chart. For example:

> *A responsibility assignment matrix does not show _____.*
> **Answer** *When people will do their jobs (time)*

Responsibility Assignment Matrix (page 206)

This chart cross-references team members with the activities or work packages they are to accomplish. Here is an example:

Activity	Team Member			
	Nicole	Morgan	Riki	Alexis
A	P		S	
B		S		P

KEY: P = Primary responsibility, S = Secondary responsibility

Organizational Breakdown Structure

Think of this as a standard company organizational chart that looks like a WBS, but only includes the company department heads and company structure.

Resource Breakdown Structure Also looks like a typical organizational chart, but this one is organized by types of resources.

Position Descriptions Usually in text format, imagine a common job description. This one is created only for project work.

Staffing Management Plan (page 208) This is a document that describes when and how team members will be added to and released from the project and how you plan to develop team members. The staffing management plan is included as part of the project management plan. Many project managers have not heard of this or created one before they get ready to take the exam, so read the following carefully.

A staffing management plan has the following components:
- How staff will be acquired
- Timetable for adding staff using a resource histogram
- When and how resources will be released from the project
- The training needs of the resources
- Recognition and rewards systems
- How you will comply with any laws, human resource policies, etc.
- How resources will be protected from safety hazards

The exam does not often ask questions as simple as, "What is included in…?" Rather, the questions jump right into more sophisticated issues to test if you really understand and use an item in the real world. This area might cause you trouble on the exam if you have never created a staffing management plan.

Resource Histogram (page 208) Is a graph that shows the number of resources used per time period and is displayed in a bar chart format. This chart shows where there is a spike in the need for resources. With such information, the project manager can arrange for the resources or change the project to minimize the peaks and valleys of resource usage (level the resources).

Recognition and Reward Systems Though included in the staffing management plan described above, this has proven to be such an alien concept for most project managers that I have separated it out to give it more importance. Read carefully!

A project manager must be able to motivate the team, especially when they are working on a project in a matrix organization. Have you ever wondered, "How do I get improved performance from people who do not report directly to me in the organization?" The more you have this problem, the less effective you are as a project manager. This is not to say that great project managers do not have issues in motivating people; they simply have the tools already in their knowledge base to prevent and to deal with problems. One of the best ways to gain cooperation is to create recognition and rewards systems. Other ways are described later in this chapter.

To create a reward system, ask yourself how you will motivate and reward not the team, but each team member individually (because of course you have already identified each one by name during planning). This involves asking and knowing what your team members and stakeholders want to get out of the project, on a professional and personal level. They might respond with such things as, "I want to learn more about XYZ," "I want to decrease the time I am allocated to this project," "I want to make sure I leave work on time on Tuesday nights because I have a family obligation," "I want to be assigned a certain piece of the project work." Such questions from the project manager are required, not optional.

The project manager takes his knowledge of the needs of the stakeholders and then creates a reward system. Such a system might include the following actions:

- Say "thank you" more often
- Award prizes such as Team Member of the Month recognition or cash prizes for performance
- Recommend team members for raises or choice work assignments, even though such actions by the project manager may not be officially part of the team member's performance review
- Send notes to their managers about great performance
- Plan milestone parties or other celebrations
- Acquire training paid for from the project budget for team members
- Adjust the project to assign people to requested activities or to remove them from disliked activities
- Work with the boss to have a team member removed from the project if they request it, and it is possible
- Assign a team member to a non-critical path activity so that he can gain more knowledge in that area

The list can go on and on, but ask yourself, do you do any of these things? Do you do them systematically? Are the above components planned in advance? They should be a part of the reward system you create. Read other sections of this chapter carefully to make sure you fully understand how to get people to perform on the project. Do not get questions wrong needlessly in this area.

Human resource planning will be included on your exam score sheet as part of Identify Project Team and Define Roles and Responsibilities.

Acquire Project Team (page 209) You have been working hard and are

now half asleep. WAKE UP! This can be confusing. Acquire project team occurs during the executing process group. "What?" you might say, "That does not make sense!" We know that the team is required to plan the project, and the team is acquired in early planning. The difference here is that the *PMBOK® Guide* is referring to large projects, where the actual people who will be doing some of the work may not be selected until shortly before the work is to begin. The final team might come from contractors or sellers, or people who will work on the project years into the future and may not even be employed by the company until needed.

 You should read the phrase "acquire project team" as "acquire final project team."

Be very careful. You are looking at an example of one of the reasons people fail the exam. They are not really managing projects, just short activities, or they only work on small projects. Get your mind around a project that would need to operate this way and read this book with a large project in mind. It will make more sense.

What about your real-world projects? Are you forced to plan the project without a final project team? Do you give the final team members a chance to have input into the project management plan before they start their work? Of course you do, because you are a great project manager and because you realize that people will not and cannot perform as well when told what to do. People want and should have input to what, for how long and when the work can be done.

Acquire the project team does not end on a project. Rarely can one say, "I have all the resources determined and they will not change." The results or outputs of acquiring the project team include project staff or work assignments, understanding resource availability, and changes to the staffing management plan resulting from acquiring additional staff.

Acquiring the project team involves the following actions:
- Know which resources are pre-assigned
- Negotiate for the best possible resources
- Hire new employees
- Hire resources through the contracting process from outside the performing organization—outsource
- Understand the possibilities and problems with using virtual teams—teams made up of people who never or rarely meet.

Enterprise Environmental Factors Enterprise environmental factors related to acquire project team include who is available, do they work well together, do they want to work on the project and how much do they cost. Get familiar with this term and its various components, as it is an input to many processes.

Organizational Process Assets The relevant inputs to acquire project team include policies for using staff on projects and hiring procedures. Get familiar with this term and its various components, as it is an input to many processes.

Negotiation (page 211) You will see negotiation frequently referenced on the exam related to gaining resources from within your organization and in contract situations. To negotiate for resources from within the organization, the project manager should understand the following:
- Know the needs of your project and its priority within the organization.
- Be able to express what is in it for the resource manager to assist you.
- Understand that the resource manager has his own work to do and that he may not gain benefits from supporting your project.
- Do not ask for the best resources if you do not need them.
- Be able to prove, by using the tools of project management such as the network diagram and project schedule, why you need better resources if you need them.
- Use the negotiation as an opportunity to discover from the resource manager what she will need from you in order to manage her own resources.
- Build a relationship so that you can call on the resource manager's expertise later in the project if necessary.
- Work with the resource manager to deal with the situation.

Notice that the discussion above goes way beyond traditional negotiation strategy, and includes elements of professional responsibility. Professional and Social Responsibility is the last chapter in this book, but the topic is discussed throughout.

Halo Effect The tendency to rate high or low on all factors due to the impression of a high or low rating on some specific factor. This can mean, "You are a great programmer. Therefore, we will make you a project manager and also expect you to be great." Such actions have a negative impact on the project and the performing organization, yet seem to be common. For the exam, understand that these types of actions should be avoided.

Acquire project team will be included on your exam score sheet as part of Implement the Procurement of Project Resources.

▬▬**Develop Project Team** (page 212) Developing the project team is done as part of executing the project. The results of developing the project team are decreased turnover, improved individual skills and improved teamwork.

Exercise What do you think needs to be done to develop a project team?

| |
| |
| |
| |
| |

Answer
- Hold team building activities from project initiating through project closing
- Gain training for team members where needed
- Establish ground rules for team member behavior
- Create and give recognitions and rewards
- Place team members in the same location; co-location
- Assess team member performance

Team Building Team building is forming the project team into a cohesive group working for the best interest of the project, in order to enhance project performance. Questions related to team building are very easy and most people can answer them based on their own experience. Make sure you know:
- It is the job of the project manager to guide, manage and improve the interaction of team members.
- The project manager should improve the trust and cohesiveness among the team.
- Project managers should incorporate team building activities into all project activities.
- Team building requires a concerted effort and continued attention throughout the life of the project.
- The WBS creation is a team building tool.
- Team building should start early in the life of the project.

Let's go back to the concept of trust. Is there trust on your project? Does the team feel that you are working in the best interest of the project, the company and them, or do they feel like you are working in your own best interest? (See also discussions of working with the team in the Professional and Social Responsibility chapter.) Trust is gained from the minute you meet each team member for the first time. If the team does not trust you, you cannot easily be successful; the team will not take your direction and follow your instructions, and the project will suffer. Most project managers never think of trust. I have often had people come to me with project problems and are surprised when I ask them if the team trusts them. "Why?" they ask. Imagine you work in a matrix organization. How do you get people to cooperate if you do not have the ability to give them a raise or a promotion? Trust, as well as reward systems, are the answer.

Trust also has to do with your reputation. Do you know what your reputation is? Everyone you might meet does. Why not ask, so you can deal with any changes you need to make.

Team building activities can include:
- Milestone parties
- Holiday and birthday celebrations
- Outside of work trips
- Creating the WBS
- Planning the project by getting everyone involved in some way

Training Any training needed by the team members in order to perform on the project or to enhance their performance should be paid for by the project. The project manager should look for such opportunities not only to help team members, but also to decrease overall project cost and schedule by increasing project efficiencies.

Ground Rules (page 214) What about trying to do something about the negative impacts of bad behavior? What behavior is acceptable and what is not acceptable on your project? This is the role of ground rules. Some project managers have addressed such things as:
- How should a team member resolve a conflict with another team member?
- When should a team member notify the project manager that she is having difficulty with an activity?
- Is it allowable for people to interrupt each other in a meeting?
- What is an acceptable way to interrupt someone talking at a meeting?
- How will you prevent people from taking over a meeting inappropriately or talking too much?
- Is it allowable for people to join a meeting late? What are the consequences?
- May people take other phone calls during the meeting?
- Who is allowed to talk to the vice president?
- Who is authorized to give direction to contractors?

Setting ground rules is more important when the team is managed virtually.

Co-Location (or War Room) (page 214) Though it might not be politically correct to say, much of great project management cannot be done with virtual teams. In other words, teams that never meet face to face will have more conflict, decreased productivity and other impacts that affect the project schedule and cost. Great project managers make an attempt to get the team physically together at least once during planning as a team building effort. If the team is located in the same city, the project manager might try to arrange for the entire team to have offices together in one place or one room. This is called co-location and has the opposite effect of virtual teams. Co-location helps communication, decreases the impact of conflict (since all parties are right there) and improves project identity for the project team and for management in a matrix organization.

Give Out Recognition and Rewards Here performance is appraised and rewards and recognitions, planned in human resource planning, are given out.

TRICKS OF THE TRADE **Team Performance Assessment** Team performance assessment is done by the project manager to evaluate and enhance the effectiveness of the team as a whole. Think of team performance assessment as "team effectiveness." This may include an analysis of how much team members' skills have improved, how well the team is performing, interacting and dealing with conflict, and the turnover rate.

Manage Project Team (page 215) Managing the project team is different from developing the team.

In order to effectively manage a project team, the project manager should do the following:
- Observe
- Use an issue log
- Keep in touch
- Complete project performance appraisals
- Actively look for and help resolve conflicts that the team cannot resolve on their own

Manage project team is done during the monitoring and controlling process group and is thus focused on measuring and controlling the project to the project management plan. In this case, the measuring relates to team members' performance. Yes, measuring team members' performance. This may be something you never do in the real world. No one likes to be measured and no one likes to measure people, yet if the project manager shies away from this, the project will suffer and the impacts to the project of actions of one team member will not be known. If you find it hard to do such measurement, let me clarify something.

Is it ethical to reprimand or penalize someone for not performing when they were not given clear direction? What if they did not agree to that direction? How many times in the workplace have you gotten in trouble for not meeting a deadline someone else set and you never agreed to? In good project management, the project team helps to create the project management plan. As a result, they find measurement to be more acceptable. "I helped create this plan, so I do not mind being held to what I agreed to," a team member might say. Think about your real world. If you ever have difficulty gaining cooperation, it might be a lack of trust, poor reward system or even the fact that team and stakeholders were not involved in creating the plan.

Another reason to measure team members' performance is for the benefit of other team members. Think of the decreased trust, increased anger and other effects when one person is not doing what she agreed to and the others are.

The results or outputs of managing the project team include:
- Requested changes
- Recommended corrective actions—what staff to change, what rewards or reward system changes are needed, disciplinary actions needed to correct problems
- Recommended preventive actions to reduce the probability or impact of problems before they occur
- Input to team members' individual performance appraisals
- Lessons learned documentation
- Changes to the project management plan

Observation and Conversation The project manager watches what is going on and also specifically talks to people to understand how things are going. Note that this does not say, "looks at the status reports." Such reports only tell part of the story and are produced after the fact. Other, more proactive actions, such as this one, are needed to control a project.

Project Performance Appraisals Evaluation of the performance of employees by those that supervise them is a common business practice around the world. This evaluation should include the employees' work on projects. The project manager can adjust the project to handle changes in performance based on these appraisals.

A new and sophisticated way to complete performance appraisals is to include input of co-workers and subordinates as well as supervisors. This may result in a clearer picture of actual performance and is called a 360-degree review.

NOTE: This assumes that those supervisors separately evaluate performance on projects in addition to the day to day work of their employees. Unfortunately, this level of support may not be present in your organization. It also assumes that the team member is being supervised by someone other than the project manager (a matrix organization).

TRICKS OF THE TRADE There are two similar concepts in this chapter that can be confusing: team performance assessment and this topic, project performance appraisals. The project manager will collect information from team members' supervisors when project performance appraisals are completed. Team performance assessment is done by the project manager in order to evaluate and improve the effectiveness of the team.

Issue Log Many project managers keep a log of the issues to be resolved on the project, but did you realize this is a tool to manage the team and stakeholders? Such logs tell people that their needs will be considered, even if they are not considered at the time the issue arises. Smart project managers control issues so that they do not impact the project.

An issue log might look like the following:

Issue #	Issue	Date Added	Raised By	Person Assigned	Resolution Due Date	Status	Date Resolved	Resolution

Powers of the Project Manager This section should be titled, "How to get cooperation from team and stakeholders." Do you have a problem with this? Project managers almost always have difficulty getting people to cooperate and perform, especially if they are working in a matrix organization. Therefore, it is important for the project manager to understand what they can do to get people to perform. These are the "powers":

- **Formal (Legitimate)** Power based on your position. "Do the work because I have been put in charge!"
- **Reward** Giving rewards. "I understand that you want to participate in the acceptance testing of this project. Because of your performance, I will assign you as part of that team!"
- **Penalty (Coercive)** Being able to penalize team members. "If this does not get done on time, I will remove you from the group going to Hawaii for the customer meeting!"
- **Expert** Being the technical or project management expert. "I hear the project manager has been very successful on other projects. Let's give her a chance!"
- **Referent** Based on the project manager referring to the authority of someone in a higher position. "The vice president has put this project at the top of his list! We will do the work on this project first."

NOTE: The best forms of power are EXPERT and REWARD. Penalty is the worst choice. FORMAL, REWARD and PENALTY are powers derived from the project manager's position in the company. EXPERT power is earned on your own.

On the exam, expect questions that describe a situation and then ask you what to do. The options will include examples using various forms of power. To answer these questions correctly, notice if penalty is being used and if it should be in the situation.

Leadership Styles   Project management is heavily dependent on managing people. Therefore, the project manager must determine the most appropriate leadership style for the needs of the project and for whatever part of the project they are in. Some of the choices are:

- **Directing** Telling others what to do
- **Facilitating** Coordinating the input of others
- **Coaching** Instructing others
- **Supporting** Providing assistance along the way
- **Autocratic** Making decisions without input
- **Consultative** Inviting ideas from others
- **Consensus** Problem solving in a group with decision-making based on group agreement

Studies disagree on which styles should be used during the various parts of the project management process. However, there is a general consensus that a project manager needs to provide more direction at the beginning of the project (only he knows what must be done to plan the project). During project executing, the project manager needs to do more coaching, facilitating and supporting. Carefully read any such questions.

TRICKS OF THE TRADE. Watch out for consensus. Many project managers believe that all decisions need to be made with the project team. This is not the case. During project executing, a project manager should have enough information about the project to make many decisions on his own. The first or best choice when a problem or issue arises may not be to call a meeting of the team.

Conflict Management (page 217) Do you remember that most of the questions on the exam are situational? Many of those situations are conflicts. To pick the best choice from many "right" answers, one might need to understand the different conflict resolution techniques and which one is best.

Is conflict bad? Should we spend time preventing the root causes of conflict? Who should solve the conflict?

Try to answer the questions just posed. Get them right and you are likely to do well on this section. The answers are no, yes, and those that have the conflict. This may need to involve the project manager.

Although many of us think conflict is bad, it actually presents opportunities for improvement. This is another situation where the understanding of many project managers differs from accepted research. Make sure your basic thinking is on the new side and not the old.

Changing Views of Conflict	
Old	New
Conflict is dysfunctional and caused by personality differences or a failure of leadership.	Conflict is an inevitable consequence of organizational interactions.
Conflict is to be avoided.	Conflict can be beneficial.
Conflict is resolved by physical separation or the intervention of upper management.	Conflict is resolved through identifying the causes, and problem solving by the people involved and their immediate managers.

Conflict is unavoidable because of the:
- Nature of projects trying to address the needs and requirements of many stakeholders
- Limited power of the project manager
- Necessity of obtaining resources from functional managers

Conflict can be avoided through the following techniques:
- Informing the team of:
  - Exactly where the project is headed
  - Project constraints and objectives
  - The contents of the project charter
  - All key decisions
  - Changes
- Clearly assigning work without ambiguity or overlapping responsibilities
- Making work assignments interesting and challenging

Note what was just said: some conflict can be avoided. Do you do the things listed above? Did you ever realize that the project manager is professionally responsible to do such things? They are not optional, they are good project management.

Many project managers think that the main source of conflict on a project is personality differences. They may be surprised to learn that this is rarely the case. It only becomes personal if the root cause of the problem is not resolved. The following describes the seven sources of conflict in order of frequency. MEMORIZE the top four and remember that personality is last:

- Schedules
- Project priorities
- Resources
- Technical opinions
- Administrative procedures
- Cost
- Personality

Conflict is best resolved by those involved in the conflict. The project manager should generally try to resolve problems and conflict as long as he or she has authority over those in conflict or the issues in conflict. If not, the sponsor or functional managers may be called in to assist. There is one exception. In instances of professional and social responsibility (breaking laws, policies, ethics) the project manager must go over the head of the person in conflict.

TRICKS OF THE TRADE When you have questions on the exam relating to this topic, make sure you first think, "Who generally has authority over the situation described in this question?" Another good phrase to remember is, "What resolution of this problem would best serve the customer's interests?" Remember to look for confronting or problem solving choices as generally the best answers, and forcing as the worst, but realize that the answer depends on the situation described. There could be situations described where withdrawal is the best option.

The following are the main conflict resolution techniques you will need to know for the exam. Make sure you notice that some have more than one title and know both.

- **Confronting (Problem Solving)** First, did you notice that this has two names? Did you realize that both names mean the same thing? Confronting means solving the real problem so that the problem goes away. Confronting leads to a win-win situation.
- **Compromising** Finding solutions that bring some degree of satisfaction to both parties. This is a lose-lose situation since no party gets everything. Did you know that compromise is not the best choice, but rather second to confronting?
- **Withdrawal (Avoidance)** Retreating or postponing a decision on a problem. Dealing with problems is a PMI-ism, therefore withdrawal is not usually the BEST choice for resolving conflict.
- **Smoothing** Emphasizing agreement rather than differences of opinion.
- **Forcing** Pushing one viewpoint at the expense of another.

Exercise Read the description of a conflict resolution and try to determine which of the techniques is being used.

Description	Form of Conflict Resolution This Represents
"It seems that the real problem here is not a lack of communication, but a lack of knowledge of what needs to be done and when. Here is a copy of the project schedule. It should help you understand what you need to know."	
"Do it my way!"	
"Let's calm down and get the job done!"	
"Let us do a little of what both of you suggest."	
"Let's deal with this issue next week."	
"Mary and Steve, both of you want this project to cause as little distraction to your departments as possible. With that in mind, I am sure we can come to an agreement on the purchase of equipment and what is best for the project."	
"We have talked about new computers enough. I do not want to get the computers and that is it!"	
"Mary, you say that the project should include the purchase of new computers and Steve, you say that the project can use existing equipment. I suggest we perform the following test on the existing equipment to determine if it needs to be replaced."	
"Since we cannot decide on the purchase of new computers, we will have to wait until our meeting next month."	
"Mary, what if we get new computers for the design activity on the project and use the existing computers for the monitoring functions?"	

Answer

Description	Form of Conflict Resolution This Represents
"It seems that the real problem here is not a lack of communication, but a lack of knowledge of what needs to be done and when. Here is a copy of the project schedule. It should help you understand what you need to know."	Confronting
"Do it my way!"	Forcing
"Let's calm down and get the job done!"	Smoothing
"Let us do a little of what both of you suggest."	Compromising
"Let's deal with this issue next week."	Withdrawal
"Mary and Steve, both of you want this project to cause as little distraction to your departments as possible. With that in mind, I am sure we can come to an agreement on the purchase of equipment and what is best for the project."	Smoothing
"We have talked about new computers enough. I do not want to get the computers and that is it!"	Forcing
"Mary, you say that the project should include the purchase of new computers and Steve, you say that the project can use existing equipment. I suggest we perform the following test on the existing equipment to determine if it needs to be replaced."	Confronting
"Since we cannot decide on the purchase of new computers, we will have to wait until our meeting next month."	Withdrawal
"Mary, what if we get new computers for the design activity on the project and use the existing computers for the monitoring functions?"	Compromising

Problem Solving Even though a project manager spends a great deal of time and energy preventing problems, there are still problems that need to be resolved. You should expect more than 100 questions (yes, that was 100 questions) that require you to solve a cost, time, human resource or other problem.

TRICKS OF THE TRADE® You must have knowledge and understanding of the contents of this entire book to answer problem solving questions correctly. Here is another trick. When you get to one of these questions, ask yourself, "What is the real problem behind the situation presented?" This can be extremely important to passing the exam! Did you realize that many people solve the wrong problem in the real world and on the exam? How about this situation:

During the executing process group, a project manager discovers that the seller did not supply the report required by the contract for the last four weeks. What should he do? If you have *PM FASTrack®*, look up this question on the software by doing a search for question number 1145. Here I am only showing you the question, not the choices. What would you do? Did you know that many people choose to investigate why the report was not supplied, when the real problem is that the seller has breached the contract and must be notified, in writing, of the error?

See how hard it can be to find the "real" problem and solve it? If you get many questions wrong in practice exams in any section of this book or on *PM FASTrack*®, one of the things you should ask yourself is, "Am I trying to solve the real problem?"

Make sure you understand the process of solving problems as outlined below. This process may also be used with stakeholders to find a fair resolution to conflicting needs. See more about this in the Professional and Social Responsibility chapter.
- Define the cause of the problem, not just the symptoms of the problem
- Analyze the problem
- Identify solutions
- Implement a decision
- Review the decision and confirm that the decision solved the problem

Expectancy Theory Employees who believe their efforts will lead to effective performance and who expect to be rewarded for their accomplishments remain productive as rewards meet their expectations.

Arbitration The hearing and resolution of a dispute performed by a neutral party.

Perquisites (perks) The giving of special rewards to some employees, such as assigned parking spaces, corner offices and executive dining.

Fringe Benefits The "standard" benefits formally given to all employees, such as education benefits, insurance and profit sharing.

Motivation Theory Were you going to skim through this topic? Caught you! If most projects are operated in a matrix environment, then one of the few things a project manager can do to gain cooperation of team members is to understand how to motivate them. This section provides answers.

Why would this be on the exam? As you have read in this chapter, the best way to gain cooperation is to give rewards. How can we reward people if we do not understand what motivates them? Questions on the exam in this area do not always directly quote motivation theorists. The questions simply describe situations and ask you what to do. The answer might depend on understanding that the person in the situation is a theory X manager, or that the project manager was motivating people in the wrong way. Take this section seriously and look for practice questions that bear out what I just said. Once you understand these concepts, questions should be easier. Here are three theories you need to understand for the exam.

McGregor's Theory of X and Y McGregor believed that all workers fit into one of two groups, X and Y. The exam uses many different ways to describe each of these theories. It can be confusing to determine which answer is the correct or even what the choices are saying. For all of you with visual memory, I will provide you with a foolproof method to answer any question on these theories.

Theory X Based on the picture, take a guess as to what theory X is.

Managers who accept this theory believe that people need to be watched every minute. People are incapable, avoid responsibility and avoid work whenever possible.

Theory Y Based on the picture, take a guess as to what theory Y is.

Managers who accept this theory believe that people are willing to work without supervision, and want to achieve. People can direct their own efforts.

Maslow's Hierarchy of Needs Maslow's message is that people do not work for security or money. They work to contribute and to use their skills. Maslow calls this "self-actualization." He created a pyramid to show how people are motivated and said that one cannot ascend to the next level until the levels below are fulfilled.

Herzberg's Theory This theory deals with hygiene factors and motivating agents.

Hygiene Factors Poor hygiene factors may destroy motivation, but improving them, under most circumstances, will not improve motivation. Hygiene factors are not sufficient to motivate people. Examples of these are:

- Working conditions
- Salary
- Personal life
- Relationships at work

- Security
- Status

Motivating Agents What motivates people is the work itself, including such things as:
- Responsibility
- Self-actualization
- Professional growth
- Recognition

The lesson to project managers—motivating people is best done by rewarding them and letting them grow. Giving raises does not do it. Many project managers initially disagree with this statement until they have a chance to think about it. Besides, the project manager may not have any influence over pay raises if the team members do not report to the project manager in the organizational structure.

Practice Exam

Human Resource Management

1. All of the following are forms of power derived from the project manager's position EXCEPT?
   A. Formal
   B. Reward
   C. Penalty
   D. Expert

2. The highest point of Maslow's hierarchy of needs is:
   A. physiological satisfaction.
   B. attainment of survival.
   C. need for association.
   D. esteem.

3. The "halo effect" refers to the tendency to:
   A. promote from within.
   B. hire the best.
   C. move people into project management because they are good in their technical fields.
   D. move people into project management because they have had project management training.

4. An obstacle to team building in a matrix organization is that the:
   A. team organization is technically focused.
   B. team members are borrowed resources and can be hard to motivate.
   C. teams are too centralized.
   D. teams are too large and therefore very hard to handle.

5. All of the following are typical concerns of matrixed team members EXCEPT?
   A. wondering who will handle their evaluations.
   B. serving multiple bosses.
   C. developing commitment.
   D. computing fringe benefits when working on multiple projects.

6. Which of the following conflict resolution techniques will generate the MOST lasting solution?
   A. Forcing
   B. Smoothing
   C. Compromise
   D. Problem solving

7. Which type of organization is BEST for managing complex projects involving cross-disciplinary efforts?
   A. Projectized
   B. Functional
   C. Line
   D. Matrix

8. The MOST common causes of conflict on a project are schedules, project priorities, and:
   A. personalities.
   B. resources.
   C. cost.
   D. management.

9. What conflict resolution technique is a project manager using when he says, "I cannot deal with this issue now!"
   A. Problem solving
   B. Forcing
   C. Withdrawal
   D. Compromising

10. What does a resource histogram show that a responsibility assignment matrix does not?
    A. Time
    B. Activity
    C. Interrelationships
    D. The person in charge of each activity

11. You have just been assigned as project manager for a large telecommunications project. This one year project is about halfway done. The project team consists of five sellers and 20 of your company's employees. You want to understand who is responsible for doing what on the project. Where would you find such information?
    A. Responsibility assignment matrix
    B. Resource histogram
    C. Bar chart
    D. Project organization chart

12. During project planning in a matrix organization, the project manager determines that additional human resources are needed. From whom would he request these resources?
    A. Project manager
    B. Functional manager
    C. Team
    D. Project sponsor

13. A project manager must publish a project schedule. Activities, start/end times and resources are identified. What should the project manager do NEXT?
    A. Distribute the project schedule according to the communications management plan.
    B. Confirm the availability of the resources.
    C. Refine the project management plan to reflect more accurate costing information.
    D. Publish a bar chart illustrating the timeline.

14. During every project team meeting, the project manager asks each team member to describe the work he or she is doing, and the project manager assigns new activities to team members. The length of these meetings has increased because there are many different activities to assign. This could be happening for all the following reasons EXCEPT?
    A. Lack of a WBS
    B. Lack of a responsibility assignment matrix
    C. Lack of resource leveling
    D. Lack of team involvement in project planning

15. You are a project manager leading a cross-functional project team in a weak matrix environment. None of your project team members report to you functionally and you do not have the ability to directly reward their performance. The project is difficult, involving tight date constraints and challenging quality standards. Which of the following types of project management power will likely be the MOST effective in this circumstance?
    A. Referent
    B. Expert
    C. Penalty
    D. Formal

16. A team member is not performing well on the project because she is inexperienced in system development work. There is no one else available who is better qualified to do the work. What is the BEST solution for the project manager?
    A. Consult with the functional manager to determine project completion incentives for the team member.
    B. Obtain a new resource more skilled in development work.
    C. Arrange for the team member to get training.
    D. Allocate some of the project schedule reserve.

17. A project manager has just found out that a major subcontractor for her project is consistently late delivering work. The project team member responsible for this part of the project does not get along with the subcontractor. To resolve the problem, the project manager says, "You both will have to give up something to solve this problem." What conflict resolution method is she using?
    A. Confrontation
    B. Compromise
    C. Smoothing
    D. Communicating

18. A project has several teams. Team C has repeatedly missed deadlines in the past. This has caused team D to have to crash the critical path several times. As the team leader for team D, you receive word that the next deadline may also be missed. You should meet with the:
    A. manager of team D.
    B. project manager alone.
    C. project manager and management.
    D. project manager and the leader of team C.

19. The new project is exciting to both the project manager and the team. This is the project manager's first assignment as project manager. The team has the feeling that they will be able to complete work that has never been tried before. There are 29 people contributing to the product description and the team consists of nine highly experienced experts in their field.

    Part of the way through planning, three highly technical team members are disagreeing about the scope of two of the deliverables. One is pointing to the draft WBS and saying that two additional work packages should be added. Another is saying that a particular work package should not even be done. The third team member agrees with both of them. How should the project manager BEST deal with the conflict?

A. He should listen to the differences of opinion, determine the best choice, and implement that choice.

B. He should postpone further discussions, meet with each individual, and determine the best approach.

C. He should listen to the differences of opinions, encourage logical discussions, and facilitate an agreement.

D. He should help the team focus on agreeable aspects of their opinions and build unity by using relaxation techniques and common focus team building.

20. The project is just starting out and consists of people from 14 different departments. The project charter was signed by one person and contains over 30 major requirements that must be met on the project. The sponsor has informed the project manager that the SPI must be kept between 0.95 and 1.1. A few minutes of investigation resulted in the identification of 34 stakeholders, and the schedule objectives on the project are constrained. A project manager has just been hired. Which of the following types of project management power will BEST help the project manager gain the cooperation of others?

A. Formal

B. Referent

C. Penalty

D. Expert

21. A project manager is trying to settle a dispute between two team members. One says the systems should be integrated before testing, and the other maintains each system should be tested before integration. The project involves over 30 people, and 12 systems need to be integrated. The sponsor is demanding that integration happen on time. What is the BEST statement the project manager can make to resolve the conflict?

A. Do it my way.

B. Let's calm down and get the job done.

C. Let's deal with this again next week after we all calm down.

D. Let's do limited testing before implementation and finish testing after implementation.

22. A project is in the middle of the executing processes when a stakeholder suggests a major new change. This change will cause the third major overhaul of the project. At the same time, the project manager discovers that a major work package was not completed because a team member's boss moved him to another project that had a higher priority. Which of the following is the best person for the project manger to address these issues with?

A. Team

B. Senior management

C. Customer

D. Sponsor

23. Work on a project is ongoing when the project manager overhears two workers arguing over what a set of instructions mean. The project manager investigates and discovers that the instructions for the construction of the concrete footings currently being

poured were poorly translated between the different languages in use on the project. Which of the following is the BEST thing for the project manager to do FIRST?

A. Get the instructions translated by a more experienced party.
B. Look for quality impacts of the poor translation of the instructions for the footings.
C. Bring the issue to the attention of the team and ask them to look for other translation problems.
D. Inform the sponsor of the problem in the next project report.

24. Conflict resolution techniques that may be used on a project include confronting, smoothing, forcing and:

A. withdrawing.
B. directing.
C. organizing.
D. controlling.

25. The installation project has a CPI of 1.03 and an SPI of 1.0. There are 14 team members and each team member had input into the final project management plan. The customer has accepted the three deliverables completed so far without complaint and the responsibility assignment matrix has not changed since the project began. The project is being completed in a matrix environment and there are no contracts needed for the project.

Though the sponsor is happy with the status of the project, one of the team members is always complaining about how much time his project work is taking. Which of the following would be the BEST thing for the project manager to do?

A. Review the reward system for the project.
B. Try to improve schedule performance of the project.
C. Meet with the customer to try to extend the schedule.
D. Gain formal acceptance in writing from the customer.

26. The project has been challenging to manage. Everyone has been on edge to complete the project on time. Unfortunately, the tension has grown to the point where team meetings have become shouting matches and little work is accomplished during the meetings. One team member asks to be excused from future team meetings, as all the shouting upsets him. Meanwhile, the sponsor has asked to attend team meetings in order to better understand how the project is going and the issues involved in completing the project, and the customer has started discussions about adding scope to the project. In this situation, it would be best for the project manager to:

A. ask the sponsor if the information needed could be send in a report rather than have him attend the meeting.
B. inform the team member who asked to be excused from the meetings of the value of communication in such meetings.
C. create new ground rules for the meetings and introduce them to the team.
D. hold a team building exercise that involves all the team members.

27. Project performance appraisals are different from team performance assessments in that project performance appraisals focus on:

A. how an individual team member is performing on the project.
B. an evaluation of the project team's effectiveness.
C. a team building effort.
D. reducing the staff turnover rate.

28. A project manager had a complex problem to solve and made a decision about what needed to be done. A few months later, the problem resurfaced. What did the project manager most likely NOT do?
    A. Proper risk analysis
    B. Confirm that the decision solved the problem
    C. Have the project sponsor validate the decision
    D. Use an Ishikawa diagram

29. The project CPI is 1.02, the benefit cost ratio is 1.7 and the latest round of performance reviews identified few needed adjustments. The project team was co-located into a new building when the project started. Everyone commented on how excited they were to have all new facilities. The sponsor is providing adequate support for the project and few unidentified risks have occurred.

    In an attempt to improve performance, the project manager spends part of the project budget on new chairs for the team members and adds the term "senior" to each team member's job title.

    Which of the following is the MOST correct thing that can be said of this project or the project manager?
    A. The project manager has misunderstood Herzberg's theory.
    B. The project is slowly spending more money than it should. The project manager should begin to watch cost more carefully.
    C. The performance review should be handled better to find more adjustments.
    D. The project manager should use good judgment to determine which variances are important.

30. You just found out that a major subcontractor for your project consistently provides deliverables late. The subcontractor approaches you and asks you to continue accepting late deliverables in exchange for a decrease in project costs. This offer is an example of:
    A. confronting.
    B. compromise.
    C. smoothing.
    D. forcing.

Human Resource Management

Human Resources Management Answers

1. **Answer** D
   Explanation When someone is given the job of project manager, they will have formal, reward and penalty power. But just having the position does not make the project manager either a technical or project management expert.

2. **Answer** D
   Explanation This question is asking which of the FOLLOWING is the highest. Self-actualization is not listed, so the next best choice is esteem.

3. **Answer** C
   Explanation Just because a person is good in his technical field does not mean he will also be a good project manager.

4. **Answer** B
   Explanation Team members are harder to motivate if their loyalty is to their functional organization rather than to the project team.

5. **Answer** D
   Explanation In a matrix organization, each team member reports to the project manager and the functional manager. Team members may therefore be worried about choices A, B and C. Since the same fringe benefits are given to all employees no matter what work they do, choice D is the exception.

6. **Answer** D
   Explanation Problem solving normally takes more time, but it gets buy-in from everyone, generating a more lasting solution.

7. **Answer** D
   Explanation The key words here are cross-disciplinary. Cross-disciplinary means that the project covers more than one department or technical area of expertise. In such a case, a matrix organization is needed with representatives from each department or discipline.

8. **Answer** B
   Explanation Know the top four sources (schedule, project priorities, resources and technical opinions), so you can answer questions such as this one. Don't be fooled because "personalities" is on the list. It is last.

9. **Answer** C
   Explanation Delaying the issue is called withdrawal.

10. **Answer** A
    Explanation Time is shown on a schedule or bar chart. The responsibility assignment matrix maps specific resources against the work packages from the WBS. On a resource histogram, the usage of resources is shown individually or by groups over time.

11. **Answer** A
    Explanation The responsibility assignment matrix maps who will do the work. The resource histogram (choice B) shows the number of resources used in each time period.

In its pure form, a bar chart (choice C) shows only activity and calendar date. An organizational chart (choice D) shows who reports to whom.

12. **Answer** B
Explanation Did you forget that in a matrix organization the functional manager controls the resources?

13. **Answer** B
Explanation The project schedule remains preliminary until resource assignments are confirmed.

14. **Answer** C
Explanation Resource leveling refers to maintaining the same number of resources on the project for each time period. Leveling has nothing to do with assigning activities or managing meetings.

15. **Answer** B
Explanation Reward and expert are the best sources of power. Reward is not listed as a choice.

16. **Answer** C
Explanation The job of the project manager includes providing or obtaining project-specific training for team members. This kind of training is a direct cost of the project.

17. **Answer** B
Explanation The act of both parties giving something defines compromise.

18. **Answer** D
Explanation Those having the problem should resolve the problem. Having had to crash the critical path several times implies that team D has already dealt with these problems. In this case, the two team leaders need to meet. The extent of this situation requires the project manager's involvement as well.

19. **Answer** C
Explanation Do not get confused by the wordiness of the question. Ask yourself what is the best way to resolve any conflict and you can get the answer. Most of the situation is a distracter. Problem solving and compromising are the two most important conflict resolution techniques. Conflict management is a key general management skill.

20. **Answer** A
Explanation: Generally, the best forms of power are reward or expert. The project manager has not had time to become a recognized expert in the company (choice D) and reward is not included as a choice here. This leaves formal power (choice A) as the only logical answer.

21. **Answer** D
Explanation: Choice D is an example of compromising.

22. **Answer** D

    Explanation It is the sponsor's role to prevent unnecessary changes and to set priorities between projects. The situation described in this question implies that such work is not being done and the project manager must therefore go to the root of the problem; the sponsor.

23. **Answer** B

    Explanation Though all of these choices are correct things to do, the question asks what to do first. What is the most immediate problem? Isn't it most urgent to find out whether the concrete footings meet your project requirements? Choice A could be done, but it does not address the immediate concern. Choice C is excellent, and something many project managers might never think of doing. However, it does not address the immediate problem. Choice D is also not taking action to solve the problem. Are the concrete footings adequate? Only choice B will help you answer that.

24. **Answer** A

    Explanation There is always the option to simply postpone dealing with the issue until later. This is withdrawing.

25. **Answer** A

    Explanation Improving schedule performance (choice B) relates to getting the project completed sooner. Though it would seem to always be a good idea to improve schedule performance, this project's performance is fine. The schedule has been approved as it is. It would be better for the project manager to spend more time controlling the project to make sure it finishes according to plan than to improve schedule performance.

    If you chose C, ask yourself why. There is nothing wrong with the schedule performance of the project that would require an extension. Did you think that the best way to deal with the complaining stakeholder was to give him more time? How do you know the team member's activities are on the critical path?

    It is always important to gain formal acceptance from the customer, as it provides an opportunity for the team to check if everything is going well. It is always good idea to get such acceptance in writing. Choice D could be done, but there is a more important problem that takes precedence here. Read on.

    The only thing glaringly wrong in this situation is that the team member is complaining. If you read the situation completely, you will notice that the team member was involved and approved the project management plan, including his own involvement in the project. Since the responsibility assignment matrix has not changed, the team member has not even been assigned different duties since the project began. There must be something else causing the team member to complain. The project manager should investigate and find out what part of the reward system is ineffective.

26. **Answer** C

    Explanation Here is a situation where all four choices could be done. Choice A could be done, but does not solve the root cause of the problem described. Choice B merely dismisses the concerns of the team member and might cause anger. A team building exercise would take planning and so could not be done right away. Remember, the sponsor might be attending the next meeting and at least one team member might not attend because of past problems. The best thing to do would be to set up new ground rules for the team governing behavior (choice C) and then plan a team building exercise (choice D).

27. **Answer** A

    Explanation Questions like this can drive one crazy on the exam because it is easy to get confused. The best thing to do is to look at the two terms used here (project performance appraisals and team performance assessment) and review in your mind what each means BEFORE looking at the choices. Choices B, C and D list aspects of team performance assessments. Only choice A is correct. Project performance appraisals deal with how each team member is performing work, rather than how well the team is working together.

28. **Answer** B

    Explanation Notice the phrasing of this question, "most likely NOT do." Expect to see questions worded on the exam in ways that can cause you to misinterpret them. You will also see questions about things we forget to do in the real world. "Who has time," you might say, "to determine if each problem is really solved?" One could respond with, "Who has time not to do this? Who has time to deal with the same problem twice?" The final steps of problem solving include: implement a decision, review it and confirm that the decision solved the problem.

29. **Answer** A

    Explanation Choice B includes the concept of cost to trick you into selecting it if you are unsure of the real answer. There is no indication that the costs are trending in any particular direction. There is no reason to think that performance reviews should turn up more adjustments (choice C). The project manager should always use good judgment (choice D) and nothing in this question talks about judgment regarding variances, so this cannot be the best choice. In this situation, the project manager is making great working conditions better. According to Herzberg's theory, fixing bad working conditions will help you to motivate, but making good ones better will not improve motivation. You need to focus on the motivating agents and not the hygiene factors.

30. **Answer** B

    Explanation Both parties are giving up something. This is a compromise.

Communications Management

How much time do you spend planning communications? How many times have you deleted a voicemail without listening to the very end of the message? Are you flooded with e-mails? How many times have you not read all the way through an e-mail?

In almost every study, including my own, communications is the number one problem a project manager has on a project. You will read in this chapter that a project manager spends 90 percent of her time communicating. Shouldn't we then do something to plan, structure and control communications?

TRICKS OF THE TRADE Beginning project managers do nothing about communications and just issue status reports. Better project managers might create a communications management plan and report more than just status. Great project managers take the previous two actions, plus the following: ask stakeholders what they need communicated to them, identify what communications they need from stakeholders, and frequently revisit communications at team meetings to limit communications problems. To pass this exam, you need to be more like the great project manager.

Although it is not particularly difficult, make sure you take this chapter seriously and find your gaps regarding communications.

TRICKS OF THE TRADE Communications questions are frequently combined with other topics. For example, a WBS is a communications tool (see the Scope chapter) and risk response strategies should be communicated (see the Risk chapter).

Rita's Process Chart—Communications Management
Where are we in the project management process?

Initiating	Planning	Executing	Monitoring & Controlling	Closing
Select project manager	**Determine how you will do planning—part of management plans**	Acquire final team	Measure against the performance measurement baselines	Develop closure procedures
Determine company culture and existing systems	Create project scope statement	Execute the PM plan	**Measure according to the management plans**	Complete contract closure
Collect processes, procedures and historical information	Determine team	Work to produce product scope	**Determine variances and if they warrant corrective action or a change**	Confirm work is done to requirements
Divide large projects into phases	Create WBS and WBS dictionary	**Recommend changes and corrective actions**	Scope verification	Gain formal acceptance of the product
Identify stakeholders	Create activity list	**Send and receive information**	Configuration management	Final performance reporting
Document business need	Create network diagram	Implement approved changes, defect repair, preventive and corrective actions	**Recommend changes, defect repair, preventive and corrective actions**	Index and archive records
Determine project objectives	Estimate resource requirements	Continuous improvement	Integrated change control	Update lessons learned knowledge base
Document assumptions and constraints	Estimate time and cost	Follow processes	Approve changes, defect repair, preventive and corrective actions	Hand off completed product
Develop project charter	Determine critical path	Team building	Risk audits	Release resources
Develop preliminary project scope statement	Develop schedule	Give recognition and rewards	Manage reserves	
	Develop budget	**Hold progress meetings**	**Use issue logs**	
	Determine quality standards, processes and metrics	Use work authorization system	Facilitate conflict resolution	
	Determine roles and responsibilities	Request seller responses	Measure team member performance	
	Determine communications requirements	Select sellers	**Report on performance**	
	Risk identification, qualitative and quantitative risk analysis and response planning		**Create forecasts**	
	Iterations—go back		Administer contracts	
	Determine what to purchase			
	Prepare procurement documents			
	Finalize the "how to execute and control" aspects of all management plans			
	Create process improvement plan			
	Develop final PM plan and performance measurement baselines			
	Gain formal approval for plan			
	Hold kickoff meeting			

The Communications Management Process

The Communications Management Process	Done During
Communications planning	Planning process group
Information distribution	Executing process group
Performance reporting	Monitoring and controlling process group
Manage stakeholders	Monitoring and controlling process group

━━Communications Planning (page 225) Communications planning involves identifying the information and communications needs of the stakeholders. This includes determining what needs to be communicated, to whom, when, with what method and how frequently. This is a very proactive approach.

The *PMBOK® Guide* often suggests work be done in a more structured way than many project managers have previously thought to do. Communication is no exception. In order to do it well, one must understand the performing organization's environment (enterprise environmental factors) such as culture and standards. One must also take into account the performing organization's processes and procedures for conducting work and communications, historical records from previous projects, lessons learned and other stored information (organizational process assets).

Early in the project management process, all the stakeholders should have been identified and their requirements and expectations determined. The requirements should not just relate to how they want the product of the project to function, but should also include their communications requirements; what do stakeholders want communicated to them, when, in what form, how frequently? Notice that such communications might include more than the average status report. How about reporting the date of the next milestone party, minor successes or lessons learned?

Whom Do We Communicate With It is important to realize that communication is not one-sided. During the early part of project planning, the project team will have had a chance to interact with other stakeholders. Have any of the stakeholders identified a large number of potential risks for the project? Why not plan to meet with them periodically throughout the project to see if they have identified any more risks. Is there a team member who is nervous about completing her assigned activities? Why not plan to find and forward relevant magazine articles or other literature to help her? These are communications, and they need to be planned.

Exercise Test yourself! Who does information need to be distributed to?

| |
| |
| |
| |
| |
| |
| |
| |
| |
| |

Answer
- Internal to the project
- External to the project
- Sponsor

- Management
- Project manager
- Team
- Team members' managers
- Other project managers
- Other stakeholders

TRICKS OF THE TRADE. Make sure such planning includes communicating in all of the following directions.

Sponsor, Functional Managers
and Team Members

Other Project Managers ⇄ **The Project** ⇄ Other Projects

Other Stakeholders

Think about other projects for a moment. Could there be projects that interact with yours with whom you might want to occasionally review those interactions? You may share resources, similar types of work or priorities within the company.

 Communications Model When was the last time you took a communications class? For most people the answer would be never. Therefore, many of us make the mistake of not ensuring that messages are properly sent and received.

The communications model looks like a circle with three parts: the sender, the message and the receiver. Each message is encoded by the sender and decoded by the receiver based on the receiver's education, experience, language and culture.

TRICKS OF THE TRADE. **Effective Communication** The sender should encode a message carefully, determine the communications method used to send it, and confirm that the message is understood.
- **Nonverbal** About 55 percent of all communications are nonverbal (e.g., based on physical mannerisms).
- **Paralingual** Pitch and tone of voice also helps to convey a message.
- **Feedback** Saying things like, "Do you understand what I have explained?"

TRICKS OF THE TRADE. **Effective Listening** The receiver should decode the message carefully and confirm the message is understood. This includes watching the speaker to pick up physical gestures and facial expressions, thinking about what you want to say before responding, asking questions, repeating and providing feedback.
- **Feedback** Saying things like, "I am not sure I understand, can you repeat what you have said?"
- **Active Listening** The receiver confirms she is listening, confirms agreement or asks for clarification.
- **Paralingual**

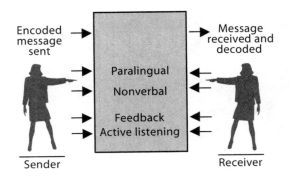

Encoded message sent → Paralingual Nonverbal Feedback Active listening → Message received and decoded

Sender — Receiver

Communications Technology (page 227, 235) Another aspect of communications planning is to determine what method should be used to communicate each item to be communicated. Communications can take place in many ways including face-to-face, by telephone, fax, e-mail or meetings (called communications technology). Communications planning involves asking questions such as:

- Would it be better to communicate the information in an e-mail or telephone call?
- Is this an issue that I need to go to see the person about?
- Should I send a letter through the mail in order for it to get real attention?

Communications Methods In order to have clear, concise communications, the project manager must handle communications in a structured manner by selecting the form of communication that is best for the situation. Communications occur internally and externally to the core project team and vertically and horizontally within the organization. A decision regarding whether the communication needs to be formal or informal, written or verbal, needs to be made for each instance of communication. Questions on communications methods should be easy if you understand the following chart:

Communications Method	When Used
Formal written	Complex problems, project management plans, project charter, communicating over long distances
Formal verbal	Presentations, speeches
Informal written	Memos, e-mail, notes
Informal verbal	Meetings, conversations

Exercise Test yourself! What is the best form of communication in the following situations?

Situation	Communications Method
Updating project management plans	
Presentations to management	
Trying to solve a complex problem	
Making notes regarding a telephone conversation	
Making changes to a contract	
Informing a team member of poor performance (first notice)	
Informing a team member of poor performance (second notice)	

Situation	Communications Method	
Scheduling a meeting		
Clarifying a work package		
Requesting additional resources		
Trying to discover the root cause of a problem		
Sending an e-mail to ask for clarification of an issue		
Holding a milestone party		
Conducting a bidder conference		

Answer Imagine these as situational questions. Exam questions may have more words, but they will boil down to straightforward situations like the ones described below.

Situation	Communications Method	
Updating project management plans	Formal written	
Presentations to management	Formal verbal	
Trying to solve a complex problem	Formal written	
Making notes regarding a telephone conversation	Informal written	
Making changes to a contract	Formal written	
Informing a team member of poor performance (first notice)	Informal verbal	
Informing a team member of poor performance (second notice)	Formal written	
Scheduling a meeting	Informal written	
Clarifying a work package	Formal written	
Requesting additional resources	Formal written	
Trying to discover the root cause of a problem	Informal verbal	
Sending an e-mail to ask for clarification of an issue	Informal written	
Holding a milestone party	Informal verbal	
Conducting a bidder conference	Formal verbal	

 Control of Communications The exam may also ask:
- Can the project manager control all communications? The answer is no! That would be impossible.
- Should the project manager try to control communications? Yes, otherwise changes, miscommunications, unclear directions and scope creep can occur.
- What percent of the project manager's time is spent communicating? About 90 percent.

Meetings The project manager may have many different types of meetings. Meetings are a problem in the real world because many project managers manage by doing everything in meetings and most meetings are not efficient.

Expect questions about the following rules for meetings (but then we already know these and follow them, don't we?)

- Set a time limit and keep to it.
- Schedule recurring meetings in advance.
- Meet with the team regularly, but not too often.
- Have a purpose for each meeting.
- Create an agenda with team input.
- Distribute the agenda beforehand.
- Stick to the agenda.
- Let people know their responsibilities in advance.
- Bring the right people together.
- Chair and lead the meeting with a set of rules.
- Assign deliverables and time limits for all work that results from meetings.
- Document and publish meeting minutes.

Communication Channels When you add one more person to the team, do communications grow linearly or exponentially? If you said exponentially, you understand why communications is a PMI-ism. The intent is for the project manager to realize that communications are complex and need to be managed. Unfortunately, there are some problems with these questions on the exam. It could be said that there are too many of them for the value of the topic to project management, and some of these questions could be poorly worded. Watch out. Expect up to four questions.

Channels can be calculated by the following formula: $[N(N-1)]/2$ where N equals the number of people. You should understand this formula. Oh, now another formula to know! You should have no problem knowing this without memorization. Just practice it. How about some tricks?

TRICKS OF THE TRADE Anytime you see a formula containing the letter "N," even if it looks slightly different from the formula above, that formula represents communication channels.

TRICKS OF THE TRADE If you have a question, "You have a team of four people, how many channels of communication are there?" simply draw the lines or channels of communication as shown below to get six channels of communication.

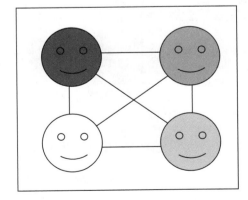

Using the formula, we would calculate 4 times 3 (which is n-1) to equal 12 and then divide by 2 to reach the answer, 6.

Now try it on your own. If you have four people on your project and you add one more, how many more communication channels do you have?

The answer is 10 of course, right? Wrong! The question asked how many more! Do you know how many people get tripped up by poorly reading questions? To use the trick, simply draw a new person and draw lines for the new person to all the other people to see there are four more channels of communication, as shown below.

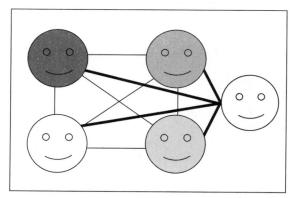

To calculate the answer, you would have to calculate the communication channels with a team of four and with a team of five and then subtract the difference. We already calculated it for four people to find six channels. The calculation for five team members is 5 times 4 equals 20, divided by 2 equals 10. 10 minus 6 = 4.

Communications Management Plan (Page 227) The output of communications planning is a communications management plan. This is so important and so valuable for all projects, even short ones!

A communications management plan documents how you will manage and control communications. Many people do not realize the extent of the information that must be distributed. Here is an exercise to help you create your own plan. It can include such categories as shown below:

What Needs to Be Communicated	Why	Between Whom	Best Method for Communicating	Respon-sibility	When and How Often

Because communications are so complex, a communications management plan should be in writing for most projects. It must address the needs of all the stakeholders. The communications management plan becomes part of the project management plan. If you have communications problems on your projects, you are not spending enough time in this area.

On some projects, a more detailed communication structure is required.

Exercise Test yourself! What information and documents need to be communicated on a project?

Answer There can be many answers to this question, depending on the nature of the project. Your answer should include:

- Project charter
- Project management plan
- Impacts of other projects
- How this project impacts other projects
- WBS
- When resources will be needed
- Meeting schedule
- Work assignments
- Status
- New risks uncovered
- Uncertainties
- Problems
- Successes
- Changes to project scope and product scope
- Updated project management plan or components of the project management plan
- Upcoming work
- Delays
- The date of the next milestone completion party
- Performance reports
- Lessons learned
- Issue logs
- Configuration management issues
- What types of e-mails will be sent to each stakeholder
- List of planned reviews of the project management plan and when updates are likely to be issued
- Contact information for all stakeholders
- Method of updating the communications management plan

Information Distribution (page 228) Information distribution involves implementing the communications management plan. In addition, since not everything can be planned, information distribution also involves creating reports or providing information that was not planned. Most of the concepts already described in communications planning are done during this process and require no further comment, except for lessons learned.

Lessons Learned (Postmortem) (throughout) If you read the early part of this book you might remember my describing that lessons learned (as part of organizational process assets) is a PMI-ism.

Exercise Test yourself! Lessons learned contain what type of information?

Answer The lessons learned document includes what was done right, wrong and what would be done differently if the project could be redone. Another way of saying this is to say that the lessons learned includes causes of the issues the project has faced and the reasoning behind the corrective actions implemented. To be as valuable as possible, lessons learned should cover three areas:

- Technical aspects of the project
- Project management (How did we do with WBS creation, risk, etc.?)
- Management (How did I do with communications and leadership as a project manager?)

TRICKS OF THE TRADE Many project managers do not understand the role of lessons learned on projects. The following graphic should help explain.

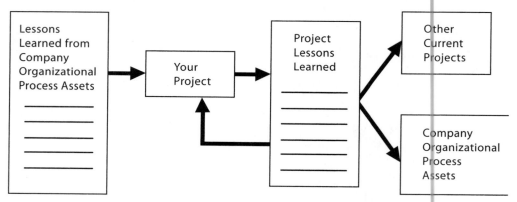

Lessons learned from similar projects are collected and reviewed before starting work on your project. Why make the same mistakes or face the same problems others have faced? Why not benefit from others' experience? Imagine you could reach into a filing cabinet and see such data for all the projects your company has worked on. How valuable would that be?

Once your project is underway, your project is required to add lessons learned to the company database (the organizational process assets). The lessons learned may be created throughout the project and then finalized during project closing or project phase closing.

Lessons learned are so valuable that a project cannot be considered complete unless the lessons learned are completed. Continuous improvement of the project management process cannot occur without lessons learned.

One should not wait until the project is over to share lessons learned with other projects. Lessons learned might be sent out as they are created, as part of information distribution activities on the project.

Exercise Test yourself! Who should contribute to creating lessons learned?

| |
| |
| |
| |
| |
| |
| |
| |
| |

Answer
- Stakeholders
- Project management team
- Team
- Project manager
- Sellers
- Customers

▬▬**Performance Reporting** (page 231) Performance reporting is really a
communications process. It collects performance data and sends it to stakeholders. Reports should provide the kinds of information and the level of detail required by stakeholders and may include:
- **Status Report** Describing where the project now stands regarding performance measurement baselines in cost, schedule, scope and quality
- **Progress Report** Describing what has been accomplished
- **Trend Report** Examining project results over time to see if performance is improving or deteriorating
- **Forecasting Report** Predicting future project status and performance
- **Variance Report** Comparing actual results to baselines
- **Earned Value** Integrating scope, cost and schedule measures to assess project performance. This report makes use of the terms described in the Cost chapter (e.g., PV, EV, AC, etc.)
- **Lessons Learned**

The key thing here is to realize that performance is reported against the performance measurement baselines set in the project management plan. Remember that you should have performance measurement baselines that can be measured, and that you are reporting on cost, schedule, scope and quality, not just schedule.

Reports help the team know where they need to recommend and implement corrective action. Included in performance reporting is the need to look into the future. Forecasts can help determine recommended corrective action needed from the team and from the sponsor. Other reports may include risk reserve reports and reports for other knowledge areas.

When completed, performance reporting should result in:
- The issuing of reports from other knowledge areas
- Feedback from those who received the reports
- Lessons learned
- Requested changes to the project management plan and communications management plan
- Reports, forecasts, requested changes and corrective actions and lessons learned documentation

▬▬**Manage Stakeholders** (page 235) This is a communications function.
Stakeholders' needs must continue to be met and their issues resolved throughout the project. When was the last time you did something like this:

A project manager knows that a stakeholder felt strongly that a certain scope should have been part of the project. Anticipating that the stakeholder will continue pressing to get the scope added, the project manager communicates the following. "Danny, I know that during project planning you wanted a certain scope to be part of the project. The entire group of sponsors on this project agreed to remove that scope from the project. It would not be worth your time to try to get it added now."

How about this situation?

During requirements gathering, a stakeholder expressed concern about how much the project would impact her department's other work. The project manager contacts her to say, "I have kept your concern in mind while planning the project. You know that there is little probability we could do this project without impacting your department, but because you were so concerned, I have put a report together telling you when we will impact your department's regular work. I will update the report on a monthly basis."

Why bother doing such work? Such actions are proactive and make the stakeholders feel that their needs and concerns are at least being considered, even if they are not agreed to. They also serve the valuable role of keeping open communication channels with the stakeholders for them to inform you of potential changes, added risks and other information.

In addition to using management skills, manage stakeholders relates to choosing the best communications method (described under communications technology in this chapter).

Issue Logs (page 236) Issue logs are discussed in the Human Resources chapter and are a means of communicating issues to concerned parties.

Communication Blockers Phrases such as "What is your game plan?" "Getting down to the nitty gritty," or even "Zero in on problems" can cause miscommunication with people from other cultures. Such comments as "What a bad idea!" also hamper effective communication. The exam has often had one or two questions that ask, "What can get in the way of communications?" The answer may include:

- Noise
- Distance
- Improper encoding of messages
- Saying "That is a bad idea"
- Hostility
- Language
- Culture

Approved Change Requests and Approved Corrective Actions (page 236) These are the results, or outputs of the manage stakeholders process in communications management. Do not get confused. Changes and corrective actions are approved through the integrated change control process. The word "approved" is used here to remind us that the stakeholders may need to approve changes and corrective actions that affect them. Make sure you understand this because there will be up to 15 questions on changes on the exam and this can slip you up.

Practice Exam

Communications Management

1. Extensive use of ___ communication is most likely to aid in solving complex problems.
   A. verbal
   B. written
   C. formal
   D. nonverbal

2. The work breakdown structure can be an effective aid for communication in which situation(s)?
   A. Internal within the project team
   B. Internal within the organization
   C. External with the customer
   D. Internal and external to the project

3. The MOST likely result of communication blockers is that:
   A. the project is delayed.
   B. trust level is enhanced.
   C. conflict occurs.
   D. senior management is displeased.

4. Communications are often enhanced when the sender ___ the receiver.
   A. speaks up to
   B. uses more physical movements when talking to
   C. talks slowly to
   D. shows concern for the perspective of

5. Formal written correspondence with the customer is required when:
   A. defects are detected.
   B. the customer requests additional work not covered under contract.
   C. the project has a schedule slippage that includes changes to the critical path.
   D. the project has cost overruns.

6. A project manager has a problem with a team member's performance. What is BEST form of communication for addressing this problem?
   A. Formal written communication
   B. Formal verbal communication
   C. Informal written communication
   D. Informal verbal communication

7. Communications under a contract should tend toward:
   A. formal written communication.
   B. formal verbal communication.
   C. informal written communication.
   D. informal verbal communication.

8. The project status report is an example of which form of communication?
   A. Formal written communication
   B. Formal verbal communication
   C. Informal written communication
   D. Informal verbal communication

9. When a project manager is engaged in negotiations, nonverbal communication skills are of:
   A. little importance.
   B. major importance.
   C. importance only when cost and schedule objectives are involved.
   D. importance only to ensure you win the negotiation.

10. A large, one-year telecommunications project is about halfway done when you take the place of the previous project manager. The project involves three different sellers and a project team of 30 people. You would like to see the project's communications requirements and what technology is being used to aid in project communications. Where will you find this information?
    A. The project management plan
    B. The information distribution plan
    C. The bar chart
    D. The communications management plan

11. Project information has been distributed according to the communications management plan. Some project deliverables have been changed in accordance with the project management plan. One stakeholder expressed surprise to the project manager upon hearing of a previously published change to a project deliverable. All stakeholders received the communication containing notification of the change. What should the project manager do?
    A. Determine why the stakeholder did not receive the information and let him know when it was published.
    B. Ask the functional manager why the stakeholder did not understand his responsibility.
    C. Review the communications management plan and make revisions if necessary.
    D. Address the situation in the next steering committee meeting so others do not miss published changes.

12. Communication is the key to the success of a project. As the project manager, you have three stakeholders with whom you need to communicate. As such, you have six channels of communication. A new stakeholder has been added that you also need to communicate with. How many communications channels do you have now?
    A. 7
    B. 10
    C. 12
    D. 16

13. Two people are arguing about what needs to be done to complete a work package. If the project manager wants to know what is going on, she should pay MOST attention to:
    A. what is being said and when.
    B. what is being said, who is saying it, and the time of day.
    C. physical mannerisms and what is being said.
    D. the pitch and tone of the voices, and physical mannerisms.

14. A project manager has a project team consisting of people in four countries. The project is very important to the company, and the project manager is concerned about its success. The length of the project schedule is acceptable. What type of communications method should he use?
    A. Informal verbal
    B. Formal written
    C. Formal verbal
    D. Informal written

15. The project status meeting is not going well. Everyone is talking at the same time, there are people who are not participating and many topics are being discussed at random. Which of the following rules for effective meetings is NOT being adhered to?
    A. Demonstrate courtesy and consideration of each other, control who is allowed to speak.
    B. Schedule meetings in advance.
    C. Have a purpose for the meeting, with the right people in attendance.
    D. Create and publish an agenda and a set of rules for controlling the meeting.

16. You have just been assigned as project manager for a large manufacturing project. This one-year project is about halfway done. It involves five different sellers and 20 members of your company on the project team. You want to quickly review where the project now stands. Which of the following reports would be the MOST helpful in finding such information?
    A. Work status
    B. Progress
    C. Forecast
    D. Communications

17. A team member is visiting the manufacturing plant of one of the suppliers. Which of the following is the MOST important thing to be done in any telephone calls the project manager might make to the team member?
    A. Ask the team member to repeat back what the project manager says.
    B. Review the list of contact information for all stakeholders.
    C. Ask the team member to look for change requests.
    D. Review the upcoming meeting schedule.

18. A project manager overhears a conversation between two stakeholders who are talking about how unhappy they are with the impacts of the project on their own departments. Stakeholder A asks if the project is on time and stakeholder B replies that the SPI is 1.05. Stakeholder A asks if the project manager for the project knows of

stakeholder B's concern. Stakeholder B responds that he is not sure. What is the BEST thing for the project manager to do?

A. Make sure the stakeholders see that the project manager overheard and then ask them to direct any questions to the project manager in writing.

B. Make a presentation to all the stakeholders regarding the status of the project.

C. Send both stakeholders a copy of the issue log and ask for additional comments.

D. Arrange a meeting with both stakeholders to allow them to voice any concerns they may have.

19. A project manager has managed four projects for the company and is being considered to join the project management office team. The following is discovered during the evaluation of his performance. The project manager's first project had an ending cost variance of -500, used two critical resources, needed to rework the project charter during project executing and was ranked 14th in priority within the company. The second project finished with a schedule variance of +100, was completed with a vastly compressed schedule and received a letter of recommendation from the sponsor, but the product of the project was not used. The third project had 23 percent more changes than expected, had an SPI of 0.90 and 25 open items in the issue log when the project was completed.

Each of these projects had a cost budget of U.S. $1,000 and 20 to 28 percent more changes than others of its size. The project management office decided not to add this project manager to the team. Which of the following BEST describes why this might have happened?

A. The project manager has only managed low priority projects and he had to compress the schedule, showing that he does not have the skill to work in the project management office.

B. Issue logs should not be used on projects of this size, showing that the project manager does not have the knowledge to work in a project management office.

C. The project manager did not effectively involve the stakeholders, showing that he does not have the knowledge to work in the project management office.

D. The project manger had two critical resources on their team and still needed to rework the project charter, showing that he does not have the discipline to work in the project management office.

20. During the middle of the project, things have been going well. The work authorization system has allowed people to know when to start work and the issue log has helped keep track of stakeholders' needs. The benefit cost ratio has been improving and the sponsor has expressed his appreciation for the team members' efforts by hosting a milestone party for the team. The project manager gets a call from a team member saying that the results from the completion of their activity's predecessor is two days late. Which of the following reasons would BEST describe why this occurred?

A. The project manager was focusing on the sponsor's needs.

B. Functional management was not included in the communications management plan.

C. The successor activities should have been watched, not the predecessors.

D. The right people were not invited to the milestone party.

21. There have been many work packages completed successfully on the project and the sponsor has made some recommendations for improvements. The project is on schedule to meet an aggressive deadline when the successor activity to a critical

path activity suffers a major setback. The activity has 14 days of float and is being completed by four people. There are two other team members with the skill set to assist the troubled activity, if needed.

The project manager receives a call that three other team members are attempting to be removed from the project because they do not feel the project can be successful. When the project manager pursues this, she discovers that those team members have issues that have not been addressed. Which of the following is the BEST thing to do to improve the project?

A. Have the team members immediately assist the troubled activity.

B. Investigate why the project schedule is aggressive.

C. See who can replace the three team members.

D. Create an issue log.

22. The project has 13 team members and affects over 15 departments in the organization. Because the project has completed 20 percent of the project to date and has had successful performance reports from five of the affected departments, the project manager holds a party to celebrate. The project manager invites to the party key stakeholders from all of the departments, in order to give those providing good reviews an informal opportunity to communicate good things to those departments that have not yet been affected by the project.

At the party, the project manager walks around to try to discover any relevant information that would help the project be more successful. He happens to hear a manager of one of the departments talking about setting up more regular meetings on the project.

The BEST thing for the project manager to do would be to FIRST:

A. record the effectiveness of the party in the project lessons learned.

B. review the information distribution methods on the project.

C. hold a meeting of all the stakeholders to discuss their concerns.

D. make sure the manager has a copy of the communications management plan so he is reminded that such concerns should be sent to the project manager.

23. A large project is underway when one of the team members reviews the project status report. He sees that the project is currently running late. As he looks at the report further, he notices that the delay will cause one of his activities to be scheduled during a time he will be out of the country and cannot work on the activity. This is of great concern because he is very committed to the project being successful and he does not want to be the cause of the project being further delayed. What is the BEST THING for him to do?

A. Contact the project manager immediately to provide him with his schedule.

B. Include the information on his next report.

C. Request that the issue be added to the project issue log.

D. Recommend corrective action.

24. Your project had a difficult time receiving formal approval of the project management plan because there were so many stakeholders whose requirements were not approved for inclusion in the project. These stakeholders argued and held up the project while they held meeting after meeting about their requirements. The

project was finally approved and work was begun six months ago. All of the following would be good preventive actions to implement EXCEPT?

A. Keep a file of what requirements were not included in the project.

B. Make sure the change control process is not used as a vehicle to add back the requirements into the project.

C. Maintain an issue log.

D. Hold meetings with the stakeholders to go over the work that will not be added to the project.

25. The project manager is expecting a deliverable to be submitted by e-mail from a team member today. At the end of the day, the project manager contacts the team member to notify them that it has not been received. The team member apologizes and says that he was not able to e-mail the deliverable, and it was sent through the mail instead. The team member goes on to explain that he notified the project manager that this would occur during a phone conversation they had while the project manager was traveling. "Wasn't that the conversation we had when I told you I could not hear you well due to poor cell phone coverage?" asks the project manager. "Yes," replies the team member. What could have avoided this problem?

A. Paralingual communication

B. Adding to the issue log after the phone call

C. Better attention to determining communications requirements

D. Feedback during the communication

26. Company procedures require the creation of a lessons learned document. Which of the following is the BEST use of lessons learned?

A. Historical records for future projects

B. Planning record for the current project

C. Informing the team about what the project manager has done

D. Informing the team about the project management plan

27. Lessons learned are BEST completed by:

A. Project manager

B. Team

C. Sponsor

D. Stakeholders

Communications Management Answers

1. **Answer** B
   Explanation Written communication allows your words to be documented, and they will go to everyone in the same form. When there are complex problems, you want everyone to receive the same thing.

2. **Answer** D
   Explanation The work breakdown structure allows communication vertically and horizontally within the organization as well as outside the project.

3. **Answer** C
   Explanation The major result of communication blockers and miscommunication as a whole is conflict.

4. **Answer** D
   Explanation Understanding the receiver's perspective allows you to direct the communication to meet his needs.

5. **Answer** B
   Explanation Everything that we do is more formal in a contract environment than in other project activities. Because choice B deals with contracts, it is the best answer.

6. **Answer** D
   Explanation The best choice is D. If informal verbal communication does not solve the problem, choice A is the next best choice. This does not mean that you do not keep records of the problem, but this question is asking about communication between two parties.

7. **Answer** A
   Explanation When we talk about contracts, everything that we do is more formal than in other project activities. Records are also important, thus the need for written communication.

8. **Answer** A
   Explanation The project status needs to be known by many people. Therefore, it is best to make this type of communication in writing so that it can be transmitted to many people. It is also formal in that it is an official report of the project. Therefore, choice A is the best answer.

9. **Answer** B
   Explanation: Nonverbal communication carries 55 percent of the message you send. With this much at stake, nonverbal communication is of major importance.

10. **Answer** D
    Explanation: Although the information is found as a sub-plan to the project management plan (choice A), the communications management plan (choice D) is the best answer because it directly answers the question.

11. **Answer** C

    Explanation Choice A cannot be correct because the question states that all stakeholders received the information. Choices B and D do not address the root cause of the problem. The problem presented here shows that there is something missing in the communications management plan. The best answer is to review the communications management plan in order to prevent future problems and find any instances of similar problems.

12. **Answer** B

    Explanation Did you realize that the project manager is part of the communication channels? Therefore, there are actually four stakeholders to begin with and six channels of communication. The question is asking how many total channels of communication do you have with a team of five people. The formula is $[N \times (N\text{-}1)]/2$ or $(5 \times 4)/2 = 10$.

13. **Answer** D

    Explanation Choices C and D both include nonverbal communication, which represents 55 percent of communication. Choice D adds paralingual communication (pitch and tone) and is thus the best choice.

14. **Answer** B

    Explanation Because of the differences in culture and the distance between team members, formal written communication is needed.

15. **Answer** D

    Explanation Choice A is not a "rule" for effective meetings. Since there is no indication that the meeting was not scheduled in advance (choice B) or that there isn't a purpose (choice C), these cannot be the best answers. "Discussed at random" implies no agenda (choice D). If an agenda is issued beforehand, people will follow the outline and should not need random discussions.

16. **Answer** B

    Explanation The key word is quickly. The status report (choice A) is too detailed for a quick look. The forecast report (choice C) only looks into the future. The progress report (choice B) will summarize project status.

17. **Answer** A

    Explanation Questions like this can drive one crazy. Although it asks for the most important thing, there are many choices that are reasonably correct. In questions like this, look for the most immediate need. In this case, the team member is in a manufacturing environment. That means that communications will most likely be blocked by noise. In order to have the issue at hand taken care of, the communication, it is BEST for the project manager to use choice A.

18. **Answer** D

    Explanation Here again is a question with more than one right answer. Would asking for something in writing be the best way to communicate here? In this particular situation, asking for the concern to be in writing might alienate the stakeholders. Therefore choice A cannot be best. The issue log (choice C) is where the issue should be listed, but the situation does not say if the project manager knows what the stakeholders' concern is. Therefore C cannot be the best choice. Why not B? Notice the use of the words "all stakeholders." Why bother other stakeholders with this problem when the project manager already knows there may be some concern of stakeholder A and B to address, not all stakeholders. Choice B refers to making a presentation. Presentations are formal verbal. This problem would likely require informal verbal communication in order to discover the real problem. Choice D is therefore the best choice.

19. **Answer** C

Explanation This is a very confusing question. Notice all the distracters that may or may not be relevant? Since most projects have their schedule compressed by the project manager during project planning, choice A is not a logical reason and so cannot be the best choice. Issue logs can be used on smaller projects, making choice B not the best choice. The number of critical (or hard to get) resources noted in choice D has no bearing on the need to rework the project charter. Since it does not make logical sense, it cannot be the best choice. Take a look at projects 2 and 3 again. In the second project, the product of the project was not used. This implies many things, including the possibilities that either the project manager did not identify the requirements of all the stakeholders or that the business need of the project changed dramatically and the project manager did not notice. This is a major flaw in the project manager's abilities. In the third project, there were 25 concerns of the stakeholders that were not addressed before the project was completed. Again, this shows a major lack of project management knowledge. The needs of the stakeholders and not just the sponsor must be taken into account on all projects. This makes choice C the best choice.

20. **Answer** B

Explanation Since there is no information about the sponsor or his needs in this situation and nothing presented here relates to sponsors, choice A cannot be best. Choice C cannot be best, as it is not a correct statement. One watches both predecessor and successor activities. Choice D cannot be best, as the attendance at the party and the issue at hand are not related. Often forgotten in communications management plans are the bosses of team members (functional management, since of course you remember that we are assuming a matrix organization). Including the bosses of team members in communications planning, requirements gathering, risk and other areas of project management helps make the project better. In addition, it helps the boss manage his own resources effectively. If the functional manager of the team member assigned to the predecessor activity had been included, he would have known when the team member was needed to do work for the project and the impact, if any, of delay. The communications management plan might also have included a method to communicate potential delays. For these reasons, choice B is best.

21. **Answer** D

Explanation Sometimes complex problems are caused by not doing simple things. The data in the first paragraph, once you read the choices, is completely extraneous. The troubled activity has float and so does not need immediate attention. Choice A may not be necessary if the amount of float will not be exceeded by the problem. None of the choices suggest investigating if the amount of float is enough to cover any delay caused by the trouble, whatever it is. Rather, the choices take one in different directions.

Choice B should have already been done before the project began. Choice C cannot be best, as replacing team members does not solve the root cause of the problem. Could there be something that the project manager is doing wrong, or could be doing that she is not, that would solve the problem without losing resources? Wouldn't it be more effective to discover the root cause of those team members' concerns so that the problem does not surface again later? The creation of an issue log will let the troubled team members know that their concerns have been heard, are noted, and will be resolved. This might be enough to stop them from leaving and avoid project delays and confusion if new team members must be added. This makes choice D the best answer.

22. **Answer** B

    Explanation Many of these choices could be done, but ask yourself, what is the most effective thing to do? The party may well generate lessons learned, and recording them (choice A) would certainly be a good idea, but the question asked what to do first. There is a more immediate issue; the manager. Choice C could also be useful, but it would require taking time of all the stakeholders' when there is only one stakeholder, the manager, who definitely has an issue. Besides, a good project manager would be holding regular meetings with the stakeholders already. Choice D might be a good idea, as the manager apparently is not communicating with the project manager. However, this would not absolutely make sure the manager does communicate.

    The manager is, in effect, saying that he is not getting the information he needs. His lack of needed information is causing him to suggest more meetings. Too many meetings are a problem on projects. The concept of information distribution (choice B) is to determine who needs what information and plan how to get it to them. A great project manager does not just add meetings, but solves the real problem in the best way. That might take the form of changing a report or sending existing reports to different people rather than adding meetings. For these reasons, choice B is best.

23. **Answer** D

    Explanation Notice that this question talks about what the team member should do? It is important for the project manager to understand the team member's role and possibly even instruct team members on how to work on projects and what is expected of them. Choices A, B and C have one thing in common. They involve the team member asking the project manager to do something. In reality, it may very well be the team member who will come up with a solution (such as decreasing the scope of the activity, fast tracking, or specific suggestions about changes to predecessor activities). Therefore choice D is the best choice. But ask yourself, how do you run your projects? Which is better, your way or this way? Lastly, please note that recommended corrective actions can come from the team or stakeholders in addition to the project manager.

24. **Answer** D

    Explanation Why would choice D be the action not to take? Isn't it similar to choice A? Yes and no. This issue should be over, but since there were so many meetings and arguments about the requirements being removed, it is unlikely that the issue will be dropped by the stakeholders. However, since it has not come up again, and the project was started six months ago, spending time in a meeting is excessive. The other choices are easier and have less impact on the project and are therefore things that could be done.

25. **Answer** D

    Explanation The pitch and tone of voice (choice A) is not relevant here, as the project manager could not even hear what was being said. There were no issues recognized after the conversation, so none could be added to the issue log (choice B). This issue is not related to communications requirements, so choice C cannot be best. Saying, "I am not sure I properly heard what you said" during the conversation or asking for the message to be repeated back to the sender would have prevented this problem. This makes choice D the best option.

26. **Answer** A

   Explanation Notice that this question asks about the use of a tool of project management. Many people can learn from a book what a lessons learned document is, but questions like this can more readily be answered if you actually use the tool and know from experience its value. Ask yourself about the other tools of project management. Why are they beneficial? The BEST use of lessons learned is choice A. There are other tools that are better for accomplishing the things listed in the other choices.

27. **Answer** D

   Explanation The best answer is stakeholders, as their input is critical for collecting all the lessons learned on each project. The term "stakeholders" includes all the other groups.

Risk Management

Quicktest

- Risk management process
- Threats
- Opportunities
- Inputs to risk management
- Risk register
- Risk management plan
- Risk response strategies
  - Avoid
  - Mitigate
  - Transfer
  - Exploit
  - Share
  - Enhance
  - Accept
- Reserves
- Reserve analysis
- Probability and impact matrix
- Risk identification techniques
- Monte Carlo analysis
- Expected monetary value
- Contingency plans
- Fallback plans
- Probability and impact
- Watchlist
- Workarounds
- Revised project management plan
- Contracting
- Risk categories
- Types of risk
- Risk response owner
- Residual risks
- Secondary risks
- Assumptions analysis
- Data quality assessment
- Risk audit
- Risk reassessments
- Risk triggers
- Risk tolerance
- Definition of uncertainty
- Decision tree
- Risk averse

Worried about this topic, are you? You should be! Let me tell you a story. Recently there were a series of hurricanes in the state of Florida in the United States, a relatively frequent occurrence there. I was talking to a project manager who had been working on a hardware/software installation project when one of the hurricanes came. You should have seen how excited he was about how quickly his team recovered from the disaster. Would you also be excited? Read on!

I said, "I am surprised your boss did not fire you." He looked at me in surprise as I continued. "Why were you doing this project that only lasted three days when there was a hurricane coming?" And yes, he should have been fired. A project manager's work should not focus on dealing with problems, it should prevent them! What do you do?

Now you can see why this might be a hard chapter for you. The exam assumes you are already doing risk management and it will therefore ask questions about situations that you should have already run into. Questions are asked on an expert level!

Another reason this chapter is extremely hard for people is that they have had no training on risk, or they think risk management means just using some software (just like people mistakenly think all you need to do to manage a project is use "project management" software).

It is important to understand that project risks can be substantially decreased. Some studies quote a 90 percent decrease in project problems through the use of risk management. Through the process of risk management, we change from the project being in control of the project manager to the project manager being in control of the project. Since risk management focuses on proactively preventing things that can go wrong and helping things to go right, it deserves more attention than just a list.

Rita's Process Chart—Risk Management
Where are we in the project management process?

Initiating	Planning	Executing	Monitoring & Controlling	Closing
Select project manager	**Determine how you will do planning—part of management plans**	Acquire final team	Measure against the performance measurement baselines	Develop closure procedures
Determine company culture and existing systems	Create project scope statement	Execute the PM plan	**Measure according to the management plans**	Complete contract closure
Collect processes, procedures and historical information	Determine team	Work to produce product scope	**Determine variances and if they warrant corrective action or a change**	Confirm work is done to requirements
Divide large projects into phases	Create WBS and WBS dictionary	Recommend changes and corrective actions		Gain formal acceptance of the product
Identify stakeholders	Create activity list	Send and receive information	Scope verification	Final performance reporting
Document business need	Create network diagram	Implement approved changes, defect repair, preventive and corrective actions	Configuration management	Index and archive records
Determine project objectives	Estimate resource requirements		**Recommend changes, defect repair, preventive and corrective actions**	Update lessons learned knowledge base
Document assumptions and constraints	Estimate time and cost	Continuous improvement		Hand off completed product
Develop project charter	Determine critical path	Follow processes	Integrated change control	Release resources
Develop preliminary project scope statement	Develop schedule	Team building	Approve changes, defect repair, preventive and corrective actions	
	Develop budget	Give recognition and rewards		
	Determine quality standards, processes and metrics	Hold progress meetings	**Risk audits**	
	Determine roles and responsibilities	Use work authorization system	**Manage reserves**	
	Determine communications requirements	Request seller responses	Use issue logs	
	Risk identification, qualitative and quantitative risk analysis and response planning	Select sellers	Facilitate conflict resolution	
	Iterations—go back		Measure team member performance	
	Determine what to purchase		Report on performance	
	Prepare procurement documents		Create forecasts	
	Finalize the "how to execute and control" aspects of all management plans		Administer contracts	
	Create process improvement plan			
	Develop final PM plan and performance measurement baselines			
	Gain formal approval for plan			
	Hold kickoff meeting			

The Risk Management Process

The Risk Management Process	Done During
Risk management planning	Planning process group
Risk identification	Planning process group
Qualitative risk analysis	Planning process group
Quantitave risk analysis	Planning process group
Risk response planning	Planning process group
Risk monitoring and control	Monitoring and controlling process group

It is also important to understand that in the real world we should have plans in place before most major "problems" occur, and not be running around trying to set up meetings to discuss how to address major problems after the fact. Now you see why you should actually learn risk management for your projects. Imagine how much fun it will be to be able to continually say on your projects, "No problem, we have a plan for that!"

Definition of Risk Management (page 237) Risk management includes risk management planning, identification, analysis, response planning and monitoring and control. The purpose of risk management is to increase the probability and impact of positive events, and decrease the probability and impact of negative events on the project.

If you are not doing very well on risk management after reading this chapter, I might suggest that you look at my book, *Risk Management Tricks of the Trade® for Project Managers*. It contains 50 more practice questions that are not available anywhere else, and it comes with information on how to use the book to help you prepare for the PMP exam.

Knowing some definitions in risk can help you find answers to exam questions. The process of risk management is very logical. Expect questions that ask, "What part of the process are you in during this situation?" or "What do you do next?" Therefore, you should understand the process of risk management and what happens when in the process. In this chapter, I have added specific references to outputs to aid you in understanding the risk process. However, expect a majority of the questions to be in the form of, "What should you do?" These are harder than the other types of questions.

This chapter will provide the overview necessary for the exam. However, you should realize that there are more tools and techniques to real-world risk management than are covered here.

Threats and Opportunities Risk is something that may or may not happen. If it does happen, it can have positive or negative impact on the project. Do not forget that there can be positive impacts; good risks, called opportunities! Opportunities can include such things as:
- The ZYX equipment is cheaper than planned
- Work package number 3.4 is completed faster than expected
- It does not take as long as expected to achieve the quality level needed on work package number 21
- Work can move faster since we were able to acquire a resource with a higher productivity level

Up to 90 percent of threats that are identified and investigated in the risk management process can be eliminated. How much better off would you be if that happened? How about the project? Your customer?

Definition of Uncertainty Uncertainty is a lack of knowledge about an event that reduces confidence in conclusions drawn from the data. The work that needs to be done, the cost, the time, the quality needs, communications needs, etc. can be uncertain. The investigation of uncertainties may help identify risks.

Risk Factors When looking at risk, one should determine:
- The probability that it will occur (what)
- The range of possible outcomes (impact or amount at stake)

- Expected timing (when) in the project life cycle
- Anticipated frequency of risk events from that source (how often)

Risk Averse
Someone who does not want to take risks is said to be risk averse.

Risk Tolerances and Thresholds
Tolerances are the areas of risk that are acceptable or unacceptable. For example, "a risk that affects our reputation will not be tolerated." Tolerance areas can include any component of the "triple constraint" as well as reputation and other intangibles that may affect the customer. A threshold is the amount of risk that is acceptable. For example, "A risk of a two week delay is okay, but nothing more."

━━━Inputs to and Outputs of Risk Management
(page 242) Have you realized yet that there are inputs to the process as a whole ("What are the inputs to risk management?") and inputs to each part of the process of risk management ("What are the inputs to risk response planning?") Did you realize that the inputs to each part of the process are almost always the outputs of the parts that came before? As a result, these should not need memorization. However, since risk management is a very step-by-step, process-oriented part of project management, expect risk input and output questions on the exam.

Inputs are merely, "What do I need to do this well?" or "What do I need before I can begin…?" Outputs are merely, "What will I have when I am done with…?"

Exercise Test yourself! Explain why each of the following inputs to risk management are needed before one can adequately perform the risk management process. This is an important test. It is the following list you should know for the exam.

Project background information	
Historical records from previous projects (part of organizational process assets)	
Past lessons learned (also part of organizational process assets)	
Other organizational process assets	
Stakeholder risk tolerance areas (part of enterprise environmental factors)	

Stakeholder risk thresholds (part of enterprise environmental factors)	
Other enterprise environmental factors	
Project charter	
Preliminary project scope statement/ project scope statement	
Team	
Work breakdown structure	
Network diagram	
Time and cost estimates	
Communications management plan	
Staffing management plan	

Procurement management plan	
Stakeholders	
Project objectives	
Assumptions	

Answer There can be many answers. Here are some possible ones.

Project background information	Information such as correspondence from before the project was approved, articles written about similar projects and other such information will help identify more risks.
Historical records from previous projects (part of organizational process assets)	Tells you risks from past, similar projects.
Past lessons learned (also part of organizational process assets)	Tells you what teams would do differently if they could do their projects again. Helps you identify, mitigate and manage risks on your project.
Other organizational process assets	Company processes and procedures for project management and risk management, or lack thereof, may lead to identifying more risks.
Stakeholder risk tolerance areas (part of enterprise environmental factors)	Knowing in which areas stakeholders are willing to accept risk helps identify the impact of risks, the highest ranked risks, and which risk response strategies you will use.
Stakeholder risk thresholds (part of enterprise environmental factors)	Knowing the amount of risk stakeholders are willing to accept helps identify the impact of risks and which risk response strategies you will use.

Other enterprise environmental factors	A company's culture and other components of enterprise environmental factors can add risk and should be considered when identifying risks.
Project charter	The project charter helps you see if the overall project objectives are generally risky or not. Helps identify risks based on what is and what is not included.
Preliminary project scope statement/ project scope statement	The preliminary project scope statement may include, among other things, the sponsor's analysis of the risks of the project. Other content, and the process of converting this to the project scope statement, will help identify additional risks. Risks can be identified from what is in the preliminary project scope statement as well as what is not included that should have been there.
Team	The project manager cannot identify all the risks alone. A group approach and the ability to share risk management responsibilities make the risk management process more accurate and timely.
Work breakdown structure	The WBS is needed because risks must be specific, not general. They should be identified at the work package level in addition to the project level.
Network diagram	This is the only place where paths that converge into one activity can be seen. Such path convergence makes the activity riskier than if there was no path convergence. The network diagram also helps determine the critical path. The 'tighter" the schedule, the more risk.
Time and cost estimates	Knowing the estimates helps you determine the risk of the project not meeting the schedule and cost objectives. Initial estimates are an input to risk management and detailed estimates are an output of risk management. Final cost and schedule cannot be determined without including risk reserves.
Communications management plan	Are there a lot of people to communicate with? Where in the project are communications so important that communication errors can actually add risk to the project? Is your communications management plan effective? Since the number one problem many people have on projects is poor communication, there is a strong connection between planning communications and decreasing risk.
Staffing management plan	What resources are available, their skill sets and how they will be moved on and off the project. Knowing this information will help you identify risks related to resources.
Procurement management plan	How many contracts will there likely be on the project? What is your expertise in handling contracts? Was the project manager involved before any contracts were signed? If not, the project will have more risk and therefore likely cost more. Contracts are a way to mitigate or transfer risks in risk response planning.

Stakeholders	Stakeholders will view the project from different perspectives, and thus will be able to see risks that the team cannot. Stakeholders are involved in many aspects of risk management.
Project objectives	Knowing the project objectives will help determine the impact of risks as well as determine additional risks related to meeting or not meeting the objectives. A project is a success if it meets the project objectives (time, cost, technical, business).
Assumptions	Assumptions are beliefs or opinions about the project that must be identified now. Project assumptions may increase or decrease risks and help in determining risk impacts. Reviewing assumptions will help uncover additional risks.

The Risk Management Process (page 237) This is an important topic. You must MEMORIZE what happens when, how risk management works on a real-world project and how it relates to the project life cycle. The six sequential risk management processes are:

1. Risk Management Planning
2. Risk Identification
3. Qualitative Risk Analysis
4. Quantitative Risk Analysis
5. Risk Response Planning
6. Risk Monitoring And Control

Risk Management Planning (page 242) The project manager, sponsor, team, customer, other stakeholders and experts can be involved in risk management planning to define how the risk process will be structured and performed for the project. Since risk management is so critical, wouldn't it be wise to think about how you will approach risk management before you do it? Plan before you act. Risk management efforts should be appropriate to the size and complexity of the project, as well as the experience and skill level of the project team. Successful risk management cannot be done with just a standardized checklist. If the project is low priority, should you spend more or less time on risk? If the project is high priority, will you spend more or less time? The risk management planning process will address these questions, as well as questions such as who and how. Company procedures for risk such as standard probability and impact matrixes are identified and then adapted to the needs of the project.

Outputs of Risk Management Planning (page 243)
- **Risk Management Plan** The risk management plan may include:
  - **Methodology** This section defines how you will perform risk management for the particular project. Remember to adapt to the needs of each project.
  - **Roles and responsibilities** Who will do what? Did you realize that non-team members may have roles and responsibilities regarding risk management?
  - **Budgeting** This section includes the cost for the risk management process.
  - **Timing** This section talks about when to do risk management for this particular project. Risk management should start as soon as you have the appropriate inputs. It should also be repeated throughout the life of the project, since new risks can be identified and may change the degree of risk on the project.
  - **Risk categories** See the next page.

- **Definitions of probability and impact** Would everyone who rates the probability a "seven" in qualitative risk analysis mean the same thing? A person who is risk averse might think of seven as very high, someone who is risk prone might think of seven as a low figure. The definitions and the standard probability and impact matrix helps standardize these interpretations and also helps compare risks between projects.
- **Stakeholder tolerances** What if the stakeholders have low risk tolerance for cost overruns? That information would be taken into account to rank cost impacts higher than they would if the low tolerance was in another area. Tolerances should not be implied, but uncovered in project initiating and clarified or refined continually.
- **Reporting formats** This section describes any reports related to risk management that will be used and what they will include.
- **Tracking** Take this to mean how the risk process will be audited, and documenting what happens with risk management activities.

Because the risk management plan contains budgets and schedules, it is an input to cost and time estimating, schedule development and cost budgeting. A risk management plan is also an input to the plan purchases and acquisitions and plan contracting processes in procurement management. This will be discussed further in the Procurement chapter of this book.

Risk Categories How many times have you forgotten a whole category of risks on your project? I have long advocated the use of a standard list of risk categories (high-level areas of risk such as technology changes or cultural issues) to make sure areas of risk are not forgotten. Risk categories are lists of common areas or sources of risk experienced by the company, or on similar projects. The categories help analyze and identify risks on each project.

Companies and project management offices should have standard lists of risk categories that all projects can use to help identify risks. Those leading risk identification should make sure that each category is considered when looking for risks.

There are many ways to classify or categorize risk such as:
- **External** Regulatory, environmental, government, market shifts
- **Internal** Time, cost, scope changes, inexperience, poor planning, people, staffing, materials, equipment
- **Technical** Changes in technology
- **Unforeseeable** Only a small portion of risks (some say about 10 percent) are actually unforeseeable

A better way is based on specific categories of risk that may occur on your company's projects. My risk research shows over 300 potential categories of risk. These include:
- **Technology**
- **Customer**
- **Project management** (yes, your lack of project management effort can add risk)
- **The customer's customers**
- **The suppliers**
- **Resistance to change**
- **Lack of knowledge of project management** by the project manager and stakeholders
- **Stakeholder-caused risks**
- **Sponsor-caused risks**
- **Cultural risks**

Another way is to categorize risks by source; "Where do risks come from?" as shown.

- **Schedule risk** "The hardware may arrive earlier than planned, allowing work package XYZ to start three days earlier."
- **Cost risk** "Because the hardware may arrive later than planned, we may need to extend our lease on the staging area at a cost of $20,000."
- **Quality risk** "The concrete may dry before winter weather sets in, allowing us to start successor work packages earlier than planned."
- **Performance or scope risk** "We might not have correctly defined the scope for the computer installation. If that proves true, we will have to add work packages at a cost of $20,000."
- **Resources risk** "Riki is such an excellent designer that he may be called away to work on the new project everyone is so excited about. If that occurs, we will have to use someone else and our schedule will slip between 100 and 275 hours."
- **Customer satisfaction (stakeholder satisfaction) risk** "There is a chance that the customer will not be happy with the XYZ deliverable and not tell us, causing at least a 20 percent increase in communication problems."

TRICKS OF THE TRADE Expect the phrases "sources of risk" and "risk categories" to be used interchangeably on the exam. They can be organized in an organizational chart or WBS-like format called a risk breakdown structure.

Risk Identification (page 246) This is where risks are identified. Any risks missed here may be harder to deal with later in the project. This effort should involve all stakeholders and might even involve literature reviews, research and talking to non-stakeholders. Sometimes the core team will begin the process and then the other members will become involved, making risk identification an iterative process.

TRICKS OF THE TRADE When you get a question about who should be involved in risk identification, the best answer is everyone! Everyone has a different perspective of the project. Take off your blinders and look beyond what you are used to.

Smart project managers begin looking for risks as soon as a project is first discussed. However, the major risk identification effort occurs during planning. Risk identification cannot be completed until a project scope statement and WBS have been created and the project team knows "what is the project." The sponsor may supply a list of risks in the preliminary project scope statement.

Because risk identification can occur during the initiating and planning process groups, the exam has often said that risk identification happens at the *onset* of the project. Risks may also be identified during any part of the project. The exam will specifically look for you to include risk identification during such activities as project changes, when working with resources, and dealing with project issues.

How do you identify risks? The *PMBOK® Guide* does not go into detail here and neither will the exam. The exam is likely to weight the questions toward project executing and project monitoring and controlling-related questions on risk. Therefore, details of risk identification are not explained in this section. It does include:

Documentation Reviews (page 247) What is and what is not included in the preliminary project scope statement, the project charter and later documents can help identify risks. Lessons learned, articles and other documents can also help uncover risks. This used to be a trick for risk management and now has become standard practice. Think about how valuable this would be in your real world.

Information Gathering Techniques (page 247) You should know there are many ways to identify risks and that risk identification can be an art form. Luckily, you need not be a risk identification expert to pass the exam. Keep it simple and just know the following!

- **Brainstorming** Brainstorming is usually done in a meeting where one idea helps generate another.
- **Delphi Technique** A technique used to build consensus of experts who participate anonymously. A request for information is sent to the experts, their responses are compiled, and the results are sent back to them for further review until consensus is reached. This technique can also be used for estimating time and cost.
- **Interviewing** Also called expert interviewing on the exam, this consists of the team or project manager interviewing project participants, stakeholders or experts to identify risks on the project or a specific element of work.
- **Root cause analysis** What if you could reorganize the risks you have uncovered by their causes? Might you see more risks? Of course, maybe many more!
- **Strengths, weaknesses, opportunities and threats analysis (SWOT)** This analysis looks at the project to identify its strengths, etc. and thereby identify risks.

Types of Risk Risks can be classified under two main types:
- **Business** Risk of a gain or loss
- **Pure (Insurable) Risk** Only a risk of loss (e.g., fire, theft, personal injury)

Checklist Analysis (page 248) The checklist of risk categories was previously described in risk management planning. One does not just go down the checklist asking "Do we have this type of risk?" Actual risks should be more specific and detailed than those in the checklist. Risks are identified using one of the techniques previously described. The checklist is then used to make sure the risk identification process has addressed all the categories of risk.

Assumptions Analysis (page 248) Analyzing what assumptions have been made on the project and if they are valid, for the purpose of identifying more risks.

Diagramming Techniques (page 248) There are many tools described in the Quality chapter that help one analyze the root causes of issues. These include cause and effect diagrams and flowcharts. When used as part of risk identification, they help identify additional risks.

Outputs of Risk Identification (page 249)
- **Risk Register** The risk register is the place where most of the risk information is kept. Think of it as one document for the whole risk management process that will be constantly updated with information as risk identification and later risk management processes are completed. The risk register becomes part of the project management plan and is also included in historical records which will be used for future projects.

 You will notice that the risk register is the only output of many of the risk management processes. Read exam questions carefully as the risk register contains different information depending on when in the risk management process the question is referencing.

At this point the risk register would include:
- **List of risks**
- **List of potential responses** Though risk response planning occurs later, one of the things experienced risk managers know is that it is not always logical to separate work on each part of risk management. There will be times when a response is identified at the same time as a risk. These responses should be added to the risk register as they are identified, and analyzed later as part of risk response planning.
- **Root causes of risks** Previously explained, these are now documented.
- **Updated risk categories** You will notice lots of places where historical records and company records are updated throughout the project management process. Make sure you are aware that lessons learned and communicating information to other projects does not just happen at the end of the project. Here, the project is providing feedback to the rest of the company regarding new categories of risk to add to the checklist previously described.

TRICKS OF THE TRADE® If I was writing a tricky question for the exam I might write, "When in the risk management process are responses documented?" You will know the answer is risk identification and risk response planning!

Qualitative Risk Analysis (page 249) You might remember that one of the later parts of risk management is to determine what you are going to do about risks. Would you want to do something about all risks identified? Of course not. That would be too expensive and you would not have enough time. Therefore, qualitative risk analysis involves creating a short list of the previously identified risks.

TRICKS OF THE TRADE® Remember that qualitative risk analysis is a *subjective* analysis of the risks identified in risk identification:
- The probability of each risk occurring (e.g., Low, Medium, High or 1 to 10)
- The impact (amount at stake, or consequences, positive or negative) of each risk occurring (e.g., Low, Medium, High or 1 to 10)

Probability and Impact Matrix (page 251) A risk rating matrix may be used to sort or rate risks to determine which ones warrant a response. These risks will be moved on through the risk process. The matrix may be standardized within the company or department, or customized to the needs of the project. Such a matrix results in a consistent evaluation of low, medium or high (or some other scale) for the project and for all projects, an improvement in the quality of the data. Use of a standardized matrix makes the risk rating process more repeatable between projects.

Different matrixes can be used for cost, time and scope if the project's thresholds for each type of risks are different.

Risk Data Quality Assessment (page 252) or "How accurate and well understood is the risk information?" Before the project manager can use the risk information collected so far, she must analyze the precision of the data—how good is the data? Is more research into "What is the risk?" required before a qualitative assessment can be done? Imagine, for example, a risk given to you on a notepad anonymously. Smart project managers might allow for anonymous contributions during risk identification, but all of the identified risks must be defined well enough to perform a qualitative assessment.

This may include determining the following for each risk:
- Extent of the understanding of the risk
- Data available about the risk
- Quality of the data
- Reliability and integrity of the data

Risk Categorization (page 253) Or in other words "What will we find if we regroup the risks by categories? By work packages?" Think about how useful it would be to not only have a subjective assessment of the amount of risk on the project, but also to know where the risks are coming from and which work packages are most affected. Such data will be helpful in risk response planning, giving you the possibility of eliminating many risks at once by eliminating one cause.

Risk Urgency Assessment (page 253) In addition to a list of risks, qualitative risk analysis includes noting risks that should move more quickly through the process. Reasons for this could include the fact that the risk may occur soon, or will require a long time to plan a response. Urgent risks may then move, independently, right into risk response planning, or they may be simply the first ones for which you plan a response.

Outputs of Qualitative Risk Analysis (page 253):
- **Risk Register** The risk register is updated to add the results of qualitative risk analysis, including:
  - **Risk ranking for the project compared to other projects** Qualitative risk analysis can lead (through means not explained here) to a number to be used to rank the project compared to others (i.e., this project has a risk score of 8.3). The impact of this is that once you complete risk response planning you can then redo qualitative risk analysis and PROVE the value of your efforts. You can now report, "The project now has a risk score of 4.8." Think how this will help you prove the value of project management!
  - **List of prioritized risks and their probability and impact ratings**
  - **Risks grouped by categories** As previously explained
  - **List of risks requiring additional analysis in the near term**
  - **List of risks for additional analysis and response** The risks that will move forward into quantitative risk analysis and/or response planning
  - **Watchlist (non-critical or non-top risks)** Documented for later revisit during risk monitoring and control
  - **Trends** Qualitative risk analysis may be redone in planning (as previously explained) or while the project work is being done. The project manager should know if risk is increasing, decreasing, or staying the same, so that trends can be analyzed.

TRICKS OF THE TRADE Qualitative risk analysis can also lead to:
- The project's risk can be compared to the overall risk of other projects
- The project may be selected, continued or terminated
- Quantitative risk analysis or risk response planning, depending on the needs of the project and the performing organization

Quantitative Risk Analysis (page 254) A numerical analysis of the
probability and impact (amount at stake or consequences) of the highest risks on the project to:
- Determine which risk events warrant a response

- Determine overall project risk (risk exposure)
- Determine the quantified probability of meeting project objectives, e.g., "We only have an 80 percent chance of completing the project within the six months required by the customer," or "We only have a 75 percent chance of completing the project within the $80,000 budget."
- Determine cost and schedule reserves
- Identify risks requiring the most attention
- Create realistic and achievable cost, schedule or scope targets

 Remember that quantitative risk analysis is a *numerical* analysis of the probability and impact (amount at stake or consequences) of the highest risks from qualitative risk analysis. Quantitative risk analysis is not required for all projects and may be skipped in favor of moving on to risk response planning. Proceed with quantitative risk analysis only if it is worth the time and money on your project. Why spend time quantitatively assessing risks for a low priority or short term project? Remember also that some projects might lend themselves to skipping the qualitative assessment and moving directly into quantitative risk analysis.

TRICKS OF THE TRADE Any time the exam uses the term *risk assessment*, think of it as risk identification through quantitative risk analysis.

Quantitative risk analysis includes:
- Further investigation into the highest risks on the project
- Determination of the type of probability distribution that will be used, e.g., triangular, normal, beta, uniform or log normal distributions (See charts, page 256)
- Sensitivity analysis – Determining which risks have the most impact on the project
- Determining how much quantified risk the project has through expected monetary value or Monte Carlo analysis. (See below.)

Determining Probability and Impact
Quantitative probability and impact can be determined in various ways, including:
- Interviewing
- Cost and time estimating
- Delphi Technique
- Use of historical records from previous projects
- Expert judgment
- Expected monetary value analysis
- Monte Carlo analysis

Expected Monetary Value
Take this to mean probability times impact. Questions on the exam can ask, "What is the expected monetary value of the following?" Expected monetary value questions can also be asked in conjunction with decision trees noted in this chapter.

Exercise Test yourself! Complete the following chart.

Work Package	Probability	Impact	Expected Monetary Value
A	10%	$20,000	
B	30%	$45,000	
C	68%	$18,000	

Answer I hope it makes you feel better that something on the exam is easy!

Work Package	Probability	Impact	Expected Monetary Value
A	10%	$20,000	$2,000
B	30%	$45,000	$13,500
C	68%	$18,000	$12,240

Monte Carlo Analysis (simulation technique) Imagine if you could prove to the sponsor that even if the project was done 5,000 times, there is only low probability that the end date they desire will happen? Valuable? Then why have you not learned risk management?

This type of result is what simulation (including Monte Carlo analysis) is all about. It uses the network diagram and estimates to "perform" the project many times and to simulate the cost or schedule results of the project. See also the discussion of this topic in the Time chapter.

There have traditionally been only one or two questions about Monte Carlo analysis on the exam, though it is mentioned as a choice a little more frequently.

 Know the following for the exam. Monte Carlo analysis:

- Evaluates the overall risk in the project
- Provides the probability of completing the project on any specific day, or for any specific amount of cost
- Provides the probability of any activity actually being on the critical path
- Takes into account path convergence (places in the network diagram where many paths converge into one activity)
- Translates uncertainties into impacts to the total project
- Can be used to assess cost and schedule impacts
- Is usually done with a computer-based Monte Carlo program because of the intricacies of the calculations
- Results in a probability distribution

Decision Tree (page 257 and a picture on page 258) Expected monetary value and Monte Carlo analysis are used in quantifying overall risk on the project. Decision trees are primarily used to make decisions regarding individual risks when there is uncertainty. Imagine using this when evaluating alternatives in risk response planning and you get the idea. Project managers are always making decisions under uncertainty (e.g., "Should I do it this way or that?"). Decisions trees are used to help make more informed decisions about such things as, "How should the work be done?" by taking into account the risks, probability and impacts.

There have traditionally been only one or two questions about decision trees on the exam. You should understand the following:

- A decision tree takes into account future events in trying to make a decision today.
- It calculates the expected monetary value (probability times impact) in more complex situations than the expected monetary value example previously presented.
- It involves mutual exclusivity (previously explained in the Quality chapter).
- A decision tree is a model of a real situation and could therefore have costs occurring early or later in the model. Look for these costs to be in different locations. You should be able to answer questions about decision trees and calculate a simple one. The exam could ask you to calculate the expected monetary value (or just "value") of a path or the value of your decision.

The following exercise shows a picture of a decision tree. The box represents a decision to be made and the circles represent what can happen as a result of the decision.

Exercise A company is trying to determine if prototyping is worthwhile on the project. They have come up with the following impacts of whether the equipment works or fails. Based on the information provided below, what is the expected monetary value of your decision?

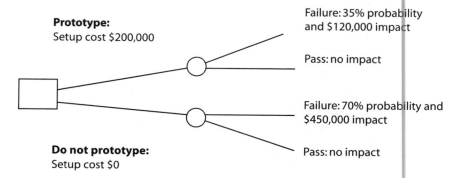

Prototype:
Setup cost $200,000

Failure: 35% probability and $120,000 impact

Pass: no impact

Failure: 70% probability and $450,000 impact

Pass: no impact

Do not prototype:
Setup cost $0

Answer If one just looks at the setup cost of prototyping it would seem like an unwise decision to spend money on prototyping. However, the analysis proves differently. Taking into account only one future event, the decision is that it would be cheaper to do the prototyping. The answer is $242,000, or to prototype.

Prototype	35% × $120,000 = $42,000 + $200,000 = $242,000
Do Not Prototype	70% × $450,000 = $315,000

Remember that probabilities and impacts can exist anywhere in a decision tree, depending on the decision modeled. Each example you see may be different.

Exercise You need to fly from one city to another. You can take airline A or B. Considering the data provided, which airline should you take, and what is the expected monetary value of your decision?

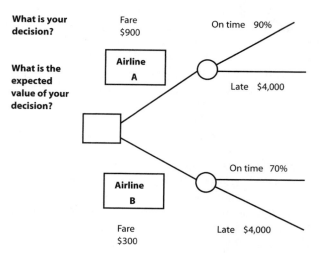

What is your decision?

What is the expected value of your decision?

Fare $900

Airline A

On time 90%

Late $4,000

On time 70%

Airline B

Fare $300

Late $4,000

Answer Notice that some of the cost impact is earlier in this example. If you just look at the cost of the airfare, you would choose airline B because it is cheaper. However, the airlines have different on time arrival rates. If the on time arrival rate for airline A is 90 percent, it must be late 10 percent of the time. We have a $4,000 impact for being late. The result is that we should choose airline A, with an expected monetary value of $1,300 as shown below.

Airline A	$(10\% \times \$4,000 = \$400) + (90\% \times \$0 = \$0) + \$900 = \$1,300$
Airline B	$(30\% \times \$4,000 = \$1,200) + (70\% \times \$0 = \$0) + \$300 = \$1,500$

TRICKS OF THE TRADE® **Proving the Value of Project Management** Project management saves time and money on projects. Sometimes getting our management to understand that is difficult. How valuable would it be to be able to prove the value of project management?

Imagine the first time you calculate the expected monetary value of all the risks that have made it through qualitative risk analysis or you have completed a Monte Carlo analysis for the project. In either case, you calculate that you need a $98,000 contingency reserve on the project to accommodate risks. That number can be used in many ways. Let's try this example. The team moves on to risk response planning and thereby eliminates some risks and reduces the probability or impact of others. The expected monetary value or Monte Carlo analysis is then redone showing a revised need for only a $12,000 reserve. You have just saved $86,000 and you have not even started the project yet! How can gaining support for project management be difficult in the real world with information like that?

Outputs of Quantitative Risk Analysis (page 259)
- **Risk Register Updates:**
  - **Prioritized list of quantified risks** What are the risks that are most likely to cause trouble? To affect the critical path? That need the most contingency reserve?
  - **Amount of contingency time and cost reserves needed** (e.g., The project requires an additional $50,000 and two months of time to accommodate the risks on the project.)
  - **Possible realistic and achievable completion dates and project costs with confidence levels versus the cost and time objectives for the project** (e.g., We are 95 percent confident that we can complete this project on May 25th for $989,000.)
  - **The quantified probability of meeting project objectives** (e.g., We only have an 80 percent chance of completing the project within the six months required by the customer, or We only have a 75 percent chance of completing the project within the $800,000 budget.)
  - **Trends in quantified risk analysis** As quantitative risk analysis is repeated during project planning, and when changes are proposed, changes to the overall risk of the project can be tracked and trends seen.

Risk Response Planning (page 260) This process involves figuring out "What are we going to do about each top risk?" It involves finding ways to make the threat smaller or eliminate it entirely, as well as finding ways to make positive risks more likely, or greater in impact. Responses may include doing one or all of the following for each top risk:
- Do something to eliminate the threats before they happen
- Decrease the probability and/or impact of threats or increase the probability and/or impact of opportunities

For the remaining (residual) risks:
- Do something if the risk happens: Contingency plans
- Do something if contingency plans are not effective: Fallback plans

Many risks can actually be eliminated, but it is not practical or possible to eliminate all risk on a project. It is important to remember that strategies are reviewed over the life of the project for appropriateness, as more information about the project becomes known.

Risk Response Strategies (Sometimes called risk mitigation strategies, page 261) When completing risk response planning, it is important to realize that many strategies for each risk can be unearthed. One or more strategy is selected that enhances opportunities and reduces threats. Sometimes strategies can be determined for each cause, rather than each risk, thereby eliminating many risks with one response.

In order to achieve these results, it is important to make sure the analysis of what can be done about each risk is thorough. Therefore, there are categories of risk responses that should be considered for each risk, or for each cause of risks. No option should be left uncovered, including changes to any component of the "triple constraint."

Some strategies involve changing the planned approach to completing the project, e.g., changes to the WBS, quality management plan, resources, communications, schedule or budget. Other strategies (called contingency responses) involve simply coming up with a plan to be implemented when and if the risk occurs.

 Communication is stressed on the exam, so do not forget the role of communicating what you are doing about risks. Communication of risks and strategies is essential.

Response strategies for threats include:
- **Avoid** Eliminate the threat by eliminating the cause (e.g., Remove the work package or person.)
- **Mitigate** Reduce the probability or the impact of a threat, thereby making it a smaller risk and removing it from the list of top risks on the project. Options for reducing the probability are looked for separately from options for reducing the impact. Any reduction will make a difference, but the option with the most reduction is often the option selected.
- **Transfer (Deflect, Allocate)** Make another party responsible for the risk through purchasing of insurance, performance bonds, warranties, guarantees or outsourcing the work. Here is where the strong connection between risk and procurement (or contracts) begins. One must complete risk assessment before a contract can be signed! Transference of risk is included in the terms and conditions of the contract.

A response to certain risks such as fire, property or personal injury (e.g., pure risks) is to purchase insurance. Insurance exchanges an unknown risk for a known risk. For example, in the event of a fire, the risk is unknown depending on the extent of the fire. But when insurance is purchased, the cost risk of fire becomes known, as it is the cost of the insurance. Purchasing insurance does not eliminate all risk. For example, there can still be schedule delays on the project caused by the fire.

 If you were to outsource work to a third party as a response strategy, would the risk go away? Transferring a risk will leave some risk behind. For example, you outsource, but the third party has trouble and therefore causes you a schedule delay.

Response strategies for opportunities include:
- **Exploit** (the reverse of avoid) Add work or change the project to make sure the opportunity occurs
- **Enhance** (the reverse of mitigate) Increase the likelihood, probability and positive impacts of the risk event
- **Share** Allocate ownership of the opportunity to a third party (forming a partnership, team or joint venture) that is best able to achieve the opportunity

Response strategy for both threats and opportunities:
- **Accept** Do nothing and say, "If it happens, it happens." Active acceptance may involve the creation of contingency plans to be implemented if the risk occurs and the allocation of time and cost reserves to the project. Passive acceptance leaves actions to be determined as needed, if (after) the risk occurs. A decision to accept a risk must be communicated to stakeholders.

Whether responding to threats or opportunities:
- Strategies must be timely
- The effort selected must be appropriate to the severity of the risk—avoid spending more money preventing the risk than the impact of the risk would cost if it occurred
- One response can be used to address more than one risk
- More than one response can be used to address the same risk
- A response can address a root cause of risk and thereby address more than one risk
- Involve the team, other stakeholders and experts in selecting a strategy

Exercise Determine the name of each risk response strategy described. Remember to include mitigate the probability and mitigate the impact.

Description of Strategy	Name of Risk Response Strategy
Remove a work package or activity from the project	
Assign a team member to visit the seller's manufacturing facilities frequently to learn about a problem with delivery as early as possible	
Move a work package to a date when a more experienced resource is available to be assigned to the project	
Begin negotiation for the equipment earlier than planned so as to secure a lower price	
Outsource a work package so as to gain an opportunity	
Notify management that there could be a cost increase if a risk occurs because no action is being taken to prevent the risk	
Remove a troublesome resource from the project	
Provide a team member who is less experienced with additional training	
Train the team on conflict resolution strategies	
Outsource difficult work to a more experienced company	
Ask the client to handle some of the work	
Prototype a risky piece of equipment	

Answer

Description of Strategy	Name of Risk Response Strategy
Remove a work package or activity from the project	Avoid
Assign a team member to visit the seller's manufacturing facilities frequently to learn about a problem with delivery as early as possible	Mitigate the impact
Move a work package to a date when a more experienced resource is available to be assigned to the project	Exploit
Begin negotiation for the equipment earlier than planned so as to secure a lower price	Enhance the impact
Outsource a work package so as to gain an opportunity	Share
Notify management that there could be a cost increase if a risk occurs because no action is being taken to prevent the risk	Accept
Remove a troublesome resource from the project	Avoid
Provide a team member who is less experienced with additional training	Mitigate the probability
Train the team on conflict resolution strategies	Mitigate the impact
Outsource difficult work to a more experienced company	Transfer
Ask the client to handle some of the work	Transfer
Prototype a risky piece of equipment	Mitigate the probability

Outputs of Risk Response Planning (page 263) The output of risk response planning is the further updated risk register plus other items.

- **Project Management Plan Updates** The efforts spent in risk management will result in changes to the risk management plan and therefore to the project management plan. Work packages or activities could be added, removed or assigned to different resources. Thus, planning is an iterative process.
- **Updates to Risk Register** including:
  - **Residual Risks** It is these risks which remain after risk response planning, and those that have been accepted for which contingency plans and fallback plans can be created. Residual risks should be properly documented and reviewed throughout the project to see if their ranking has changed.
  - **Contingency Plans** Contingency plans are plans describing the specific actions that will be taken if the opportunity or threat occurs.
  - **Risk Response Owners** (page 260) A key concept in risk response planning is that the project manager does not have to do it all and neither does the team. Each risk must be assigned to someone who may help develop the risk response and who will be assigned to carry out the risk response or "own" the risk. The risk response owner can be a stakeholder rather than a team member.

    Think about how the application of risk management can change your real-world projects. The risk occurs; the risk response owner takes the pre-arranged and pre-approved plan for action determined in project planning and informs the project manager. No meeting is needed, just action! How powerful is this!

- **Secondary Risks** Included in risk response planning should be an analysis of the new risks created by the implementation of selected risk response strategies. Frequently, what is done to respond to one risk will cause other risks to occur. For example, a risk of fire can be allocated to an insurance company, potentially causing the risk of cash flow problems. Cash flow should then be analyzed and if appropriate, added to the risk management process.
- **Risk Triggers** Events that trigger the contingency response. A project manager should identify the early warning signs (indirect manifestations of actual risk events) for each risk on a project so that they will know when to take action.
- **Contracts** A project manager must be involved before a contract is signed. Before the contract is finalized, the project manager will have completed a risk analysis and included contract terms and conditions required to mitigate or allocate threats and to enhance opportunities.
- **Fallback Plans** (page 264) Specific actions that will be taken if the contingency plan is not effective. Think how prepared you will feel if you have plans for what to do if a risk occurs and what to do if that original plan does not work.
- **Reserves** (contingency, page 264) Let's spend a little more time talking about this. First, realize that having reserves for schedule and cost is a required part of project management. You cannot come up with a schedule or budget for the project without them. Reserves are covered in the Cost chapter, but it makes sense to cover them here as well.

  There can be two kinds of reserves for time and cost; contingency reserves and management reserves. Contingency reserves account for "known unknowns;" items you identified in risk management. They cover the residual risks in the project. Management reserves account for "unknown unknowns," items you did not or could not identify in risk management. Projects can have both kinds. The contingency reserve is calculated and is made part of the cost baseline. Management reserves are estimated (e.g., 5 percent of the project cost) and are made a part of the project budget, not the baseline. Therefore, management approval is needed to make use of management reserves.

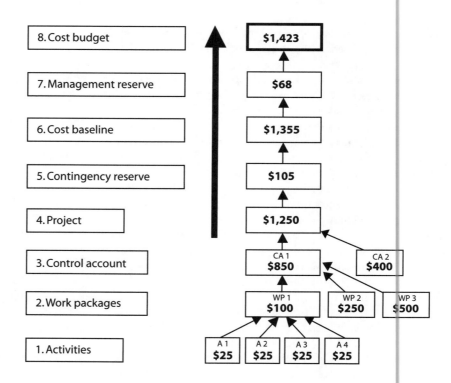

8. Cost budget		**$1,423**
7. Management reserve		**$68**
6. Cost baseline		**$1,355**
5. Contingency reserve		**$105**
4. Project		**$1,250**
3. Control account		CA 1 **$850** CA 2 **$400**
2. Work packages		WP 1 **$100** WP 2 **$250** WP 3 **$500**
1. Activities		A 1 **$25** A 2 **$25** A 3 **$25** A 4 **$25**

Reserves should be managed and guarded throughout the project life cycle. Let's try an example of calculating contingency reserve.

Exercise You are planning the manufacture of an existing product's modifications. Your analysis has come up with the following. What is the cost contingency reserve that you would use?

- 30 percent probability of a delay in the receipt of parts with a cost to the project of $9,000
- 20 percent probability that the parts will be $10,000 cheaper than expected
- 25 percent probability that two parts will not fit together when installed, costing an extra $3,500
- 30 percent probability that the manufacture may be simpler than expected, saving $2,500
- 5 percent probability of a design defect, causing $5,000 of rework

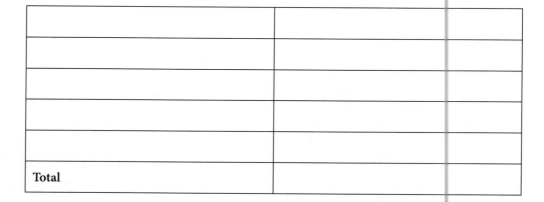

Total	

Answer The answer is $1,075.

30% × $9,000	Add $2,700
20% × $10,000	Subtract $2,000
25% × $3,500	Add $875
30% × $2,500	Subtract $750
5% × $5,000	Add $250
Total	**$1,075**

TRICKS OF THE TRADE Let's understand the process better by looking at it in a chart form.

Exercise Create a flowchart of the risk process from risk identification through risk response planning.

Answer Creating this chart will help you make sure you understand what you have read. Remember that your flowchart might be different than mine.

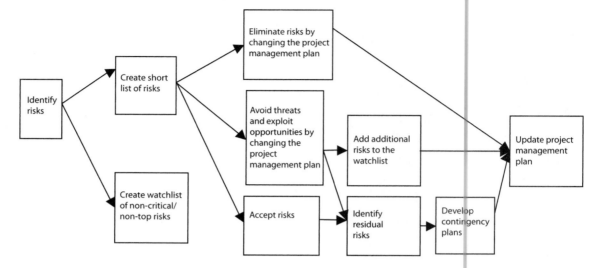

The exam often asks questions such as:
>   *What do you do with non-critical risks?*
>   **Answer** *Document in a watchlist and revisit periodically.*
>
>   *Would you select only one risk response strategy?*
>   **Answer** *No, you can choose a combination of choices.*
>
>   *What risk management activities are done during the execution of the project?*
>   **Answer** *Watching out for watchlisted (non-critical) risks that become more important.*
>
>   *What is the most important item to address in project team meetings?*
>   **Answer** *Risk.*
>
>   *How would risks be addressed in project meetings?*
>   **Answer** *By asking, "What is the status of risks? Any new risks? Any change to the order of importance?"*

▬▬ Risk Monitoring and Control (page 264)

Risk questions are asked assuming that you have done proper project management and assuming that you have risk response owners, you have contingency plans already in place and other such activities. The exam also assumes that the project is substantially less risky than it would have been if you had not planned the project. If you do not have experience using risk management in the real world, these exam questions may be hard.

Exercise Think about the paragraph above. What should the project manager be doing related to risk while the project work is ongoing? Spend time really thinking this through. Once you have completed your own list of actions, look at mine to make sure you do them all. You could include things that are not on my list, but check each one of those for validity before determining that they are accurate additions to your list.

Actions	Included Below?

Answer This process involves managing the project according to the risk response plan and may include the following actions:

- Look for the occurrence of risk triggers
- Monitor residual risks
- Identify, analyze and plan for new risks (REMEMBER: Risk identification is done during risk identification as well as risk monitoring and controlling!)
- Ensure the execution of risk management plans
- Evaluate the effectiveness of risk management plans
- Develop new risk responses
- Collect and communicate risk status
- Communicate with stakeholders about risks
- Determine if assumptions are still valid
- Ensure proper risk management procedures are being followed
- Revisit the watchlist to see if additional risk responses need to be determined
- Implement corrective actions to adjust to the severity of actual risk events
- Look for any unexpected effects or consequences of risk events
- Reevaluate risk identification, qualitative and quantitative risk analysis when the project deviates from the baseline
- Update risk management and response plans

- Look at the need to recommend corrective actions and change requests to see if they lead to identifying more risks
- Make changes to the project management plan when new risk responses are developed
- Create a database of risk data that may be used throughout the organization on other projects
- Perform variance and trend analysis on project performance data
- Use contingency reserves and adjust for approved changes

Other terms to know include:

Workarounds (page 267) Whereas contingency responses are developed in advance, workarounds are unplanned responses developed to deal with the occurrence of unanticipated risk events.

Risk Audits (page 266) Imagine having a team of auditors descend upon you asking you to prove you have identified all the risks that can be or should be identified for your project, that you have plans for each of the major risks and that risk response owners are prepared to take action. This is a risk audit. It results in identification of lessons learned for the project and for other projects in the organization.

Risk Reassessments (page 266) Questions always seem to come up on the exam that require you to know the team needs to periodically review risk management plans and adjust as required. Many items in the previous exercise relate to this. Remember, a result of such reviews may be additional qualitative or quantitative risk analysis, as well as further risk response planning.

Status Meetings (page 267) I have often said that only bad project managers hold "go around the room" type status meetings (see the free tip on this subject on our Web site: www.rmcproject.com). Risk should be a major topic at status meetings (I call them team meetings) to keep focus on risks, to continue to identify new risks and to make sure plans remain appropriate.

Reserve Analysis (page 266) Everyone will try to use the management or contingency reserve for changes. It is the project manager's role to manage the reserve, use it only for risks and to keep track of the risk of the project. Additional reserve might need to be requested or reserve could be decreased if expected threats do not occur or expected opportunities do occur.

Closing of Risks That Are No Longer Applicable The time when each identified risk could logically occur will eventually pass. Closing of risks allows the team to focus on managing those risks that are still open.

Outputs of Risk Monitoring and Control (page 267):
- **Risk Register Updates** Risk monitoring and control will add to the risk register the following:
  - Outcomes of the risk reassessments and risk audits
  - Updates to previous parts of risk management
  - Closing of risks that are no longer applicable
  - Details of what happened when risks occurred
  - Lessons learned

- **Requested Changes** Risk monitoring and control will uncover changes needed to the project management plan. These changes are reviewed in integrated change control and then implemented in direct and manage project execution and risk monitoring and control, as necessary.
- **Recommended Corrective and Preventive Actions**
- **Updates to the Project Management Plan**
- **Organizational Process Assets Updates** The risk process will lead to the creation of risk templates, risk register including project risks and risk responses, checklists and other data to be used as historical records for future projects.

Common Risk Management Errors The following is a synopsis of my presentation, "Common Stumbling Blocks in Risk Management," designed to help you think about common risk management errors and thus help you prepare for the exam.

- Risk identification is completed without knowing enough about the project. (See inputs to risk management.)
- Project risk is evaluated using only a questionnaire, interview or Monte Carlo analysis and thus does not provide specific risks.
- Risk identification ends too soon, resulting in a brief list (20 risks) rather than an extensive list (hundreds) of risks.
- Risk identification through quantitative risk analysis are blended, resulting in risks that are evaluated or judged as they come to light. This decreases the number of total risks identified and causes people to stop participating in risk identification.
- The risks identified are general rather than specific (e.g., "communications" rather than "poor communication of customers' needs regarding installation of system XXX causing two weeks of rework").
- Some things considered to be risks are not uncertain, but facts, and are therefore not risks.
- Whole categories of risks are missed such as technology, cultural or marketplace.
- Only one method is used to identify risks (i.e., only using a checklist) rather than a combination of methods. A combination helps ensure that more risks are identified.
- The first risk response strategy identified is selected without looking at other options and finding the best option or combination of options.
- Risk management is not given enough attention during project executing.
- Project managers do not explain the risk management process to their team during project planning.
- Contracts are usually signed long BEFORE risks to the project are discussed.

The Risk Management Process Exercise There can be many questions about the process of risk management on the exam. The following exercise tests if you understand what you have read.

Exercise Re-create the risk management process, including the outputs, on the form on the next page. Check your answers to the contents of this chapter when you are done. Even with one reading of this book, you should get most of the actions and outputs correct. The second and third times you read the chapter, you should be almost 100 percent accurate. This exercise is about remembering key parts of risk management, not memorization. Create the chart three times and you should know it well enough for the exam.

Risk Manage- ment Planning	Risk Identifica- tion	Qualitative Risk Analysis	Quantitative Risk Analysis	Risk Re- sponse Planning	Risk Moni- toring and Controlling
Actions					
Outputs					

Practice Exam

Risk Management

1. All of the following are factors in the assessment of project risk EXCEPT?
   A. Risk event
   B. Risk probability
   C. Amount at stake
   D. Insurance premiums

2. If a project has a 60 percent chance of a U.S. $100,000 profit and a 40 percent chance of a U.S. $100,000 loss, the expected monetary value for the project is:
   A. $100,000 profit
   B. $60,000 loss
   C. $20,000 profit
   D. $40,000 loss

3. Assuming that the ends of a range of estimates are +/- 3 sigma from the mean, which of the following range estimates involves the LEAST risk?
   A. 30 days, plus or minus 5 days
   B. 22–30 days
   C. Optimistic = 26 days, most likely = 30 days, pessimistic = 33 days
   D. Mean of 28 days

4. Which of the following risk events is MOST likely to interfere with attaining a project's schedule objective?
   A. Delays in obtaining required approvals
   B. Substantial increases in the cost of purchased materials
   C. Contract disputes that generate claims for increased payments
   D. Slippage of the planned post-implementation review meeting

5. If a risk has a 20 percent chance of happening in a given month, and the project is expected to last five months, what is the probability that this risk event will occur during the fourth month of the project?
   A. Less than 1 percent
   B. 20 percent
   C. 60 percent
   D. 80 percent

6. If a risk event has a 90 percent chance of occurring, and the consequences will be U.S. $10,000, what does U.S. $9,000 represent?
   A. Risk value
   B. Present value
   C. Expected monetary value
   D. Contingency budget

7. Risks will be identified during which risk management process(es)?
   A. Quantitative risk analysis and risk identification
   B. Risk identification and risk monitoring and control
   C. Qualitative risk analysis and risk monitoring and control
   D. Risk identification

8. **What should be done with risks on the watchlist?**
   A. Document them for historical use on other projects.
   B. Document them and revisit during project monitoring and controlling.
   C. Document them and set them aside because they are already covered in your contingency plans.
   D. Document them and give them to the customer.

9. **All of the following are always inputs to the risk management process EXCEPT:**
   A. historical information.
   B. lessons learned.
   C. work breakdown structure.
   D. project status reports.

10. **Risk tolerances are determined in order to help:**
    A. the team rank the project risks.
    B. the project manager estimate the project.
    C. the team schedule the project.
    D. management know how other managers will act on the project.

11. **All of the following are common results of risk management EXCEPT?**
    A. Contract terms and conditions are created.
    B. The project management plan is changed.
    C. The communications management plan is changed.
    D. The project charter is changed.

12. **Purchasing insurance is BEST considered an example of risk:**
    A. mitigation.
    B. transfer.
    C. acceptance.
    D. avoidance.

13. **You are finding it difficult to evaluate the exact cost impact of risks. You should evaluate on a(n):**
    A. quantitative basis.
    B. numerical basis.
    C. qualitative basis.
    D. econometric basis.

14. **An output of risk response planning is:**
    A. residual risks.
    B. risks identified.
    C. prioritized list of risks.
    D. impacts identified.

15. **Workarounds are determined during which risk management process?**
    A. Risk identification
    B. Quantitative risk analysis
    C. Risk response planning
    D. Risk monitoring and control

16. During which risk management process is a determination to transfer a risk made?
    A. Risk identification
    B. Quantitative risk analysis
    C. Risk response planning
    D. Risk monitoring and control

17. A project manager has just finished the risk response plan for a U.S. $387,000 engineering project. Which of the following should he probably do NEXT?
    A. Determine the overall risk rating of the project.
    B. Begin to analyze the risks that show up in the project drawings.
    C. Add work packages to the project work breakdown structure.
    D. Hold a project risk reassessment.

18. A project manager asked various stakeholders to determine the probability and impact of a number of risks. He then analyzed assumptions. He is about to move to the next step of risk management. Based on this information, what has the project manager forgotten to do?
    A. Evaluate trends in risk analysis.
    B. Identify triggers.
    C. Provide a standardized risk rating matrix.
    D. Create a fallback plan.

19. A project manager has assembled the project team, identified 56 risks on the project, determined what would trigger the risks, rated them on a risk rating matrix, tested their assumptions and assessed the quality of the data used. The team is continuing to move through the risk management process. What has the project manager forgotten to do?
    A. Simulation
    B. Risk mitigation
    C. Overall risk ranking for the project
    D. Involvement of other stakeholders

20. You are a project manager for a construction of a major new manufacturing plant that has never been done before. The project cost is estimated at U.S. $30,000,000 and will make use of three sellers. Once begun, the project cannot be cancelled, as there will be a large expenditure on plant and equipment. As the project manager, it would be MOST important to carefully:
    A. review all cost proposals from the sellers.
    B. examine the budget reserves.
    C. complete the project charter.
    D. perform an identification of risks.

21. During risk management planning, your team has come up with 434 risks and 16 major causes of those risks. The project is the last of a series of projects which the team has worked on together. The sponsor is very supportive and a lot of time was

invested in making sure the project charter was complete and signed off by all key stakeholders.

During project planning, the team cannot come up with an effective way to mitigate or insure against a risk. It is not work that can be outsourced, nor can it be deleted. What would be the BEST solution?

A. Accept the risk.

B. Continue to investigate ways to mitigate the risk.

C. Look for ways to avoid the risk.

D. Look for ways to transfer the risk.

22. **A project manager is quantifying risk for her project. Several of her experts are offsite, but wish to be included. How can this be done?**

A. Use Monte Carlo analysis using the Internet as a tool.

B. Apply the critical path method.

C. Determine options for recommended corrective action.

D. Apply the Delphi Technique.

23. **An experienced project manager has just begun working for a large information technology integrator. Her manager provides her with a draft project charter and immediately asks her to provide an analysis of the risks on the project. Which of the following would BEST help in this effort?**

A. An article from PM Network Magazine

B. Her project scope statement from the project planning process

C. Her resource plan from the project planning process

D. A conversation with a team member from a similar project that failed in the past

24. **You have been appointed as the manager of a new, large and complex project. Because this project is business-critical and very visible, senior management has told you to analyze the project's risks and prepare response strategies for them as soon as possible. The organization has risk management procedures that are seldom used or followed, and has had a history of handling risks badly. The project's first milestone is in two weeks. In preparing the risk response plan, input from which of the following is generally LEAST important?**

A. Project team members

B. Project sponsor

C. Individuals responsible for risk management policies and templates

D. Key stakeholders

25. **You were in the middle of a two-year project to deploy new technology to field offices across the country. A hurricane caused power outages just when the upgrade was near completion. When the power was restored, all of the project reports and historical data were lost with no way of retrieving them. What should have been done to mitigate this risk?**

A. Purchase insurance.

B. Plan for a reserve fund.

C. Monitor the weather and have a contingency plan.

D. Schedule the installation outside of the hurricane season.

26. A system development project is nearing project closing when a previously unidentified risk is discovered. This could potentially affect the project's overall ability to deliver. What should be done NEXT?
    A. Alert the project sponsor of potential impacts to cost, scope or schedule.
    B. Qualify the risk.
    C. Mitigate this risk by developing a risk response plan.
    D. Develop a workaround.

27. The cost performance index (CPI) of a project is 0.6 and the schedule performance index (SPI) is 0.71. The project has 625 work packages and is being completed over a four year period. The team members are very inexperienced and the project received little support for proper planning. Which of the following is the BEST thing to do?
    A. Update risk identification and analysis.
    B. Spend more time improving the cost estimates.
    C. Remove as many work packages as possible.
    D. Reorganize the responsibility assignment matrix.

28. While preparing your risk responses, you identify additional risks. What should you do?
    A. Add reserves to the project to accommodate the new risks and notify management.
    B. Document the risk items and calculate the expected monetary value based on probability and impact that result from the occurrences.
    C. Determine the risk events and the associated cost, then add the cost to the project budget as a reserve.
    D. Add a 10 percent contingency to the project budget and notify the customer.

29. You have just been assigned as the project manager for a new telecommunications project that is entering the second phase of the project. There appear to be many risks on this project, but no one has evaluated them to assess the range of possible project outcomes. What needs to be done?
    A. Risk management planning
    B. Quantitative risk analysis
    C. Risk response planning
    D. Risk monitoring and control

30. During project executing, a team member identifies a risk that is not in the risk register. What should you do?
    A. Get further information on how the team member identified the risk, because you already performed a detailed analysis and did not identify this risk.
    B. Disregard the risk, because risks were identified during project planning.
    C. Inform the customer about the risk.
    D. Analyze the risk.

31. During project executing, a major problem occurs that was not included in the risk register. What should you do FIRST?
    A. Create a workaround.
    B. Reevaluate the risk identification process.
    C. Look for any unexpected effects of the problem.
    D. Tell management.

32. The customer requests a change to the project that would increase the project risk. Which of the following should you do before all the others?
    A. Include the expected monetary value of the risk in the new cost estimate.
    B. Talk to the customer about the impact of the change.
    C. Analyze the impacts of the change with the team.
    D. Change the risk management plan.

33. Which of the following is a chief characteristic of the Delphi Technique?
    A. Extrapolation from historical records from previous projects
    B. Expert opinion
    C. Analytical hierarchy process
    D. Bottom-up approach

34. A project has had some problems, but now seems under control. In the last few months almost all the reserve has been used up and most of the negative impacts of events that had been predicted have occurred. There are only four activities left and two of them are on the critical path. Management now informs the project manager that it would be in the performing organization's best interest to finish the project two weeks earlier than scheduled in order to receive an additional profit. In response, the project manager sends out a request for proposal for some work that the team was going to do, in the hopes that another company might be able to do the work faster. The project manager can BEST be said to be attempting to work with:
    A. reserve.
    B. opportunities.
    C. scope verification.
    D. threats.

Risk Management Answers

1. **Answer** D
   Explanation Insurance premiums come into play when you determine which risk response strategy you will use.

2. **Answer** C
   Explanation Expected monetary value (EMV) is computed by EMV = Probability × Impact. We need to compute both positive and negative values and then sum them. 0.6 × $100,000 = $60,000. 0.4 × ($100,000) = ($40,000). Expected Monetary Value = $60,000 - $40,000 = $20,000 profit.

3. **Answer** C
   Explanation This one drove you crazy didn't it? Reread the question! When you look at the ranges of each choice, you will see that choice A is ten days, choice B is eight days and choice C is seven days. The range of estimates with the smallest range is the least risky. Therefore, the answer is C. The words +/- 3 sigma are extraneous. Practice reading questions that are wordy and have extraneous data.

4. **Answer** A
   Explanation Cost increases (choice B) and contract disputes (choice C) will not necessarily interfere with schedule. Notice the words "post-implementation" in choice D. It will not definitely interfere with the project schedule. Choice A is the only one that deals with a time delay.

5. **Answer** B
   Explanation Don't feel too silly. Many people miss this one. No calculation is needed. If there is a 20 percent chance in any one month, the chance in the fourth month must therefore be 20 percent.

6. **Answer** C
   Explanation Expected monetary value is computed by multiplying the probability times the impact. In this case, EMV = 0.9 × $10,000 = $9,000.

7. **Answer** B
   Explanation This is a tricky question. Risks are identified during risk identification, naturally, but newly emerging risks are identified in risk monitoring and control.

8. **Answer** B
   Explanation Risks change throughout the project. You need to review risks at intervals during the project to ensure that non-critical risks have not become critical.

9. **Answer** D
   Explanation Project status reports (choice D) can be an input to risk management. However, when completing risk management for the first time, you would not have project status reports. Therefore, project status reports are not always an input to risk management.

10. **Answer** A
    Explanation If you know the tolerances of the stakeholders, you can determine how they might react to different situations and risk events. You use this information to help assign levels of risk on each work package or activity.

11. **Answer** D

    Explanation A change to the project charter is not always necessary. In fact, a change to the charter is a fundamental change to the project and may require a major adjustment to all aspects of the project management plan. There are many reasons the other choices could happen as a result of risk. Since a contract can only be created after risks are known (a contract is a tool to transfer risks) it is common sense that choice A cannot be the exception. The project management plan (choice B) could change to include a modified WBS and new work packages related to mitigating risk. The communications management plan (choice C) could change as a way to address a risk. Choice D is the best answer.

12. **Answer** B

    Explanation To mitigate risk (choice A) we either reduce the probability of the event happening or reduce its impact. Many people think of using insurance as a way of decreasing impact. However, mitigating risk is taking action before a risk event occurs. Buying insurance is not such an action. Acceptance of risk (choice C) does not involve such action as purchasing insurance. Avoidance of risk (choice D) means we change the way we will execute the project so the risk is no longer a factor. Transference is passing the risk off to another party.

13. **Answer** C

    Explanation If you cannot determine an exact cost impact to the event, use qualitative estimates such as Low, Medium, High, etc.

14. **Answer** A

    Explanation Risks are identified (choice B) during risk identification and risk monitoring and control. Prioritized risks (choice C) are documented during qualitative and quantitative risk analysis. Impacts (choice D) are generally determined during quantitative risk analysis. The best answer is A.

15. **Answer** D

    Explanation A workaround refers to determining how to handle a risk that occurs but is not included in the risk register. The project must be in risk monitoring and control if risks have occurred.

16. **Answer** C

    Explanation Transference is a risk response strategy.

17. **Answer** C

    Explanation This situation is occurring during project planning. Planning must be completed before moving on. Determining the risk rating of the project (choice A) is done during qualitative risk analysis, and should have already been done. Choice B is work that is done during project executing. Project risk reassessment (choice D) occurs during risk monitoring and control, the next step in the risk process after response planning. But the question does not ask what is next in the risk management process, just what is next. Only choice C comes after risk in project planning. Do you know the order of planning yet?

18. **Answer** C

    Explanation The activities of qualitative risk analysis are probability and impact definition, assumptions testing and probability and impact matrix development.

19. **Answer** D

    Explanation The process they have used so far is fine, except the input of other stakeholders is needed in order to identify more risks.

20. **Answer** D

    Explanation Choice A could be done, but it is not a pressing issue based on the situation provided. Choice B could also be done, but not until risk planning is completed. It is always important to carefully complete a project charter, choice C, but there are other issues needing detailed attention in this situation, so choice C cannot be best. Since this project has never been done before, and there will be a large cost outlay, it would be best for the project manager to spend more time on risk management. Risk identification is the most proactive response and would have the greatest positive impact on the project.

21. **Answer** A

    Explanation This question relates real-world situations to the risk types. Did you realize that the entire first paragraph is extraneous? Based on the question, you cannot delete the work to avoid it, nor can you insure or outsource to transfer the risk. This leaves acceptance as the only correct choice.

22. **Answer** D

    Explanation The Delphi Technique is most commonly used to obtain expert opinions on technical issues, the necessary project or product scope, or the risks.

23. **Answer** D

    Explanation Did you realize that this situation is taking place during the initiating process group? Choices B and C are created in the project planning process and so are not yet available. Therefore, we are left with deciding if choice A or choice D provides the greater value. Since the information gained in choice D is more specific to your company, it is the best choice.

24. **Answer** B

    Explanation Team members (choice A) will have knowledge of the project and the product of the project and will thus have a lot to contribute to risk responses. Those responsible for risk templates (choice C) will be able to provide the templates from past projects (historical records) and therefore will be very important. Key stakeholders (choice D) will know more about the technical working of the project to help plan "What are we going to do about it?" so choice D is not likely to be the least important. The sponsor (choice B) may have the least knowledge of what will work to solve the problems. Sponsors need to be involved in the project and help identify risks. They may even approve the response plans created by others, but they would not generally be major contributors to response plans. This makes B the best choice.

25. **Answer** C

    Explanation The risk is the loss of data due to a power outage. Choice A is not related to "mitigating" the problem. It transfers the risk. A reserve fund (choice B) is acceptance and would help address the cost factors after the power failure, but would not reduce the probablilty or impact of it. Avoiding the hurricane by scheduling the installation at a different time (choice D) mitigates the power outage risk but could have a large negative impact on the project schedule and so is not the best choice. The better choice of the mitigation options (choices C and D) is to monitor the weather and know when to implement the contingency plan. It is relevant that this is a two-year project. If the project was shorter, choice D may have been a more appropriate choice.

26. **Answer** B
Explanation You would need to analyze the problem before you would talk to the sponsor (choice A). You could not mitigate the risk (choice C) until you qualified the risk. A workaround (choice D) is an unplanned response to a risk that is occurring. This risk is identified, not occurring, so there is no need to take action by creating a workaround. Qualifying the risk (choice B) will give you an indication of how great the risk is. That information will help you determine how to proceed.

27. **Answer** A
Explanation This project has deviated so far from the baseline that updated risk identification and risk analysis should be performed.

28. **Answer** B
Explanation When a new risk is identified, it should go through the risk management process. Choice A cannot be the best choice, as you first need to determine the probability and impact of the risk and then try to diminish impact through risk response planning. Only after these efforts should you add reserves. Choice C addresses only costs, when there could also be a time impact. This choice also ignores risk response planning work. Choice D cannot be the best choice because it is better to determine reserves based on a detailed analysis of risk. Therefore the best choice is B.

29. **Answer** A
Explanation Did you notice that this project has already begun? Risk management is a required element of project management. You must complete the risk management process, starting with risk management planning, making choice A the correct choice.

30. **Answer** D
Explanation First you want to determine what the risk entails and the impact to the project, then determine what actions you will take regarding the risk.

31. **Answer** A
Explanation Notice that this is a problem that has occurred, rather than a problem that has just been identified. Following the right process is part of professional and social responsibility. Because an unidentified problem or risk occurred, it is important to perform choices B and C. However, they are not your first choices. You might need to inform management (choice D) but this is reactive, not proactive, and not the first thing you should do.

32. **Answer** C
Explanation This is a recurring theme. First, you should evaluate the impact of the change. Next, determine options. Then go to management and the customer.

33. **Answer** B
Explanation The Delphi Technique uses experts and builds to consensus; therefore expert opinion is the chief characteristic.

34. **Answer** B

    Explanation The wording of this question can be confusing. Reserve (choice A) is mentioned in the situation, but the project manager is not dealing with reserves in the actions he is taking. Choice C involves meeting with the customer to gain formal acceptance, so it cannot be the best choice. Choice D cannot be the best choice since the project manager is trying to make something good happen, not dealing with a negative impact, or threat, that may or may not occur. The project manager is working to make a positive impact on the project more likely to occur, therefore choice B is best.

Procurement Management

Quicktest

- Procurement management process
- Procurement management plan
- Contract management plan
- Contract types
  - CR, CPFF, CPPC, CPIF, T&M, FP, FPIF, FPEPA, Purchase order
- How is project management different in each contract form
- Advantages/disadvantages of each contract form
- Contract change control system
- Termination
- Breach
- What is a contract
- Project manager's role in procurement
- Procurement documents: RFP, IFB, RFQ
- Contract administration work
- Non-competitive forms of procurement
- Types of contract statements of work
- Buyer-conducted performance review
- Claims administration
- Make-or-buy
- Formal acceptance
- Inputs to procurement
- Records management system
- Bidder conferences
- Risk and contract type
- Waiver
- Financial closure
- Final contract performance reporting
- Conflict with contract administrator
- Procurement audit
- Product verification
- Evaluation criteria
- Incentives
- Special provisions
- Standard contract
- Terms and conditions
- Negotiation objectives/tactics
- Privity
- Qualified seller lists
- Advertising
- Centralized/decentralized contracting
- Contract interpretation
- Letter of intent
- Presentations
- Lessons learned
- Contract file
- Non-disclosure agreement
- What makes a legal contract
- Force majeure

I once had a student in my project management class who was very experienced, yet he was very upset about a situation at work. He said that he had arranged a meeting with a seller and the seller did not show up. He then rescheduled and the seller still did not show up. I asked him what kind of contract he had. He had to contact his office to find out that he had a fixed price contract. My next question? Where in the contract did it say the seller had to attend such meetings? After some investigation, he said it was not listed in the contract. My response? Why would the seller attend such meetings if he was not getting paid for it?

Think about it. We are not talking about the role of an attorney, or a contracts or procurement office. We are talking about the project manager's role. The basic knowledge and skills of a project manager should include being able to help create and then read and manage contracts.

For some people, procurement management is one of the hardest knowledge areas on the exam. If you have worked with contracts before, you might have to fine-tune your knowledge and learn the terms for what you already do. You might also have to understand the project manager's role a little better, but you should score well on these questions.

TRICKS OF THE TRADE® If you have not worked with contracts before, I strongly suggest that you obtain from your company some sample contracts, requests for proposals and the resulting proposals and look at them before reading on. It might also be valuable to get in touch with your contract, procurement or legal department. You have an opportunity to build an extremely worthwhile relationship when you ask them what you should know about contracts and then have an opportunity to tell them about project management. Try it!

The project manager should interact with a legal, contracting or procurement department to deal with

Rita's Process Chart—Procurement Management
Where are we in the project management process?

Initiating	Planning	Executing	Monitoring & Controlling	Closing
Select project manager	**Determine how you will do planning—part of management plans**	Acquire final team	Measure against the performance measurement baselines	Develop closure procedures
Determine company culture and existing systems	Create project scope statement	Execute the PM plan	**Measure according to the management plans**	**Complete contract closure**
Collect processes, procedures and historical information	Determine team	Work to produce product scope	**Determine variances and if they warrant corrective action or a change**	**Confirm work is done to requirements**
	Create WBS and WBS dictionary	**Recommend changes and corrective actions**		
	Create activity list	Send and receive information		**Gain formal acceptance of the product**
Divide large projects into phases	Create network diagram	Implement approved changes, defect repair, preventive and corrective actions	Scope verification	Final performance reporting
Identify stakeholders	Estimate resource requirements		Configuration management	**Index and archive records**
Document business need	Estimate time and cost	Continuous improvement	**Recommend changes, defect repair, preventive and corrective actions**	**Update lessons learned knowledge base**
	Determine critical path	Follow processes		
	Develop schedule	Team building		
Determine project objectives	Develop budget	Give recognition and rewards	Integrated change control	Hand off completed product
Document assumptions and constraints	Determine quality standards, processes and metrics	Hold progress meetings	Approve changes, defect repair, preventive and corrective actions	Release resources
	Determine roles and responsibilities	Use work authorization system		
Develop project charter	Determine communications requirements	**Request seller responses**	Risk audits	
	Risk identification, qualitative and quantitative risk analysis and response planning	**Select sellers**	Manage reserves	
Develop preliminary project scope statement			Use issue logs	
	Iterations—go back		Facilitate conflict resolution	
	Determine what to purchase		Measure team member performance	
	Prepare procurement documents		Report on performance	
	Finalize the "how to execute and control" aspects of all management plans		Create forecasts	
	Create process improvement plan		**Administer contracts**	
	Develop final PM plan and performance measurement baselines			
	Gain formal approval for plan			
	Hold kickoff meeting			

The Procurement Management Process

The Procurement Management Process	Done During
Plan purchases and acquisitions	Planning process group
Plan contracting	Planning process group
Request seller responses	Executing process group
Select sellers	Executing process group
Contract administration	Monitoring and controlling process group
Contract closure	Closing process group

contracts. In many cases, it is one of those departments that have the primary responsibility to create and administer contracts. They may also be the only ones who can approve a change to the contract. People in these departments could be called the procurement manager, procurement officer, contract officer or contract manager. For brevity's sake, I will just use the term contract manager in this chapter.

In the real world, there are terms such as contractor, subcontractor, owner, designer, etc. The *PMBOK® Guide* has narrowed all of these down to two; you are either a buyer or a seller in any procurement. Many companies are a buyer in one procurement and a seller in another. Be careful as this has also been an area that has troubled people on the exam.

TRICKS OF THE TRADE® If you are a seller in your real world work, it is an important trick to know that the questions are all written from the buyer's perspective unless stated otherwise. The exam also assumes the seller is not supplying people to adjunct the buyer's team, meaning that the seller remains external to the project team. Remember this and get four more questions right! Sellers should get used to thinking from the buyer's perspective when answering practice questions.

TRICKS OF THE TRADE® Keep in mind the following general rules, especially if you find a question where the answer is not immediately apparent:
- Contracts require formality
- All product and project management requirements should be specifically stated in the contract
- If it is not in the contract, it can only be done if a change is issued
- If it is in the contract, it must be done or a change order, signed by both parties issued
- Changes must be in writing
- Contracts are legally binding
- Contracts should help diminish project risk
- Most governments back all contracts by providing a court system for dispute resolution

NOTE TO STUDENTS OUTSIDE OF THE UNITED STATES: The exam has very few references to international contracts, but you should be aware that government contracting specialists in the United States wrote many of these questions. PMI's process for procurement management closely follows what is done in the United States, but it is different from the way procurement is handled in many other parts of the world. In many parts of the world, the contract is an informal document and the relationship between the parties is more important than the contract.

TRICKS OF THE TRADE® If you are not from the United States, a key trick is to take a more formal approach to the procurement process when answering questions. The contract is most important. It must be followed and everything provided in it must be done. Study this chapter carefully.

TRICKS OF THE TRADE® ## Project Manager's Role in Procurement The project manager must be involved in the creation of contracts and fulfills the following key roles:
- Know the procurement process
- Understand contract terms and conditions
- Make sure the contract contains all the project management requirements such as attendance at meetings, reports, actions and communications deemed necessary
- Identify risks and incorporate mitigation and allocation of risks into the contract
- Help tailor the contract to the unique needs of the project
- Fit the schedule for completion of the procurement process into the schedule for the project

- Be involved during contract negotiation to protect the relationship with the seller
- Protect the integrity of the project and the ability to get the work done
- Uphold the entire contract, not just the contract statement of work
- Work with the contract manager to manage changes to the contract

The project manager must be assigned before a contract is signed! This allows the project manager to complete a risk analysis before a contract is signed. However, if yours is like many companies, this comes as something of a shock. In companies where projects are created through winning a contract from an outside client, sales and marketing will have handled the whole proposal process and signed a contract before the project manager is assigned. The project manager then is handed a project that already may be in trouble because the contract, its terms and conditions, and even the contract statement of work may not be appropriate.

Centralized/Decentralized Contracting
There are many ways a contract department can be organized. In a centralized contracting environment, there is a contracting department and a contract manager may handle contracts on many projects. In a decentralized contracting environment, a contract manager is assigned to one project full time and reports directly to the project manager.

Exercise Without more help, try the following exercise. Do well and you do not have to study this much. Identify the advantages and disadvantages of each type of contracting organization.

Centralized

Advantages	Disadvantages

Decentralized

Advantages	Disadvantages

Answer

Centralized

Advantages	Disadvantages
Increased expertise in contracting	One contracts person may work on many projects
A contracting department will provide its employees with continuous improvement, training and shared lessons learned	May be more difficult to obtain contracting help when needed
Standardized company practices	
Contracting professionals have a clearly defined career path in the contracting profession	

Decentralized

Advantages	Disadvantages
Easier access to contracting expertise because contract experts are on the team	No home department for the contracts person to return to after the project is completed
More loyalty to the project	Difficult to maintain a high level of contracting expertise in the company
More focused contracting experience	Duplication of expertise and inefficient use of contracting resources across projects
	Little standardization of contracting practices from one project to the next
	Tendency to have a lack of defined career path in the contracting profession

The Procurement Management Process (page 269) Project managers often
come to contract managers saying, "I need a seller NOW!" Contract managers would like to
say, "There is a procurement process designed to obtain the best seller at the most reasonable
price. That process includes waiting time for the sellers to look at our needs and respond. The
process can take from one to three months for this type of procurement. Why did you not
manage your project well enough to account for this time in your schedule?" This is one of
the reasons a project manager must understand the procurement process. Not only does the
project manager need to be involved along the way, assisting the procurement or contracting
office with project input, but he also needs to plan for the time procurements take.

Many questions relating to the procurement process are similar to those in risk
management and the project management process. You must MEMORIZE what happens
when, how procurement management works on a real project and how it relates to the
project life cycle. The six sequential procurement processes are:

1. Plan Purchases and Acquisitions
2. Plan Contracting
3. Request Seller Responses
4. Select Sellers
5. Contract Administration
6. Contract Closure

▬Inputs to the Procurement Management Process (or "What do you need before you begin the procurement process?") Procurement is the one area that has a lot of templates, procedures and information available in order to make the procurement process faster and easier.

- **Enterprise environmental factors** Company culture and existing systems that your project will have to deal with or can make use of. For procurement, this includes marketplace conditions and what services are available to be purchased.
- **Organizational process assets** Procurement procedures, standard contracts, lessons learned from past projects, lists of pre-qualified sellers.
- **Contract manager assigned** This may come later depending on the amount of contracting.
- **Project scope statement**
- **WBS and WBS dictionary**
- **Risk register** An understanding of risk uncovered to date. Remember, risk analysis of the project should be completed before contracts can be signed.
- **Any contracts already in place on the project** The project manager must manage the interface between multiple sellers and multiple contracts on one project.
- **Resources** that may be lacking in the performing organization.
- **What work is needed**
- **The project schedule**
- **Initial cost estimates for work to be contracted**
- **Cost baseline for the project**

Exercise So you think you read it well! Try to recreate what you just read and see what you forgot. Then spend time thinking about what you forgot to make sure you do not forget it again.

▬Plan Purchases and Acquisitions (page 274) Answers the question, "What goods and services do we need to buy for this project?" Plan purchases and acquisitions includes the following activities:

Make-or-Buy Analysis (page 276) The performing organization can make all it needs, buy all it needs, or any range of solutions in between. (As simple as this sounds, it has been a question on the exam!) The actual out-of-pocket costs to purchase the product as well as the indirect cost of managing the procurement should be considered in any "make-or-buy" decision. The cost savings to purchase may be outweighed by the cost of managing the procurement.

One of the main reasons to buy is to decrease risk to any component of the "triple constraint." It is better to "make" if:
- You have an idle plant or workforce
- You want to retain control
- The work involves proprietary information or procedures

Sometimes the make-or-buy analysis involves a buy or lease question such as:

You are trying to decide whether to lease or buy an item for your project. The daily lease cost is $120. To purchase the item the investment cost is $1,000 and the daily cost is $20. How long will it take for the lease cost to be the same as the purchase cost?

> **Answer** *Let D equal the number of days when the purchase and lease costs are equal.*
>
> $120D = $1,000 + $20D
>
> $120D - $20D = $1,000
>
> $100D = $1,000
>
> *D= 10. The lease cost will be the same as the purchase cost after ten days. If you think you will need the item for more than ten days, you should consider purchasing it to reduce total costs.*

Contract Type Selection (page 277) This is an important topic! You must understand the following contract types and be able to tell the difference. You should be able to answer situational questions describing what you would do differently depending on the contract type. There are also questions that require you to pick the most appropriate contract type based on a described situation. Think through this section carefully!

The goal of contract type selection is to have reasonable distribution of risk between the buyer and seller and the greatest incentive for the seller's efficient and economical performance.

There are generally three types of contracts:
- Cost reimbursable (CR)
- Time and material (T&M)
- Fixed price (FP)

The following factors may influence the type of contract selected:
- How well-defined the contract statement of work is or can be
- The amount or frequency of changes expected after project start
- The level of effort and expertise the buyer can devote to managing the seller
- Industry standards of the type of contract used
- Amount of market competition
- Amount of risk

Cost Reimbursable (CR) (page 278) The seller's costs are reimbursed, plus an additional amount. The buyer has the most cost risk because the total costs are unknown. This form of contract is often used when the buyer can only describe what is needed, rather than what to do (e.g., when the complete contract statement of work or requirements is unknown, as in situations of buying unique knowledge). The seller will therefore write the detailed contract statement of work. Research and development or information technology projects where the scope is unknown are typical examples of cost reimbursable contracts.

Common forms of cost-reimbursable contracts include:

Cost Plus Fee (CPF) or Cost Plus Percentage of Costs (CPPC) This type of contract is not allowed for either U.S. federal acquisitions or procurements under federal acquisition regulations, and is bad for buyers everywhere. Can you guess why?

This type of cost reimbursable contract requires the buyer to pay for all costs plus a percent of costs as a fee. Sellers are not motivated to control costs because the seller will get paid profit on every cost without limit.

Example
Contract = Cost plus 10% of costs as fee.

Cost Plus Fixed Fee (CPFF) This is the most common type of cost reimbursable contract. In this type, the buyer pays all costs, but the fee (or profit) is fixed at a specific dollar amount. This helps to keep the seller's costs in line because a cost overrun will not generate any additional fee or profit. Fees only change with approved change orders.

Example
Contract = Cost plus a fee of $100,000.

Cost Plus Incentive Fee (CPIF) This type of cost reimbursable contract pays all costs and an agreed upon fee, plus a bonus for beating the performance objectives stated in the contract. See more on incentives at the end of this topic.

Cost Plus Award Fee (CPAF) This type of cost reimbursable contract pays all costs and an apportionment of a bonus based on performance. This is very similar to the CPIF contract except the award amount is determined in advance and apportioned out depending on performance. For example, the buyer might say that there is a $50,000 award fee available. It will be apportioned out at the rate of $5,000 for every month production on the project is over a certain amount.

Time and Material (T&M) or Unit Price (page 278) This type of contract is usually used for small dollar amounts. The contract is priced on a per hour or per item basis and has elements of a fixed price contract (in the fixed price per hour) and a cost reimbursable contract (in the material costs and the fact that the total cost is unknown).

In this type, the buyer has a medium amount of cost risk compared to CR and FP because the contract is usually for small dollar amounts and for a shorter length of time.

Example
Contract = $100 per hour plus expenses or materials at cost or $5 per linear meter of wood.

Fixed Price (FP, or Lump Sum, Firm Fixed Price) (page 277) This is the most common type of contract in the world. In this type of contract, one price is agreed upon for all the work. The buyer has the least cost risk, provided the buyer has a completely defined scope, because the risk of higher costs is borne by the seller. Therefore, it could be said that the seller is most concerned with the contract statement of work in this type of contract.

This type of contract is most appropriate when the buyer can completely describe the contract statement of work. (Do you see anything different from what you are doing in the real world? Maybe having the wrong contract type is the root cause of some of your problems!)

> ### Example
> Contract = $1,100,000.

Fixed Price Incentive Fee (FPIF) There are also incentives for fixed price contracts. The incentive is the same as CPIF.

> ### Example
> Contract = $1,100,000. For every month early the project is finished, an additional $10,000 is paid to the seller.

Fixed Price Economic Price Adjustment (FPEPA) Sometimes a fixed price contract allows for price increases if the contract is for multiple years.

> ### Example
> Contract = $1,100,000 but a price increase will be allowed in year two based on the U.S. Consumer Price Increase report for year one. Or the contract price is $1,100,000 but a price increase will be allowed in year two to account for increases in specific material costs.

Purchase Order A purchase order is the simplest type of fixed price contract. This type of contract is normally unilateral (signed by one party) instead of bilateral (signed by both parties). It is usually used for simple commodity procurements. Purchase orders are considered contracts when they are accepted either by performance (i.e., equipment is shipped by the seller—a unilateral PO) or by signing a purchase order (a bilateral PO).

> ### Example
> Contract to purchase 30 linear meters of wood at $9 per meter.

Advantages and Disadvantages of Each Contract Type A trick on the exam is to realize that in the real world, the buyer must select the appropriate type of contract for what they are buying. This exercise helps test whether you really understand the different types of contracts. It will help you select the appropriate type of contract on the exam.

Exercise 1 In the chart below, write the advantages and disadvantages of each form of contract from the perspective of the BUYER.

Cost Reimbursable

Advantages	Disadvantages

Time and Material

Advantages	Disadvantages

Fixed Price

Advantages	Disadvantages

Answer There can be more answers than listed here. Did you identify and understand these?

Cost Reimbursable

Advantages	Disadvantages
Simpler contract statement of work	Requires auditing seller's invoices
Usually requires less work to write the scope than fixed price	Requires more work for the buyer to manage
Generally lower cost than fixed price because the seller does not have to add as much for risk	Seller has only a moderate incentive to control costs
	Total price is unknown

Time and Material

Advantages	Disadvantages
Quick to create	Profit is in every hour billed
Contract duration is brief	Seller has no incentive to control costs
Good choice when you are hiring "bodies" or people to augment your staff	Appropriate only for small projects
	Requires the most day to day oversight from the buyer

Fixed Price

Advantages	Disadvantages
Less work for buyer to manage	Seller may underprice the work and try to make up profits on change orders
Seller has a strong incentive to control costs	Seller may not complete some of the contract statement of work if they begin to lose money
Companies have experience with this type	More work for buyer to write the contract statement of work
Buyer knows the total price at project start	Can be more expensive than CR if the contract statement of work is incomplete The seller will need to add to the price for their increased risk

Exercise 2 Name the most appropriate contract type to use in the situation described.

Situation	Type of Contract to Use
You need work to begin right away	
You want to buy expertise in determining what needs to be done	
You know exactly what needs to be done	
You are buying the services of a programmer to augment your staff	
You need work done but you don't have time to audit invoices on this work	

Answer 2 Try to think of other situations that you would use each type of contract.

Situation	Type of Contract to Use
You need work to begin right away	T&M
You want to buy expertise in determining what needs to be done	CR
You know exactly what needs to be done	FP
You are buying the services of a programmer to augment your staff	T&M
You need work done but you don't have time to audit invoices on this work	FP

Risk and Contract Type The exam may ask questions that connect risk with the different types of contracts. The diagram below shows the amount of risk the buyer has with each contract type. Use it to better understand the different contract types, and also to answer questions such as:

> *Who has the risk in a cost reimbursable contract, the buyer or seller?*
> **Answer** *Buyer. If the costs increase, the buyer pays the added costs.*
>
> *Who has the cost risk in a fixed price contract, the buyer or seller?*
> **Answer** *Seller! If costs increase, the seller pays the costs and makes less profit.*

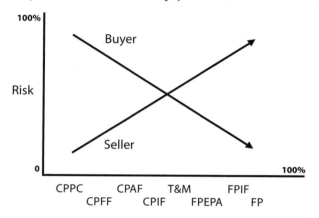

Incentives Allows an incentive (or bonus) on top of the agreed upon price for exceeding time or cost as specified in the contract. An incentive helps bring the seller's objectives in line with those of the buyer. With an incentive, both buyer and seller work toward the same objective, for instance, completing the project on time.

You should have some experience calculating the revised fee and total costs associated with this type of contract (see the next exercise). Such questions occasionally appear on the exam.

Exercise In this cost reimbursable contract, the cost is estimated at $210,000 and the fee at $25,000. If the seller beats that cost they will share the savings; 80 percent to the buyer and 20 percent to the seller. If the actual costs come in at $200,000, what is the final fee and final price?

Answer

Target cost	$210,000
Target fee	$25,000
Target price	$235,000
Sharing ratio	80/20
Actual cost	$200,000

Fee	$210,000 − $200,000 = $10,000 × 20% = $2,000 $25,000 target fee + $2,000 = $27,000 fee
Final Price	$200,000 + $27,000 = $227,000

Types of Contract Statements of Work (page 280) Based on the project scope statement, the contract statement of work describes what work is to be completed under the contract. It must be as clear, complete and concise as possible, and describe all the work and activities the seller is required to complete.

Let's say that again, you read it too fast! The contract statement of work must be as clear, complete and concise as possible and describe all the work and activities the seller is required to complete. Yes, all the work. This should include all meetings, all reports, all communications. If not included, the cost of adding them later can be more than adding them now. This should also lead you to think of the amount of work required to create a complete contract statement of work. Remember that a contract is a document used to manage a contracted activity. It does not sit in a drawer. Therefore, both parties to the contract should always be asking, "What does the contract say?" Contract problems are not easy to resolve. The trick is to prevent the problems. Having a complete contract statement of work is important.

What does the word "complete" mean? It depends on what you are buying. If you are buying expertise (such as software design or legal services), your contract statement of work (in addition to meetings, reports and communications required) will just include your functional and/or performance requirements. If you are buying the construction of a building, your requirements will be extremely specific, outlining things like the type of wood to be used, the process that must be followed and even a work schedule. If you are hiring staff that you will direct (a programmer to be added to the team), your contract statement of work will likely contain more details of what you want.

The contract statement of work may be revised during the procurement process, but should become finalized (excluding changes) by the time the contract is signed. There are many types of contract statements of work. Your choice should depend on the nature of the work and the type of industry.
- **Performance** Conveys what the final product should be able to accomplish, rather than how it should be built or what its design characteristics should be (e.g., "I want a car that will go zero to 120 kilometers per hour in 4.2 seconds.")
- **Functional** Conveys the end purpose or result, rather than specific procedures, etc. It is to be used in the performance of the work and may also include a statement of the minimum essential characteristics of the product (e.g., "I want a car with 23 cup holders." [OK, why can't I try to be funny?])
- **Design** Conveys precisely what work is to be done (e.g., "Build it exactly as shown on these drawings.")

Performance and functional contract statements of work are commonly used for information systems, information technology, high-tech, research and development and projects that have never been done before. Design is most commonly used in construction, equipment purchasing and other types of projects.

Components of a contract statement of work can include drawings, specifications, technical and descriptive wording, etc. No matter what it contains, you should realize that the contract statement of work becomes part of the contract.

Exercise Complete the following to describe how detailed the contract statement of work must be for each type of contract.

For a CR Contract?	
For a T&M Contract?	
For a FP Contract?	

Answer

For a CR Contract?	In this case, the contract statement of work describes only the performance or requirements because we are buying the expertise of "how to do the work." We may not be able to say exactly what to do or when.
For a T&M Contract?	The contract statement of work can be any of the choices (performance, functional or design), but it will be brief, describing limited performance, functional, or design requirements.
For a FP Contract?	The contract statement of work must be extraordinarily complete because we are buying "do it," not "how to do it." In order for the seller to fix the price they need to know, in advance, ALL the work they are required to do.

Be careful, this is a general approach. There are many reasons to handle contracts differently. However, using an inappropriate contract form can result in increased risk, conflict and project failure.

Procurement Management Plan (page 279) Like all management plans, the procurement management plan will describe how the procurement process will be planned, managed and executed. Think about how different this might be from your real world and get your mind around the concept of management plans. They have been in almost every chapter. Do you understand them now?

——Plan Contracting (page 281) This process consists primarily of putting together the procurement documents that will be sent to prospective sellers describing the buyer's need, how to respond and the criteria by which the buyer will select a seller.

Procurement Documents (bid documents) The documents put together by the buyer to tell the seller its needs. Procurement documents may take one of the following forms:
- **Request for Proposal (RFP,** sometimes called **Request for Tender)** Requests a price, but also a detailed proposal on how the work will be accomplished, who will do it, resumes, company experience, etc.
- **Invitation for Bid (IFB,** or **Request for Bid, RFB)** Requests one price to do all the work
- **Request for Quotation (RFQ)** Requests a price quote per item, hour or foot

Procurement documents may include the following:
- Information for sellers
  - Background information
  - Procedures for replying
  - Guidelines for preparation of the response
  - Form of response required
  - Evaluation criteria (described later)
  - Pricing forms
- Contract statement of work
- Proposed terms and conditions of the contract (legal and business)

Note that the proposed contract is included in the procurement documents. Can you answer why? The terms and conditions of the contract are also work that needs to be done and have costs associated with them (warranties, ownership, etc.). The seller must be aware of *all* the work that needs to be completed to adequately understand and price the project.

Well-designed procurement documents can have the following effects on the project:
- Easier comparison of sellers' responses
- More complete responses
- More accurate pricing
- Decrease in the number of changes to the project

You should understand that sellers could make suggestions for changes to the procurement documents, including the contract statement of work and the project management plan.

TRICKS OF THE TRADE A trick for the exam is to realize that the choice of which procurement document to use depends on the form of contract statement of work and contract type selected. See the next exercise.

Exercise Test yourself! In the space provided below, write the contract type (FP, CR, T&M) that applies next to the procurement document, and the type of contract statement of work (Performance, Functional or Design) to be used.

Procurement Documents	Contract Type	Contract Statement of Work
Request for Proposal (RFP)		
Invitation for Bid (IFB)		
Request for Quotation (RFQ)		

Answer This is a general approach to promote understanding. In the world of contracts, an infinite variety of procurement documents and contract types exist. The exam keeps things simple.

Procurement Documents	Contract Type	Contract Statement of Work
Request for Proposal (RFP)	CR	Performance or Functional
Invitation for Bid (IFB)	FP	Design
Request for Quotation (RFQ)	T&M	Any

Non-Disclosure Agreement This is an agreement between the buyer and any prospective sellers stating what information or documents they will hold confidential and control, and who in their organization will gain access to the confidential information. With a non-disclosure agreement in place, the buyer can talk more openly about its needs without fear that one of the buyer's competitors will gain access to the information shared. Like any agreement, a non-disclosure agreement has consequences if violated.

Standard Contract Companies frequently have standard, preauthorized contracts for the purchase of goods or services. These types of standard contracts need no further legal review if used as they are. If signed without changes, they are legally sufficient. The exam requires that you understand standard contracts, but also realize the project manager's role in special provisions (described next).

Special Provisions (Special Conditions) The project manager must be able to read and understand standard terms and conditions, and determine what needs to be added, changed or removed from the standard provisions, so that the resulting contract addresses the particular needs of the project. The project manager meets with the contract manager to discuss the needs of the project and determine the final contract terms and conditions. These additions, changes or removals are sometimes called special provisions and are a result of:
- Risk analysis
- The requirements of the project
- The type of project
- Administrative, legal or business requirements

Terms and Conditions Let's start out with a story. A project manager needed to have his team members trained on using some equipment. He contacted a seller to do the work and then proceeded to have his contracts department send the seller a contract. Meanwhile, he arranged to have the team members fly in from around the world for the training. The contract the project manager's contracts department sent included terms and conditions that said that the project manager's company would have the rights to create derivative works and make copies of any handouts from class. Those handouts were proprietary and already copyrighted. The seller could not and would not sign such a contract.

The class had to be cancelled at the last minute, after many people were already on planes to attend the training. Whose fault was this? It was the project manager's fault. He should have made sure the contracts department understood what they were buying and also taken a look at the contract before it was sent, to make sure that any inappropriate language was removed. Creating a contract requires the involvement of both the project manager and the contract manager. Do you do this?

The other side of understanding contract language is being able to enforce it. Remember, if it is in the contract, it must be done unless both sides agree and a change is issued!

One day the head of a company called the project manager asking where the seller's reports were. The project manager did not know what reports the company head was asking about and so had not received them from the seller. It turned out that those reports seemed minor to the project manager when he finally read the contract, but had major legal significance to the company. Not receiving them cost the buyer's company an extra $50,000 in costs. The lesson? Know what is in your contracts and why.

In another situation, (tired of stories yet?), a seller did not submit testing information required in the contract to the buyer, and the project manager did not notice it was not received. After four weeks, the company head asked for the testing information and found out it was not received. The project manager then asked the seller to send the information. The seller argued, "You did not receive the testing reports for four weeks and you did not say anything. You have therefore waived your rights to ever get them." They refused to give the reports without a change to the contract and additional payment. This issue went to a court of law to resolve. There is no clear answer with such limited information to say who was right in this story. The lesson? Read the contract and enforce all that is there.

Following are some of the terms and conditions that can make up standard and special provisions. You should be generally familiar with what all of these mean. Don't get overwhelmed! You do not need to memorize these, just be familiar with the impact they have on you, the project manager. These will often be used in sentences (e.g., "There was a force majeure," or "There was a huge flood that caused the seller to not be able to perform").

- **Acceptance** How will you specifically know if the work is acceptable?
- **Agent** Who is an authorized representative of each party?
- **Arbitration** A method to resolve disputes that uses private third parties to render a decision on the dispute. Arbitration is paid for by the parties and is used because it is usually faster and cheaper than the courts.
- **Assignment** Describes the circumstances under which one party can assign its rights or obligations under the contract to another.
- **Authority** Who has the power to do what?
- **Bonds** Describes the payment or performance bonds, if any, that must be purchased. For example, a payment bond would protect the buyer from claims of non-payment by the seller.
- **Breach/Default** A breach occurs when any obligation of the contract is not met. Watch out, a breach on the seller's part cannot be fixed by a breach on the buyer's part, e.g., not completing an item in the contract statement of work (seller's breach) cannot be handled by the buyer stopping ALL payments (buyer's breach).

    This is an extremely serious event. The exam will give you questions where seemingly little things in the contract are not done. The response to a breach must always be the issuing of a letter formally notifying the other party of the breach. The project manager must understand the legal implications of his actions. If he does not watch out for and send official notice of breach, the project manager's company could lose their right to claim breach later.
- **Changes** How will changes be made, what forms used, timeframes for notice and turnaround?
- **Confidentiality** What information must not be made known or given to third parties?
- **Force majeure** A situation that can be considered an act of God, such as fire or freak electrical storm, that is an allowable excuse for either party not meeting contract requirements. If a force majeure occurs, it is considered to be neither party's fault. It is usually resolved by the seller receiving an extension of time on the project. (See also **Risk of loss**.) Who pays for the cost of the items destroyed in the fire? If the items were for the project, the risk of loss here is usually borne by the seller and hopefully covered by insurance.
- **Incentives** What benefits can the seller receive for aligning with the buyer's objectives of time, cost, quality, risk and performance?
- **Indemnification (liability)** Who is liable for personal injury, damage, accidents?
- **Independent contractor** States that the seller is not an employee of the buyer.

- **Inspection** Does anyone have a right to inspect the work during execution of the project? Under what circumstances?
- **Intellectual property** Who owns the intellectual property (patents, trademarks, copyrights, processes, source code, books) used in connection with or developed as part of the contract? May include warranties of the right to use certain intellectual property in performance of the contract.
- **Invoicing** When sent, what supporting documents are required and to whom are they sent?
- **Liquidated damages** Estimated damages for specific defaults, described in advance.
- **Management requirements** Attendance at meetings, approval of staff assigned to the project, etc.
- **Material breach** A breach so large that it may not be possible to complete the work under the contract.
- **Notice** To whom should certain correspondence be sent?
- **Ownership** Who will own the tangible items (materials, buildings, equipment) used in connection with or developed as part of the contract?
- **Payments** When will they be made, late payment fees, reasons for nonpayment? Watch out for payment management questions. For example, as a response to inaccurate invoices, the buyer cannot stop ALL payments; this would be a breach. They can, however, stop payments on disputed amounts.
- **Reporting** What reports are required, at what frequency, from and to whom?
- **Retainage** An amount of money, usually 5 percent or 10 percent, withheld from each payment. This money is paid when all the final work is completed and helps ensure completion.
- **Risk of loss** Allocates the risk between the parties to a contract in the event goods or services are lost or destroyed during the performance of a contract.
- **Contract statement of work** If not listed separately.
- **Site access** Any requirements for access to the site where the work will be performed.
- **Termination** Stopping the work before it is completed.
- **Time is of the essence** Delivery is strictly binding. Seller is on notice that time is very important and that any delay is a material breach.
- **Waivers** Statements saying that rights under the contract may not be waived or modified other than by express agreement of the parties. A project manager must realize they can intentionally or unintentionally give up a right in the contract through conduct, inadvertent failure to enforce or lack of oversight. Therefore, a project manager must understand all aspects of the legal and other contract parts to enforce them, even if a contract manager is available to administer the contract.
- **Warranties** Promises of quality for the goods or services delivered under the contract, usually restricted to a certain time period.
- **Work for hire** The work provided under the contract will be owned by the buyer.

Letter of Intent You should understand this is normally NOT a contract but simply a letter, without legal binding, that says the buyer intends to hire the seller.

Privity Means a contractual relationship. You should understand the following because it explains privity and shows you how questions on this topic are asked.

> *Company A hires company B to do some work for them. Company B subcontracts to company C. The project manager for A is at the job site and tells company C to stop work. Generally, does company C have to listen?*
>
> **Answer** *No. Companies C and A have no contractual relationship. A needs to talk to B who needs to talk to C.*

Non-Competitive Forms of Procurement What if there is only one seller, or you want to work with a company you have worked with before? Do you have to go through the procurement process? No. There is no reason that you must go through the procurement process unless the procurement is for a government, or the performing organization has rules restricting such procurements. You would, however, lose the value of competition.

When would you award work to a company without competition? The following is a more complete list.

- The project is under extreme schedule pressure.
- A seller has unique qualifications.
- There is only one seller.
- A seller holds a patent for the item you need.
- Other mechanisms exist to ensure that the seller's prices are reasonable.

You should be familiar with the following forms of non-competitive procurements:

- **Single Source** Contract directly with your preferred seller without going through the procurement process. This might be a company that you have worked with before and, for various reasons, you do not want to look for another.
- **Sole Source** There is only one seller. This might be a company that owns a patent.

You may save time not having to do the procurement process before bids or proposals are received, but you will have to spend the time (perform extra work) after they are received to come up with a contract.

TRICKS OF THE TRADE Most of the questions on the exam will present various situations and ask you questions about those situations. In procurement, tricky questions can include addressing concepts that you many have not dealt with before, such as describing the work that would need to be done to negotiate a contract when there is no competition. The following exercise will help.

Exercise Test yourself! What topics must be addressed in creating a contract for non-competitive procurement that would not need as much attention in a competitive environment?

For Single Source—Preferred Supplier

For Sole Source—There Is Only One Supplier	

Answer

For Single Source—Preferred Supplier
- **Scope** More work will be needed to document all the items received free in the past to make sure you get them now. Only what is in the contract will be received.
- **Scope** There could be a tendency for the performing organization to say, "The seller knows us and we know them, we do not have to spend so much time determining our requirements and completing a contract statement of work. They know what we want."
- **Quality** The seller may never be asked to prove they have the experience, cash flow and manpower to complete the new work.
- **Cost** Time will need to be spent to compare previous costs to the new cost to check for reasonableness.
- **Schedule** Now that the seller knows they have you as a longer term customer, they may not be as responsive to your needs.
- **Customer satisfaction** Now that the seller knows they have you as a longer term customer, they may not be as responsive to your needs.
- **Risk** The risk can be weighted more toward the buyer unless the above are investigated.

For Sole Source—There Is Only One Supplier
- What if the seller owns a patent and goes out of business?
- If the seller owns a patent and goes bankrupt, who owns the patent?
- **Quality** You may have to take what you get rather than request a certain quality level.
- **Cost** Multiple year agreements will be required for the purchase of items to prevent a price increase in the future.
- **Schedule** The seller has little incentive to agree to a schedule.
- **Scope** You may have to change the project to accommodate the procurement rather than change the procurement to accommodate the project.
- **Customer satisfaction** The seller has little incentive to be concerned with the buyer's needs and desires.
- **Risk** The overall risk can be weighted more toward the buyer unless the above are investigated and resolved.

Make sure you read questions on the exam carefully. They might ask what to watch out for, or what needs to be negotiated in non-competitive procurements. They may simply ask about the procurement process. Wouldn't your efforts during the contracting process be different if there wasn't another company to go to for the goods or service?

Evaluation Criteria (page 283) Evaluation criteria are included in the procurement document to give the seller an understanding of the buyer's needs and help them decide if they should bid or make a proposal on the work. During select sellers, evaluation criteria become the basis by which the bids or proposals are evaluated by the buyer.

If the buyer is purchasing a commodity like linear meters of wood, the evaluation criteria may be just the lowest price. If they are buying construction services, the evaluation criteria may be price plus experience. If the buyer is buying services only, the evaluation criteria will be more extensive. In the latter case, such evaluation criteria may include:
- Understanding of need
- Overall or life cycle cost (see definition in the Cost chapter)
- Technical ability
- Management approach
- Financial capacity
- Project management ability (I had to put this in! Shouldn't you require your sellers or vendors to use the project management techniques you have learned? How about asking for a WBS, network diagram and risk analysis?)

━━ Request Seller Responses (page 284) This process consists of getting the procurement documents into the hands of sellers, answering the sellers' questions and the sellers preparing the proposals.

Bidder Conferences (Contractor Conferences, Vendor Conferences, Pre-Bid Conferences) (page 285) In order to maintain the integrity of the procurement and to make sure all sellers are bidding or proposing on the same work with the same knowledge, the buyer will control who can talk to the prospective sellers and what can be said.

To make sure all the sellers' questions are answered, the buyer invites the sellers to attend a meeting where they can tour the buyer's facilities (if relevant to the project) and ask questions about the procurement. The questions and answers are written down and sent to all prospective bidders to make sure all prospective sellers have the same information. The questions and answers are also added to the procurement documents as addenda.

Getting answers to questions can be important because many procurement documents will include a provision that says by submitting the bid or proposal, the seller warrants that the bid covers all the work. This meeting is also an opportunity for the buyer to discover anything that is missing.

A bidder conference can be the key to making sure the pricing in the seller's response matches the work that needs to be done and is therefore the lowest price. Bidder conferences benefit both the buyer and seller. Many project managers do not attend these meetings or realize their importance. The exam often asks what things the project manager must watch out for in a bidder conference:
- Collusion
- Sellers not asking their questions in front of their competition
- Making sure all questions and answers are put in writing and issued to all potential sellers by the buyer as addenda to the procurement documents. This ensures that all sellers are responding to the same contract statement of work.

Advertising (page 285) To attract additional sellers, an advertisement may be placed in newspapers, magazines and other places. NOTE: The U.S. government is required to advertise most of its procurements.

Qualified Seller List (or pre-qualified seller list, page 285) The process of finding prospective sellers can take months. Another option, especially if a buyer purchases the same type of service often, is to find, investigate and check the credentials of prospective sellers in advance. This will speed up the purchase and help make sure the sellers' qualifications are well researched before they are awarded contracts. This information may be a part of organizational process assets, or can be developed by the project team. The procurement documents for specific projects would then be sent only to the pre-qualified sellers.

Proposal (or Bid) This is what the seller's response to the procurement document is called. A proposal is usually the response to a request for proposal (RFP), a price quote is usually the response to a request for quote (RFQ), and a bid is usually the response to an invitation for bid (IFB). The proposal represents an official offer from the seller. Here is what takes time. Sellers may have many RFPs or IFBs sent to them. They need time to review them and determine which are worth responding to. If you are looking for the best sellers to be interested, the procurement documents should be as complete and straightforward as possible.

Once the seller decides they will respond, they need to form a team, evaluate the buyer's needs, attend the bidder conference and create a response. This can sometimes take as long as a month. The buyer's project manager should plan for this time and the time for the rest of the procurement process in the project schedule.

Request seller responses and select sellers (see next topic) will be included on your exam score sheet as part of Implement the Procurement of Project Resources.

━━Select Sellers (page 286) This process consists of receiving and reviewing the proposals and selecting a seller. The evaluation criteria identified in the plan contracting process are used to assess the potential sellers' ability and willingness to provide the requested products or services. Because they are measurable, the criteria provide a basis for quantitatively evaluating proposals to minimize the influence of personal prejudices. In this process:
- A seller may simply be selected and asked to sign a standard contract
- A seller may be asked to make a presentation and then, if all goes well, go on to negotiations
- The list of sellers may be narrowed down ("short-listed") to a few
- The short-listed sellers may be asked to make presentations and the selected seller then asked to go on to negotiations
- The buyer can negotiate with more than one seller
- Or some combination of presentations and negotiations

The choice of methods depends on the importance of the procurement, the number of interested sellers and the type of work to be performed.

The sellers' proposals may be reviewed, compared or selected by any one of the following:

Weighting System Weighting the evaluation criteria according to your priorities, and comparing sellers to choose the one who best meets your criteria.

Independent Estimate Comparing the cost to an estimate created in-house or with outside assistance. This allows the discovery of significant differences between what the buyer and seller intend in the contract statement of work. The buyer must have his or her own estimates to check reasonableness and cannot rely solely on the seller's cost estimates.

Screening System Eliminating sellers that do not meet minimum requirements of the evaluation criteria.

Past Performance History Looking at the seller's past history with the buyer.

Presentations In many cases, some of the sellers will be asked to make presentations of their proposals to the buyer so the buyer can pick the most appropriate seller. This is often a formal meeting of the buyer's and seller's teams. It provides the seller with an opportunity to present their proposal, team and approach to completing the work. Buyers get a chance to see the team they may hire and ask questions to assess competency, knowledge and ability. Presentations are used most often when a cost reimbursable contract is used, but they can be used in other situations (there is more to assess, and how the seller is going to do the work is of prime importance).

Negotiation (page 288) The exam usually has only one or two questions about contract negotiations. Procurement may or may not involve negotiations. The project manager may be involved during negotiations to clarify project requirements, and if for no other reason than to protect the relationship with the other side. Many projects go bad because of how negotiations were handled.

Objectives of Negotiation The objectives of negotiation are to:
- Obtain a fair and reasonable price
- Develop a good relationship with the seller

The second item surprises most people. If you press too strongly during negotiations and the negotiations turn from a win-win (preferable) situation to a win-lose situation, the seller will be less concerned with completing the work than with recovering what they lost in negotiation. If negotiations are win-lose (in favor of the buyer), the buyer's project manager will have to spend time making sure that the seller does not add extra costs, propose unnecessary work or initiate other activities to "win" back what they lost during negotiation.

Negotiation Tactics This is another topic that can be included on the exam, that is not covered in the *PMBOK® Guide*. You should be familiar with the following types of negotiation tactics. Do not memorize them. Simply be able to pick the negotiation tactic being used in a situation.
- **Attacks** "If you don't know the details of your own company, perhaps you should get out of the business!"
- **Personal Insults** "If you do not understand what you are doing, perhaps you should find another job!"
- **Good Guy/Bad Guy** One person is helpful to the other side while another is difficult to deal with.
- **Deadline** "We have a flight leaving at 5 P.M. today and must finish negotiations before that time."
- **Lying** Not telling the truth. This may be obvious or hidden.

- **Limited Authority** "I can't agree to shorten the schedule by six months. I only have been authorized to offer three months." Limited authority statements may or may not be true.
- **Missing Man** "Only my boss can agree to that request, and he isn't here. Why don't we agree to only do _____? I can agree to that."
- **Fair and Reasonable** "Let's be fair and reasonable. Accept this offer as it stands."
- **Delay** "Let us revisit this issue the next time we get together." This may also take the form of never actually getting down to negotiating until the last day of a planned visit.
- **Extreme Demands** "We planned to give you a computer manufactured in 1988 to meet the requirement to deliver 'a computer' in the contract."
- **Withdrawal** This can either be an emotional withdrawal or a physical withdrawal and can show a lessening of interest.
- **Fait Accompli** A done deal. "These government terms and conditions must be in all our contracts."

Main Items to Negotiate (page 288) The main items to address while negotiating a contract are:

- Responsibilities
- Authority
- Applicable law—Under whose law will the contract fall
- Technical and business management approaches
- Contract financing
- Schedule
- Payments and price

Remember that price may not be the primary selection criteria or the primary negotiating item. Also note that this list may differ from the real world.

TRICKS OF THE TRADE **What Is a Contract** When you think of the word contract, what comes to mind? If you are like many others, you will think of all the legal words such as indemnification, intellectual property and other legal small print. People often think of only the preprinted or standard contract—boilerplate contracts—supplied to them from the contracts or legal departments. They are only partially correct.

The word contract actually refers to the entire agreement between both parties. Therefore, it includes boilerplate language, but it also includes business terms regarding payments, reporting requirements, marketing literature, the proposal, and the contract statement of work—all the requirements of the project.

Many project managers and business professionals think that the only relevant part of a contract is the contract statement of work, because they are naturally most familiar with that aspect of the contract. However, the contract statement of work does not include all the requirements. In fact, some of the boilerplate language can be more relevant than the contract statement of work. For example, think of a project to develop new software. Who owns the resulting program? Who owns the resulting program if it contains modules or pieces of programs previously used and planned for future reuse? How do you protect your rights and ensure that all source code is delivered? The ownership clause in a contract for such services might be more relevant than the contract statement of work itself.

A contract is a legally binding document. Therefore, all terms and conditions in the contract must be met. One cannot choose to not conform or to not do something required in the contract. Changes to the contract are made formally in writing.

What Do You Need to Have a Legal Contract?
- An offer
- Acceptance
- Consideration   Something of value, not necessarily money
- Legal capacity   Separate legal parties, competent parties
- Legal purpose   You cannot have a contract for the sale of illegal goods

A contract, offer or acceptance may be oral or written, though written is preferred.

Try out this story. You need plumbing work done on your home. You contact a plumber, who sends you a price with a notice that says, "If you want me to do the work on your home, send me a copy of the design drawings." Three weeks later, that plumber shows up at your home to start work, but you are surprised as you signed a contract with another plumber. The plumber says that you also have a contract with him because you sent the drawings. Is the plumber right? Yes; acceptance can be an action or it can be verbal. You have a difficult situation on your hands and you will likely have to pay this plumber something. The trick is to avoid these situations by understanding contracts.

Contract Management Plan (page 290) Whereas the procurement management plan will address how all procurements on a project will be managed, the contract management plan is specific to one contract and talks only about contract administration. Imagine you have a 100 page contract. A trick used by contract professionals is to summarize the key milestones, reporting and other requirements of the contract that both the buyer and seller have to meet. The result is a list (referring back to the detailed contract) of all the to-do items in the contract.

——Contract Administration (page 290) Contract administration consists of assuring that the performance of both parties to the contract meets contractual requirements. This is an important area on the exam.

TRICKS OF THE TRADE You have to know what to watch out for, what the project manager should do, that all things in the contract must be done, however small, and that the project manager must help uphold all parts of the contract, not just the project scope.

Take a moment and think of what work must be done during contract administration and try the next exercises.

Exercise 1 Describe what needs to occur during contract administration.

Answer 1 Actions during this process may include:

- Review invoices
- Complete integrated change control
- Documentation
- Make and handle changes
- Authorize payments
- Interpret what is and what is not in the contract
- Interpret what the contract means
- Resolve disputes
- Make sure only authorized people are communicating with the seller
- Deal with the contract manager regarding changes and contract compliance
- Hold meetings
- Report on performance
- Monitor cost, schedule and technical performance against the contract including all of its components (terms and conditions, contract statement of work, etc.)
- Understand the legal implications of action taken
- Control quality
- Review claims
- Authorize the seller's work at the appropriate time
- Correspondence
- Keep records
- Disseminate changes to the appropriate parties
- Verify scope
- Identify risks
- Monitor and control risk

Now the hard part. The exam will require you to know that your management efforts are different under each form of contract, meaning there will be different things you will need to do depending on the type of contract you have. Be wary, not only does this apply to the real world but there could be up to seven questions that require you to understand this. So let's try an exercise. Spend a lot of time making sure you understand this topic.

Exercise 2 Hopefully, you have built a strong working relationship with the seller. That means you are working well with each other. What if the seller has financial troubles, changes owners, or did not include in their own estimate major pieces of the work? The good relationship can go bad in an instant. Describe what specific things you must watch out for (spend your time managing) during contract administration for each of the three main forms of contracts, no matter what the relationship between the buyer and seller. Think about your real-world experience.

Cost Reimbursable

Time and Material

Fixed Price

Answer 2 This is not a complete list! Think of what other actions may be taken.

Cost Reimbursable
Make sure all the costs charged are applicable to the project
Audit every invoice
Make sure the seller's work is progressing efficiently
Watch for the seller adding resources to your project that do not add value or perform real work
Watch for resources being shifted from what was said in the original proposal (More experienced people proposed and less experienced used, but charged at the higher rate)
Watch for seller charges that were not part of the original plan
Re-estimate the cost of the project

Time and Material
Provide day-to-day direction to the seller
Attempt to get concrete deliverables
Make sure the project length is not extended
Make sure the number of hours spent on work is reasonable
Watch for situations when switching to a different form of contract makes sense (You determine the contract statement of work under a T&M contract and then switch to a fixed price contract for completion of the project)

Fixed Price
Watch for seller cutting scope
Watch for seller cutting quality
Watch for seller charging the buyer for costs they have not yet incurred (unless allowable in the contract)
Watch for overpriced change orders
Check for scope misunderstandings

Conflict In most projects where a contract is used, another person controls the contract. This person may be called the contract manager or contract administrator and, in many cases, IS THE ONLY ONE WITH AUTHORITY TO CHANGE THE CONTRACT. We have already said that the contract includes the contract statement of work. You can see the potential for conflict between the contract manager and the project manager. This type of conflict is frequently a subject of exam questions.

Contract Change Control System (page 292) A process for modifying the contract that should be included in the contract.

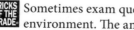 Sometimes exam questions ask how project control is different in a contracted environment. The answer may include:

- You need to deal with a different company's set of procedures
- It is not as easy to "see" problems
- Greater reliance on reports to determine if a problem exists
- Greater reliance on relationships between the buyer's and seller's project managers

All contracts, like all projects, have changes. The first step to handling changes that arise on the contracted project is to analyze the impacts to the project, just as it would be on a project without contracts or purchase orders. The change procedures in the contract must also be followed and all changes should be made formally. Changes are requested through the procurement process and are handled as part of the project integrated change control efforts.

A large number of changes on a project are a major problem because it is difficult, if not impossible, to continue work on an activity if you are not certain the change will be approved. In instances where there are many changes, it might be best to terminate the contract, if both parties agree, and start fresh through negotiating a new contract or finding a new seller. This is a drastic step to be done only when the existing contract no longer serves the purposes of defining all the work, roles and responsibilities.

TRICKS OF THE TRADE: Expect situations where your actions regarding changes are different depending on the type of contract used! Also expect situational questions to require that you know how to evaluate and formally make every change.

Buyer-Conducted Performance Review (page 293) This is a meeting where all the available data is brought together to see if the seller is performing. Often the seller is present to review the data and most importantly talk about what the buyer can do differently to help the work along. The purpose of this review is to determine and recommend needed corrective and preventive actions and to request formal changes.

Claims Administration (page 293) A claim is an assertion that the buyer did something that has hurt the seller and the seller asking for compensation. Another way of looking at claims is that they are a form of seller's change requests. Claims can get nasty. Imagine a seller that is not making as much profit as he hoped for, issuing claims for every action taken by the buyer. Imagine working with a fixed price contract and an incomplete scope. Many claims are not resolved until the work is completed.

Records Management System (page 293) A contract is a formal, legal document. Recordkeeping can be critical if actions taken or situations faced during a project are ever in question after the work is completed. This can happen related to unresolved claims or legal actions, or even in order to satisfy insurance needs. On many projects, every e-mail, every payment, every written and oral communication must be recorded, kept and stored. On other projects the weather each day and the number of people on the buyers' property each day may also be required. Whatever is appropriate for the particular industry and project is kept.

A record management system can be quite extensive, with one person assigned just to manage these records. They can also include indexing systems, archiving systems and information retrieval systems for projects with extensive documentation.

Contract Interpretation In the real world, project managers are always faced with the need to interpret the contract to answer many questions including "What does the contract really say?" and "Who is responsible for what part of the contract statement of work?"

Contract interpretation is never easy and frequently requires the assistance of a lawyer. However, the exam may describe a simple situation about a conflict over interpretation of a contract and ask you to determine the correct answer.

Procurement Management

TRICKS OF THE TRADE. Contract interpretation is based on an analysis of the intent of the parties to the contract and a few guidelines. One such guideline is that the contract supersedes any memos, conversations or discussions that may have occurred prior to the contract signing. Therefore, if a requirement is not in the contract, it does not have to be met, even if it was agreed upon prior to signing the contract. The following is an exercise on intent.

Exercise In each row, circle the item on the left side or the right side that would "win" in a dispute over contract interpretation.

Contract language	or	A memo drafted by one of the parties describing proposed changes after the contract is signed
Contract language	or	A memo signed by both parties before the contract is signed that describes what was agreed to during negotiations
Contract terms and conditions	or	Contract statement of work
Common definition	or	The intended meaning (without supplying a definition)
Industry use of the term	or	Common use of the term
Special provisions	or	General provisions
Typed-over wording on the contract	or	A handwritten comment on the contract that is also initialed
Numbers	or	Words
Detailed terms	or	General terms

Answer The correct answers (in bold) show more clearly the intent of the parties to the contract.

Contract language	or	A memo drafted by one of the parties describing proposed changes after the contract is signed
Contract language	or	A memo signed by both parties before the contract is signed that describes what was agreed to during negotiations
Contract terms and conditions	or	Contract statement of work
The answer depends on the Order of Precedence Clause in the contract that describes which terms and conditions take precedence over the others in the event of a conflict between them.		
Common definition	or	The intended meaning (without supplying a definition)
Industry use of the term	or	Common use of the term
Special provisions	or	General provisions
Typed-over wording on the contract	or	**A handwritten comment on the contract that is also initialed**
Numbers	or	**Words**
Detailed terms	or	General terms

═══ **Contract Closure** (page 295) This process consists of finishing all the loose ends of the contract. Be prepared for up to six questions about this topic. Contract closure is

part of the close project process described in Integration. Make sure you reread that part of the Integration chapter as you read this section.

Contract closure is done:
- When a contract ends
- When a contract is terminated before the work is completed

All contracts must be closed out no matter the circumstances under which they stop, are terminated or completed. Closure provides value to the performing organization and the customer and should not be eliminated under any circumstances. You will see situational questions on the exam asking if the project is closed. The exam also asks for the difference between administrative closure and contract closure. Depending on what choices the exam gives you, the answer could be:
- Contract closure occurs first. All contracts must be closed out before the project is closed out. Therefore, at the end of the contract, the project manager performs a procurement audit for each contract, administratively closes out the contract, and then administratively closes out the project when the whole project is completed.
- Administrative closure may be done at the end of each project phase and at the end of the project as a whole. Contract closure is done only once, at the end of the contract.
- Administrative closure uses the term "lessons learned" and contract closure uses the term "procurement audit."

Contract closure requires more recordkeeping and must be done more formally than is generally required for administrative closure, in order to make sure to protect the legal interests of both parties. Remember these for the exam!

Exercise Describe what work must be done during contract closure.

Answer Such closure will include:
- **Product Verification** Checking to see if all the work was completed correctly and satisfactorily. Was the product of the contract the same as what was requested? Did the product of the contract meet the needs of the customer?
- **Financial Closure** Making final payments and completing cost records.
- **Update Records in the Records Management System**
- **Final Contract Performance Reporting** Analyzing and documenting the success and effectiveness of the contract.

- **Contract File** (Project archives in administrative closure) Putting records of the contract into an organized file. This file will be stored for use as historical records and help protect the project in case of arguments or legal action regarding what was done and not done on the contract. The file should include:
  - Contract
  - Changes (approved and rejected)
  - Submittals from the seller
  - Seller performance reports
  - Financial information
  - Inspection results
  - Lessons learned
- **Procurement Audit** A structured review of the procurement process. Do not think of this as an audit of costs, rather think of it as a lessons learned of the procurement process that can help improve other procurements. The seller may be involved in procurement audits and/or lessons learned activities.
- **Lessons Learned** Lessons learned are created with the seller relating to the contract work and become part of the lessons learned for the project.
- **Other** There could also be additional activities in contract closure such as:
  - Arranging for storage of contract records and drawings
  - Creating and delivering legal documents such as release of lien documents and formal acceptance letters
  - Return of property used on the contract to its owner
- **Formal Acceptance and Closure** Once closure is completed and formal sign-off that the products of the contract are acceptable is received from the buyer, the contract is closed. Expect many questions on the exam that provide you with situations and require you to determine if the contract is closed. In gaining formal acceptance the seller is also working to measure customer satisfaction. Often a formal customer satisfaction survey may be included in contract closure.

Termination The contract should have provisions for stopping work before completion. Termination can be for cause or for convenience. The buyer may terminate a contract for cause if the seller breaches the contract (e.g., does not perform). The buyer can also terminate the contract because they no longer want the work done (termination for convenience). It is rare to allow the seller to terminate a contract, but it could be appropriate on some projects. Termination automatically puts the project into the closing process group.

The Procurement Process Exercise Now that you know so much about procurement, test your knowledge by completing the following chart. Notice the word "ACTIONS." **You need to know for the exam, among other things, what needs to be done during each step and what are the outputs.**

Exercise 1 Re-create the procurement management process, including the outputs, on the form opposite. Check your answers to the contents of this chapter when you are done. Even with one reading of this book, you should get most of the actions and outputs correct. The second and third times you read the chapter, you should be almost 100 percent accurate. This exercise is about remembering key parts of procurement management, not memorization. Create the chart three times and you should know it well enough for the exam.

Procurement Management

Plan Purchases and Acquisitions	Plan Contracting	Request Seller Responses	Select Sellers	Contract Administration	Contract Closure

Actions

Outputs

> **TRICKS OF THE TRADE.** Here is a trick for understanding the process without memorizing the whole thing—know only the outputs! If a question describes some activity and that activity is after the proposal is created and before the contract is signed, then it must be taking place as part of select sellers. If is taking place after the contract is signed, but before the work is substantially done, it must be occurring during contract administration.

Exercise 2 Here is another exercise. You must understand the project manager's role in contracts in order to pass the exam. After reading this chapter, how would you describe the project manager's role?

Answer 2
- Know the procurement process
- Understand contract terms and conditions
- Make sure the contract contains all the project management requirements such as attendance at meetings, reports, actions and communications deemed necessary
- Identify risks and incorporate mitigation and allocation of risks into the contract
- Help tailor the contract to the unique needs of the project
- Fit the schedule for completion of the procurement process into the schedule for the project
- Be involved during contract negotiation to protect the relationship with the seller
- Protect the integrity of the project and the ability to get the work done
- Uphold the entire contract, not just the contract statement of work
- Work with the contract manager to manage changes to the contract

Practice Exam

Procurement Management

1. **Once signed, a contract is legally binding unless:**
   A. one party is unable to perform.
   B. one party is unable to finance its part of the work.
   C. it is in violation of applicable law.
   D. it is declared null and void by either party's legal counsel.

2. **With a clear contract statement of work, a seller completes work as specified, but the buyer is not pleased with the results. The contract is considered to be:**
   A. null and void.
   B. incomplete.
   C. complete.
   D. waived.

3. **All of the following statements concerning bid documentation are incorrect EXCEPT?**
   A. Well-designed bid documents can simplify comparison of responses.
   B. Bid documentation must be rigorous with no flexibility to allow consideration of seller suggestions.
   C. In general, bid documents should not include evaluation criteria.
   D. Well-designed bid documents do not include a contract statement of work.

4. **A project manager for the seller is told by her management that the project should do whatever possible to be awarded incentive money. The primary objective of incentive clauses in a contract is to:**
   A. reduce costs for the buyer.
   B. help the seller control costs.
   C. synchronize objectives.
   D. reduce risk for the seller by shifting risk to the buyer.

5. **All the following statements about change control are incorrect EXCEPT?**
   A. A fixed price contract will minimize the need for change control.
   B. Changes seldom provide real benefits to the project.
   C. Contracts should include procedures to accommodate changes.
   D. More detailed specifications eliminate the causes of changes.

6. **A routine audit of a cost reimbursable (CR) contract determines that overcharges are being made. If the contract does not specify corrective action, the buyer should:**
   A. continue to make project payments.
   B. halt payments until the problem is corrected.
   C. void the contract and start legal action to recover overpayments.
   D. change the contract to require more frequent audits.

7. **The primary objective of contract negotiations is to:**
   A. get the most from the other side.
   B. protect the relationship.
   C. get the highest monetary return.
   D. define objectives and stick to them.

8. A seller is working on a cost reimbursable (CR) contract when the buyer decides he would like to expand the scope of services and change to a fixed price (FP) contract. All of the following are the seller's options EXCEPT?
   A. Completing the original work on a cost reimbursable basis and then negotiating a fixed price for the additional work
   B. Completing the original work and rejecting the additional work
   C. Negotiating a fixed price contract that includes all the work
   D. Starting over with a new contract

9. Bidder conferences are part of:
   A. plan contracting.
   B. contract administration.
   C. request seller responses.
   D. plan purchases and acquisitions.

10. All of the following MUST be present to have a contract EXCEPT?
    A. Contract statement of work
    B. Acceptance
    C. Address of the seller
    D. Buyers' signatures

11. Which of the following BEST describes the project manager's role during the contracting process?
    A. Project manager has only minor involvement.
    B. Project manager should be the negotiator.
    C. Project manager should supply an understanding of the risks of the project.
    D. Project manager should tell the contract manager how the contracting process should be handled.

12. What is one of the KEY objectives during contract negotiations?
    A. Obtain a fair and reasonable price.
    B. Negotiate a price under the seller's estimate.
    C. Ensure that all project risks are thoroughly delineated.
    D. Ensure that an effective communications management plan is established.

13. Which of the following activities occurs during plan purchases and acquisitions?
    A. Make-or-buy decisions
    B. Answering sellers' questions about the bid documents
    C. Creating the contract terms and conditions
    D. Creating the request for proposal or bid documents

14. Which of the following is the BEST thing for a project manager to do in the request seller responses part of procurement management?
    A. Evaluate risks
    B. Confirm that submittals have been sent
    C. Confirm that changes to the contract are made
    D. Answer sellers' questions about bid documents

15. The sponsor is worried about the seller deriving extra profit on the cost plus fixed fee (CPFF) contract. Each month he requires the project manager to submit CPI

calculations and an analysis of the cost to complete. The project manager explains to the sponsor that extra profits should not be a worry on this project because?

A. The team is making sure the seller does not cut scope.
B. All costs invoiced are being audited.
C. There can only be a maximum 10 percent increase if there is an unexpected cost overrun.
D. The fee is only received by the seller when the project is completed.

16. **In a fixed price (FP) contract, the fee or profit is:**

A. unknown.
B. part of the negotiation involved in paying every invoice.
C. applied as a line item to every invoice.
D. determined with the other party at the end of the project.

17. **A project performed under a cost reimbursable contract has finally entered the closing process. What must the buyer remember to do?**

A. Decrease the risk rating of the project.
B. Audit seller's cost submittals.
C. Evaluate the fee he is paying.
D. Make sure that the seller is not adding resources.

18. **The sponsor and the project manager are discussing what type of contract the project manager plans to use on the project. The buyer points out that the performing organization spent a lot of money hiring a design team to come up with the design.**

The project manager is concerned that the risk for the buyer be as small as possible. An advantage of a fixed price contract for the buyer is:

A. cost risk is lower.
B. cost risk is higher.
C. there is little risk.
D. risk is shared by all parties.

19. **As part of the records management system, you are trying to make sure that all records from the procurement are documented and indexed. Which of the following do you NOT have to worry about?**

A. Proposal
B. Statement of work
C. Terms and conditions
D. Negotiation process

20. **You are in the middle of a complex negotiation when the other party says, "We need to finish in one hour because I have to catch my plane." That person is using which of the following negotiation strategies?**

A. Good guy, bad guy
B. Delay
C. Deadline
D. Extreme demands

21. Which of the following is an advantage of centralized contracting?
    A. Gives easier access to contracting expertise
    B. Increases company expertise in contracting
    C. Gives more loyalty to the project
    D. Allows a contracts person to work on a single project

22. With which type of contract is the seller MOST concerned about project scope?
    A. Fixed price
    B. Cost plus fixed fee
    C. Time and material
    D. Purchase order

23. Your company has an emergency and needs contracted work done as soon as possible. Under these circumstances, which of the following would be the MOST helpful to add to the contract?
    A. A clear contract statement of work
    B. Requirements as to which subcontractors can be used
    C. Incentives
    D. A force majeure clause

24. During what part of the procurement process does contract negotiation occur?
    A. Plan purchases and acquisitions
    B. Plan contracting
    C. Request seller responses
    D. Select sellers

25. The project team is arguing about the prospective sellers who have submitted proposals. One team member argues for a certain seller while another team member wants the project awarded to a different seller. What part of the procurement process is the team in?
    A. Plan purchases and acquisitions
    B. Plan contracting
    C. Request seller responses
    D. Select sellers

26. The project team seems to like to argue; they have argued about everything. Luckily the project manager has set in place a reward system and team building sessions that will help and encourage the team to cooperate more. The latest thing they are arguing about is if they should complete a work package themselves or outsource the work to someone else. What part of the procurement process must they be in?
    A. Contract administration
    B. Plan purchases and acquisitions
    C. Request seller responses
    D. Select sellers

27. A project manager is in the middle of creating a request for proposal (RFP). What part of the procurement process is he in?
    A. Plan purchases and acquisitions
    B. Plan contracting
    C. Request seller responses
    D. Select sellers

28. Your program manager has come to you, the project manager, for help with a bid for her newest project. You want to protect your company from financial risk. You have limited scope definition. What is the BEST type of contract to choose?
    A. Fixed price (FP)
    B. Cost plus percent of cost (CPPC)
    C. Time and material (T&M)
    D. Cost plus fixed fee (CPFF)

29. Negotiations between two parties are becoming complex, so party A makes some notes that both parties sign. However, when the work is being done, party B claims that they are not required to provide an item they both agreed to during negotiations, because it was not included in the subsequent contract. In this case, party B is:
    A. incorrect, because both parties must comply with what they agreed upon.
    B. correct, because there was an offer.
    C. generally correct, because both parties are only required to perform what is in the contract.
    D. generally incorrect, because all agreements must be upheld.

30. Your project has just been fast tracked and you are looking at bringing in a subcontractor to complete networking quickly. There is no time to issue a request for proposal (RFP), so you choose to use a company you have used many times before for software development. A PRIMARY concern in this situation is:
    A. collusion between subcontractors.
    B. the subcontractor's qualifications.
    C. the subcontractor's evaluation criteria.
    D. holding a bidder conference.

31. The project manager and project sponsor are discussing the project costs and whether it is better to have their own company do part of the project or hire another company to do the work. If they asked for your opinion, you might say it would be better to do the work yourself if:
    A. there is a lot of proprietary data.
    B. you have the expertise but you do not have the available manpower.
    C. you do not need control over the work.
    D. your company resources are limited.

32. After much excitement and hard work, the contract statement of work for the project is completed. Even after gaining agreement that the contract statement of work is complete, the project manager is still concerned whether it actually addresses all the buyer's needs. The project manager is about to attend the bidder conference. He asks you for advice on what to do during the session. Which of the following is the BEST advice you can give him?
    A. You do not need to attend this session. The contract manager will hold it.
    B. Make sure you negotiate project scope.
    C. Make sure you give all the sellers enough time to ask questions. They may not want to ask questions while their competitors are in the room.
    D. Let the project sponsor handle the meeting so you can be the good guy in the negotiation session.

33. A seller is awarded a contract to build a pipeline. The contract terms and conditions require that a work plan be issued for the buyer's approval prior to commencing

work, but the seller fails to provide one. Which of the following is the BEST thing for the buyer's project manager to do?
A. File a letter of intent.
B. Develop the work plan and issue it to the seller to move things along.
C. Issue a default letter.
D. Issue a stop work order to the seller until a work plan is prepared.

34. Contract closure is different from administrative closure in that contract closure:
A. occurs before administrative closure.
B. is the only one to involve the customer.
C. includes the return of property.
D. may be done more than once for each contract.

35. You have just started administrating a contract when management decides to terminate the contract. What should you do FIRST?
A. Go back to request seller responses.
B. Go back to plan contracting.
C. Finish contract administration.
D. Go to contract closure.

36. The project team is arguing about the prospective sellers who have submitted proposals. One team member argues for a certain seller, while another team member wants the project to be awarded to a different seller. The BEST thing the project manager should remind the team to focus on in order to make a selection is the:
A. procurement documents.
B. procurement audits.
C. evaluation criteria.
D. procurement management plan.

37. The performing organization is trying to decide whether to split the contracts department and assign contracting responsibilities to departments directly responsible for the projects. A contract professional might not want this split to occur because they would lose _____ in a decentralized contracting environment.
A. standardized company project management practices
B. loyalty to the project
C. experience
D. access to others with similar expertise

38. During project executing, your project team member delivers a project deliverable to the buyer. However, the buyer refuses the deliverable, stating that it does not meet the requirement on page 300 of the technical specifications. You review the document and find that you agree. What is the BEST thing to do?
A. Explain that the contract is wrong and should be changed.
B. Issue a change order.
C. Review the requirements and meet with the responsible team member to review the WBS dictionary.
D. Call a meeting of the team to review the requirement on page 300.

39. **What type of contract do you NOT want to use if you do not have enough labor to audit invoices?**
    A. Cost plus fixed fee (CPFF)
    B. Time & material (T&M)
    C. Fixed price (FP)
    D. Fixed price incentive fee (FPIF)

40. **A new project manager is about to begin creating the contract statement of work. One stakeholder wants to add many items to the contract statement of work. Another stakeholder only wants to describe the functional requirements. The project is important for the project manager's company, but a seller will do the work. How would you advise the project manager?**
    A. The contract statement of work should be general to allow the seller to make his own decisions.
    B. The contract statement of work should be general to allow clarification later.
    C. The contract statement of work should be detailed to allow clarification later.
    D. The contract statement of work should be as detailed as necessary for the type of project.

41. **A customer has given you a contract statement of work for a complex, eight month project that has a few unknowns. The customer has asked you to just "get it done" and only wants to see you at the end of eight months when you deliver the finished project. Under these circumstances, which of the following is the BEST thing to do?**
    A. Complete the project as requested, but verify its scope with the customer occasionally throughout.
    B. Complete the project within eight months without contacting the customer during this time.
    C. Ask management to check in with the customer occasionally.
    D. Complete the project, but document that the customer did not want contact.

Procurement Management

Procurement Management Answers

1. **Answer** C

   Explanation Once signed, a contract is binding. Generally, the inability to perform, get financing or one party's belief that the contract is null and void does not change the fact that the contract is binding. If, however, both sides agree to terminate the contract, the contract can move into closure and it is considered completed.

2. **Answer** C

   Explanation If the seller completes the work specified in the contract statement of work, the contract is considered complete. That does not mean the same thing as contract closed. Contract closure must still occur. However, in this situation, the contract work is completed. Tricky!

3. **Answer** A

   Explanation Often the seller is required to inform the buyer of anything that is missing or unclear in the bid documents (choice B). It is in the buyer's best interest to discover missing items, since it will save the buyer money and trouble to correct the problem early. Bid documents must contain terms and conditions and evaluation criteria (choice C) as well as all the work that is to be done, including the contract statement of work (choice D). This is so the seller can price the project and know what is most important to the buyer. Choice A is an important point for the real world and is the best answer.

4. **Answer** C

   Explanation Incentives are meant to bring the objectives of the seller in line with those of the buyer. That way both are progressing toward the same objective.

5. **Answer** C

   Explanation Since there can be changes in any form of contract, choice A is not the best answer. There are always good ideas (changes) that can add benefit to the project, so choice B cannot be the best answer. In choice D, the word "eliminate" implies that changes will not occur. As that is not true, this cannot be the best answer.

6. **Answer** A

   Explanation Notice that choice B is really saying "halt ALL payments." Halting all payments would be a breach of contract on the buyer's part. Choice C is too severe and cannot be done unilaterally. Choice D does not solve the problem presented. A choice that said, "Halt payments on the disputed amount" would probably be the best answer, but it is not offered. Therefore, the best answer is A.

7. **Answer** B

   Explanation As a project manager, you want to develop a relationship during negotiations that will last throughout the project.

8. **Answer** D

   Explanation The seller does not have the choice to start over. The contract that exists is binding. Both parties could agree to start over, but this is a drastic step.

9. **Answer** C

   Explanation Expect many questions on the exam that require you to know in what part of the procurement process activities are done.

10. **Answer** C

    Explanation Many people miss the fact that a contract includes a contract statement of work (choice A). To have a contract, you must also have acceptance (choice B). One set of signatures is not enough; you must have sign-off (i.e., acceptance) from both parties, so choice D is only partially correct. The address of the seller (choice C) is not required, and therefore is the exception.

11. **Answer** C

    Explanation As the project manager, you know what the project risks are. You need to make sure that provisions are included in the contract to address these risks.

12. **Answer** A

    Explanation Choices C and D are good ideas, but not the key objective. Negotiations should be win/win, so choice B is not the best choice. A fair and equitable price (choice A) will create a good working atmosphere. Otherwise, you will pay later, on change orders.

13. **Answer** A

    Explanation Answering sellers' questions (choice B) occurs during request seller responses; the contract and RFP (choices C and D) are created during plan contracting.

14. **Answer** D

    Explanation During request seller responses, you normally answer questions submitted by the sellers. Risk identification (choice A) is done before the procurement process begins, as procurement is a risk mitigation and transference tool. Submittals (choice B) is another name for deliverables that are sent during contract administration. Contract changes (choice C) may be made in select sellers and contract administration.

15. **Answer** B

    Explanation Choice A cannot be best because cutting scope decreases profits on this type of contract. Choice C cannot be best, as CPFF contracts generally do not limit fee increases. Choice D cannot be best, as the fee in a CPFF contract is usually paid out on a continuous basis during the life of the project. One of the ways to change the profit in a cost plus fixed fee contract is to invoice for items not chargeable to the project (choice B).

16. **Answer** A

    Explanation To the seller, it is known, but this question is from the buyer's perspective. You do not know what profit the seller included in the contract.

17. **Answer** B

    Explanation Though a reserve might be decreased for the project overall when one of its contracts enters closure, the risk rating of the project (choice A) may not be affected. Choice C should have been done during select sellers. Although choice D may be a concern during contract administration, it is not common during closure. Choice B, audit seller's cost submittals, is part of the procurement audit and is a required aspect of contract closure.

18. **Answer** A

    Explanation If you had trouble with this one, you might remember that the questions are asked from the buyer's perspective unless otherwise noted. In this case, the seller has the most cost risk and the buyer's risk is lower.

19. **Answer** D

    Explanation You will see long, wordy questions consisting of many paragraphs on the exam, but do not let them worry you. Sometimes the briefer questions are harder. To answer this question, you need to know what a record management system is and that it would not be used to keep track of negotiations. The negotiation process is not a document.

20. **Answer** C

    Explanation Giving a time limit to the negotiation is an example of deadline.

21. **Answer** B

    Explanation Choices A, C and D are all advantages of decentralized contracting. With centralizing contracting, you increase the company's expertise in contracting, allowing individuals to learn from each other.

22. **Answer** A

    Explanation In a fixed price contract, the seller has the cost risk and therefore wants to completely understand the contract statement of work before bidding.

23. **Answer** C

    Explanation If you follow the proper project management process, you ALWAYS have good definition of scope (choice A). In this situation, you are in a time crunch. Both good scope definition and incentives are required to make it happen. Which provides the better answer? Along with good scope definition, you need the seller to feel your need for speed. Incentives bring the seller's objectives in line with the buyer's and thus would be the MOST helpful. Good scope definition alone does not ensure speed.

24. **Answer** D

    Explanation Negotiation occurs during select sellers.

25. **Answer** D

    Explanation The seller creates his proposal during request seller responses, but it is not received and reviewed until select sellers.

26. **Answer** B

    Explanation Notice that much of this question is irrelevant? Did you also notice that the words "make-or-buy decision" were not used in the question? Instead, the question used the definition of make-or-buy. Watch out for this on the exam. A make-or-buy decision is needed before the rest of the procurement process can occur. It therefore must be one of the earlier steps of the procurement process.

27. **Answer** B

    Explanation In plan contracting, we create the documents that will be sent out during request seller responses. The request for proposal is one of those documents.

28. **Answer** D
    Explanation Of the options given, the only contract that limits fees for large projects with limited scope definition is CPFF.

29. **Answer** C
    Explanation Party B is only required to deliver what is defined in the contract.

30. **Answer** B
    Explanation Although you have used this contractor before, how can you be sure the company is qualified to do the new work, since it is not exactly like the previous work? This is the risk you are taking.

31. **Answer** A
    Explanation It is generally better to do the work yourself if using an outside company means you have to turn over proprietary data to the other company.

32. **Answer** C
    Explanation The project manager should attend the bidder conference, so choice A is incorrect. Did you select choice B because the question referred to a concern about scope? Then read the choice again. It talks about negotiation, and negotiation occurs after the seller is selected, not during the bidder conference. The contract manager usually holds the bidder conference, so choice D is incorrect. Choice C describes one of the many challenges of a bidder conference and is therefore the best answer.

33. **Answer** C
    Explanation Any time that a seller does not perform according to the contract, the project manager must take action. The preferred choice might be to contact the seller and ask what is going on, but that choice is not available here. Therefore, the best choice is to let him know he is in default (choice C).

34. **Answer** A
    Explanation Choice B cannot be correct since the customer may be involved in lessons learned and procurement audits and would certainly be involved in formal acceptance. Choice C cannot be correct since both contract closure and administrative closure involve the return of property. Contract closure is done only once, at the end of the contract, so choice D cannot be correct. Choice A is correct because contracts are closed out before the project is closed out with administrative closure.

35. **Answer** D
    Explanation If the contract is terminated, the project needs to enter closure. You need those results for historical purposes.

36. **Answer** C
    Explanation The evaluation criteria are the primary tools for evaluating potential sellers and should be used by the entire team in order to make a selection.

37. **Answer** D
    Explanation Choice A is incorrect, as the change would not impact the entire project management process, only contracting. Loyalty to the project (choice B) would be gained, not lost, in a decentralized environment. In a decentralized contracting

situation, there is less focus on maintaining the skill or expertise of the contracting function, making choice D the best answer.

38. **Answer** C
Explanation In choice A, the contract could be wrong, or the customer could be wrong, but this would have/should have been discovered earlier if proper project management was followed. If you picked choice B, you have forgotten that a seller cannot issue a change order (although he could request one). Did you select choice D? If so, remember that project management is not about making every decision with ALL the team members. Choice C involves meeting with the appropriate team member. If such a problem has arisen, it could mean something was wrong in the WBS dictionary or in how the team member completed the work.

39. **Answer** A
Explanation If you got this question wrong, reread it. You need to audit invoices in all contract types, so how do you choose? Look for the answer that is BEST. In this case, it would be the choice that requires the greatest effort.

Invoices need to be audited in a fixed price contract because the seller could be charging you before they pay out the money, thus taking the payment and investing it until they need to pay it out. A T&M contract (choice B) should be for small dollars and short duration (remember that a T&M contract has no incentive to finish) so it does not have a great risk. Choices C and D cannot be best because the risk to the buyer is limited—they are still only going to pay the contract price. In a CPFF contract the buyer pays all costs. The seller could be charging the buyer for costs that should not be allocated to the buyer. Because of the size and dollar amount of these type of contracts and because the risk to the buyer is great, CPFF contracts need the most auditing. Since this question asked for which one you do not want to use, the answer must be choice A.

40. **Answer** D
Explanation When the seller has more expertise than the buyer, the contract statement of work should describe performance or function rather than a complete list of work. In any case, the contract statement of work should be as detailed as possible.

41. **Answer** A
Explanation Notice the use of the term contract statement of work. This is used to refer to the part of the project work that will be done by a seller.

It is unethical to ignore scope verification, as it will add risk that the project will not meet the customer's needs. Therefore, choice A is the best answer. In a real-world situation, one would probably work with the customer to efficiently handle verification so as to cause as little disruption as possible.

Professional and Social Responsibility

Quicktest

- Do the right thing
- Follow the right process
- Act ethically, fairly and professionally toward team and resource owners
- Watch for conflicts of interest
- Report violations
- Put the project's needs before your own
- Share lessons learned
- Deal with problems
- Ensure individual integrity
- Contribute to the project management knowledge base
- Enhance personal professional competence
- Promote interaction among stakeholders
- Balance stakeholders' interests
- Interact with team and stakeholders in a professional and cooperative manner

There can be about 18 questions out of 200 on the exam covering professional and social responsibility. When you take a PMP simulation, or take the actual exam, you should not get more than six questions wrong in this area. Those who score poorly in other areas of the exam also score poorly here. Those who score well in other areas of the exam also score well here.

Some people think that professional and social responsibility relates to ethics, and that is partially correct. Then why would people answer any questions wrong in this area? Are people unethical? No, but there may be lapses in your knowledge that trip you up on the exam. Read this chapter carefully and be honest with yourself. Remember, questions on the exam are written to uncover what you are really like as a project manager.

You should review and understand PMI's Code of Professional Conduct shown at the end of this chapter, since many questions relate to that code. It seems that the more ambiguous questions on the exam are ones relating to professional and social responsibility. Read ambiguous questions carefully.

As certified project managers (or soon to be), we have a responsibility to uphold and support the integrity and ethics of the profession. This involves ensuring that our actions are always in line with legal requirements and ethical standards. Sounds easy, right? But ethics also relates to the proper use of project management. Did you realize it could be considered unethical to publish a project schedule that is not accurate? That it could be considered unethical to start a project without a project charter, or to start a project without a complete scope or a plan to deal with the incomplete scope? The lack of project management knowledge and lack of application of that knowledge causes many project managers to act in ways that are considered unethical.

Rita's Process Chart—Professional and Social Responsibility
Where are we in the project management process?

Professional and social responsibility should be maintained throughout the project management process.

Initiating	Planning	Executing	Monitoring & Controlling	Closing
Select project manager	Determine how you will do planning—part of management plans	Acquire final team	Measure against the performance measurement baselines	Develop closure procedures
Determine company culture and existing systems	Create project scope statement	Execute the PM plan	Measure according to the management plans	Complete contract closure
Collect processes, procedures and historical information	Determine team	Work to produce product scope	Determine variances and if they warrant corrective action or a change	Confirm work is done to requirements
Divide large projects into phases	Create WBS and WBS dictionary	Recommend changes and corrective actions		Gain formal acceptance of the product
Identify stakeholders	Create activity list	Send and receive information	Scope verification	Final performance reporting
Document business need	Create network diagram	Implement approved changes, defect repair, preventive and corrective actions	Configuration management	Index and archive records
Determine project objectives	Estimate resource requirements	Continuous improvement	Recommend changes, defect repair, preventive and corrective actions	Update lessons learned knowledge base
Document assumptions and constraints	Estimate time and cost	Follow processes	Integrated change control	Hand off completed product
Develop project charter	Determine critical path	Team building	Approve changes, defect repair, preventive and corrective actions	Release resources
Develop preliminary project scope statement	Develop schedule	Give recognition and rewards	Risk audits	
	Develop budget	Hold progress meetings	Manage reserves	
	Determine quality standards, processes and metrics	Use work authorization system	Use issue logs	
	Determine roles and responsibilities	Request seller responses	Facilitate conflict resolution	
	Determine communications requirements	Select sellers	Measure team member performance	
	Risk identification, qualitative and quantitative risk analysis and response planning		Report on performance	
	Iterations—go back		Create forecasts	
	Determine what to purchase		Administer contracts	
	Prepare procurement documents			
	Finalize the "how to execute and control" aspects of all management plans			
	Create process improvement plan			
	Develop final PM plan and performance measurement baselines			
	Gain formal approval for plan			
	Hold kickoff meeting			

Professional and social responsibility can be broken down into the following categories:
- Ensure individual integrity
- Contribute to the project management knowledge base
- Enhance personal professional competence
- Promote interaction among stakeholders

These sound easy, but they are not. Pay particular attention to ensure individual integrity and promote interaction among stakeholders.

Ensure Individual Integrity This topic may require you to know that a project manager must:
- Tell the truth in reports, conversations and other communications
- Follow copyright and other laws
- Not divulge company data to unauthorized parties
- Value and protect intellectual (non-tangible) property
- Not put personal gain over the needs of the project
- Prevent conflicts of interest or the appearance of conflicts of interest and deal with them when they do occur
- Not give or take bribes or inappropriate gifts
- Treat everyone with respect
- Follow PMI's Code of Professional Conduct
- Do the right thing
- Follow the right process
- Report violations of laws, business policies, ethics and other rules

Tell the Truth in Reports, Conversations and Other Communications You should realize what this means. An example is reporting the real project status (e.g., that the project is currently behind schedule) in project reports, conversations and meetings, even if you are asked not to.

Follow Copyright Laws When was the last time you made a copy of an article or made a copy of a music CD and gave that copy to others? Did you know that such actions could be violating copyright laws? How about taking excerpts from this book, or any book, and putting them in a company report or in the material used for a training class without written permission of the copyright owner? Is that allowable? This is also a likely violation of copyright laws.

International copyright laws give the owner of the copyright the exclusive rights to make copies of the work and to prepare derivative works based on the work. It is illegal to infringe upon these rights—that is, to use the copyrighted work in certain ways without the owner's permission. For example, without the copyright owner's permission, no one may copy or reproduce any part of a book, create new material based on or incorporating any part of a book, or sell or distribute copies of a book except in limited instances covered by the Fair Use Doctrine. A copyright notice on the document is not required in order for something to be considered copyrighted. Be careful, many people are completely uninformed about copyright law and can easily be tripped up on questions in this area.

When you are working with copyrighted materials you should always be mindful of the following issues:
- Is it appropriate to copy software?

- If you're a contractor asked to create a copyrightable work, who owns the copyright, you or the company that hired you to create it?
- If you're an employee and create a work, do you own the copyright or does your employer?
- If someone asks you to copy and distribute a work created by someone else, should you do it?

These are some basic issues confronting project managers who deal with copyrighted works. A project manager should ask the questions before taking any action that could be perceived as copyright infringement.

Put the Project's Needs Before Your Own This one sounds simple doesn't it? Watch out though. If the question was asked directly, everyone would get it right, but most questions are not asked directly. What about instances where the project is suffering and the project manager does not want to do anything about the real issue because it will make his manager angry? The correct or professionally responsible thing to do would be to deal with the issue hurting the project, to put the needs of the project before your own. Questions on the exam may be hard if you do not follow this rule in the real world.

Do Not Give or Take Bribes or Inappropriate Gifts Did you know that in many countries bribery is punishable as a crime and that can mean jail time? What is a bribe? Is it a bribe if someone asks you to pay a fee in order to bring machinery through a city? How about requesting a payment for police protection?

In many countries, fees for services such as protection and bringing machinery through a town, or fees for issuing permits and other official documents are allowable and are not considered bribes. Payments to convince a government official to select your company are bribes. Many companies have policies or codes of business conduct to help prevent bribes or other illegal activity.

What about other "payments"? Would it be appropriate to accept a free automobile or a free weekend holiday for you and your family? These are probably not allowable. Tom Donaldson, in *The Ethics of International Business*, suggests that a practice is permissible if you can answer "No" to both of the following questions:
1. Is it permissible to conduct business successfully in the host country without undertaking the practice?
2. Is the practice a clear violation of a fundamental international right?

Fundamental rights include such rights as the right to food, a fair trial, non-discriminating treatment, minimal education, physical safety and freedom of speech.

There will be few questions on this area on the exam. However, if you need more help, see the exercise on the following page, and the many questions on this topic in our PMP exam simulation software, *PM FASTrack*®.

Do the Right Thing Many of these topics are interrelated. Do the right thing means being ethical, reporting violations, treating others with respect and following the right project management process. Notice this as you continue reading the rest of this chapter.

Follow the Right Process This is one of the hardest topics in professional and social responsibility! Professional and social responsibility REQUIRES you to follow the project management process. It means that you MUST have a project charter, in fact it is unethical not to. It means that you MUST have a work breakdown structure, it is unethical not to. Why?

You should realize that not having a project charter hurts your project and at the least, causes increased costs and wasted time. Not having a WBS means that the project will have rework and that work will remain undefined until later in the project.

In previous sections of this book, I have strongly suggested that you understand and memorize Rita's Process Chart. Now you can see why. A project manager must understand the project management process in order to do the right thing!

Often the project manager is not given the authority required to get the project done. Imagine a situation where the project manager is given only the authority to write reports and transmit them to others. With no one directing the integration of the work, the project will probably be late and individuals working on the project will waste valuable time in rework. Professional responsibility REQUIRES the project manager to obtain the authority necessary to manage the project.

Project managers are often given unrealistic project completion deadlines or milestones. Many project managers just make the project happen as best as they can and wait to see what happens. Professional and social responsibility REQUIRES the project manager to handle an unrealistic schedule problem upfront. This may mean saying, "Assign the project to someone else!" or "You have requested that the project be completed within six months. Our analysis makes us very certain that we can meet that due date only if we adjust the scope, cost or quality on this project. If we cannot make any changes, the project will be completed in eight months."

Professional and social responsibility in today's project management world also means saying, "I am sorry that you do not want to support my efforts in planning the project and want me to get started producing work right away. As a certified PMP, I am ethically bound to do project management correctly for the best interests of the project and the company. This means that I must have a project charter and at least a high-level work breakdown structure." The project manager is REQUIRED to do the right thing and stand up for the right process! When you pass the exam, start showing this book to your management. They can blame me instead of you when you want to do the right thing.

Exercise

1. Your management has told you that you will receive part of the incentive fee from the customer if you can bring the project in early. While finalizing a major deliverable, your team informs you that the deliverable meets the requirements in the contract, but will not provide the functionality the customer needs. If the deliverable is late, you know that the project will not be completed early. What action should you take?

2. You are asked to make a copy of a magazine article and include it in new software you are writing. You see that the article has a copyright notice. What is the best thing to do?

3. Your company is in competition to win a major project for the government of country X. You are told that you must make a large payment to the foreign minister in order to be considered for the project. What is the best thing to do?

4. You provide a project cost estimate for the project to the project sponsor. He is unhappy with the estimate, because he thinks the price should be lower. He asks you to cut 15 percent off the project estimate. What should you do?

Answers The answers depend on the exact wording of the choices, but generally:
1. Review the situation with the customer; review what is required in the contract
2. Ask the copyright owner for permission
3. Find out if there are any laws against such a payment
4. Look for options such as schedule compression, re-estimating or changing scope

Report Violations Ask yourself what you would do if someone in your company told you that they do not follow a certain company procedure. The correct answer is to report them to those responsible for the policy.

"What?" you might say. Questions like this can annoy you. Let me help by explaining why the ethical choice is to report the violation. You are probably not the one who created the policy and you are therefore not the best person to explain the reasons behind the policy. If you attempt to explain it to the person, you could make an error and therefore cost the company time and money. It is best to leave such things to those whose responsibility it is. Seem more logical now? Many questions on the exam require the project manager to immediately report violations of policies, laws or ethics to a manager or supervisor. Questions on these topics should be reviewed carefully before answering.

▰▰Contribute to the Project Management Knowledge Base
This is a relatively easy topic to understand.

This topic may require you to know that a project manager should:
- Share lessons learned from the project with other project managers in the company
- Write articles about project management
- Support the education of other project managers and stakeholders about project management
- Coach or mentor other project managers and project team members
- Perform research to discover best practices for the use of project management and share the results with others
- Perform research on projects done within the company for the purpose of calculating performance metrics

▰▰Enhance Personal Professional Competence
This is also a relatively easy topic to understand.

This topic may require you to know that project managers should:
- Work to understand their personal strengths and weaknesses
- Continue to learn to apply the science of project management
- Plan their own professional development
- Constantly look for new information and practices that will help the company or its projects
- Continue to learn about the industry or industries where they work

Project managers are busy! When was the last time you took a more formal approach to any of these bulleted items? Notice how each is introspective? Do you know your strengths and weaknesses? How do you know you are right? What is your plan for improving on your strengths?

Promote Interaction Among Stakeholders

Balance Stakeholders' Interests   Product-related and project-related requirements and project objectives are developed early in the project and are documented in the project charter and project scope statement. There should be an attempt to balance stakeholders' interests during project initiating and project planning in order to determine the final project objectives. During project planning, the issue is to balance the overall project objectives with the requirements in order to answer the question, "Can all of the project requirements be met within the project objectives?" If they cannot, then you need to look for options to adjust the competing demands of scope, time, cost, quality, resources and risk. For example, see the discussion of schedule compression and other related topics in the Time chapter. Do you perform such activities now?

There is also a need to balance stakeholders' interests during the life of the project. Over the life of the project, the project manager will discover that stakeholders have interests which may or may not match those of the project or those of other stakeholders. These interests must be balanced against the interests of the project and any conflicts resolved. There are also those stakeholder interests which may not conflict with those of the project objectives, but still need to be managed by the project manager.

Balancing stakeholders' interests is never easy or quick, but it is an impossible effort if you do not have clear project objectives, if you have not previously identified ALL the stakeholders and determined ALL their requirements. Being able to balance their interests implies that you also know the priority of their requirements. Do you spend the effort in the real world to get as close to final requirements as possible? Are your requirements ranked by order of importance? Think about this to improve your real-world projects. Assume that efforts have been expended to determine all requirements and that those requirements are ranked when answering exam questions.

Exercise   What a project manager should do is outlined in this exercise. Spend some time THINKING about balancing stakeholders' interests while getting ready for the exam. This exercise will help you determine if you really understand the process summarized here. Go through each topic and put a checkmark next to the ones you understand. Put an X next to the ones you are able to do in the real world. Further study all boxes without marks.

Topic	Under-stand ✔	Can Do X
Work to get as clear and complete requirements as possible before starting the project (See the next section.)		
Understand all the stakeholders on the project and their needs, wants and expectations		
Know the team cannot resolve competing interests during the project if they did not identify all the stakeholders and determine all their requirements before project executing		
Resolve stakeholders' competing interests based on how they affect the project (See the next section.)		
Know that if any needs conflict with those of the customer, the customer's needs normally take precedence		
Use quality management to ensure that the project will satisfy the needs for which it was undertaken		
Look for competing interests during project planning, don't just wait for them to show up during project executing		
Deal with problems and conflicts as soon as they arise (See the next section.)		
Realize that the project manager will have to say "No" (and have the authority to say "No") to some of the competing interests		
Realize that the project manager can call on management to help resolve competing interests that the project manager and the team cannot resolve on their own		
Fix the project when the project starts to deviate from the requirements, rather than changing or lowering the requirements to meet the results of the project		
Know what the project manager and the team will need to look for—including options for resolving competing interests and alternative ways of completing the project activities		
Work toward fair resolution of disputes that consider all stakeholders' interests as well as the needs of the project		
Use the conflict resolution techniques explained in the Human Resources chapter		
Use negotiation techniques to resolve disputes between stakeholders		
Plan and implement effective communication as explained in the Communications chapter (Do not just read this, think, "What is effective communication?")		
Gather, assess and integrate information into the project		

Resolve Competing Interests Many project managers have no idea how to weight interests. What if the engineering department wants the project to focus on decreasing defects and the accounting department wants the project costs to be smaller? Can both needs be met? What if the engineering department is the primary stakeholder or even the sponsor of the project? Do their needs outweigh the needs of the accounting department?

What if the needs of the engineering department actually hurt the accounting department? Some issues are so complex they cannot be resolved by the project manager alone, and require management intervention. There are some standard guidelines for balancing stakeholders' interests. One trick is to walk through the following list for each interest.

TRICKS OF THE TRADE The project manager should facilitate the resolution of competing interests by accepting those that best comply with the following:
- The reason the project was initiated (market demand, legal requirement, etc.)
- The project charter
- The preliminary project scope statement
- The project scope statement
- The components of the "triple constraint"

Therefore, a stakeholder request to do or add something to the project that is not related to the reason the project was initiated should be rejected! If it is related to the reason the project was initiated, but does not fall within the project charter, the request is rejected! If the most important component of the "triple constraint" is schedule, then any needs or objectives that would delay the schedule would not likely be accepted. Those that enhance the schedule (without serious impact on the other components of the "triple constraint") would more likely be accepted.

In order to deal with competing interests, the project manager would take the following actions:
- Determine and understand the interests of all stakeholders
- Actively look for competing interests
- Get management involved when the team cannot resolve the competing interests
- Determine options for fair resolution of conflict
- Use conflict resolution, communication, negotiation, information distribution, team building and problem solving skills (see those topics in this book)
- Review the competing interests against those listed above (Those needs that are in line with the items listed above may be accepted, those that are not are rejected and may become a parts of a future project)
- Look for options including: schedule compression, re-estimating, brainstorming and other project management and management-related techniques
- Hold meetings, interviews and discussions to facilitate resolution of competing interests
- Make decisions and changes that do not impact the reason the project was initiated, the project charter, the preliminary project scope statement, the project scope statement or the components of the "triple constraint"
- Bring suggested changes to the project charter to the sponsor's attention for approval
- Escalate when a fair and equitable solution cannot be facilitated

Deal With Problems and Conflicts As They Arise Many people prefer to avoid conflict (withdraw) instead of solving the problem. Imagine a senior manager who is arbitrarily adding work to your project that does not fit within its charter. Would you deal with it, or delay action? Why would dealing with problems fall under the area of ethics? Because when a problem is not dealt with, its effect on the project increases. Questions in this area are not always easy. Imagine the following:

A seller on your project is four weeks late in submitting a report required in the contract. What would you do? Would you call them and investigate why it was late? If so, you would get the answer wrong. In a contract situation, the seller has breached the contract, making the required action sending a letter to notify them of the breach. In other words, your lack of project management knowledge might cause you to select a choice to a question that is not the proper way to deal with the problem. For those with a lack of experience managing large projects, this can be a large gap to fill!

Interact With Team and Stakeholders in a Professional and Cooperative Manner

Think about resource managers. Are you in the habit of going to them and asking for the immediate assignment of needed resources for your project? If so, then you are one of the people who will have great difficulty with this, one of the most difficult Professional Responsibility topics.

Put yourself in the shoes of a resource manager for a moment. Resource managers are usually compensated for how well their do their own work, not how well they support projects. Resource managers have their own needs, yet project managers tend to treat them as existing only to serve the project. The project manager has an ethical responsibility to provide resource managers with advance notice of what resources they need and when, and the impact to the project if those resources are not available. By providing them with a realistic schedule, the project manager informs the resource managers of when their resources will be used on the project. This enables the resource managers to better manage project work with their other work. Professional and social responsibility questions can require you to know the proper use of project management tools, techniques and practices in order to get these questions right.

Now let's look at the team. Have you ever realized the reputation of each of your team members is in your hands? How well the project goes will reflect on their careers. If a team member believes the project will be unsuccessful, he will remove himself from as much work on the project as possible so it does not tarnish him. The project manager has a duty to team members to make sure there is a realistic schedule so the team members can know when they really need to complete work on the project. They need to be provided with a reward system. They need to be asked their opinions and to contribute to the development of the project management plan. They need to help control the project. Do you treat them as servants?

Believe it or not, most project managers do not properly treat resource managers and team members, and therefore do not score well in this area. When you also consider the project manager's responsibility to stakeholders (i.e., properly reporting to them, keeping them appropriately involved in the project, etc.), you can start to see why you might want to read this whole section over again. Spend time thinking about what you do incorrectly in the real world, so you don't miss questions on the exam. Remember that most of the questions are not direct (e.g., What should you provide resource managers?) Rather, they describe a situation and see if you understand this concept well enough to choose the proper thing to do.

There is even more here. This topic also may require you to know that a project manager must:
- Respect the needs of resource managers
- Realize that team members' reputations can be negatively affected by the project
- Identify and understand cultural differences
- Uncover communication preferences when identifying stakeholders
- Uncover and respect different work ethics and practices of team members

- Provide formal and informal training to stakeholders as needed for them to effectively work on the project
- Follow the practices in use in other countries as long as they do not violate laws

Identify and Understand Cultural Differences Cultural differences can mean differences in language, cultural values, nonverbal actions and cultural practices. Without planning and monitoring and controlling, these can easily impede the project. Cultural differences do not only occur between people from different countries. They may also occur between people from the same country. In many countries there are cultural differences between those from different areas within it. Therefore, a project manager will do all the following, and more, to diminish the negative impact and gain positive impact of cultural differences. Such actions include:

- Embrace diversity. Cultural differences can make a project more fun.
- Prevent culture shock. The disorientation that occurs when you find yourself working with other cultures in a different environment. Training and advance research about the different cultures will help prevent culture shock.
- Expect cultural differences to surface on the project.
- Use clear communication to the right people and in the right form, as outlined in the Communications chapter, to prevent cultural differences from becoming a problem.
- Uncover cultural differences when identifying stakeholders.
- Ask for clarification whenever a cultural difference arises.
- Discuss the topic of cultural differences at team meetings as needed.

Uncover Communication Preferences When Identifying Stakeholders Would you be shocked if someone you worked for asked you what is the best way to communicate with you about various topics? Should they call you, e-mail you, send a letter? If you would be shocked, you might score poorly here because such actions should be commonplace. Not only does asking such questions show respect for the other person, but it also helps effectively plan communications.

The following exercise will help you remember what you have learned and help you to make the concepts more real-world.

Exercise This is an extensive list of the professional and social responsibility topics on the exam. Make sure you get your mind around any differences between the responsibilities listed here and how you manage your real-world projects! There is no need to spend hours reading about it or memorizing the following topics. The process of going through this exercise (in a study group if possible) will help you to prepare for the exam!

Test yourself! For each topic listed next, give an example of the area of professional and social responsibility occurring in the real world. This is not an easy exercise, and because of the wide variety of possible responses, there are no "answers" provided.

Area of Professional and Social Responsibility	Describe a Real-World Situation
Ensure individual integrity	
Adhere to legal requirements and ethical standards	

Area of Professional and Social Responsibility	Describe a Real-World Situation	
Protect stakeholders		
Share lessons learned and relevant information with others within and outside the performing organization		
Build the capabilities of colleagues		
Advance the profession of project management		
Improve your competencies as a project manager		
Balance stakeholders' interests on the project		
Strive for fair resolutions		
Satisfy competing interests		
Interact with others in a professional manner		
Respect personal, ethnic and cultural differences		
Ensure a collaborative project management environment		
Comply with all organizational rules and policies		
Provide accurate and truthful representations in cost estimates		
Provide accurate and truthful representations in project reports		
Report violations of policies, procedures and codes of ethics		

Area of Professional and Social Responsibility	Describe a Real-World Situation
Be responsible for satisfying the complete scope and objectives of customer requirements	
Maintain and respect confidential information	
Ensure that a conflict of interest does not compromise the customer's legitimate interests	
Ensure that a conflict of interest does not interfere with professional judgment	
Disclose conflicts of interest to the customer, sponsor and others	
Disclose circumstances that could be construed as conflicts of interest	
Refrain from offering or accepting inappropriate payments, gifts or other forms of compensation	
Adhere to all applicable laws or customs of the country where services are being provided	
Respect intellectual property developed or owned by others	
Act in an accurate, truthful and competent manner	

  TRICKS OF THE TRADE The trick for all the professional and social responsibility questions is to MEMORIZE the following phrases. In a broad sense, professional and social responsibility means:

- Do the right thing
- Follow the right process
- Act ethically, fairly and professionally toward team and resource owners
- Watch for conflicts of interest
- Report violations
- Deal with problems
- Put the project's needs before your own
- Share lessons learned
- Enhance your competence

PMI's PMP® Code of Professional Conduct

Many of the questions on professional and social responsibility directly relate to PMI's PMP Code of Professional Conduct.

As a PMI® Project Management Professional, I agree to support and adhere to the responsibilities described in the PMI PMP Code of Professional Conduct.

I. **Responsibilities to the Profession**
   a. **Compliance with all organizational rules and policies**
      i. Responsibility to provide accurate and truthful representations concerning all information directly or indirectly related to all aspects of the PMI Certification Program, including but not limited to the following: examination applications, test item banks, examinations, answer sheets, candidate information and PMI Continuing Certification Requirements Program reporting forms.
      ii. Upon a reasonable and clear factual basis, responsibility to report possible violations of the PMP Code of Professional Conduct by individuals in the field of project management.
      iii. Responsibility to cooperate with PMI concerning ethics violations and the collection of related information.
      iv. Responsibility to disclose to clients, customers, owners or contractors, significant circumstances that could be construed as a conflict of interest or an appearance of impropriety.
   b. **Candidate/Certificant Professional Practice**
      i. Responsibility to provide accurate, truthful advertising and representations concerning qualifications, experience and performance of services.
      ii. Responsibility to comply with laws, regulations and ethical standards governing professional practice in the state/province and/or country when providing project management services.
   c. **Advancement of the Profession**
      i. Responsibility to recognize and respect intellectual property developed or owned by others, and to otherwise act in an accurate, truthful and complete manner, including all activities related to professional work and research.
      ii. Responsibility to support and disseminate the PMP Code of Professional Conduct to other PMP certificants.
II. **Responsibilities to Customers and the Public**
   a. **Qualifications, experience and performance of professional services**
      i. Responsibility to provide accurate and truthful representations to the public in advertising, public statements and in the preparation of estimates concerning costs, services and expected results.
      ii. Responsibility to maintain and satisfy the scope and objectives of the professional services, unless otherwise directed by the customer.
      iii. Responsibility to maintain and respect the confidentiality of sensitive information obtained in the course of professional activities or otherwise where a clear obligation exists.
   b. **Conflict of interest situations and other prohibited professional conduct**
      i. Responsibility to ensure that a conflict of interest does not compromise legitimate interests of a client or customer, or influence/interfere with professional judgments.
      ii. Responsibility to refrain from offering or accepting inappropriate payments, gifts or other forms of compensation for personal gain, unless in conformity with applicable laws or customs of the country where project management services are being provided.

Used with permission of the Project Management Institute

Practice Exam

Professional and Social Responsibility

1. Near the end of your last project, additional requirements were demanded by a group of stakeholders when they learned they would be affected by your project. This became a problem because you had not included the time or cost in the project management plan for these requirements. What is the BEST thing you can do to prevent such a problem on future projects?
   A. Review the WBS dictionary more thoroughly, looking for incomplete descriptions.
   B. Review the project charter more thoroughly, examining the business case for "holes."
   C. Do a more thorough job of contract planning.
   D. Pay more attention to stakeholder management.

2. The software development project is not going well. There are over 30 stakeholders, and no one can agree on the project objectives. One stakeholder believes the project can achieve a 30 percent improvement while another believes a 50 percent improvement is possible. The project manager thinks a 10 percent improvement is more realistic. What is the BEST course of action?
   A. Move forward with the project and look for more information later to settle the issue.
   B. Average the numbers and use that as an objective.
   C. Perform a feasibility analysis.
   D. Ask the sponsor to make the final decision.

3. A project team has completed, and the customer has accepted, the completed project scope. However, the lessons learned required by the project management office have not been completed. What is the status of the project?
   A. The project is incomplete because the project needs to be re-planned.
   B. The project is incomplete until all project and product deliverables are complete and accepted.
   C. The project is complete because the customer has accepted the deliverables.
   D. The project is complete because the project has reached the due date.

4. You are in the middle of a new product development for your publicly traded company when you discover that the previous project manager made a U.S. $3,000,000 payment that was not approved in accordance with your company policies. Luckily, the project cost performance index (CPI) is 1.2. What should you do?
   A. Contact your manager.
   B. Put the payment in an escrow account.
   C. Bury the cost in the largest cost center available.
   D. Ignore the payment.

5. During a meeting with some of the project stakeholders, the project manager is asked to add work to the project scope. The project manager had access to correspondence about the project before the project charter was signed and remembers that the

project sponsor specifically denied funding for the scope mentioned by these stakeholders. The BEST thing for the project manager to do would be to:

A. let the sponsor know of the stakeholders' request.
B. evaluate the impact of adding the scope.
C. tell the stakeholders the scope cannot be added.
D. add the work if there is time available in the project schedule.

6. When checking the calendar of a team member to schedule a meeting, you see she has scheduled a meeting with a key stakeholder that you were not informed of. The BEST approach would be to:

A. avoid mentioning it to the team member but continue to watch her activities.
B. notify your boss about the problem.
C. address the concern with the team member's boss.
D. address the concern with the team member.

7. The project manager is having a very difficult time keeping a project schedule on track. The project requires 220 people to complete it. All of the project problems have been fixed to the project manager's satisfaction, the schedule performance index (SPI) is currently 0.67, the cost performance index (CPI) is 1.26, there are 23 activities on the critical path and the project PERT duration is 26. Under these circumstances, the monthly status report should report:

A. that the project is doing well.
B. that the project will be late.
C. that the project cost is behind budget.
D. the issues and options.

8. Your employee is three days late with a report. Five minutes before the meeting where the topic of the report is to be discussed, she hands you the report. You notice some serious errors in it. What should you do?

A. Cancel the meeting and reschedule when the report is fixed.
B. Go to the meeting and tell the other attendees there are errors in the report.
C. Force the employee to do the presentation and remain silent as the other attendees find the errors.
D. Cancel the meeting and rewrite the report yourself.

9. A manager has responsibility for a project that has the support of a senior manager. From the beginning, you have disagreed with the manager as to how the project should proceed and what the deliverables should be. You and she have disagreed over many issues in the past. Your department has been tasked with providing some key work packages for the project. What should you do?

A. Provide the manager with what she needs.
B. Inform your manager of your concerns to get her support.
C. Sit down with the manager at the beginning of the project and attempt to describe why you object to the project, and discover a way to solve the problem.
D. Ask to be removed from the project.

10. A large, complex construction project in a foreign country requires coordination to move the required equipment through crowded city streets. To ensure the equipment

is transported successfully, your contact in that country informs you that you will have to pay the local police a fee for coordinating traffic. What should you do?

A. Do not pay the fee because it is a bribe.

B. Eliminate the work.

C. Pay the fee.

D. Do not pay the fee if it is not part of the project estimate.

11. A major negotiation with a potential subcontractor is scheduled for tomorrow when you discover there is a good chance the project will be cancelled. What should you do?

A. Do not spend too much time preparing for the negotiations.

B. Cut the negotiations short.

C. Only negotiate major items.

D. Postpone the negotiations.

12. You've been assigned to take over managing a project that should be half complete according to the schedule. After an extensive evaluation, you discover that the project is running far behind schedule, and that the project will probably take twice the time originally estimated by the previous project manager. However, the sponsor has been told that the project is on schedule. What is the BEST course of action?

A. Try to restructure the schedule to meet the project deadline.

B. Report your assessment to the sponsor.

C. Turn the project back to the previous project manager.

D. Move forward with the schedule as planned by the previous project manager and report at the first missed milestone.

13. You are halfway through a major network rollout. There are 300 locations in the United States with another 20 in England. A software seller has just released a major software upgrade for some of the equipment being installed. The upgrade would provide the customer with functionality they requested that was not available at the time the project began. What is the BEST course of action under these circumstances?

A. Continue as planned, your customer has not requested a change.

B. Inform the customer of the upgrade and the impacts to the project's timeline and functionality.

C. Implement the change and adjust the schedule as necessary because this supports the customer's original request.

D. Implement the change to the remaining sites and continue with the schedule.

14. You are working on your research and development project when your customer asks you to include a particular component in the project. You know this represents new work, and you do not have excess funds available. What should you do?

A. Delete a lower priority work package to make more time and funds available.

B. Use funds from the contingency reserve to cover the cost.

C. Follow the contract change control process.

D. Ask for more funds from the project sponsor.

15. You are a project manager for one of many projects in a large and important program. At a high-level status meeting, you note that another project manager has reported her project on schedule. Looking back on your project over the last few

weeks, you remember many deliverables from the other project that arrived late. What should you do?

A. Meet with the program manager.

B. Develop a risk control plan.

C. Discuss the issue with your boss.

D. Meet with the other project manager.

16. You have always been asked by your management to cut your project estimate by ten percent after you have given it to them. The scope of your new project is unclear and there are over 30 stakeholders. Management expects a 25 percent reduction in downtime as a result of the project. Which of the following is the BEST course of action in this situation?

A. Re-plan to achieve a 35 percent improvement in downtime.

B. Reduce the estimates and note the changes in the risk response plan.

C. Provide an accurate estimate of the actual costs and be able to support it.

D. Meet with the team to identify where you can find 10 percent savings.

17. Your employee is three days late with a report. She walks into a meeting where the report is to be discussed and hands you a copy five minutes before the topic is to be discussed. You notice some serious errors in the report. How could this have been prevented?

A. Require periodic updates from the employee.

B. Coach and mentor the employee.

C. Make sure the employee was competent to do the work.

D. Cancel the meeting earlier because you did not have a chance to review the report.

18. You are in the middle of a project when you discover that a software seller for your project is having major difficulty keeping employees due to a labor dispute. Many other projects in your company are also using the company's services. What should you do?

A. Attempt to keep the required people on your project.

B. Tell the other project managers in your company about the labor problem.

C. Contact the company and advise it that you will cancel its work on the project unless it settles its labor dispute.

D. Cease doing business with the company.

19. All of the following are the responsibility of a project manager EXCEPT?

A. Maintain the confidentiality of customer confidential information.

B. Determine the legality of company procedures.

C. Ensure that a conflict of interest does not compromise the legitimate interest of the customer.

D. Provide accurate and truthful representations in cost estimates.

20. In order to complete work on your projects, you have been provided confidential information from all of your clients. A university contacts you to help it in its research. Such assistance would require you to provide the university with some of the client data from your files. What should you do?

A. Release the information, but remove all references to the clients' names.

B. Provide high-level information only.

C. Contact your clients and seek permission to disclose the information.

D. Disclose the information.

21. Management has promised you part of the incentive fee from the customer if you complete the project early. While finalizing a major deliverable, your team informs you that the deliverable meets the requirements in the contract but will not provide the functionality the customer needs. If the deliverable is late, the project will not be completed early. What action should you take?
    A. Provide the deliverable as it is.
    B. Inform the customer of the situation and work out a mutually agreeable solution.
    C. Start to compile a list of delays caused by the customer to prepare for negotiations.
    D. Cut out other activities in a way that will be unnoticed to provide more time to fix the deliverable.

22. You have just discovered an error in the implementation plan that will prevent you from meeting a milestone date. The BEST thing you can do is:
    A. develop options to meet the milestone date.
    B. change the milestone date.
    C. remove any discussion about due dates in the project status report.
    D. educate the team about the need to meet milestone dates.

23. While testing the strength of concrete poured on your project, you discover that over 35 percent of the concrete does not meet your company's quality standards. You feel certain the concrete will function as it is, and you don't think the concrete needs to meet the quality level specified. What should you do?
    A. Change the quality standards to meet the level achieved.
    B. List in your reports that the concrete simply "meets our quality needs."
    C. Ensure the remaining concrete meets the standard.
    D. Report the lesser quality level and try to find a solution.

24. You are the project manager for a new international project and your project team includes people from four countries. Most of the team members have not worked on similar projects before, but the project has strong support from senior management. What is the BEST thing to do to ensure that cultural differences do not interfere with the project?
    A. Spend a little more time creating the work breakdown structure and making sure it is complete.
    B. As the project manager, make sure you choose your words carefully whenever you communicate.
    C. Ask one person at each team meeting to describe something unique about their culture.
    D. Carefully encode all of the project manager's communications.

25. A project has a tight budget when you begin negotiating with a seller for a piece of equipment. The seller has told you that the equipment price is fixed. Your manager has told you to negotiate the cost with the seller. What is your BEST course of action?
    A. Make a good faith effort to find a way to decrease the cost.
    B. Postpone negotiations until you can convince your manager to change his mind.
    C. Hold the negotiations, but only negotiate other aspects of the project.
    D. Cancel the negotiations.

26. You are working on a large construction project that is progressing within the baselines. Resource usage has remained steady, and your boss has just awarded you a prize for your performance. One of your team members returns from a meeting with

the customer and tells you that the customer is not happy with the project progress. What is the FIRST thing you should do?
A. Tell your manager.
B. Complete a team building exercise and invite the customer's representatives.
C. Change the schedule baseline.
D. Meet with the customer to uncover details.

27. A project manager discovers a defect in a deliverable that is due to the customer under contract today. The project manager knows the customer does not have the technical understanding to notice the defect. The deliverable meets the contract requirements, but it does not meet the project manager's quality standard. What should the project manager do in this situation?
A. Issue the deliverable and get formal acceptance from the customer.
B. Note the problem in the lessons learned so future projects do not encounter the same problem.
C. Discuss the issue with the customer.
D. Inform the customer that the deliverable will be late.

28. Management tells a project manager to subcontract part of the project to a company that management has worked with many times. Under these circumstances, the project manager should be MOST concerned about:
A. making sure the company has the qualifications to complete the project.
B. meeting management expectations of time.
C. the cost of the subcontracted work.
D. the contract terms and conditions.

29. The customer on a project tells the project manager he has run out of money to pay for the project. What should the project manager do FIRST?
A. Shift more of the work to later in the schedule to allow time for the customer to get the funds.
B. Enter administrative closure.
C. Stop work.
D. Release part of the project team.

30. You are the project manager for a large project under contract with the government. The contract for this two year, multi-million dollar project was signed six months ago. You were not involved in contract negotiations or setting up procedures for managing changes, but now you are swamped with changes from the customer and from people inside your organization. Who is normally responsible for formally reviewing major changes to the project/contract?
A. The change control board
B. The contracting/legal department
C. The project manager
D. Senior management

31. The engineering department wants the project objective to be a 10 percent improvement in throughput. The information technology department wants no more than five percent of its resources to be used on the project. Management, who

is also your boss, wants the project team to decrease tax liability. The BEST thing you can do is:

A. put a plan together that meets all the objectives.
B. have these people get together and agree on one objective.
C. include the engineering and information technology objectives but hold further meetings regarding management's objective.
D. include only management's objective.

Professional and Social Responsibility Answers

1. **Answer** D
   Explanation Choices A and B are good ideas, but they do not solve the problem presented in the question. The WBS (choice A) and the project charter (choice B) do not identify stakeholders. Choice C is a procurement function.

2. **Answer** C
   Explanation This type of issue must be settled early in the project, because the content and extent of the entire project management plan depends on the deliverables and objectives. The best way to resolve the issue is choice C, which is a problem solving method. The other choices are really smoothing or forcing.

3. **Answer** B
   Explanation Re-planning (choice A) is uncalled for by the situation described. A project is complete when all work, including all project management work, is complete and the product of the project, not just deliverables, accepted. The lessons learned are project management deliverables, so choice C cannot be correct. Proper work must be done, not just a date passed, for a project to be complete, so choice D cannot be best.

4. **Answer** A
   Explanation Project managers must deal with potentially unethical situations like the situation described. Choices B and C hide it. Choice D ignores it. Only choice A deals with it.

5. **Answer** C
   Explanation Based on the information presented, there is no reason to try to convince the sponsor to add the work (choices B and D). Though one could let the sponsor know (choice A) the best choice would be to say no. An even better choice would be to find the root cause of the problem, but that choice is not listed here.

6. **Answer** D
   Explanation Always look for the choice that deals with and solves the problem. Choice A is withdrawal. Choices B and C would not be appropriate until you learn the root cause of the problem.

7. **Answer** D
   Explanation The professional and social responsibility of the project manager requires that the truth be told. Choice A is lying and unethical. Choice B is not the correct choice because you do not KNOW the project will be late. There is time to fix the problems. Choice C is not correct because there are no cost problems illustrated in the question. As in any report, you need to state the issues and options.

8. **Answer** A
   Explanation Choice C is penalizing the employee and making her lose face. Choices B, C and D all involve decreasing the employee's morale. Therefore the best choice, and the one that does not waste everyone's time, is to cancel the meeting, get to the root cause of the problem and then fix it and reschedule the meeting (partially described in choice A).

9. **Answer** A

   Explanation We assume that proper project management was followed and your opinion was considered during project initiating. Therefore, the best choice would be choice A. You need to provide the work as approved by management.

10. **Answer** C

    Explanation This is fee for service paid to a government official and is therefore not a bribe.

11. **Answer** D

    Explanation Choice D is more ethical and demonstrates good faith. Why spend time in negotiations?

12. **Answer** B

    Explanation Choice C is not possible as the previous project manager may have left the company or he may be busy with new projects. It is a form of withdrawal. Moving ahead (choice D) also withdraws from the problem, and withdrawal is not the best choice. There are two problems described here; the project is behind and the sponsor does not know it. There seem to be two possible right answers, choices A and B. Which is the best thing to deal with? Certainly it would be to work to get the project on schedule, but look at what choice A says. It limits the effort to restructuring the schedule and does not consider other options, such as cutting scope, that might more effectively deal with the problem. Choice A is too limiting. What if the sponsor would agree to change the due date? The best choice in THIS situation is to inform the sponsor of the revised completion time estimate.

13. **Answer** B

    Explanation Professional and social responsibility includes looking after the customer's best interests. Therefore, choice A cannot be best. In this case, the schedule and scope are already approved and all changes must go through the change control process. Therefore choices C and D cannot be best.

14. **Answer** C

    Explanation This is a common occurrence on many projects. When you take the exam, always assume that a change requires evaluation and formal change (choice C) unless it says otherwise. The request from the customer is a change and should be handled as a change. Choices A and D could be done, but only after evaluation and customer approval and as part of choice C. Choice B could be done only if the situation was identified as a risk and included in the reserve.

15. **Answer** D

    Explanation Professional and social responsibility dictates that you should confront the situation first with the other project manager (choice D) to find out if the other project is really on schedule and thereby confirm or deny your information. Choice A or C would be the second step if choice D validates your concern. Choice B would be a more likely choice if it referred to an earlier step in risk. But choice D remains the best answer.

16. **Answer** C

    Explanation This is a common problem on projects that many inexperienced project managers handle by doing choice B or D. If your estimates are accurate, you are ethically bound to stand by them (choice C). Management's only option to cut cost is to support the project manager's looking for options related to the components of the "triple constraint." Choice A does not address the issue at hand, costs.

17. **Answer** D
Explanation Both A and D could have prevented the outcome, but D is the only one that would ensure you were not sitting in a meeting with a document that had not been reviewed.

18. **Answer** B
Explanation Choice A puts your interests over those of your company so it cannot be the best choice. There is no indication that the labor dispute has caused any problems, so there is no need to cancel its work (choice C) or to cease doing business with the company (choice D). The best choice would be to inform others in your company.

19. **Answer** B
Explanation The project manager is neither empowered nor competent to determine the legality of company procedures. NOTE: There is an important distinction between practices and procedures. All unethical practices should be reported. For example, a project manager must report an act of fraud. Fraud is not a company procedure (normally). However, a project manager is not in a position to determine whether company procedures comply with existing law.

20. **Answer** C
Explanation Confidential information should be respected (not disclosed to third parties without the express approval of the client). If you picked choice A, remember that the clients own the confidential information. See, not all professional and social responsibility questions are tough!

21. **Answer** B
Explanation Choices A and D ignore the customer's best interests. Any delays would have already been resolved with other change orders, so choice C is not appropriate. The ethical solution is to talk with the customer (choice B). You might still be able to win the incentive fee and find a mutually agreeable solution. Think of the good will that will come from telling the customer.

22. **Answer** A
Explanation Choices B, C and D do not solve the problem, while choice A does. Choice B is unethical. Choice C violates the rule to report honestly.

23. **Answer** D
Explanation Can you explain why choices A and B are unethical? Choice C simply withdraws from the problem and is therefore not the best solution. The only possible choice is D. That choice would involve quality and other experts to find a resolution.

24. **Answer** C
Explanation You should have noticed that only choices A and C involve more people than just the project manager. Since this is an issue involving everyone, everyone should be involved. Choice A may be a good idea in all cases; however, it does not specifically address cultural issues. Therefore, the answer must be C.

25. **Answer** A

   Explanation There is always a way to decrease costs on the project. How about offering to feature the seller in your next television ad? The best choice is A.

26. **Answer** D

   Explanation You should look for a choice that solves the problem. Choice A is not assertive enough for a project manager. Also, you need more information before talking to your manager. Choice B might be nice, but it does not address the customer's concerns with the project. Changing the baseline (choice C) is not ethical under these circumstances. Problem solving begins with defining the causes of the problem. Therefore, choice D is the only answer.

27. **Answer** C

   Explanation Choice A does not follow the rule to protect the best interests of the customer. Choice B does not solve the problem. Choice D will cause a default of contract. Although the deliverable meets the contractual requirements, it is best to bring the problem to the customer's attention (choice C) so an option that does no harm can be found.

28. **Answer** A

   Explanation The first thing that should come to mind is whether this is an ethical situation and whether it violates any company rules or laws. If it does not violate any of these, it would be best to check qualifications (choice A). There is no justification to rate choices B, C or D higher than any other choice.

29. **Answer** B

   Explanation Every project must be closed, as administrative closure provides benefit to the performing organization. This makes stopping work (choice C) not the best choice. Choices A and D do not solve the problem, they just postpone dealing with it.

30. **Answer** A

   Explanation It is the role of the change control board to review and approve changes. That board may include people representative of all of the other choices. The contracting office signs any approved changes.

31. **Answer** C

   Explanation Did this one catch you? All deliverables must be quantifiable. Management's objective cannot be measured and therefore, needs more work. That means choice A is not correct. All parties rarely agree on all objectives (choice B). All the objectives should be met, but they must be quantifiable, so choice D is not correct. You need to have more discussions with management so you can make their objective quantifiable.

Formulas to Know for the Exam

Title	Formula	PMP® Exam Prep chapter reference
PERT	$\dfrac{P + 4M + O}{6}$	Time (can also be used for Cost)
Standard deviation of an activity	$\dfrac{P - O}{6}$	Time (can also be used for Cost)
Variance of an activity	$\left[\dfrac{P - O}{6}\right]^2$ Also stated as standard deviation squared	Time (can also be used for Cost)
Total float	LS - ES *or* LF - EF	Time
Cost Variance (CV)	EV - AC	Cost
Schedule Variance (SV)	EV - PV	Cost
Cost Performance Index (CPI)	$\dfrac{EV}{AC}$	Cost
Schedule Performance Index (SPI)	$\dfrac{EV}{PV}$	Cost
Estimate at Completion (EAC)	$\dfrac{BAC}{CPI}$	Cost
Estimate at Completion (EAC)	AC + ETC	Cost
Estimate at Completion (EAC)	AC + (BAC - EV)	Cost
Estimate at Completion (EAC)	$AC + \dfrac{(BAC - EV)}{CPI}$	Cost
Estimate to Complete (ETC)	EAC - AC	Cost
Variance at Completion (VAC)	BAC - EAC	Cost
Cumulative CPI	$CPI^C = EV^C / AC^C$	Cost
Present Value (*do not memorize for the exam)	$PV = \dfrac{FV}{(1 + r)^n}$	Cost
Communication channels	[N(N-1)]/2	Communications
Expected Monetary Value	EMV = P x I	Risk